infants

infants
Development and Relationships

Mollie S. Smart / Russell C. Smart

Department of Child Development and Family Relations
University of Rhode Island

THE MACMILLAN COMPANY, NEW YORK
Collier-Macmillan Limited, London

Reprinted with modifications from *Children: Development and Relationships*, Second Edition, by Mollie S. Smart and Russell C. Smart, copyright © 1967 and 1972 by The Macmillan Company and *Readings in Child Development and Relationships*, by Russell C. Smart and Mollie S. Smart, copyright © 1972 by The Macmillan Company.

The Macmillan Company
866 Third Avenue, New York, New York 10022

Collier-Macmillan Canada, Ltd., Toronto, Ontario

Library of Congress catalog card number: 72–75857

Printing: 5 6 7 8   Year: 5 6 7 8 9

contents

introduction

Of all ages and stages of childhood, infancy seems to be the most fascinating to researchers. Along with the preschool stage, it also is most promising to practitioners. In his immaturity and flexibility, the human newborn has exciting potential. The prenatal period is even more mysterious and just as full of promise, due to the recent development of methods for studying and controlling heredity, pregnancy, and prenatal development. Teachers usually enjoy teaching about infancy because it illustrates many principles of development. The ethologists suggest that we are all programmed or innately equipped to respond positively to the diminutive proportions of immature creatures. Indeed, the world loves a baby!

The final chapter is a general one about human life and growth. It deals with the various ways in which children interact with the physical and social surroundings, thereby changing, developing, and restructuring their bodies, minds, and personalities. Some principles of development are stated. Different ways of learning and maturing are discussed. The readings for the final chapter were chosen in order to show man as part of an ecosystem and to introduce the reader to the thoughts and styles of the great developmentalists.

The first four chapters of the book are about infancy, the period from conception to about 2 years of age. During this brief span of time, the human being develops from a speck of fertilized ovum into a real person who can walk, talk, make decisions, and build relationships. Never again will he grow as fast as he grows during his first days and weeks of existence. Never again will he have such a wide range of possibilities for development.

The dynamic interplay and interdependence of mother and baby is punctuated by the dramatic crisis of birth, when the relationship of the two must be reorganized. The father, whose prenatal influence was only through the mother, can now interact directly with the baby. Cognitive stimulation and development occur in the give and take of mother and baby and also as the father and other people participate in the infant's expanding world. Infant intellectual growth comprises the sensorimotor period of intelligence, during which the child learns to control his movements in space and establishes the notion of the permanence of objects. He comes to realize that *he* is an object in space, an object among objects. These achievements contribute to his sense of trust, whose growth is crucial at this age. He learns to expect certain regularities in the world. He learns that he can count on himself to accomplish certain acts and that he can count on his mother, father, and other persons to comfort him and to make life interesting.

During the latter part of the period of sensorimotor intelligence, the toddler becomes involved in a new stage of personality growth, the development of the sense of autonomy. Problems of autonomy occupy him for about the first half of the preschool period. The time from 18 months to 2 years, when the child is called a toddler, is a transition period in both intellect and personality. Intellectually, the toddler enjoys the new ability to represent actions and objects to himself, through the use of mental images. He demonstrates that he can do so when he pretends and imitates. He can use very primitive foresight and planning. Language emerges at this time, greatly expanding his powers. The end of infancy is marked by the use of language for both communication and thinking. The growth of the sense of autonomy is facilitated by these new mental abilities, through which he begins to know himself as a person-among-persons. Growing physical powers and motor coordination also contribute to his feelings of being an individual who can make decisions and who can succeed. His testing grounds and workshop include both objects and people. Through interactions with them, he develops in one direction or another. He makes his family into a different family, its members into new people. Our consideration of development and relationships therefore is very concerned with those interactions.

Chapter 1

Halvar Loken

Prenatal Development and Birth

The individual's first relationship is as a baby inside his mother. As an embryo and then a fetus, he influences his mother and is influenced by her. The stress in this chapter will be on the physical and psychological development of the baby, explained in the light of the mother's development and the mutuality of the two individuals.

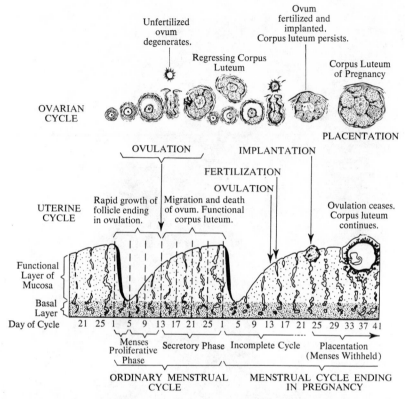

OVARIAN CYCLE

Unfertilized ovum degenerates.

Regressing Corpus Luteum

Ovum fertilized and implanted. Corpus luteum persists.

Corpus Luteum of Pregnancy

PLACENTATION

OVULATION   IMPLANTATION

FERTILIZATION

OVULATION

UTERINE CYCLE

Rapid growth of follicle ending in ovulation.

Migration and death of ovum. Functional corpus luteum.

Ovulation ceases. Corpus luteum continues.

Functional Layer of Mucosa

Basal Layer

Day of Cycle   21 25 1   5   9   13 17 21 25   1   5   9   13 17 21 25 29 33 37 41

Menses Proliferative Phase   Secretory Phase   Incomplete Cycle   Placentation (Menses Withheld)

ORDINARY MENSTRUAL CYCLE   MENSTRUAL CYCLE ENDING IN PREGNANCY

Figure 1–1. Changes taking place in the ovary and uterus during an ordinary menstrual cycle and during the beginning stage of a pregnancy. (Modified from Schroder in B. M. Patten *Human Embryology*, 2nd edition. Copyright 1953. McGraw-Hill Book Company. Used by permission.)

Stages of Prenatal Development

From Fertilization to Implantation

The time when the baby can begin depends upon ovulation. At about the middle of each menstrual cycle (the thirteenth or fourteenth day of a 28-day cycle), a mature ovum reaches the middle of the Fallopian tube in its journey from the ovary to the uterus. Figure 1–1 shows the sequence and timing of events in the menstrual cycle.

The ovum is a little ball about the size of a dot which looks much like a chicken egg if seen under a microscope. It has a yellow yolk in the middle of clear fluid, surrounded by a gummy shell. Figure 1–2 shows a greatly magnified human egg. Unable to move by itself, the ovum is swept down the tube by suction, expansion, and contraction of the tube, and hairlike parts of the tube which lash back and forth. The sperm that must meet it partway down the tube if fertilization is to take place is one of 500 million, more or less, contributed by the father some time during the past 48 hours. Ever so much smaller than the egg, the sperm swims by lashing its long tail. Figure 1–3 shows several sperm cells. Probably many sperm bump against

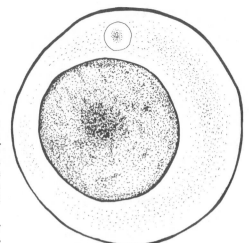

Figure 1–2. A human egg, about 800 times actual size. A tough membrane encloses a layer of whitish fluid, inside which is a yolk-like central portion. The little ball inside the white layer is a polar body, containing unused chromosomes.

SOURCE: After a photograph by Landrum Shettles in E. H. Haveman, *Birth control*. Time, Inc., 1967.

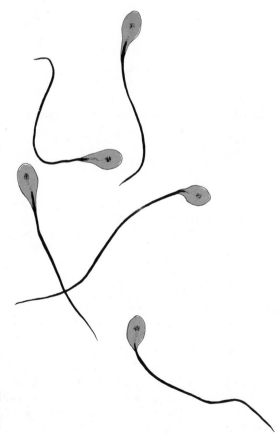

Figure 1–3. Several sperm cells magnified about 900 times.

SOURCE: After a photograph by Landrum Shettles in E. H. Haveman, *Birth control*. Time, Inc., 1967.

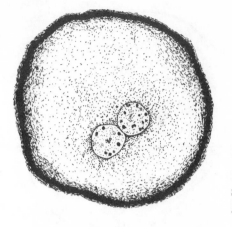

Figure 1–4. A fertilized egg. Male and female nuclei lie side by side for a few hours before uniting.

SOURCE: After a photograph by Landrum Shettles in E. H. Haveman, *Birth control.* Time, Inc., 1967.

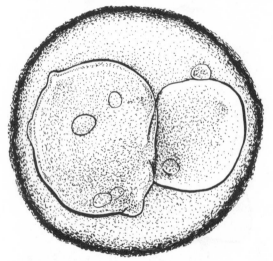

Figure 1–5. A few hours after the male and female nuclei merge, the egg splits into two cells.

SOURCE: After a photograph by Landrum Shettles in E. H. Haveman, *Birth control.* Time, Inc., 1967.

the egg before one succeeds in penetrating the tough outer membrane. Although more than one may penetrate the membrane, only one sperm's nucleus unites with the nucleus of the egg. The male and female nucleus lie side by side for a few hours, as seen in Figure 1–4, before they merge to form the zygote, the fertilized egg, the beginning of a new individual. The egg splits into 2 cells, as can be seen in Figure 1–5. The 2 cells form 4 cells and the 4 cells 8. After 72 hours, the ovum has grown into 32 cells, as shown in Figure 1–6, and after four days, it consists of 90 cells and looks like Figure 1–7. Note that there is a cavity in the center, and cells are clustered around it. It is in this state that the organism, now called a blastocyst, leaves the Fallopian tube and enters the uterus, where it floats for one or two days before settling itself into the lining of the uterus. The outer layer of cells, the trophoblast, produces tendrils, or villi, which burrow into the uterine lining and connect the ovum with the uterine wall. This process, called implantation, marks the end of the stage of the ovum and the beginning of the stage of the embryo.

The question of when this organism can be considered a human being is an important one, since we have the means of diagnosing many abnormalities in utero.

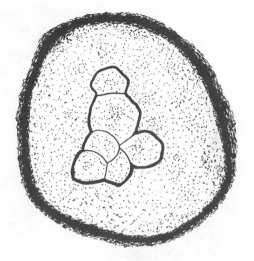

Figure 1–6. During the first 72 hours of life, the ovum grows into 32 cells.

SOURCE: After a photograph by Landrum Shettles in E. H. Haveman, *Birth control.* Time, Inc., 1967.

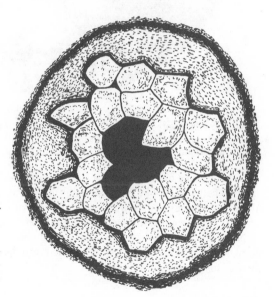

Figure 1–7. At four days of age, the ovum consists of about 90 cells.

SOURCE: After a photograph by Landrum Shettles in E. H. Haveman, *Birth control.* Time, Inc., 1967.

A properly performed abortion carries less risk than a tonsillectomy and a great deal less discomfort. In addition, a growing number of people are coming to believe that every woman has a right to decide for herself whether she shall bear a child. English common law and the laws of the Roman Catholic Church until the nineteenth century were permissive as long as the abortion took place before the quickening, the time when the fetus was first felt moving by the mother. During the nineteenth century, restrictive laws were passed, and the Roman Catholic Church redefined the point of humanity as being fertilization. More liberal trends are again in evidence. Scholars point out that before implantation, the ovum has no dependence on the mother and that the embryo is not an individual life until it becomes a fetus and produces hormones of its own [2]. Others say, "Scientifically,

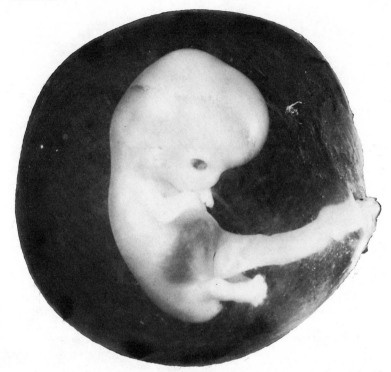

By courtesy of the Carnegie Institution of Washington.

Figure 1-8. The embryo at 7 weeks. This photograph is about four times life size. Notice the human-looking face, with eyes, ears, nose, and lips. The arms have hands, with fingers and thumbs. The legs have knees, ankles, and toes.

the fetus is not a human being for the simple reason that it cannot survive, even with outside help" [23]. The cultural definition of full human status varies throughout the world, from the notion of the fertilized ovum being human to the idea that the child is not a real person until several months after birth [37].

None of the events of the period of the ovum can be felt by the mother, not even implantation. Her offspring is well settled into her body before she has any indication of his presence.

The Embryo

The individual is called an embryo during the time that the various organs and tissues are being differentiated and formed, from the end of the second week to the end of the second month. Mosslike villi extend from the embryo into the blood spaces of the maternal uterus, forming a means of exchanging body fluids. Protective and supportive membranes, the chorion and amnion, take form. The amniotic sac enclosing the embryo begins to fill with fluid.

The head comes first in the developmental timetable. The head of the embryo is one half of its total length; of the newborn, one quarter; of the adult, one tenth. These ratios illustrate the principle of developmental direction, described in Chapter 5, which holds for lower animals as well as for man and for function as well as for structure—that is, *development proceeds from anterior to posterior.*

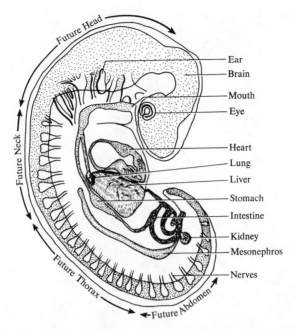

Figure 1–9. The month-old embryo has the foundations of many organs and systems.
SOURCE: Reproduced by permission from M. S. Gilbert, *Biography of the Unborn*. Baltimore: The
Williams & Wilkins Co., 1938.

The 18-day embryo has the beginning of a heart, which begins to beat at the end
of the third week. By 4 weeks the embryo has a system of blood vessels connected
with the heart and two tubes which are the beginnings of the gastrointestinal tract
and the cerebrospinal canal. He has eyeballs with lenses, pits which will be parts
of the nose, semicircular canals, a primitive kidney, lung sacs, and limb buds.
Figure 1–9 shows some of these structures.

Development is very rapid during the second 4 weeks. During this time the
embryo comes to look a little like a human being. Figure 1–10 indicates how quickly
length and weight increase. Since measurements of the embryo and fetus vary
considerably from one study to another, these graphs should be taken as approximations and not as exact representations.

The Fetus

At 8 weeks, the organism is recognizable, at least to the practiced eye, as a
human being, and a new name is applied. From the end of the eighth week until
he is born, the individual is called *fetus* instead of *embryo*. Complete with face,
neck, arms, legs, fingers, toes, some calcification of his bones, functioning internal
organs and muscles, the fetus is ready to build upon the basic form that has been
laid down.

Development during the third month includes differentiation between the sexes,
the tooth buds and sockets for the temporary teeth, the vocal chords and, of course,

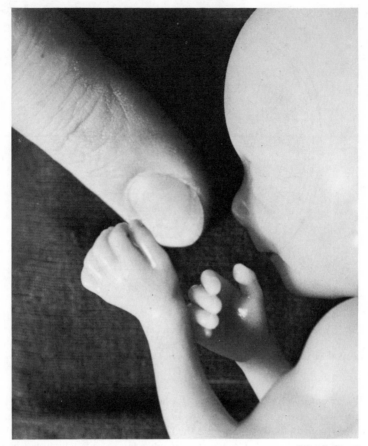

Ellen S. Smart

Figure 1-10. Fetus at about four months.

growth in size and complexity. The third and fourth months are a time of tremendous growth in size; 6 or 8 inches are added to his length. At 4 months the fetus has reached half of what its length will be at birth. At 6 months the vernix caseosa, formed from skin cells and a fatty secretion, protects the thin, delicate skin. The skin is red and wrinkled until subcutaneous fat is deposited under it, during the last 3 months of prenatal life. The fetus swallows, makes breathing movements, secretes enzymes and hormones, digests, and secretes urine. He makes hiccuplike movements and is thought to suck his thumb. All of these functions indicate the maturing of the nervous system.

The baby in utero is an aquatic creature who has been described as "a sort of combination astronaut and underwater swimmer" [35]. The surrounding amniotic fluid supports him in an almost weightless state, protects him from shocks and jarring, and gives him freedom to move. "His movements to and fro, round and round, up and down, have the wonderfully relaxed grace which we see in films of life under water . . . he is really very busy, swimming around in his private space capsule" [35].

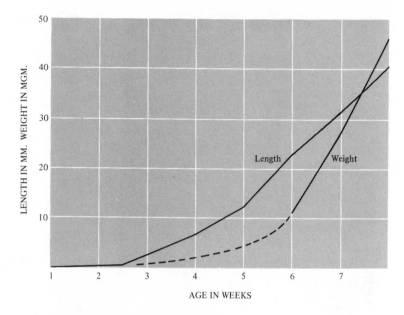

2. Flat embryonic disc with three germ layers
3. Disc arches to form cylinder, beginning alimentary canal, kidney, heart, nervous system, muscles.
4. C shape with large head end, tail, limb buds, gill slits, bulging beating heart. Beginnings of eyes, nose pits, ears, lungs, jaws.
6. Face forming, with lips. Eyes on sides. Paddle-like limbs. Cartilage beginning. Brain growing rapidly, bending forward.
8. Looks human, with jaws, ears, fingers and toes. Tail almost covered. Head about half of total length. Forehead bulges with large brain. Ossification centers. Testes and ovaries distinguishable.

Figure 1–11a. Summary of development during the period of the embryo.

SOURCES: G. S. Dodds, *The Essentials of Human Embryology*, 3rd edit., John Wiley & Sons, 1946. M. S. Gilbert, *Biography of the Unborn*, Williams & Wilkins, 1938. B. M. Patten, *Human Embryology*, 2nd edit., McGraw-Hill, 1953.

By 12 weeks the head extends when the trunk flexes, the rump flexes more rapidly, and one arm moves farther back than its opposite. To a lesser degree, the legs also move independently of the trunk and asymmetrically, suggesting the beginning of alternating movements. Thus the anterior portion shows more behavior than the posterior portion, illustrating again the principle that development proceeds from the anterior to posterior. Another principle specified in Chapter 5 is demonstrated also, namely that *development proceeds through differentiation and integration.* The generalized movement of the fetus at 8 weeks, when the limbs move along with the trunk, is differentiated to a unit of movement in which arms and legs are independent of the trunk but coordinated with it.

The fetus is 16 to 20 weeks old when his mother first feels him moving like a butterfly inside her. Before long, he will thump her interior instead of tickling it. Already he has a large repertory of movements which includes blinking, sucking, turning the head and gripping, and a wide variety of movements of limbs, hands, and feet.

The motor behavior of the baby before birth is related to his behavior after birth, as might be expected [61]. Thirty-five women kept records of fetal movements

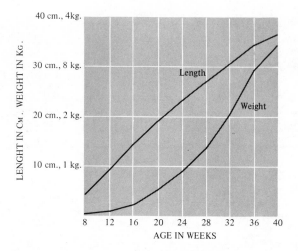

12. Sex distinguishable. Eyelids sealed shut. Buds for deciduous teeth. Vocal cords. Digestive tract, kidneys and liver secrete.
16. Head about one third of total length. Nose plugged. Lips visible. Fine hair on body. Pads on hands and feet. Skin dark red, loose, wrinkled.
20. Body axis straightens. Vernix caseosa covers skin as skin glands develop. Internal organs move toward mature positions.
24-28. Eyes open. Taste buds present. If born, can breathe, cry and live for a few hours.
28-40. Fat deposited. Rapid brain growth. Nails develop. Permanent tooth buds. Testes descend. Becomes viable.

Figure 1–11b. Summary of development during the fetal period.
Sources: As in 1–11a.

during the last three months of pregnancy. Gesell tests done on the babies at 12, 24, and 36 weeks showed positive relationships between amount of fetal activity and motor and total scores at each level.

The last half of prenatal life is a period of preparation for birth and independent living. Most important is the maturing of the nervous system, which must organize and coordinate all the other systems. The establishment of breathing, the most precarious step into the outside world, will be determined largely by the condition of the nervous system. Figure 1–11 shows growth in length and height during the prenatal period, along with some landmarks of development.

The Placenta and Cord

The placenta, an organ that serves the unborn baby's growth needs, might be thought of as a part of the fetus which is discarded at birth. Derived from the trophoblast, which sends tendrils into the endometrial tissue (uterine lining) of the mother, the placenta grows into an inch-thick disc, about 7 inches across. One side of it is attached to the mother's uterus and the other side to the baby's umbilical cord. In the early stages of pregnancy, the placenta does the work of kidney, intestine, liver, endocrines, and lungs for the baby, adjusting its functions as the fetus grows its internal organs. Through the placenta the baby gets nutrients and oxygen from his mother and sends carbon dioxide and other waste products into her body for disposal. The baby's and mother's blood stream do not mix, however, except for the occasional escape of small amounts of the baby's blood into the mother's. They exchange products through the walls of tiny blood vessels which lie close to each other but do not run into each other. This system is the placental barrier. Bodies carrying immunity pass through the barrier from mother to fetus, thus protecting him for several months after birth from the diseases to which his mother is immune. The placenta makes hormones that affect both baby and mother, directing development of the mother's body in ways that nurture the fetus and prepare her body for birth and lactation.

The umbilical cord is derived from the body stock which is differentiated out of the trophoblast. Connecting the baby and placenta, the cord in utero looks like a stiff rope or tube, about 20 inches long. Blood flows through the cord at a high rate, as much as a half pint per minute [35]. Since the cord is under pressure, it is not flexible enough to knot in the uterus. Only during the birth processes, when it becomes slack, is there any possibility of danger from the baby entangling himself in it. At that point, of course, the physician or midwife will take care of such an emergency.

Stages of Maternal Development and Experience

Since the zygote is free-floating and self-contained for about a week, the mother has no reactions to pregnancy until after implantation.

Symptoms and Diagnosis

Failure to menstruate is usually the first symptom of pregnancy, although it is not a conclusive symptom. Absence of menses can be due to a variety of reasons, including age, illness, and emotional upset; menstruation during the first two or three months of pregnancy is possible. Breast changes may announce pregnancy: fullness, tingling, and hypersensitivity may occur even before the first period.

Nausea or queasiness may begin when the first period is overdue. For those who are nauseated, the common pattern is morning queasiness, which disappears gradually in about eight weeks. Recent studies indicate that about one out of two pregnant women has some nausea during pregnancy. The most common pattern is a mild disturbance, consisting of morning queasiness which disappears during the day. Such symptoms are most likely due to biochemical changes rather than to psychological maladjustment [21]. Severe, pathological vomiting, which occurs in a small percentage of women, is more likely to have some psychological origins. Research on nausea of pregnancy has yielded conflicting results, however, and these conclusions are only tentative [21]. Fatigue and the need for extra sleep, frequent during the early months of pregnancy, probably represent a protective mechanism for facilitating physical changes. Frequency of urination is another early symptom.

The physician can diagnose pregnancy through laboratory tests soon after the first missed period. The classic and conclusive signs are hearing the fetal heartbeat, feeling fetal movements, and seeing the fetal skeleton in an X ray—all possible between the sixteenth and twentieth weeks.

Physical Changes

The whole body is affected by pregnancy. The first stage seems to be one of reorganization. The middle stage is normally one of smooth functioning, when the mother feels and looks blooming, settles into her job of supplying the fetus. Later stages involve more preparations for the birth process.

Foundations for childbearing are laid early in the mother's life, even at her conception, since pregnancy and birth are affected by the whole of her development and health [30]. The woman who begins pregnancy with a normal, fully mature, healthy, well-nourished body, in contrast to one in poor nutritional condition, is less likely to have complications in pregnancy, premature birth, and a baby in poor condition [46]. It is difficult to compensate for inadequacies in certain nutritional elements during pregnancy. For example, if the mother has a good supply of calcium already stored in her bones, she will be more likely to keep herself and her baby well supplied with calcium than will a mother with inadequate stores, even though both have a good diet during pregnancy. Similarly with nitrogen retention and hemoglobin level, a healthy condition in the beginning makes it easier to maintain good levels through pregnancy [57].

Special diets for the bride-to-be are a feature of some non-Western societies— a very functional feature. Even husbands-to-be have been known to receive nutritional supervision. Where a fat girl is beautiful, as in some African cultures, the standard of beauty may contribute to the nutritional preparation of mothers. In America, where slenderness is beautiful and high fashion models are scrawny, teen-age girls often eat inadequate diets which put them into poor condition for motherhood. Recent evidence pushes the important period for nutrition back into childhood, indicating that the adolescent years are only part of the time when a girl's nutrition has implications for her offspring: "... the mother's opportunity to grow during her childhood is perhaps the single strongest determining factor for her obstetrical and reproductive performance" [3].

Reproductive System. The uterus grows in weight from 2 ounces to over 2 pounds, in capacity from a half teaspoon to 4 or 5 quarts. Muscle fibers grow to 10 times their former length. The preparation of the muscular layer of the uterus is extremely important, since it will open the cervix, help to push the baby out, and form ligatures to cut off the blood vessels supplying the lining of the uterus. The lining provides the spot where the blastocyst implants and takes part in forming the placenta. It provides a mucous plug to close the entrance to the uterus. The cervix, or neck of the uterus, softens as its muscle fibers diminish in number and size, connective tissue grows thinner, and blood supply increases. The vagina increases in length and capacity as its muscle fibers hypertrophy, connective tissue loosens, and more blood is supplied. All perineal structures, the tissues surrounding the birth canal, are loosened, becoming more distensible. Vaginal secretions increase in quantity and in bacteriocidal action.

Hormones from the placenta prepare the breasts for lactation. The breasts increase in size due to an increase in mammary gland tissue and an increased blood supply. The pigmented area darkens. From the fourth month on, colostrum, a clear yellow fluid, is excreted from the nipple.

Circulatory System. The blood vessels supplying the uterus elongate, dilate, and become tortuous. The blood volume increases by one fifth, but has a progressively lower specific gravity and lower hemoglobin count. Although this condition is not true anemia, good hygiene is important in order to prevent anemia. Because of the changing specific gravity, the ordinary balance of fluids in the lymph system and certain veins may be upset. Balance is encouraged by breathing movements and muscular activity and upset by inactivity and gravity. When too much blood accu-

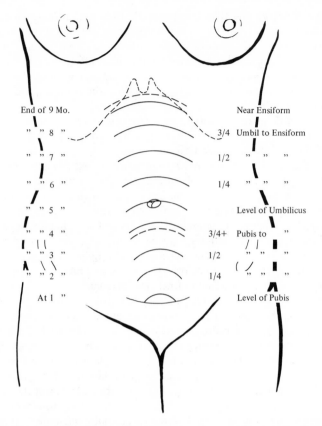

Figure 1–12. The height reached by the uterus at each successive month of pregnancy.
SOURCE: Reproduced by permission from J. P. Greenhill. *Obstetrics* (13th ed.) Philadelphia: W. B. Saunders Company, 1965.

mulates in the vessels of the legs and the perineal and anal regions, drainage is improved by resting with the feet up.

Systemic Functions. Changes in the hormonal balance occur. Pregnancy affects various glands, including the thyroid, parathyroid, pituitary, and suprarenals. Metabolism is increased and improved after the third month. The capacity to store essential elements increases. The kidneys must work harder to take care of the products of increased metabolism and excretion of the fetus. The pelvis of the kidney dilates to double its former capacity. Sweat and sebaceous glands become more active.

Psychological Aspects

Pregnancy is a crisis period. New feelings go along with the pervading physical changes and reorganization. The first pregnancy brings sensations that a woman has not known before. Perhaps there has been something like it, but not exactly in this form. She has been tired before, but not so eager for an afternoon nap. She has experienced an upset stomach, but not the consistent daily cycle of hovering on the brink of nausea and then conquering it. The deep, alive, tingling sensation in the breasts may remind her of premenstrual sensations, but it is more than that. Then, as the pregnancy advances, there is the perception of fetal movements, which is like nothing else. She may describe it first as a fluttering. The spectrum of new bodily experiences demands attention. The pregnant woman, therefore, turns some of her attention inward, thinking about what she is feeling and about what is happening to her body.

The burden of pregnancy is carried easily by some women and not so easily by others. It is a burden in a literal sense. Simply transporting 20 to 25 extra pounds requires additional muscular exertion and more work done by the lungs, heart, kidneys—in fact, all of the body. When some parts of the body are found to be not quite up to carrying their share of the burden, their performance, resulting in discomfort, adds to the perceived burden. Common discomforts of pregnancy include varicose veins (the bulging of loaded blood vessels), heartburn (the product of the stomach's imperfect functioning), and shortness of breath (resulting from squeezed lungs). Such discomforts may be slight or severe, depending on such physical factors as bodily structure, nutrition, and fatigue. Medical care and good hygiene help to alleviate the difficulties. The woman's reactions to pregnancy are also the product of her culture and of her own personality.

Little girls are taught what to anticipate as they look forward to growing up and having babies of their own. Their mothers set an example when carrying baby brothers and sisters. Overheard conversations are influential. So are glances, nuances, and conversations that stop in midair as the child approaches. If mothers tell their children that pregnancy and birth are simple, natural, and beautiful and yet the children hear them exchanging stories with their friends which depict these processes as frightening and agonizing, they will surely not accept the first version confidently. Children also give each other information and misinformation. They may read news items and see films and television that contribute to their attitude toward pregnancy and childbirth. The reality of the situation is not lost in those looking forward to pregnancy. They notice how pregnant women are regarded in their culture. The range and variety of attitudes toward pregnancy in the various cultures of the world are quite amazing. There are those who regard pregnancy as a time of illness and an abnormal condition, as do certain peoples in South, Central, and North America; other tribes in South America and in the Pacific regard it as very normal and natural; some African tribes think that pregnancy is the height of happiness. Birth may be considered defiling and unclean, so that a woman is dirty afterwards and must be purified by a religious ritual. Birth may be thought supernatural, a time when a woman hovers between life and death or is especially vulnerable to demons [37].

The wide diversity of cultures in America results in wide variation in attitudes toward pregnancy. While today, in contrast to half a century ago, there is no taboo on pregnant women appearing in public and carrying on their ordinary activities, substantial fears, superstitions, and anxieties linger on because of ignorance. Many a girl in a pretty maternity dress, unembarrassed at her bulge in front, is afraid of the unknown she will have to meet in the labor room. The luckier ones have had a good sex education and preparation for childbirth. An aspect of today's reality is the comparative ease and safety with which human reproduction occurs. Because of medical knowledge and techniques, drugs, nutrition, and health care, girls do not hear very often about women dying in childbirth or of their being almost frightened to death. They do hear, however, of children being born with physical and mental defects. They may be even more aware of these children than their grandmothers were, since there are more of them around. Modern medicine, although doing marvels to correct defects, maintains life in increasing numbers of defective children. Pregnant women commonly fear that their children will not be normal.

The personality of the expectant mother plays a large part in her reactions to pregnancy. If she has coped successfully with the problems of identity and has a marriage in which her sense of intimacy has developed, then, most likely, she welcomes parenthood with a feeling of confidence and happy anticipation. Nobody is unshakable in his self concepts, and nobody has perfect communication and sharing with another. Therefore, even the healthiest pregnant woman will have occasional doubts about herself: her potential as a mother and her ability to cope with the more complicated family which will result from the birth of her baby. The woman who had difficult problems before her pregnancy is likely to find life harder now. The demands upon her would understandably increase fears about sex, modesty, physical adequacy, and family difficulties. Sick role expectations have also been found to be associated with low social and educational status, low levels of aspiration, and disturbances in social relationships [47].

A pregnant mother's emotions are understandably affected by whether she wants the pregnancy or not. There is evidence that many pregnancies are unwelcome. For example, during the year in which abortions were legalized in Japan, it is estimated that about 2 million abortions were performed, approximately the same number as there were live births [22]. In the United States an estimate of between 1 and 2 million illegal abortions to $3\frac{1}{2}$ million births does not accurately reflect the number of unwanted pregnancies but only those unwanted to the point of desperation. Poor Americans, much more than those on higher economic levels, are likely to have more children than they want [44]. These are the women on whom pregnancy would be the greatest burden, physically and emotionally. And of course the unhappy state of the mother during an unwanted pregnancy is only the beginning of an unfortunate and avoidable situation.

The Expectant Father. A man can contribute to the well-being of his unborn child through the help and support he gives to his wife. Feeling vulnerable as she does, her confidence in him as provider and protector is constructive in making her relaxed and secure. She appreciates reassurance that she is still attractive in spite of her increasing girth and decreasing agility. She may want some sympathy for the aches, pains, annoyances, and limitations on activity. If she has fears about the pain of delivery and the well-being of the baby or fears about her competence as a mother, she may seek reassurance from her husband. A mature man, who has coped successfully with his own personality growth, can give his pregnant wife a great deal of comfort through his understanding, sympathy, and confidence. Many men, even while trying to be supportive, find the role of expectant father a very difficult one to play.

With a first pregnancy, the natural turning inward of the woman's attention may constitute the first time in the marriage when the husband feels displaced in her thoughts. He may realize that the worst is yet to come, when the infant will require a great deal of the time and attention which used to belong to him. He may feel deprived sexually, since the doctor may limit intercourse. The father will probably feel added financial responsibility, since a new baby costs something even before birth and then costs more and more as the years go by. New, larger, costlier living quarters may be indicated. The thoughts of college expenses may cross his mind. If the pregnancy is an unwanted one, especially if it threatens the mother's health and the family's solvency, then the expectant father is likely to feel strong guilt.

The husband may find himself being the main, or even only, emotional support of his pregnant wife. When a young American couple move to another part of the country, leaving family and friends behind, they are dependent, at least for a while, on the resources they have as a pair. In contrast, an extended family offers vast aid and support to a pregnant woman. If not already living with the older generation, the young woman may go home to her mother's house, where she is surrounded with affectionate care until after her baby is born and adjusted to life. Or her mother may come to her, taking authoritative command of what is considered woman's affairs, thus relieving the young father of much of the burden he would have to carry in a nuclear family consisting of husband, wife, and child.

In order to fill in some of the emotional and technical gaps created by the change from extended to nuclear family life, many communities offer education for childbirth. Pregnant mothers, with the permission of their doctors, learn about the changes taking place within themselves, how delivery takes place, how to care for themselves and how to care for their babies. Fathers go to classes that focus on what they want to know, what is happening to mother and baby, their own hereditary contribution, what they can do psychologically, and something about infant care and development. Through discussions, both parents clarify their own feelings and share with other expectant parents. Thus they derive much of the security offered in other cultures by experienced family members, while they enjoy the added advantage of applying knowledge from modern research. The International Childbirth Education Association is a federation of groups and individuals interested in family-centered maternity and infant care. This association holds conferences and sponsors programs and provides educational materials on preparation for childbirth and breast feeding and promotes medical and hospital practices which support sound parent–child and husband–wife relationships. (The address of the association is 1840 South Elena, Suite 205, Redondo Beach, California 90277.)

When There Is No Father. With increasing numbers of out-of-wedlock pregnancies occurring in the United States, it is appropriate to wonder how a pregnant woman manages without a partner's help and love. Much depends on the woman's motivation for becoming pregnant and upon her social group's evaluation of illegitimate pregnancies. When the pregnancy represents rebellion against parents and/or society, then obviously the young woman is immature and in serious emotional conflict. When, on the other hand, an unmarried girl is pregnant in a social setting where illegitimate pregnancies are frequent and easily accepted, then she may have little or no psychological trauma. Her own mother may take over much responsibility, giving her the protection and security that a married woman would get from her husband. Out-of-wedlock pregnancy usually causes shame and anxiety to middle-class Americans, while some women in subcultures of poverty may accept it more casually [43]. Statistics concerning illegitimate pregnancies are hard to interpret because of the socioeconomic factors involved. However, studies of such pregnancies do show the following: they occur at all social levels, but in greater numbers at lower levels; the women tend to be young, many of them under 20; mothers are more likely to work late in pregnancy, to receive little or no prenatal

Halvar Loken

care, and to live in poor housing; death rates for mothers and babies are higher than in legitimate pregnancies; low birth weights and higher prematurity rates are more frequent [30].

Prenatal Influence

The question of whether and how a woman can influence her unborn baby is one which has intrigued people since the dawn of history. Some societies have maintained that specific thoughts and experiences could mark the baby in specific ways, such as the notion that if a rabbit ran across the pregnant woman's path, she would bear a baby with a harelip, or if she squashed a strawberry, her baby would have a red birthmark. Less specific, but just as unfounded, is the notion that by listening to good music and viewing great paintings, a woman could confer talent upon the child within her. As scientific knowledge about pregnancy and birth became widespread, more and more people realized that the baby's blood system was separate from the mother's, exchanging nutrients and products of excretion through membranes, but not exchanging blood. As the old superstitions, such as those of the harelip and strawberry mark, were swept away, many people got the idea that nutrition was the *only* prenatal influence. It is now known that chronic or severe stress of the mother constitutes danger to the baby and that there are indeed additional ways in which an unborn baby can be affected through its mother.

Nutrition

The woman who starts her pregnancy in good nutritional condition is fortunate, since she can thus provide the optimal environment for her baby right from the beginning. A nutritional defect is difficult to correct when the demands upon the body are increased by pregnancy. The very fact of being well nourished shows that the woman has established a pattern of eating an adequate selection of foods in amounts suited to her. She will not have to change her ways of eating other than to increase the amounts slightly as pregnancy advances.

While nearly all people in all parts of the world believe that diet during pregnancy is important, the nutritional adaptations prescibed for pregnant women are not always helpful. Meat and fish are often forbidden, as in the tribe who prohibited owl monkey meat for fear that that it would influence the baby to stay awake at night.

Gross Results of Malnutritrition. Until recently, adequacy of prenatal nutrition was estimated largely in rather gross terms, such as number of miscarriages and stillbirths, birth weight, and abnormalities of labor. These indices are still valuable in pointing up the importance of a good diet in pregnancy, but now there are additional pieces of evidence for the vital role of prenatal nutrition. One gross statistic, which is nevertheless impressive, comes from a study on infant mortality rates in 17 African tribes. Among those tribes who had adequate diets or who supplemented inadequate diets sufficiently during pregnancy, the infant mortality rate was 96.8 per thousand births; in tribes with inadequate diets and no supplementation, the rate was 181.1 deaths per thousand births [24]. Wars and other disasters have provided famine conditions under which the effects of serious nutritional deficiencies can be studied. Toward the end of World War II and immediately afterward, the birth weight of babies was reduced in parts of Holland, Germany, and Russia [12, 53]. The siege of Leningrad resulted in severe food restrictions for pregnant mothers who were already malnourished. In 1942 the stillbirth rate doubled, and premature births increased by 41 percent [57]. The effects of improving an inadequate diet were demonstrated by Canadian physicians who supplemented the diets of half of a group of nutritionally deficient pregnant women [16]. The experimental group of mothers (those with improved diets) had fewer cases of anemia, toxemia, miscarriages, and premature births. Their average length of labor was shorter. Their babies were in better condition at birth and were healthier infants than those of the control group. Another way of focusing on the problem of poor prenatal nutrition was to examine the histories of stillborn infants, infants who died in the first few days of life, prematures, and babies with congenital defects [6]. Almost all of the mothers of these infants had had very poor diets during pregnancy.

Some Specific Results of Malnutrition. Since nutrition deprivation studies cannot be done on human beings because of moral considerations, researchers use animals to study the effects of prenatal starvation and malnutrition. While results cannot be applied directly to human beings, they give insight into what happens when the developing baby does not have enough body-building materials. In the early stages of cleavage, when the fertilized ovum is first dividing, the ovum's use of oxygen is significantly retarded in animals on a low protein diet [41]. Baby rats whose mothers were underfed while pregnant did not show marked size reduction at birth, but their ultimate growth potential was reduced, they were unable to utilize food efficiently, and they showed abnormalities and delays in behavior and motor development [52]. When pregnant rats were fed low protein diets during the latter half of pregnancy, their offspring were slow learners [7].

Feeding the Pregnant Woman. Pregnant American women are often placed in conflict over what they should eat [37]. It is common medical practice to restrict weight gain. Doctors often give out a diet sheet prescribing a diet of good quality while restricting calories. The rationale for limiting weight gain is usually threefold: the mother will have less fat to lose after delivery and hence will look better;

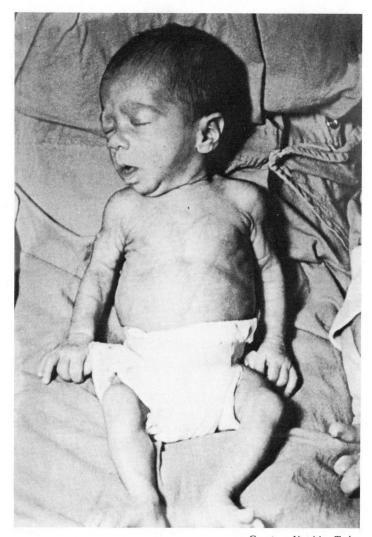

Courtesy *Nutrition Today*

Figure 1–13. Typical underweight newborn baby.

From R. E. Shank, "A Chink in Our Armor," *Nutrition Today*, 1970, **5**:2, p. 2. Copyright © 1970, Enloe, Stalvey and Associates.

chances of toxemia will be decreased; the baby will take what he needs, anyway. Sometimes a fourth is added: the baby will be smaller at birth and hence easier to deliver. A recent report of the Food and Nutrition Board of the National Research Council calls for important changes in the nutritional management of pregnancy [51]. The average optimal gain in pregnancy is 24 pounds, and there is no scientific reason for limiting it to lesser amounts. When well-fed, younger women will tend to gain a little more, thin women more, fat women less, and women having their first babies more. Pregnancy is not a time for fat women to try to reduce. Severe

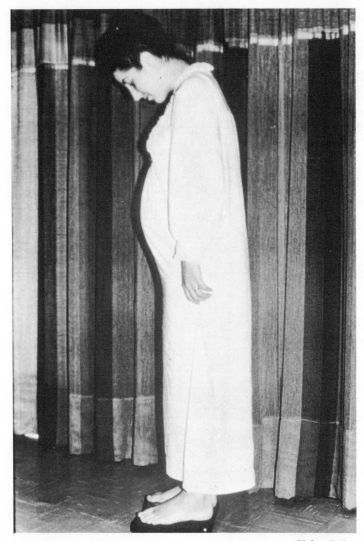

Halvar Loken

restriction of calories is potentially harmful to both mother and baby. The mother should eat what she wants, as long as her diet is balanced. There is no evidence that weight gain due to accumulation of fat is associated with toxemia. The committee also recommends supplements of iron and folic acid and cautions against routine restriction of salt. Normal weight gain and the distribution of the weight are shown in Figures 1–14.

The notion that the baby will somehow draw what he needs out of his mother's body is an old wives' tale. Animal experiments show that calorie and protein restrictions in the mother's diet drastically affect litter size, survival, birth weight, growth patterns, and behavior of offspring [51]. Human studies have shown a strong association between weight gain of mother and birth weight of baby. Birth weight

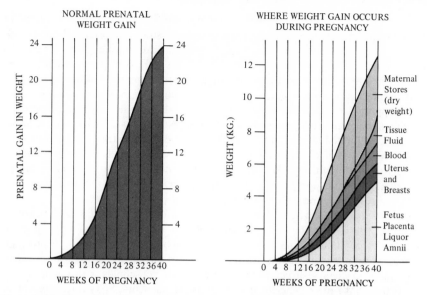

NORMAL PRENATAL
WEIGHT GAIN

WHERE WEIGHT GAIN OCCURS
DURING PREGNANCY

PRENATAL GAIN IN WEIGHT

WEIGHT (KG.)

Maternal
Stores
(dry
weight)

Tissue
Fluid

Blood

Uterus
and
Breasts

Fetus
Placenta
Liquor
Amnii

WEEKS OF PREGNANCY

WEEKS OF PREGNANCY

Figure 1–14. Normal prenatal weight gain and where weight gain occurs during pregnancy.
SOURCE: Reprinted by permission from R. E. Shank, "A Chink in Our Armor," *Nutrition Today*, 1970, 5:2, p. 6. Copyright © 1970, Enloe, Stalvey and Associates.

of baby is linked to survival, normalcy, and health of the infant. A specific example of the baby's inability to get what he needs if the mother does not supply enough is that of 8-month-old babies whose mothers had had low iodine levels in their blood during pregnancies which were otherwise normal [27]. When compared with babies of mothers who had had normal iodine levels, the experimental group scored significantly lower on motor and mental tests and showed higher incidences of cerebral palsy, mental deficiency, visual and hearing loss and other impairments. A more drastic illustration of the importance of adequate *intake* is the case of pregnant rats that were deprived of zinc. Ninety percent of their babies had malformation, including cleft lip, missing limbs, brain anomalies, and curved spines [29]. Analyses of the mothers' bodies showed no losses of zinc from their bones and livers. The zinc was actually in the mothers' bodies, but the fetuses could not withdraw it. Apparently they had to get their supply from zinc in the current diet, not out of the mothers' reserves.

Malnutrition and Mental Retardation. A growing body of evidence links prenatal malnutrition to mental retardation in children. Brain growth is very rapid during the prenatal period for both animals and humans. Eighty percent of adult brain size is reached at 4 weeks by the rat, 8 to 10 weeks by pigs, and 3 years by human children [50]. When a human baby is born, his brain is gaining weight at the rate of 1 to 2 milligrams each minute. Because of such a rapid growth rate, the brain is especially sensitive to nutritional deprivation when the organism is very young. (The principle of critical periods, described in Chapter 5, is illustrated here.) Brain growth is thought to begin with increasing the number of cells (by cell division) and then to continue with increases in number of cells and size of cells, ending with a period of increase in size of cells [65]. Pregnant rats who were fed a low protein diet produced babies whose brains were different in weight, protein content, and number of cells [69]. In human children it is difficult to separate the effects of prenatal and postnatal nutrition. However, many studies of young children who were severely malnourished have shown them to have unusually small head circumferences, suggesting abnormally small brains [50]. Autopsies of infants who died of malnutrition showed that all had a subnormal number of brain cells [39].

A number of studies of malnourished young children in underdeveloped countries support the likelihood that malnourishment during the early stages of growth produces impaired intelligence, inadequate integration between seeing and hearing, apathy, and limited learning ability [10]. A more definitive study has recently been done on American children of mothers who lost abnormally large amounts of protein during pregnancy [39]. At 4 years these children, who must have had an inadequate protein supply prenatally, had significantly lower IQ scores than children whose mothers retained normal amounts of protein.

Poverty and Malnutrition. Mental retardation, apathy, and impaired learning ability are serious problems in underdeveloped countries and among the poor people in the United States. While sufficient income does not assure a pregnant woman of an adequate diet, a low income means virtual certainty of a poor diet. An American dietary survey found 37 percent of households with incomes over $10,000 to have diets deficient in one or more nutrients. Sixty-three percent of households with incomes under $3000 had deficient diets. Half of all the families surveyed had diets that did not meet all nutritional requirements. The nutrients most often lacking were calcium, vitamin A, and ascorbic acid [60]. Customs and knowledge are also important. In India, where the average income is $86 a year, and in much of Asia, for example, the wife eats after her husband and children have eaten. What is more, it is not easy to get enough protein from a vegetarian diet, and most Indians are vegetarians. In parts of Nigeria, pregnant women may not eat vegetables or fruits. After delivery, they are not supposed to eat soup containing meat or fish [8].

Importance of Nutrition Education. Even when enough good food is available, most women need education and guidance in planning their diets. Probably the best place to begin is in nutrition education for all high school girls. More specific guidance during pregnancy is offered by classes for mothers, often taught as part of a comprehensive maternal care program in a hospital or clinic, or by public health nurses in the community. Countries with strong maternal and child health programs, such as New Zealand and Sweden, teach and help a large proportion of pregnant women. Their infant and maternal mortality statistics reflect the value of such programs. (See Figures 1–15a and 1–15b.)

Requirements vary from one woman to another, and there are a variety of ways in which requirements can be met. When deficiencies occur, they can harm either mother or baby but they are likely to harm both. Dietary deficiencies can contribute to premature and otherwise abnormal births, stillbirth, death within the first few days of life, congenital defects, small size, and illnesses during infancy. The importance of adequate, individualized prenatal care is emphasized by the role of nutrition in assuring the health and safety of mother and baby.

Sensory Stimuli

The fetus responds to a wide variety of tones and to loud and sudden noises with increased motor activity and heart rate. Although this behavior has been

MATERNAL MORTALITY RATES

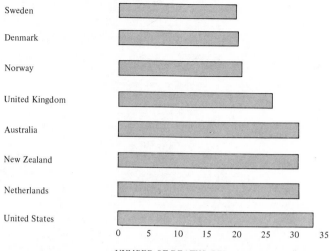

Figure 1–15a. Maternal mortality in prosperous countries.

SOURCE: Data from *Statistical Bulletin*, Metropolitan Life Insurance Company, 1968, **49**, p. 4. Also from 1969 World Population Data Sheet, *Obstetrical and Gynecological News*, 1969, **4**:10, p. 28.

studied in detail [55], it is not known whether there are any lasting effects from stimulating the unborn baby in this way. Probably every baby receives some loud and sudden stimuli before birth—when his mother drops a pot in the kitchen, at a concert, in heavy traffic, when a siren blows, and so on. Mothers report that their fetuses do react to such noises by moving. The baby can be conditioned during the last two months of pregnancy to give a startle response. In one study, the primary stimulus, a loud noise, was paired with a vibrotactile stimulus (an electric doorbell with the gong removed). The latter called forth no fetal response when originally applied to the mother's abdomen, but after 15 or 20 trials with the loud noise, the vibrotactile stimulus alone elicited a startle response [56].

The baby's eyes open in utero. The mother's internal organs make noises that in all likelihood her baby can hear. Her breathing is rhythmic, too, with some tactile and kinesthetic stimulation along with auditory. An interesting suggestion is that "if she should drink a glass of champagne or a bottle of beer, the sounds, to her unborn baby, would be something akin to rockets being shot off all around" [35]. The baby surely hears his mother talking, coughing, sneezing, and swallowing. Her heartbeat is a rhythmic sound that may take on important significance at this time, when the infant receives steady auditory stimulation from it over a long period.

The following chapter includes a description of experiments with babies and toddlers, using a heartbeat sound. Because the sound was found soothing to infants and children, it seems worthwhile to consider what meaning it may have prenatally. The heartbeat sound has the criteria of an imprinting stimulus being intermittent and repetitious and occurring early in the life of the organism, before it experiences fear [48]. Later, when the organism is exposed to fear, it is reassured by the stimulus

INFANT MORTALITY RATES (BIRTH – 1 YEAR)

NUMBER OF DEATHS (PER 1,000 LIVE BIRTHS)

Figure 1–15b. Infant mortality in prosperous countries.
SOURCE: As in 1–15a.

to which it has been imprinted. Thus it seems quite possible that the unborn baby interacts with his environment in such a way that the rhythms of sounds and pressures prepare him for coping with some of the difficulties he will encounter after he is born. Seeking to comfort his distress and express their love, his parents and other people will hold him in their arms and walk with him or rock and jiggle him. The resulting sounds and pressures will reassure him, perhaps because he was imprinted prenatally to such stimuli.

Maternal Emotions
Fetal behavior has been studied at the Fels Institute for several decades. Emotional disturbances in the mother have been shown to be associated with high

activity in the fetus [54]. Infants of mothers who had suffered emotional upsets during pregnancy were likely to show frequent irritability, excessive crying, and gastrointestinal disturbances, such as regurgitation, dyspepsia, and diarrhea. These difficulties are thought to be of autonomic origin and to be caused by intra-uterine conditions.

Severe stress of the pregnant mother is associated with complications of pregnancy and with poor condition and abnormality of the baby. When a stress is measured by objective situations, such as marriage problems, injury, death or illness of the husband or a child, severe housing problems, or economic difficulties, some studies have shown an association between maternal shock and defects in babies [21]. Stress may be more or less harmful at different stages occurring between fertilization and implantation and may result in death of the fertilized ovum [45].

Further evidence of the significance of maternal emotional upset comes from a study of factors connected with birth difficulties and infant abnormalities. A highly anxious group of mothers was found to experience more complications of delivery and abnormalities in their babies [11]. A state of general moodiness, depression, and overdependency in pregnant mothers was found to be associated with physical complications of childbirth [26]. Another group of mothers who indicated negative attitudes on a questionnaire produced babies whose behavior was deviant during a rating period of the first five days of life, in terms of amount of crying, sleeping, bowel movements, feeding, and irritability [19]. The connection between maternal emotions and fetal upset is made through several steps, but it can be explained in physical terms [38].

The nervous and endocrine systems communicate through the blood. An experience of the mother is registered in her cerebral cortex from which impulses pass to the thalamus, hypothalamus, and into the autonomic nervous system. The autonomic system acts on the endocrines, which pour their products into the blood. The blood takes the products of the endocrines to the placenta, through which some of them pass to the fetal blood and to the nervous system of the fetus.

Another explanation is suggested by Salk's [48] explorations with a gallop heartbeat rhythm and a very fast heartbeat. The newborn infants who had quieted to the sound of a normal heartbeat showed an immediate increase in crying and disturbance to these unusual heartbeats and also to a hissing sound which the machine accidentally developed. A frightened or disturbed pregnant mother could be expected to show variations from the normal pattern of heartbeat and breathing. Her baby then might be disturbed by the resulting tactile, auditory, and kinesthetic stimuli. Either by themselves, or added to the effects of the endocrines in the blood, these stimuli could be a significant prenatal influence. Proof of their influence awaits further research.

If an unborn baby can suffer from his mother's extreme emotional upset, then could the opposite be true? What happens to the fetus whose mother has an unusually happy, safe, secure time? At birth, is he different from babies whose mothers have had an average or disturbed pregnancy? Definitive answers to these questions are not available. However, the multiplicity of studies on harmful influences makes one very much aware of what can go wrong prenatally. Perhaps a happy, relaxed pregnancy contributes physical and mental health to the baby. There is nothing to lose and possibly much to gain when the father and other family members are understanding, considerate, and affectionate with the expectant mother, not only for her sake, but also for the baby's. This is not to say that the pregnant mother cannot safely deal with everyday problems and work, but only that she benefits from having the general tone of her life a positive one.

Physical and Chemical Agents

Heavy labor during pregnancy constitutes a stress on the fetus as well as on the mother. Extreme summer heat is another kind of stress [40]. Massive X-ray doses are lethal or seriously damaging to the unborn child. After World War II, effects of atom bomb radiation on children who had been in utero at the time included increased anomalies and morbidity [42, 67].

Many drugs taken by the pregnant mother can affect the baby, some apparently temporarily and some drastically and permanently. Quinine can cause deafness. At least five studies show that smoking during pregnancy increases the risk of producing a premature baby or a baby of low birth weight [40]. There is some evidence that the lower the socioeconomic status, the greater the effect of smoking during pregnancy. A possible explanation is that the very poor mothers lower their protein intake significantly when they smoke, whereas protein intake is not much affected by smoking in the upper economic brackets. Heavy doses of certain barbiturates produce asphyxiation and brain damage. The tranquilizer thalidomide caused thousands of tragic births in Germany, England, and Canada, where its prenatal use produced babies lacking limbs or with limbs in early stages of embryonic development. When heroin-addicted mothers were admitted to a hospital for childbirth, the heroin was withdrawn from them. Their babies were born with withdrawal symptoms, from which they recovered in two or three days. Their sleep patterns were then studied, revealing sleep that differed significantly from normal newborn sleep patterns. The heroin-affected babies had more rapid eye movements, greater variability in heart rates, and no truly quiet sleep, indicating that their central nervous systems had been affected [49].

Since extremely noxious and dangerous stimuli and agents cannot be used experimentally on human beings, a great deal of research is being carried on with animals to find out exactly how radiation and drugs affect them. It has been shown that the stage at which the agents are administered is important in determining the extent of injury and that within certain ranges of stimuli, the stage is more important than the strength [63]. These findings illustrate the growth principle of *critical periods*, described in Chapter 5.

A positive result from abdominal decompression has been reported [13]. Developed by a South African physician, the technique requires an airtight suit or bubble which is placed on the pregnant mother's abdomen. The air pressure is lowered, allowing the fetus to rise in the body cavity. This technique has been used during the last three months of pregnancy. The babies whose mothers have had this treatment have had Gesell developmental quotients that were significantly higher than average. The babies who had the greater number of prenatal decompression treatments had the higher quotients. The inventor of the technique suggests that babies do not get enough oxygen for optimal development during the last stages of prenatal life and that the decompression improves the oxygen supply.

Infections and Blood Incompatibility

German measles, or rubella, which is preventable by immunization, is a serious threat to the baby in utero. A review of studies of rubella in the Baltimore–

Washington area shows that over 50 percent of the women who contracted the disease during the first three months of pregnancy had either miscarriages, still-births, or handicapped infants [25]. The handicaps included profound hearing loss, severe mental retardation, cataracts, heart defects, low birth weight, growth failure, and abnormalities of blood, bones, and other organs. In children whose mothers had rubella during the second and third three months, handicaps were less severe and included communications problems, hearing defects, mild mental retardation, and small body size [25]. A program of immunizing all children can wipe out rubella [25]. Immunization against rubella is now possible, but it must be done at least three months *before* the beginning of pregnancy. In the meantime, abortion is an answer for some of the pregnant women who contract rubella. Some other diseases dangerous to the fetus are syphilis, smallpox, chicken pox, measles, mumps, scarlet fever, tuberculosis, and malarial parasites.

About 1 pregnancy in 200 results in some disturbance from incompatibility between the blood of the mother and baby. The Rh factor is a substance that occurs in the red blood cells of about 85 percent of white people, 93 percent of blacks, and 99 percent of Mongolian peoples. The remaining minorities are Rh negative [2]. When the mother's blood is Rh negative and the fetus' blood is Rh positive, there is one chance in ten that the infant will have some of his red blood cells destroyed. The way it happens is that the fetus produces antigens which go through the placenta into the mother's blood. Her blood then makes antibodies which go back through the placenta to the baby's blood stream. Results include miscarriage, stillbirth, death after birth, brain damage, jaundice, and anemia. Adequate prenatal care requires a blood test that will detect negative Rh. The physician discovering it would then determine the husband's blood type and learn the chances of incompatibility arising between fetus and mother. Taking into account the finding that the danger from Rh factors increases with each baby after the first, he would be ready to cope with symptoms likely to arise. Much can be done to alleviate the condition immediately after birth or even before birth. Harm to future babies can be prevented immediately after the birth of an Rh positive baby to an Rh negative mother. She can be given medication that will prevent damage to subsequent babies through blood incompatibility.

Age and Parity of the Mother

The only time a woman of 35 is considered elderly is when she is having her first baby. In this case, she is called, by the medical profession an "elderly primipara," a logical term in light of the fact that the childbearing period is more than two-thirds over. At age 35 and older, the average length of labor is increased beyond the overall average by an hour and a half, and the risk to mother and baby is increased slightly. Maternal mortality, by age and race, is shown in Figure 1–16. Note that the hazards of age are enormously increased if the woman is black, but only slightly increased if she is white. These figures reflect the depressed economic conditions under which many blacks live.

When risk to the baby is estimated, it makes a difference which portion of the first year of life is considered. Although death rates are stated in terms of the mother's age and parity (number of pregnancies she has had), it must be remembered that both age and parity have different significance in different sociocultural settings. Stillbirths rise with increasing age and fall with parity up to the fourth

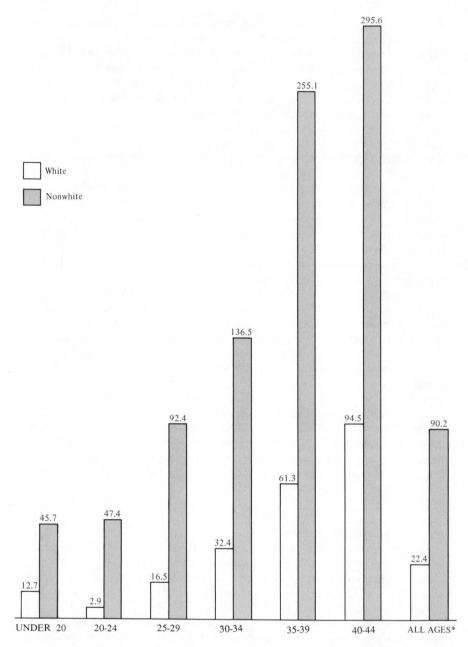

295.6

255.1

136.5

92.4

94.5

90.2

61.3

45.7

47.4

32.4

22.4

16.5

12.7

2.9

White

Nonwhite

UNDER 20   20-24   25-29   30-34   35-39   40-44   ALL AGES*

*Including ages 45 and over.

Figure 1–16. Number of maternal deaths for each 100,000 live births, given for nonwhite and white women (United States 1963–65), by age.

SOURCE: Data from *Statistical Bulletin*, Metropolitan Life Insurance Co., December, 1968, p. 2.

pregnancy. The lowest rates are in the 20- to 24-year-age group and the highest in mothers 35 and over. Death within the first month occurs most often with high parity in the youngest age group and next often to mothers of high parity in the oldest age group. The death rate between 1 month and 11 months rises with increasing parity and falls with increasing age. Prematurity rates are highest in 15- to 19-year-old mothers, with the exception of first babies born to mothers over 35, who have the highest prematurity rate of all [30]. Older mothers are also more likely to produce mongoloid children. Before age 30, the risk of having a mongoloid baby is 1 in 1000, while at age 40 it is 1 in 100, and at age 45, 1 in 45 [15]. When defects of all kinds are counted, very young mothers and older mothers produce more impaired infants than do mothers in the ages in between [40].

From all these findings there follows a generalization that the first birth carries an extra risk and that aging and repeated births also add risk. Frequently repeated births carry a risk to the normalcy of the child, as well as to his life. Babies born within one year of a previous gestation were matched with controls born two to five years after the previous gestation. Matching was done for sex, race, hospital of birth, and socioeconomic status [28]. Their gestation ages were equal, but the babies produced in rapid succession averaged significantly smaller birth weights, lower scores on the Bayley tests at 8 months, and lower Stanford–Binet IQs at 4 years. At 1 year of age, the average baby in the experimental group had a smaller head and delayed motor development. A survey of development of 16,000 7-year-old children in Scotland leads the investigator to conclude: "today, in Aberdeen at least, it is clear that the woman who has five or more children—no matter what class she belongs to officially—is likely to have children with IQ scores well below average" [1].

Teen-Age Mothers

Adolescent Mothers, A Special Problem

Of all the prosperous countries in the world, the United States has the largest number of adolescent mothers. They account at least in part for our poor showing in regard to infant mortality rates. Before completing their own growth, 197,372 girls produced babies during a recent 12-month period. Among them, 29,000 mothers were 15 years old or under. The baby's growth needs are thus superimposed upon the mother's growth needs. The impact of pregnancy upon the body of a growing mother has not been determined, but the impact on her baby is well known, as has been indicated above.

Physical Adequacy of the Mother

Studies from several different countries have shown a relationship between height of mother and reproductive performance. Mothers judged poor in physique tended to be short and to have flattening of the pelvic brim. Short mothers are more likely to have complications of pregnancy and delivery, and to produce babies with lower birth weights, greater prematurity, more birth trauma, and more stillbirths. The relationship between stature of mother and physical well-being of baby is not thought to be a direct one, but, rather, both conditions are results of a socioeconomic environment. A poor environment, supplying inadequate food, housing, clothing, sanitation, and education, will stunt the physical and mental growth of children living in it. Short stature is thus associated with low education, early marriage, premarital pregnancy, premature delivery, longer labor, absence of family planning, frequent pregnancies, poor diet, poor housing, and poor use of information, health services, and social services [30].

The Birth Process

The developments described thus far occur in the course of about nine months. The obstetrician names the delivery date on the pregnant woman's first visit, by adding 280 days to the first day of her last menstrual period. He will warn her, though, that this date is an approximation. Only 4 percent of women deliver on the 280th day; 46 percent deliver within a week of that date; and 74 percent within two weeks of it. Being born and giving birth are physical crises for the two most concerned. The crises are emotional, also, for the two and their family. Thus birth must be understood in various contexts.

The Processes and Stages of Labor

Labor is the work that the mother does in giving birth. Three distinct stages can be described. *The first stage*, requiring the major portion of the duration of labor, is the opening of the cervix or neck of the uterus. It begins with rhythmic uterine contractions, usually felt as pains. The two types of muscular forces working to enlarge the cervical openings are indicated in Figure 1–17. The uterus resembles a pear-shaped balloon whose walls are made of very strong muscle fibers. The fibers contract, exerting about 30 pounds of pressure on the fluids surrounding the baby. The membranes enclosing the fluids press on the tiny opening in the lower end of the uterus. After the membranes break (the mother cannot feel this), the baby presses on the opening. At the same time another set of muscle fibers, which surround the tiny opening, are relaxing to allow the opening to enlarge. As these muscular processes continue, the tissues of the cervix are pulled back into the general roundish shape of the uterus. When the cervix is completely dilated, the diameter of the opening is about 4 inches.

The muscular processes of the first stage of labor are involuntary. The only way in which a woman can influence them is through relaxation. Although it is still a debatable subject, it is commonly believed that general bodily relaxation, due to absence of fear, plus confidence, hastens relaxation of the muscle fibers surrounding the cervix; fear and tension are thought to increase their resistance to stretching and to result in pain. One of the purposes of education for childbirth is to induce this kind of relaxation.

The second stage lasts from the time that the cervix is completely open until the baby emerges from his mother. For a first baby this stage requires an hour and a half on the average; for the second, half as long. The uterus continues to push the baby out. The mother adds a bearing-down action to it, pushing with her diaphragm, but involving her whole body. (See Figure 1–18.) Although she bears down spontaneously, without teaching or conscious thought, a great deal of this activity can be placed under conscious control. Education for childbirth includes teaching the mother to breathe, relax, and bear down in a manner calculated to facilitate the natural labor processes. The confidence factor is just as important in the second stage as in the first in promoting control and either eliminating pain,

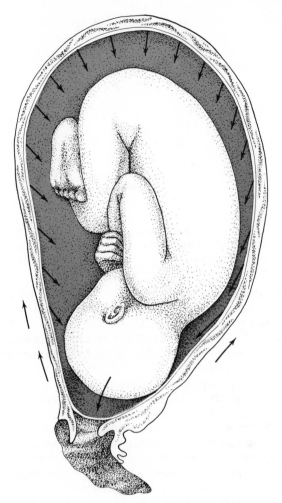

Figure 1–17. The baby during the first stages of labor. Uterine contractions push him downward while the muscle fibers surrounding the opening are pulled upward by the upper segment of the uterus, thus enlarging the opening.

SOURCE: Reproduced by permission from J. P. Greenhill, *Obstetrics*, 13th edition. Philadelphia: W. B. Saunders Company, 1965.

reducing it, or making it more bearable. The *third stage* is the expelling of the placenta and membranes. It lasts only a few minutes.

When women discuss the length of labor with each other, they often mark its beginning with the trip to the hospital. Or the beginning may be considered the time when labor contractions become severe. To be accurate, labor length has to be measured from the time of the first contraction to the moment when the placenta and membranes are completely expelled. Therefore, the average figures for length of labor may look formidably long to the woman who takes her neighbor's experience as the norm.

An overall average for length of labor is about 14 hours, divided among the three stages about like this: first stage 12½ hours; second stage 80 minutes; third stage

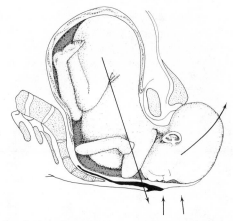

Figure 1–18. The baby during the second stage of labor. The mother's bearing-down action, pushing with her diaphragm, adds to the uterine forces pushing the baby out.
SOURCE: Reproduced by permission from J. B. DeLee and J. P. Greenhill, *Principles and Practices of Obstetrics*. Philadelphia: W. B. Saunders Company, 1947.

10 minutes. The second stage requires about 20 contractions for a first baby and 10 or less for subsequent babies. For a first baby, half of the women in a study of nearly 15,000 cases took less than 11 hours; half took more. The commonest length of labor was 7 hours. Women who had already had at least one baby had shorter labors; half under approximately 6 hours, half over, with the commonest length of labor 4 hours [15].

When a normal birth is impossible or dangerous, the baby may be delivered by Caesarian section, a procedure of cutting the mother's abdomen and uterus to remove the baby and then, of course, the placenta. Although this surgical procedure used to be very dangerous, it now carries relatively slight risk. A Caesarian section is much safer for mother and baby than a difficult forceps delivery or a breech birth through a narrowed pelvis. Although there is no limit to the number of Caesarian births one patient can have, each repetition means that the scar in the uterus is stretched by the pregnancy and hence runs a small risk of rupturing. Many physicians recommend sterilizing with the third Caesarian operation.

Emotional Aspects

The culture in which she has grown up will set the broad outlines of a woman's attitude toward labor. The Judeo-Christian tradition, for example, builds up considerable expectation of pain and tears. According to Mead [59, p. 28],

> in some African tribes, women are expected to shriek, scream, writhe and go through the most terrific expressions of agony, and all the little girl children are brought along to watch, so they will know how to have a baby. In other societies, women are enjoined to the greatest stoicism, and to utter a single cry would be to proclaim yourself not a woman, and again the little girls are brought along to see that they behave like this.

Education and specific experiences are important in setting the mother's expectations of pain and danger and her confidence in her own abilities. The ways in which she handles the fear and pain involved will depend not only on herself, however, but on the support and help she receives during labor. Her husband, the hospital staff and, most of all, the doctor have important emotional functions. Directly connected with the mother's fear or confidence, tension or relaxation, pain or easiness, is the amount and type of anesthetic she will receive. A woman who feels confident and in command of herself and who also feels trust in the help she is receiving will most likely need a minimum of drugs. The terrified patient will seek a maximum, including amnesiacs. (Abnormal physical conditions may require maximum use of drugs too.)

A famous obstetrical event in the animal kingdom pointed up the life-and-death aspects of emotions during labor. A live baby elephant was delivered successfully at the Portland (Oregon) Zoo, after months of anxious waiting and speculation as how to avoid the fiascoes of past elephant reproduction in captivity. One of the innovations which may have spelled success was the presence of several female elephants in the labor pen. These "aunties" were warmly and actively concerned with the mother, even massaging her with their trunks. In contrast to the frantic concern of isolated elephants-in-labor, this mother conducted herself with calm efficiency.

A growing use of psychological means of relieving and controlling pain in labor is probably the result of two trends. First is an increased interest in having childbirth a positive, rewarding experience for the mother and father instead of a trial to be endured. Second is a growing body of evidence that drugs carry more risk to babies than was previously thought to be true. Anesthesia and analgesia during labor and delivery have been shown to have a depressing effect on sensorimotor functioning for at least the first four weeks [4]. Amount of medication was related to muscular, visual, and neural development and to ability to inhibit response to an auditory stimulus. Analgesics have also been found to depress sucking [32] and visual attention [58]. Refined methods of testing for central nervous damage and records kept over long periods of time are yielding indications that analgesics and anesthetics considered normal in America may cause some long-term neurological impairment [9, 33].

There are two well-known methods of preparation for childbirth which have brought pain relief, confidence, and often joy to many women in childbirth. Both methods include teaching of the processes of labor, exercises, and breathing. Neither excludes anesthetics, but uses them moderately when patient and doctor consider them indicated. The Read method, originated by an English obstetrician, stresses emotional education and relief of fear through relaxation and knowledge. The LaMaze (pronounced LaMahz) method, contributed by a French obstetrician, uses conditioning to eliminate or diminish pain. LaMaze courses are available in many if not most parts of the United States and can be located through the International Childbirth Association. Obviously, the approval and cooperation of the physician in charge is a requirement for using any method of education for childbirth. Some skilled and sensitive obstetricians have their own successful ways of giving psychological support and may feel that their patients do not need courses. Many others see childbirth education as a time-consuming operation which can be successfully delegated to specialists trained for that purpose.

The Baby during Labor

Being born is a difficult and risky experience that has claimed the attention of philosophers and psychiatrists, as well as physicians and lay people. The great

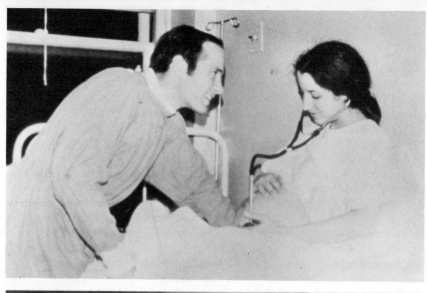

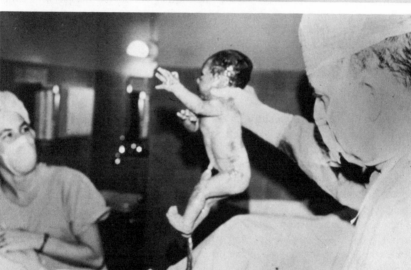

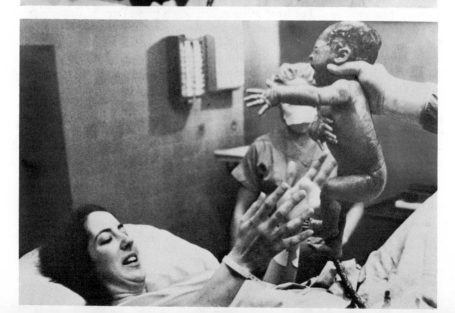

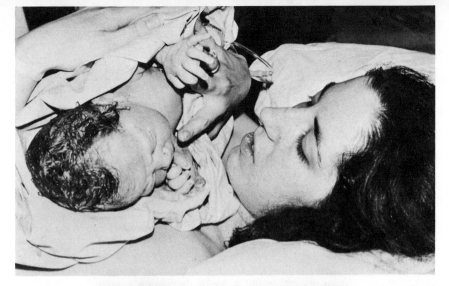

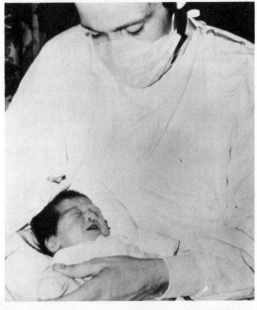

Halvar Loken

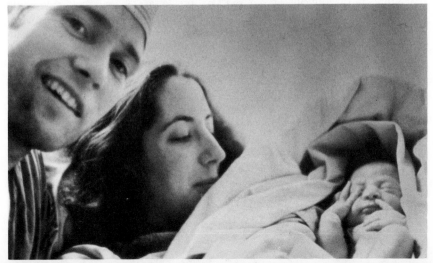

obstetrician DeLee believed that babies suffered pain while being born. The fact that babies give little evidence of a skin pain sense in the early postnatal days is not proof that the global experience of birth is without trauma.

The important bones of the baby's head are separated by the sutures, membranous spaces that feel soft to the touch. Where several sutures meet, the space is called a fontanelle. Figure 1–19 shows the anterior and posterior fontanelles on the top of a baby's head. During labor, the infant's head adapts by becoming narrower as the bones squeeze closer together. They may even overlap. The molding, or squeezing together, may result in a head that looks misshapen at birth, but within a few days, the head resumes a normal shape.

The fetal heartbeat responds to each uterine contraction by speeding up, slowing down, and then speeding up again. As labor progresses, the fetal heart beats very fast, slowly, or irregularly. During a strong uterine contraction, the fetal blood cannot get oxygen from the placenta. The increasing concentration of carbon dioxide stimulates the respiratory center and hence the beginning of breathing after birth. Amniotic fluid and mucus escape from the baby's air passages during expulsion of the baby, due to compression of his chest. The attendant may remove excess mucus from the mouth and throat, using a soft rubber ear syringe. Most babies begin breathing by themselves. If an infant does not breathe, slapping, cold water, and other stimulants are no longer used, but rather a careful resuscitation [15].

The emotional significance of the birth experience is a matter of conjecture. Some schools of thought hold that birth has a lasting psychological influence, while others maintain that the organism is too immature to record experience meaningfully. There is no question but that birth is a critical physical experience and no argument with the fact that the newborn needs adequate physical care if he is to survive.

Injuries from Abnormal Conditions of Childbearing

The wonderful protective and adaptive resources of both mother and baby result in most infants being born intact. A minority of babies suffer from conditions existing prenatally and during the birth process. Such damage can result in fetal death, stillbirth, death soon after birth, cerebral palsy, epilepsy, mental retardation, behavior disorders, and perhaps speech and reading disorders [40]. The dangerous conditions include complications of pregnancy such as toxemias and bleeding, premature birth, difficult, prolonged, or precipitate labor, malpresentation, general anesthetic, and major illnesses of the mother.

Research is revealing increasingly the milder aspects of birth injury. Follow-up tests of motor, adaptive, and language behavior of babies who suffered stress at birth showed that the effects of stress showed up more in the second six months than during the first six months [31]. A study of infants who had suffered oxygen deprivation during birth, contrasting them with normal babies during the first five days of life, showed the traumatized infants to be significantly less sensitive to pain stimulation and visual stimulation, less integrated in motor behavior patterns, more irritable, and more tense and rigid muscularly [20]. Another study of infants who suffered oxygen deprivation at birth showed them to differ intellectually from normal children at age 3. The oxygen-deprived children averaged 8 points lower in IQ and did less well on tests of concept formation [18]. The longest follow-up study to date is on a group of 16- to 22-year-olds whose breathing had

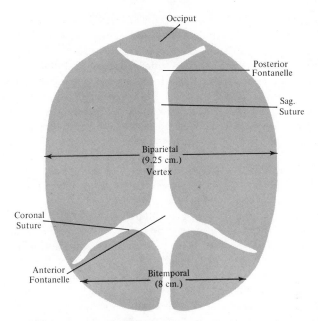

Figure 1–19. The fontanelles, or membranous spaces, on the top of a newborn baby's head. (After N. J. Eastman and L. M. Hellman, *Williams Obstetrics*. Appleton-Century-Crofts, 1966. Fig. 5, page 196.)

been delayed for one minute or more after birth [33]. Instead of the normal pattern of having a definite superiority of the preferred hand over nonpreferred in a balancing test, they showed little difference between hands. Oxygen deprivation at birth, then, depressed the score for the preferred hand 16 to 22 years later, showing a permanent effect on the central nervous system.

Prematurity

Premature birth is a hazard to life, health, and growth, both physical and mental. A baby is called premature if his gestation period is less than 37 weeks or his weight is under 5½ pounds. Birth weight is not the most accurate indicator of prematurity, as shown by recent studies. A combination of figures for birth weight and gestation period has been found useful for predicting survival and planning care [68]. Low birth weight plus short gestation usually means a more difficult time adapting immediately after birth, requiring a longer stay in the hospital and incubator. After surviving the first few months, however, these babies have a better prognosis than low birth weight babies of longer gestation. The latter had five times as many severe congenital anomalies as did the former.

Head circumference is the best single measurement for estimating gestation age [17]. Since certain abnormalities cause changes in head circumference, probably the most accurate way of estimating maturity is with a combination of head circumference, electroencephalographic data, other neurological data, and motor performance. Many babies with very low birth weights die and among those who survive, about half suffer neurological damage which ranges from minimal to severe mental deficiency [66]. About a third of cerebral palsied children were premature babies. The more premature the child or the lower the birth weight, the greater are his chances of being handicapped and the more severe the handicaps are likely to be [5, 36]. He is likely to suffer more physical illness during the first two years [14]. The premature child tends to score lower on developmental tests in infancy and on intelligence tests in childhood, children of lower socioeconomic status being more depressed in scores than those of higher status [14]. At age 12–13, children of low birth weight showed impaired reading and were below average in grade placement [64]. Prematures are more prone to behavior disorders and social and emotional difficulties. Subtle brain damage, specific reading problems, and hearing losses were suspected when prematures with normal IQs did not do as well as average in school, at age 10 [36]. Abnormal patterns of brain waves have been found in prematures. Physical growth, too, tends to be retarded. Premature infants are likely to be below average in size as children and as adults [36]. Blindness as a result of prematurity is not so frequent now as it was in the 1940s and 50s, when oxygen was routinely given liberally to premature babies. After the discovery that this practice often caused severe damage to the retina, oxygen has been used much more cautiously, but sometimes a choice has to be made between the baby's life and a high risk of injury to his eyes.

The ways in which prematurity is associated with defects are complex. First, the neurological and behavior disorders associated with prematurity may be the results of the same prenatal disorders that caused the baby to be born early. Second, the immature condition of the prematurely born baby makes him less able to stand the stresses and strains of birth and postnatal life. Third, he is treated differently from full-term babies. Kept in an incubator and extra sanitary environment, he is deprived of normal skin contacts and other stimulation. He is probably not breast-fed and may not even be able to seek, find, and suck his food. Later on, the anxiety surrounding his early days may evoke special handling from his family, encouraging dependency.

Since the last two months of intrauterine life is the time when the fat is laid down under the skin, a premature baby looks red and wrinkled, as compared with a full-term baby. His head looks extra big for his tiny body. Depending on how immature he is, he may or may not be able to suck and swallow. Feeding him the right nutriments is a problem, even though mechanical devices can put the food into his stomach. Many hospitals encourage mothers to express their own milk for their prematures, or they may use a human milk bank. Leads on what to feed prematures are being sought through studying marsupials and the secretions that they give to their immature young while in the pouch. The small stature observed in children and adults who were born prematurely may be the result of inadequate nutrition during a critical growth period. All aspects of prematurity are receiving the attention of research scientists, the social as well as the biological. It has been found that parents of damaged prematures respond well to counseling, especially when offered early [66].

After this dreary recital of what can go wrong with a premature child, we want to reassure our readers that some prematures grow up normal. After all, only 40 to 60 percent of infants in the studies surveyed have shown defects. An example of a premature baby who has shown only a slight, temporary problem stemming from it is Laura, to whom this book is dedicated. With a gestation of 36 weeks and a birth weight of 4½ pounds, she could suck and swallow and showed normal neonatal reflexes. As a young child, she had a speech defect that was cured by a few weeks of speech therapy. At age 22, she is a successful businesswoman, a graduate student, a member of Phi Beta Kappa and a happy wife.

Fetology, the new branch of medical science which deals with the fetus, is yielding techniques for diagnosing and treating fetal illnesses and imperfections, thus making it possible to prevent many birth defects. One of the new techniques is amniocentesis, the drawing off of amniotic fluid through a tube put through the mother's abdominal and uterine walls and into the amniotic sac. Analysis of the fluid can show genetic defects, such as Mongolism. The sex of the baby can be determined, and this may be important in a family that is known to have sex-linked defects, such as hemophilia. The fluid can also show if the baby is ill and how ill he is from causes such as blood incompatibility. The baby might be saved by a blood transfusion or a Caesarian delivery. Another diagnostic technique is examination with an amnioscope, an instrument for lighting and viewing the inside of the uterus from the birth canal. It is possible to draw a blood sample from the baby's head through the birth canal. Fetal surgery is performed by making a small opening in the mother's abdomen and uterus, inserting a catheter into the baby or giving other treatment, and then closing the incisions in the mother [2]. Research on animals has demonstrated the possibility of much more complicated fetal surgery [34]. Other techniques that have stimulated advances in diagnosis and treatment include thermography, a way of mapping the pregnant mother through heat waves, ultrasonics, or mapping of the fetus by sound waves and electrocardiograms of the fetus.

Significance of Socioeconomic Conditions for Childbearing

Birth control, in the form of both contraception and abortion, is less available to poor, uneducated people, than it is to the middle and upper class. For this reason, among other reasons, more unplanned and unwanted children, in fact, more children, are born to the poor. Thus more pregnancies and more closely spaced pregnancies occur among the women who have the most inadequate diets, the most stressful physical environments, and the most exposure to crises of many kinds. The most careful studies of fetal and infant death, related to socioeconomic status, have been done in Britain [30]. American studies show relationships between mortality and skin color which are highly related to socioeconomic conditions. In Scotland, fetal loss and stillbirths have been higher for semiskilled and unskilled laborers than for professionals and managers ever since statistics have been recorded. When death rates have gone down, the ratio between the classes has been maintained. In the United States, the color differences in perinatal mortality is strongly in favor of whites. The ratio has increased in recent years. Maternal mortality figures reflect the same socioeconomic differences seen in the statistics for infants. Figures 1–15, 1–16, and 1–20 illustrate these differences.

Poor countries show poor performance in childbearing as compared with prosperous countries, just as do the poor in a given country as compared with the well-to-do. Low birth weights occur in 4 percent of Scandinavian births, 7 or 8 percent of British, 7 percent of white American, 10 percent of black American, 18 percent of South African Indians, and 35 percent of Indian births in Madras [45].

The production of children of excellent quality, then, is the outcome of many factors. Poverty is associated with all the factors that work against excellence in

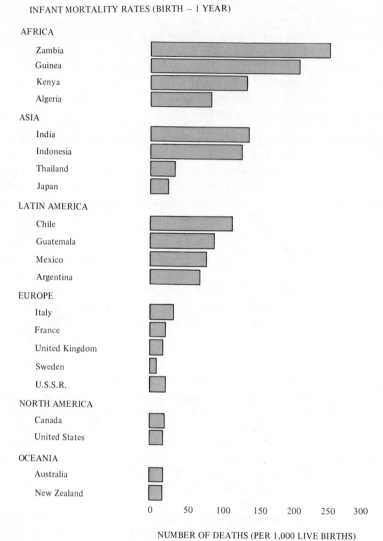

INFANT MORTALITY RATES (BIRTH – 1 YEAR)

AFRICA
Zambia
Guinea
Kenya
Algeria

ASIA
India
Indonesia
Thailand
Japan

LATIN AMERICA
Chile
Guatemala
Mexico
Argentina

EUROPE
Italy
France
United Kingdom
Sweden
U.S.S.R.

NORTH AMERICA
Canada
United States

OCEANIA
Australia
New Zealand

0   50   100   150   200   250   300

NUMBER OF DEATHS (PER 1,000 LIVE BIRTHS)

Figure 1–20. Infant mortality in selected nations.

SOURCE: Data from 1969 World Population Data Sheet, *Obstetrical and Gynecological News*, 1969, 4:10, p. 28. Also from *Demographic Yearbook* 1967, 19th issue; Special topic: Mortality Statistics, Statistical Office of the U.N. Dept. of Economic and Social Affairs, N.Y.: United Nations, 1968.

reproduction. Quantity dilutes quality. A limited number of high-quality babies can be born under certain conditions. Excellent infants require prenatal conditions that assure them of good nutrition, absence of stress and disease, an environment provided by a woman of appropriate age, adequate medical supervision of pregnancy and birth. Since family planning and, when indicated, heredity counseling are now essential for parents who want to give their children the best chance for full development, education is very pertinent to successful childbearing.

Summary

Fertilization occurs in the middle of a menstrual cycle, when a spermatazoon penetrates a mature ovum. After subdividing for three or four days, the fertilized egg implants itself in the lining of the uterus. Differentiation of the organs and tissues takes place during the first 2 months of life, during which time the organism is called an embryo. Fluid fills the amniotic sac, which encloses and protects the embryo. Having acquired a more human appearance, the embryo's name is changed to *fetus* when he reaches 8 weeks of age. Further differentiation of organs and tissues takes place along the basic form which has been laid down. The organs begin to function. The fetus moves freely and performs many reflex acts. The head end is better developed than the tail end, both physically and functionally.

Pregnancy can be diagnosed through laboratory tests soon after the first missed menstrual period. The mother's awareness of pregnancy may occur even before this time, or it may be delayed until much later, depending upon the symptoms she experiences. The first three months of pregnancy is a time of physiological reorganization which usually involves fatigue. New feelings and emotions go along with the pervasive bodily changes which affect all the systems. Adjustment to pregnancy is affected by physical and psychological preparation for it, by the natural resources of the mother, and by the care and experiences she has during pregnancy. The small, nuclear family tends to place the main burden of emotional support upon the husband. Out-of-wedlock pregnancies show higher rates of physical and psychological disturbances.

Infant and mother are affected by the nutritional state of the mother when the pregnancy is begun, as well as by the adequacy of nutrition throughout the pregnancy. Since mothers vary considerably in their needs, individual nutritional guidance is very desirable. Serious nutritional deficiencies are associated with complications of pregnancy, labor, and delivery, and with defective development of the baby.

Babies respond prenatally to loud sudden sounds by moving, often in sudden movements which are probably similar to the startle response of the newborn. Maternal emotional disturbance, also, is associated with high activity in the fetus. Emotional well-being of the mother probably contributes to the emotional well-being of the baby. Prenatal influence also occurs through physical, chemical, and biological means. X rays, beyond a certain level, are damaging and even lethal. Many drugs, such as quinine, certain barbiturates, and tranquilizers, will damage the unborn baby. Cigaret smoking is associated with premature birth. Many diseases, such as measles, are likely to damage the embryo or fetus. Incompatibility between the mother's blood and the baby's blood will, under certain conditions, harm the baby. Certain risks to mother and baby are increased when the mother is in the later years of childbearing.

Birth is a physical and emotional crisis for the mother, baby, and family. Labor. the work which the mother does in giving birth, consists of three stages. The first stage, the opening of the cervix, is accomplished by muscles which are not under voluntary control. The confident, secure mother can probably help the process by relaxing. The second stage, pushing the baby out, is partially involuntary and partially controllable by the mother. Education for childbirth prepares her to function here. The third stage, a brief process, is the expelling of the placenta. The duration of labor varies considerably, the most common length for a first labor being 7 hours, and for subsequent labors, 4 hours. A Caesarian birth is safer for mother and baby than is a difficult natural delivery.

The mother's emotions and her experience of pain during labor are determined to some extent by what she has been taught to expect. Education for childbirth can be a very positive influence. "Prepared childbirth" uses education, emotional preparation, and support during labor.

The baby is equipped with mechanisms for adapting to the birth process. Some of his responses to this process prepare him for beginning to breathe. A few babies are injured at birth and others are damaged prenatally. Premature birth is associated with neurological disorders. Hereditary defects account for some abnormalities. Most seriously malformed fetuses do not live to full term. Good obstetrical care includes prenatal supervision and education as well as skilled help to the mother and baby during labor and delivery and afterward.

Poverty and lack of education are associated with higher maternal mortality and with greater numbers of children with birth defects, including low birth weights which are associated with below par development. The production of children in excellent condition at birth and with excellent chances of good development is associated both with greater income and greater knowledge and education.

References

1. Baird, D. Quoted in *San Francisco Chronicle*, January 18, 1969.
2. Berrill, N. J. *The person in the womb*. New York: Dodd, Mead, 1968.
3. Birch, H. Research issues in child health IV: Some philosophic and methodological issues. In E. Grotberg (Ed.), *Critical issues in research related to disadvantaged children*. Princeton, N.J.: Educational Testing Service, 1969.
4. Bowes, W. A., Brackbill, Y., Conway, E., & Steinschneider, A. The effects of obstetrical medication on fetus and infant. *Mono. Soc. Res. Child Devel.*, 1970, **35**:4.
5. Braine, M. D. S., et al. Factors associated with impairment of the early development of prematures. *Mono. Soc. Res. Child Devel.*, 1966, **31**:4.
6. Burke, B. S., Beal, V. A., Kirkwood, S. B., & Stuart, H. C. The influence of nutrition during pregnancy upon the condition of the infant at birth. *J. Nutrition*, 1943, **26**, 569–583.
7. Caldwell, D. F., & Churchill, J. A. Learning ability in the progeny of rats administered a protein-deficient diet during the second half of gestation. *Neurology*, 1967, 17–95.
8. Collis, W. F. R., & Janes, M. Multifactorial causation of malnutrition and retarded growth and development. In N. S. Scrimshaw & J. E. Gordon (Eds.), *Malnutrition, learning and Behavior*. Cambridge, Mass.: M.I.T. Press, 1967, pp. 55–80.
9. Conway, E., & Brackbill, Y. Effects of obstetrical medication on the infant's sensorimotor behavior. Paper presented at the meeting of the Society for Research in Child Development, Santa Monica, Calif., March 27, 1969.
10. Cravioto, J. Nutritional deficiencies and mental performance in childhood. In D. C. Glass (Ed.), *Environmental influences*. New York: Rockefeller University Press, 1968, pp. 3–51.
11. Davids, A., DeVault, S., & Talmadge, M. Anxiety, pregnancy, and childbirth abnormalities. *J. Consult. Psychol.*, 1961, **25**, 74–77.

12. Dean, R. F. A. The size of the baby at birth and the yield of breast milk. Studies of undernutrition. Wuppertal, 1946–1949. *Special Report Series, Medical Research Council*, 275. London: Her Majesty's Stationery Office, 1951.

13. Denenberg, V. H. Stimulation in infancy, emotional reactivity, and exploratory behavior. In D. C. Glass (Ed.), *Neurophysiology and emotion*. New York: Rockefeller University Press and Russell Sage Foundation, 1967, pp. 161–190.

14. Drillien, C. M. The growth and development of the prematurely born infant. Baltimore: Williams & Wilkins, 1964.

15. Eastman, N. J., & Hellman, L. M. *Williams obstetrics* (13th ed.). New York: Appleton-Century-Crofts, 1966.

16. Ebbs, J. N., Tisdall, F. F., & Scott, W. A. Influence of prenatal diet on mother and child. *J. Nutrition*, 1941, **22**, 515–526.

17. Eichorn, D. H. Biology of gestation and infancy: Fatherland and frontier. *Merrill-Palmer Quart.*, 1968, **14**, 47–81.

18. Ernhart, C. B., Graham, F. K., & Thurston, D. Relationship of neonatal apnea to development at three years. *Arch. Neurol.*, 1960, **2**, 504–510.

19. Ferreira, A. J. The pregnant woman's emotional attitude and its reflection on the newborn. *Am. J. Orthopsychiat.*, 1960, **30**, 553–561.

20. Graham, F. K., Mantarazzo, R. G., & Caldwell, B. M. Behavioral differences between normal and traumatized newborns. *Psychol. Mono.*, 1956, **70**, 20 & 21, Numbers 427–428.

21. Grimm, E. R. Psychological and social factors in pregnancy, delivery and outcome. In S. A. Richardson & A. F. Guttmacher [45], pp. 1–52.

22. Guttmacher, A. F. Speech at Brown University, Providence, R. I., January 23, 1969.

23. Hall, R. E. His birth without permission. *Sat. Rev.*, December 7, 1968, 78–79.

24. Hamer, J. H. The cultural aspects of infant mortality in Subsaharan Africa. (Ph.D. thesis in Anthropology, Northwestern Univeristy) Ann Arbor, Mich.: University Microfilms, 1962.

25. Hardy, J. B. Rubella and its aftermath. *Children*, 1969, **16**(3), 91–96.

26. Heinstein, M. I. Expressed attitudes and feelings of pregnant women and their relations to physical complications of pregnancy. *Merrill-Palmer Quart.*, 1967, **13**, 217–236.

27. Holden, R. H., Man, E. B., & Jones, W. P. Maternal hypothyroxinemia and developmental consequences during the first year of life. Paper presented at the meeting of the Society for Research in Child Development, Santa Monica, Calif., March 27, 1969.

28. Holley, W. L., Rosenbaum, A. L., & Churchill, J. A. Effects of rapid succession of pregnancy. In *Perinatal factors affecting human development*, Pan American Health Organization, Pan American Sanitary Bureau, Regional Office of World Health Organization, 1969, pp. 41–45.

29. Hurley, L. S. The consequences of fetal impoverishment. *Nutrition Today*, 1968, **3**(4), 2–10.

30. Illsley, R. The sociological study of reproduction and its outcome. In S. A. Richardson & A. F. Guttmacher [45], pp. 75–141.

31. Klatskin, E. H., McGarry, M. E., & Steward, M. S. Variability in developmental test patterns as a sequel to neonatal stress. *Child Devel.*, 1966, **37**, 819–826.

32. Kron, R. E., Stein, M., & Goddard, K. E. Newborn sucking behavior affected by obstetric sedation. *Pediat.*, 1966, **37**, 1012–1016.

33. Leventhal, D. S. Specialized manual skill and personality adjustment 16–22 years after delayed breathing at birth (perinatal apnea): A replication and extension. Paper presented at the meeting of the Society for Research in Child Development, Santa Monica, Calif., March 27, 1969.

34. *Life* magazine. Control of life. September 10, 1965, 55–77.

35. Liley, H. M. I. *Modern motherhood.* New York: Random House, 1967.

36. Lubchenco, L. O., et al. Sequelae of premature birth. *Am. J. Dis. Child.*, 1963, **106**, 101–115.

37. Mead, M., & Newton, N. Cultural patterning of perinatal behavior. In S. A. Richardson & A. F. Guttmacher [45], pp. 142–244.

38. Montagu, M. F. A. *Prenatal influences.* Springfield, Ill.: Charles C Thomas, 1962.

39. *New York Times.* It really may be food for thought. July 28, 1968 (interview with John Churchill).

40. Pasamanick, B., & Knobloch, H. Retrospective studies on the epidemiology of reproductive causality: Old and new. *Merrill-Palmer Quart.*, 1966, **12**, 7–26.

41. Platt, B. S., Barrett, I. M., & Christie, B. A. The effect of chronic dietary protein-calorie deficiency on reproductive performance of rats: Respiratory metabolism of ova (in press). Cited in *Perspectives on human deprivation.* Washington, D.C.: U.S. Dept. of Health, Education, and Welfare, 1966, p. 244.

42. Plummer, G. Anomalies occurring in children exposed in utero to the atomic bomb in Hiroshima. *Pediat.*, 1952, **10**, 687–693.

43. Pope, H. Negro-white differences in decisions regarding illegitimate children *J. Marr. Fam.*, 1969, **31**, 756–764.

44. Rainwater, L. *And the poor get children.* Chicago: Quadrangle, 1960.

45. Richardson, S. A., & Guttmacher, A. F. (Eds.). *Childbearing—Its social & psychological aspects.* Baltimore: Williams & Wilkins, 1967.

46. Robinson, C. H. *Fundamentals of normal nutrition.* New York: Macmillan, 1968.

47. Rosengren, W. R. Social sources of pregnancy as illness or normality. *Social Forces*, 1961, **39**, 260–267.

48. Salk, L. Mother's heartbeat as an imprinting stimulus. *Trans. N.Y. Acad. Sci.*, Ser. II, 1962, **24**, 753–763.

49. Schulman, C. A. Sleep patterns in newborn infants as a function of suspected neurological impairment of maternal heroin addiction. Paper presented at the meeting of the Society for Research in Child Development. Santa Monica, Calif., March 27, 1969.

50. Scrimshaw, N. S. Malnutrition, learning and behavior. *Am. J. Clinical Nutrition*, 1967, **20**, 493–502.

51. Shank, R. E. A chink in our armor. *Nutrition Today*, 1970, **5**:2.

52. Sherwin, R. W. Perinatal nutrition as a developmental determinant. *Nutrition News*, 1967, **30**(4), 13–14.

53. Smith, C. A. Effects of maternal undernutrition upon the newborn infant in Holland, *J. Pediat.*, 1947, **30**, 229–243.

54. Sontag, L. W. Significance of fetal environmental differences. *Am. J. Obstet. Gynecol.*, 1941, **54**, 994–1003.

55. Sontag, L. W., & Richards, T. W. Studies in fetal behavior. I: Fetal heart rate as a behavior indicator. *Mono. Soc. Res. Child Devel.*, 1938, 3:4.

56. Spelt, D. K. The conditioning of the human fetus in utero. *J. Exptl. Psychol.*, 1948, **38**, 338–346.

57. Stearns, G. Nutritional state of the mother prior to conception. *J. Am. Med. Assoc.*, 1958, **168**, 1655–1659.

58. Stechler, G. Newborn attention affected by medication during labor. *Sci.*, **144**, 315–317.

59. Tanner, J. M., & Inhelder, B. *Discussions on child development*. Vol. 3. New York: International Universities, 1958.

60. United States Department of Agriculture. *Dietary levels of households in the United States, Spring, 1965, A preliminary report*. Washington, D.C.: U.S. Govt. Printing Office, 1968.

61. Walters, C. E. Prediction of postnatal development from fetal activity. *Child Devel.*, 1965, **36**, 801–808.

62. Watson, E. H., & Lowrey, G. H. *Growth and development of children* (5th ed.). Chicago: Year Book, 1967.

63. Werboff, J. Prenatal factors determining later behavior. In A. J. Schuster (Ed.) *The teaching of infant development*. Detroit: Merrill-Palmer Institute, 1962, 98–105.

64. Wiener, G. Scholastic achievement at age 12–13 of prematurely born infants. *J. Special Educ.*, 1968, **2**, 237–250.

65. Winnick, M., & Noble, A. Cellular response with increased feeding in neonatal rats. *J. Nutrition*, 1967, **91**, 179–182.

66. Wortis, H. Social class and premature birth. *Social Casework*, 1963, **45**, 541–543.

67. Yamazaki, J. N., et al. Outcome of pregnancy in women exposed to the atomic bomb in Nagasaki. *Am. J. Dis. Child.*, 1954, **87**, 448–463.

68. Yerushalmy, J. The low-birthweight baby. *Hospital Practice*, 1968, **3**, 62–69.

69. Zamenhof, S., Van Marthens, E., & Margolis, F. L. DNA (cell number) and protein in neonatal brain: Alteration by maternal dietary protein restriction. *Science*, 1968, **160**, 322–323.

Readings in
Prenatal Development and Birth

Between conception and birth the human being grows from a single cell to a mass of about 7 pounds. The single cell, although simple as compared with the myriad cells composing the newborn infant, is itself a complex organism. The factors operating to shape the nine-month growth are numerous; the interrelationships among the factors are subtle. It used to be generally agreed that the prenatal child was a tyrannical parasite, taking what it needed from the mother's bloodstream, at her expense, if need be. It is now apparent that deprivation of the mother deprives her unborn child.

Even the social settings of childbearing are significant for the baby and the mother. A Scottish sociologist, Raymond Illsley of the University of Aberdeen, traces the complicated interrelationships between social class and the performance of mothers in childbearing. In the process he uses data from large numbers of women and shows that, on the average, women from more deprived cultural settings produce more handicapped children than women from favored settings.

It is not the social setting itself which affects prenatal development, but factors within the social setting, such as nutrition and personal hygiene. Therefore inadequate nutrition and poor personal hygiene, if they occur in a wealthy, otherwise advantaged person, also will have an adverse effect.

Anthropologist Margaret Mead and psychologist Niles Newton discuss the varieties of family structures within which men and women develop as parents. The main focus of this article is on fatherhood. Biological fatherhood is only a brief episode in many animals' lives. The roles and responsibilities of human fatherhood, essential for the survival and development of the child, as developed in various cultures, are the subject matter in this article. (See also the article by Biller in Smart and Smart, Preschool Children, *Macmillan, 1973, which reports research on American boys whose fathers were not present in the homes in which the boys were growing up.) What a man does for and with his children after they are born is subject to a great deal of variation.*

In the next article Carlo Valenti, a research obstetrician, describes modern techniques for intrauterine diagnosis and treatment. He outlines the hereditary basis of Mongolism and gives the case history of a mother who was saved from producing a Mongoloid child. Valenti faces the reader with the new moral decisions and social adaptations required by recent progress in medicine.

In the last article, a series of excerpts from a longer article, Shank discusses the most recent knowledge regarding optimum nutrition in pregnancy. It is clear that although there are nutritional needs that are unique to pregnancy, optimum nutrition of pregnancy does not begin at conception, or end at birth. The woman's body needs to have good stores of the

46

nutritional elements before conception. Equally important are the eating habits which result in the woman's nutritional state. Because eating habits are resistant to change, it would be extremely difficult for a woman to improve poor eating patterns to the point of providing good nutrition during the short period of nine months.

Significance of Class Differences to Childbearing

Raymond Illsley

UNIVERSITY OF ABERDEEN, SCOTLAND

Socio-economic status does not itself affect biological functioning. For purposes of epidemiological research, it is best regarded as an abstraction, a classificatory system designed to subdivide populations according to their social background, characteristics, behavior, and values. Class differences in reproductive behavior merely indicate the possible existence of environmental influences. As a research tool, social class is perhaps comparable to the physician's thermometer, which may indicate that a problem exists but cannot provide a diagnosis. Social classes differ in status origin, education, diet, housing, types of activity, age at marriage and childbirth, parity, physical health, etc.; the difficult but essential task is to identify which of these and many other social influences, acting singly or in combination, produce high obstetric risks.

There is no reason to assume that the same class-related factor is responsible for variations in each pregnancy complication or that for a specific complication the same social etiology applies at different times and places. The components of class reflect the culture of the time and place. This point is illustrated below in a discussion of the difficulties encountered in comparing class performance from decade to decade and from area to area.

The decrease in infant mortality since the beginning of the century has occurred most strikingly for causes of death associated with poor living conditions. One might therefore have expected a long-term tendency toward an equalization of rates. Yet, as reported above, class differentials have hardly changed in Britain (the only country for which data are available) over 40 years of great social, economic, and medical change. Various theories have been advanced to explain these surprising results. Most of these theories are based on the concept of time lag; methods of treatment, the availability of health services, even income, it was argued, could perhaps be changed suddenly, but other, less tangible influences changed slowly—e.g., housing conditions, the physical environment of large towns, habits of hygiene, methods of infant care, the actual use of health facilities, and so forth. Indeed, in the short run,

Reprinted from S. A. Richardson & A. F. Guttmacher (eds.), *Childbearing—Its Social and Psychological Aspects.* Baltimore: Williams and Wilkins, 1967, pp. 82–86, 105–108. By permission of the Association for the Aid of Crippled Children.

it might well be that the educated middle classes would benefit most because their education enabled them to take immediate advantage of improved medical and social services. Thus, decreasing death rates might initially be accompanied by wider class differences, followed, after an interval, by a gradual tendency toward equalization. The history of public health services and the results of health campaigns lend weight to this type of argument; in current campaigns for the early detection of cervical cancer, it is the middle-class woman with a low disease risk who receives the regular check-up.

Another, supplementary explanation has been advanced by Illsley (1955). He showed that women brought up in the lower socio-economic groups who married professional or skilled workers tended to be taller and of better physique than those who remained in the lower social classes at marriage. They also gave birth to heavier babies and had fewer perinatal deaths. Women who moved down the social scale at marriage had high prematurity and perinatal death rates. Illsley postulated a continuous process of social mobility which tended to concentrate healthy women in the upper social groups and the least healthy in the lower social groups, a process which would keep class mortality rates apart as long as social inequality existed. The decreasing size of the semiskilled and unskilled groups, combined with selective upward mobility would, more-over, increase the concentration of less healthy mothers in these groups, thus counteracting any tendency to improvement in their mortality rates.

This argument highlights a property of current methods of status classification which makes them inappropriate for certain types of investigation. If we compare, over time, the mortality rates of two groups, each of which marries entirely within itself (e.g., two castes), and the one with the higher mortality rate is given preferential social and medical care, the two rates should eventually move together. Comparisons over time between countries or regions, between white and colored, are of this kind. Such comparisons would be vitiated, however, if group boundaries were substantially loosened by intermarriage or migration so that the group receiving preferential treatment eventually lost its healthy members to the other group and received their least healthy in return. This is frequently the case in class comparisons, because those members of the lower class who receive preferential treatment as children tend simul-taneously to grow into healthy adults and to rise in the social scale. Preferential treatment of one group, as children, results, 20 years later, in the superior health of adults in the other social group.

If we wish to know whether improved living conditions for low-status groups have produced women more capable of producing viable babies, we should classify perinatal or infant mortality rates not by the social status which women reach as adults (their husband's social class) but by their status in childhood (their father's social class). This argument applies to all status groups in a mobile society, to individual occupations as much as to general social classes, because the status reached in adult life reflects the conditions of upbringing which made that status possible.

Time comparisons are complicated by a further technical property of most social classifications. The range of social variation between upper- and lower-status groups depends on their size. Thus, if we compare the upper and lower 5 percent of a population, the range will be greater than if we compare the upper and lower quartiles. Unfortunately, the boundaries of status or class groups are usually fixed by external factors—the percentage of the population possessing certain defined social characteristics—and cannot be manipulated for analytical convenience. In the British example, the lowest social class is defined as "unskilled workers," who formed a considerable proportion of the population 50 years ago but are a relatively small category today. Thus, in comparing the mortality rates of the lowest social class in 1910 and 1960 we might be comparing the lowest quartile of the 1910 population with a highly concentrated 10 percent of the 1960 population. The upper class, on the other hand, will have increased its relative size. For purposes of time comparison, it would be more appropriate to use a "percentile" type of classification so that, for example, the highest and lowest ranking 10 percent could be compared with each other at each time point.

Parallel difficulties occur when we compare the meaning of class from one area to another. The problem is illustrated in Figure 1, derived from the British Perinatal Mortality Survey (Butler and Bonham, 1963). The same criteria of classification were applied to occupations of husbands in the Northern, Midland, and Southern regions of Britain to produce four class categories: professional and managerial, clerical, skilled manual workers, and semiskilled and unskilled workers. Perinatal death rates are expressed as a ratio of the

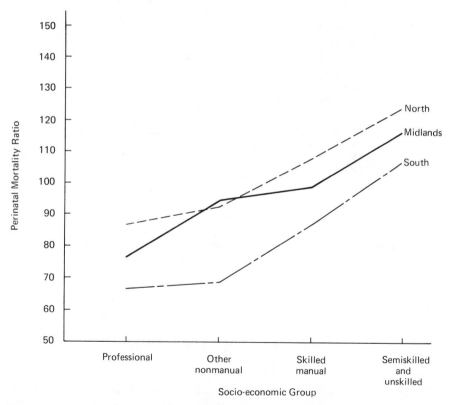

FIGURE 1.   *Perinatal death rates in each region and socio-economic group in Great Britain in 1958 expressed as a ratio of the national rate (Great Britain = 100).*

over-all British rate. It is clear that the rates of each class vary consistently with the region. Indeed, they vary so sharply that professional workers in the North are equivalent to skilled manual workers in the South. Thus, similarity of socio-economic status (as defined by our crude indices) is no guarantee of social identity. There are many reasons for this, some technical, some more truly sociological.

1. When we use classifications which distinguish individuals with a given characteristic—e.g., professional workers, or unskilled workers, people above or below a certain income level, etc.—we may select quite different proportions of the populations in two areas. We may, as in the time comparison discussed above, be comparing the lowest ranking 10 percent of one community with the lowest ranking 25 percent of another. This possibility is even more likely if we deal with selected clinic or hospital populations from different areas.

In most instances such disparity in relative size tends to obscure class differences. In the example given in Figure 1, semiskilled and unskilled workers constituted 31 percent of the population in the north of Great Britain compared with 21 percent in the south. If the Southern group were increased to 31 percent by the reclassification of the lowest ranking skilled workers as semiskilled, the regional differential in the perinatal death rates of semiskilled and unskilled workers would be even greater. On the other hand, in hospital populations, with their overt and hidden biases, class differentials may be obscured; where, for example, private hospital patients in a relatively poor community are compared with those in public hospitals in a richer community, real differences between classes in the two communities may easily be eliminated.

The use of a "percentile" approach avoids this problem but poses an alternative dilemma: equivalent ranks in two communities may have little in common other than their percentile position.

2. Groups with the same nominal class in two areas may, because of heterogeneity within a single class, be widely different in other respects. Thus "skilled workers" in one area may denote craftsmen, whereas in others the term may mean workers in heavy industry, miners, agricultural workers, etc.

3. Behind these technical problems of classification there lies a further sociological problem: within even a relatively small area, separate communities may exist which differ so much in their ways of life that the pooling together of nominally similar social classes from each community may be a meaningless operation. . . .

THE INTERRELATIONSHIP OF SOCIAL AND OBSTETRIC PROCESSES

Each of . . . these factors . . .—social class; country, region, and area; illegitimacy; age; parity; and maternal height—is clearly associated with many aspects of reproductive functioning. The range of differences along a single axis is in each case strongly marked. Although all these factors are interrelated, there is some reason to assume that each may exercise an "independent" effect or indicate the presence of a further causal factor so that when they occur together their impact is cumulative. The range of perinatal death rates occurring between tall wives of professional men in the south of England and short wives of manual workers in the north of Britain is itself large (mortality ratio of 58 compared to 140); if simultaneous data were available on age and parity and the analysis were extended over a wider geographic and ethnic range, these differences would be further widened (Illsley and Kincaid, 1963). It is clearly important to study the interrelationships among these factors and the social processes by which they become interrelated and through which they jointly relate to obstetric behavior. The intrinsic effect of other specific factors, such as nutrition in pregnancy, smoking, physical activity, etc., can then be viewed against the general socio-medical background.

The period of infancy, childhood, and adolescence may be regarded not only as one of growth and learning but also as one of differentiation. The child undergoes environmental experiences, both physical and cultural, which shape his physique and health and his emotional and intellectual growth and simultaneously implant the social values and habits which will characterize his behavior as an adult. The physical and cultural stimuli are not independent of one another: the socio-economic conditions which influence education, social values, aspirations, and opportunities also affect the child's material environment and nutrition; and the nutritional experience which influences his growth simultaneously patterns his later dietary habits.

In the highly diversified, mobile, changing society of the industrial West, this is a complex process; the increasingly technological nature of the economy demands the emergence from lower socio-economic strata of huge population groups with skills and values different from those of their parents, and the informal educational institutions of the family and the social group are systematically supplemented by the vast educational machinery of the modern state. This is a selective movement: persons move up into the higher socio-economic strata whose material and cultural environment has most fitted them to take advantage of increasing educational and occupational opportunities. There is a corresponding downward movement of individuals and groups who, for many reasons, have been unable to grasp these opportunities. The vast literature on the subject cannot be summarized here (see Glass, 1954; Lipset and Bendix, 1959) but its implications are important, for it leads to the existence of adult groups with characteristic patterns of social and biological inter-correlations. It is this process of socialization, selection, and acculturation that produces the tendency for certain biological characteristics and social habits and values to hang together. Thus each of the various socio-economic groups is characterized not only by similarity in wealth but also by broadly similar educational levels, nutritional habits, housing and work conditions, habits in relation to age at marriage, attitudes to family size, spacing and methods of birth control, access to and motivation to use health services, and also by their physical build and their basic health status.

In terms of the variables discussed above, the lower social classes tend to marry early, to have many children at short intervals, to be drawn from poorer regions and housing areas, and to be short in stature. Around these basic factors are clustered other typical characteristics: illegitimacy, prenuptial conception, poor diet, infectious environments; heavy manual work, late or inadequate antenatal care, lack of ready access to information and advice, poor motivation to seek such help, limited knowledge of biological functioning, lack of control over their environment and consequent anxiety, inadequate or ill-balanced dietary intakes, etc. These characteristics do not, of course, all occur uniformly in all members of lower socio-economic groups, and they may be modified by ethnic or religious influences in a heterogeneous society; each characteristic, however, occurs most frequently in these groups and there is an internal logic in their simultaneous manifestation.

Many implications flow from such patterns. In studying the etiology of a pregnancy condition, the simultaneous occurrence of many factors inevitably leads to accidental correlations. The term "young multipara," for example, connotes many factors besides youth and multiparity; depending on the culture in which it is applied, it may connote short, unhealthy women, poor antenatal and obstetric care, economic disadvantage (nonwhite, unskilled workers, unemployed, etc.), and a host of related factors. Its implications may not always lead in the same direction. As we have seen, youth appears to be a favorable factor in relation to stillbirth, and stillbirth rates are relatively low for young women and for second and third pregnancies, but youth and multiparity in combination are associated with high stillbirth and infant death rates. The "elderly primigravida" has the low infant mortality rates appropriate to her favorable social characteristics and the high stillbirth rates associated with age.

Systematic study of the specific influence of a biological variable seems to require, therefore, detailed knowledge of the operation and interrelation of social and biological factors as they apply in the culture being studied—a requirement very rarely met. This requirement becomes more important when (1) the sampling basis of the study population is unknown; and (2) smaller groups from different populations or institutions are being added together to form a large total sample.

These are the conditions under which research is normally conducted in most centers. A hospital located in one area of a large city is likely to draw its population from the surrounding neighborhood; this is likely to be socially selected. Certain socio-economic groups may already have been drawn off to be patients of private or specialized hospitals and, where home confinement is common, self-selection of another and biased kind may also have important effects. Valid conclusions may still be drawn from such studies, but the validity will depend on the nature of the population, the problem being studied, the strength of diagnostic tools, the clinical insight of the medical practitioner, etc. Some of the difficulties arising in such studies will be considered in more detail later.

A second series of implications affects those studies dealing with the consequences of the birth process for the functioning of the child. A low level of functioning in a child may result from a multiplicity of genetic, intrauterine, perinatal, and postnatal influence, some biological, some social and psychological. When the level of functioning of children whose birth was characterized by a particular condition (e.g., low birth weight) is below average, there is at least a prima facie case for arguing that the condition itself affected the child's functioning. This, however, is one of several possibilities which, in terms of low birth weight and infant I.Q., may be stated as follows:

1. A direct causal link exists (as stated above).

2. Women of low I.Q. may be prone to bear small babies, many of whom thus inherit a low intellectual potential.

3. Low birth weight and low infant I.Q. may both independently be resultants of maternal pregnancy pathology.

4. Low-birth-weight babies may be born into postnatal environments relatively unfavorable to intellectual growth.

A number of variations could be played on a combination of such hypotheses, either for premature babies in general or for clinical subcategories.

We are thus dealing with genetic, perinatal, and sociopsychological processes which may each have its own pathways but which may be and usually are interconnected. The association of birth weight with social status and maternal height, for example, already introduces the problem of genetic and social factors in the determination of stature, their joint effect on birth weight, the relationship of each to other aspects of maternal functioning, the genetic inheritance of intelligence, and the effect of parental socio-economic status on intellectual development. The problem is, of course, complicated if studies are based on partial and biased populations where one or all of the processes involved may be distorted by selection.

References

BUTLER, N. R., and BONHAM, D. G., 1963: *Perinatal Mortality*. Edinburgh: Livingstone.

GLASS, D. (ed.), 1954: *Social Mobility in Great Britain*. London: Routledge, Kegan and Paul.

ILLSLEY, R., 1955: Social class selection and class differences in relation to stillbirths and infant deaths, *Brit. Med. J.*, 2:1520–4.

——, and KINCAID, J. C., 1963: ".Social Correlates of Perinatal Mortality," in *Perinatal Mortality*, N. R. Butler and D. G. Bonham (eds.). Edinburgh: Livingstone.

LIPSET, S. M., and BENDIX, R., 1959: *Social Mobility in Industrial Society*. London: Heineman.

Fatherhood

Margaret Mead

THE MUSEUM OF NATURAL HISTORY

Niles Newton

NORTHWESTERN UNIVERSITY

Mead (1949) has emphasized that human fatherhood is a fundamental social invention. In all human societies there is at least some help given by some men to childbearing women. "Which woman and which children are provided

Reprinted from S. A. Richardson and A. F. Guttmacher (Eds.), *Childbearing—Its Social and Psychological Aspects*. Baltimore: Williams and Wilkins, 1967, pp. 189–192. By permission of the Association for the Aid of Crippled Children.

for is entirely a matter of social arrangements although the central pattern seems to be that of a man's providing for the woman who is his sexual partner and whatever children she may happen to have."

There are, of course, many variations on the basic theme reviewed by Mead. Some societies have brothers who help sisters with all aspects of child-bearing except fertilization. In many societies some men do not help directly with childbearing, preferring instead the life of a monk or other nonfamily types of living. Some highly organized societies may substitute the state for some aspects of fatherly care by taxing men and other wage earners in order to provide allowances for mothers.

Mead (1949) points out also that fatherly behavior is disrupted by slavery and some forms of indentured labor and serfdom as well as during periods of extreme social unrest, such as wars, revolutions, famines, epidemics, or abrupt transition from one kind of economy to another. "Men may flounder badly in these periods, during which the primary unit may again become mother and child."

Possibly because it is so easy under some conditions for men not to assume nurturing and assisting behavior toward childbearing women and children, many societies have developed ways of emphasizing the responsibilities of men. The Arapesh are an example of a society that begins to develop very active feelings of responsibility for women and children at a young age. The betrothed of an Arapesh boy, who should be about six years younger than he, moves into his house when she is seven or eight years old. The boy is required to grow yams, work sago, and hunt meat to feed his future wife (Mead, 1935).

Most societies emphasize responsibilities toward women and children somewhat later, through economic exchanges and rituals preceding cohabitation or during the first pregnancy. Whether the money is paid to the groom in the form of a dowry to ensure his feeling a moral obligation for future economic support of the woman and child, or whether the money is paid in the form of a bride price to the wife's family, or whether the economic exchange between families tends to be fairly equal does not matter so much as the fact that in all these cases the responsibility of men for women and their children is emphasized.

Many primitive cultures very directly stress the father's role during childbearing. The father feels personally responsible for the growth of the fetus because of the common belief that what the father does during pregnancy, as well as what the mother does, affects the health and development of the fetus. Food and activity restrictions involve not only the mother but the father also. The Ifugao of the Philippines do not permit the husband to cut or kill anything during his wife's pregnancy. Relatives must even cut wood for him, which he then carries home (Ford, 1945). The Pacific Ocean Easter Islander father gets a real sense of participation in birth by having his wife recline against him during labor and delivery (Métraux, 1940). The Kurtatchi father of the Pacific Islands is excluded from the labor, which takes place in another hut, but the importance of his impending fatherhood is emphasized by the fact that he must stop work and remain in seclusion. On no account may he lift anything heavy or touch a sharp instrument (Blackwood, 1935).

Very often the regulations cover both husband and wife, thus emphasizing the mutual nature of the undertaking. The Ila husband and wife avoid the flesh of a hartebeest, since the young of this animal are born blind and they fear the human infant will be born blind if hartebeest flesh is eaten by the parents (Smith and Dale, 1920).

Ceremonies involving husband as well as wife also emphasize fatherhood. Among the Lepcha, for example, both parents have a ceremonial cleansing in the fifth month of pregnancy (Gorer, 1938). The custom of couvade occurs in many parts of the world. Essentially it involves a period of activity restriction and "regulation" for the father as well as the mother for a time after birth. Ford's sample (1945) of 64 cultures contains records of the customs of 18 tribes in this regard. Seventeen tribes from Asia, North America, Oceania, and South America involved the father in couvade after delivery. In only one group was it definitely recorded that there was no couvade. There may be real survival value in this custom as it may particularly emphasize the father's role and responsibilities at the crucial time as each child is born. It may help him to identify with mother and baby.

In American middle-class culture, often particular emphasis is put on the wedding ceremony rather than on the later phases of fatherhood. A very elaborate wedding ceremony emphasizes man's assumption of economic responsibility for a woman and her future children. This ceremony involves name changing on the part of the woman and changes in the residence, tax status, and financial liability of both. This suitably expresses the American concept that the father's role is particularly concerned with monetary support. In fact, the American man is often actively discouraged from aiding his wife directly at the time of parturition, seldom being permitted in the delivery room and being restricted in the times he may visit with his wife in the post-delivery hospital phase. During this period, too, he may be permitted to see his baby for a few minutes behind nursery glass, but touching his baby is taboo in most hospitals. However, he is permitted to call attention to his new fatherhood by giving gifts of cigars to other men, and very recently participation in pregnancy has developed in some areas in the form of "parents' classes" which the husband as well as his expectant wife attend.

BIOLOGICAL PATERNITY AND ILLEGITIMACY

Social paternity is probably a very ancient custom, since some responsibility to nurture women and children by men is felt in all known societies, but biological paternity and concepts of illegitimacy are, in contrast, probably fairly recent. The Trobrianders, living near New Guinea, and the Aranda (Ford, 1945) believe that coitus exists merely for pleasure. They do not recognize its direct connection with conception and thus do not have the concept of physiological paternity.

Other societies know about biological paternity but regard it as a fact of minor significance. For example, the Ila young man is rather pleased if his bride has a fatherless child as thus he already has the start of a family (Smith and Dale, 1920). The Lepcha woman with an illegitimate child may be sought after and get a richer husband owing to her demonstrated fertility (Morris, 1938), although on her marriage her child usually stays with her family, the social father role being assumed by the grandfather rather than the husband of the woman. The Pukapuka (Beaglehole and Beaglehole, 1938) do not have a word for the physiological state of virginity; sexual experience takes place quite irrespective of marriage. A woman with an out-of-wedlock child is regarded as one who has proven herself fertile and thus able to carry on the patrilineal line.

In Antigua, in the West Indies, "the unmarried mother outnumbers the married mother by two to one, and there is no social or other stigma associated with this state of affairs." The teenager starting on her first pregnancy feels she will be treated better by her boy friend if she is not legally married to him. Here perhaps better social fathering occurs when marriage is not solemnized. It is interesting that under these conditions an extensive demographic study found no significant difference in the stillbirth rate between illegitimate and legitimate children (Uttley, 1961).

Other societies, however, have greatly emphasized the fact of physical paternity. In these societies the type of care the woman receives in pregnancy and the type of care her child receives are very definitely related to whether the child is the biological child of a duly wedded husband. If the child is illegitimate, its right to live is often jeopardized. Induced abortion of illegitimate conceptions occurs in many societies in which great shame is attached to illegitimacy. In some cultures even the mother may be killed. The custom in Jordan some years ago was to kill the unmarried mother; and even in 1925 no child born of an unmarried woman could be registered in the village. Granqvist (1950) comments: "Although the fellaheen fear punishment by Government, their ideas of morality still demand that the child and the mother must die."

Still other societies do not see legitimacy and illegitimacy in simple, dichotomous terms but have developed various degrees of legitimacy symbolizing different degrees of status. Among the Vietnamese, "children born of a second wife are not exactly illegitimate but do not have the same rights as children born of the first wife" (Dê, 1951). The Tupinamba had five categories of illegitimacy (d'Evreux, 1864), the highest status accruing to the offspring of the Tupinamba man and woman, and the lowest to the offspring of a Frenchman and slave of the Tupinamba.

On the other hand, low social status may make the illegitimate child more welcome. Thus the child of an unmarried Bambara mother may not live to cry more than once, but the child of an unmarried slave of the Bambara is welcome (Henry, 1910). In Goajiro, among very poor families, the illegitimately pregnant woman is merely ridiculed, whereas the woman of high class is nearly always abandoned by her relatives (Gutierrez de Pineda, 1948).

Thus in some cases illegitimacy is so construed as to deny the child any help or protection from any men, whereas in other cases the child is helped by the men of the mother's family rather than by the biological father. In still others the child is helped by the husband of his mother. In terms of outcome of the pregnancy, illegitimacy can mean death, negligent care, or care that is as good as that furnished to legitimate babies and their mothers in the same cultures, depending on social attitudes and customs. . . .

References

References originating from the Human Relations Area Files are marked with an asterisk. In cases where Human Relations Area Files foreign language texts have been quoted in this paper, the translations into English are those of the Human Relations Area Files.

*BEAGLEHOLE, E., and BEAGLEHOLE, P., 1938: "Ethnology of Pukapuka," *Bernice P. Bishop Museum Bulletin 150*, Honolulu.
*BLACKWOOD, B., 1935: *Both Sides of Buka Passage*. Oxford: Clarendon Press.
*DÊ, T. D., 1951: "Notes on Birth and Reproduction in Vietnam," unpublished manuscript by Margaret Coughlin.
*GORER, G., 1938: *Himalayan Village: An Account of the Lepchas of Sikkim*. London: Michael Joseph.
*GRANQVIST, H., 1950: *Child Problems Among the Arabs*. Helsingfors: Söderström.
*GUTIERREZ DE PINEDA, V., 1948: "Organizacion social en la Guajira," *Rev. Inst Etnolog. Nac. (Bogota)*, 3.
*HENRY, J., 1910: "L'ame d'un peuple Africain," *Bibliotheque-Anthropos*, *1*, No. 2.
*MEAD, M., 1935: *Sex and Temperament in Three Primitive Societies*. New York: William Morrow.
———, 1949: *Male and Female*. New York: William Morrow.
*MÉTRAUX, A., 1940: "Ethnology of Easter Island," *Bernice P. Bishop Museum Bulletin 160*. Honolulu.
*MORRIS, J., 1938: *Living with Lepchas: A Book about the Sikkim Himalayas*. London: William Heinemann.
*SMITH, E. W., and DALE, A. M., 1920: *The Ila-Speaking Peoples of Northern Rhodesia*. London: Macmillan.
UTTLEY, K. H., 1961: The birth, stillbirth, death and fertility rates in the coloured population of Antigua, West Indies, from 1857 to 1956, *Trans. Roy. Soc. Trop. Med. Hyg.*, *55*:59–78.

The Child: His Right to Be Normal

Carlo Valenti

DOWNSTATE MEDICAL CENTER, STATE UNIVERSITY OF NEW YORK

In his new classic of modern biology, *The Person in the Womb*, Dr. N. J. Berrill makes this, among other, declarations:

> If a human right exists at all, it is the right to be born with normal body and mind, with the prospect of developing further to fulfillment. If this is to be denied, then life and conscience are mockery and a chance should be made for another throw of the ovarian dice.

Reprinted from *Saturday Review*, December 7, 1968, pp. 75–78. Copyright © 1968 Saturday Review, Inc. By permission.

In accord with this philosophy, I draw attention to some favorable prospects for "another throw."

About one in fifty babies is born with a greater or less degree of abnormality inherited from its parents. These weaknesses, more than 500 of them severe enough to be classified as diseases (diabetes, for example), are ordered by the genes carried on the chromosomes. No one has ever seen a gene, but we can identify chromosomes under the microscope. Every normal person has a complement of forty-six of them, paired in twenty-three sets. One of the twenty-three pairs determines sex. The determination is made by chance and occurs as follows (see Figure 1).

The female sex chromosomes are paired XX. In any division of the germ cell in preparation for mating with a male sperm, the female half of the marriage will therefore always be X.

The male sex chromosomes are paired XY. When the division of this germ cell occurs, the sperm may be X or it may be Y.

When a female egg is penetrated by an X sperm, the nuclei of the egg and the sperm will fuse XX and the offspring will be female.

When a female egg is penetrated by a Y sperm, the offspring will be XY, or male.

The choice is simple when everything goes well in the reproductive process. However, faulty working of the ovaries or testes sometimes produces fertilized XXX eggs (super-females, not always fertile), XXYs (outwardly male, but without sperm), XOs (outwardly female, but without ovaries and therefore without eggs), XXXXYs (typically defective mentally), and XYYs (typically defective mentally, often aggressive to a criminal extent).

The other twenty-two pairs of chromosomes suffer displacements when parents bring together certain genetic characteristics. The results can be very sad. For example, the chromosome pairs numbered 13-14-15 are catalogued by the letter D. Pairs No. 21 and 22 are catalogued by the letter G. Sometimes one chromosome of these two pairs is displaced in what is called a D/G translocation. What happens is that one of the No. 21 pair crosses over to and joins up with one of the No. 15 pair, riding piggyback as it were and giving that one No. 15 a lopsided appearance.

The person who bears this particular pattern of chromosomes is a balanced carrier, for Mongolism. We say "balanced" because the total amount of genetic material on the chromosomes is normal, although the number of chromosomes is only forty-five. But the chromosomal pattern is thrown off balance when the balanced carrier's offspring inherits the lopsided chromosome from the carrier along with a 21 from the carrier and a 21 from the other parent. The total inheritance then is three 21s, two in the normal position and one on the lopsided chromosome. The three 21s doom their possessor to Mongolism.

Why focus on the Mongoloid?

A Mongoloid child—in medical terms, he is a victim of "Down's syndrome"—has folded eyes and a flat-rooted nose (the Mongolian-like features from which the popular name of the anomaly derives), small head, fissured protruding tongue, peculiarities in the lines of the palms of the hands and the soles of the feet, retarded intellectual development ranging from idiocy to a maximum prospective mental age of seven years.

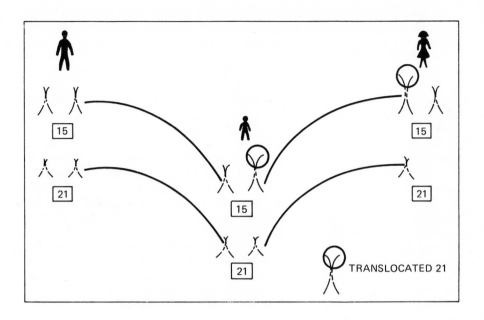

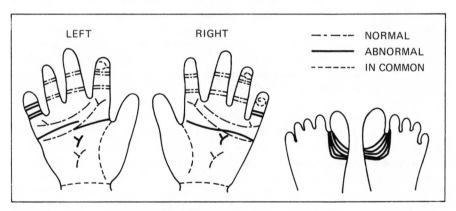

FIGURE 1.   *How Mongolism is transmitted through a "balanced carrier" to an offspring is demonstrated above. Only two of the twenty-three sets of chromosomes—the No. 15s and the No. 21s—are shown. Note that whereas the father has the normal 21 pair, the mother has one 21 in its normal place and the other upside down on the lopsided No. 15. When chance deals the child the lopsided 15, he has three 21s and is doomed. Palm prints and sole prints of Mongoloid child are below.*

Once given life, a Mongoloid is a poignant burden on its parents. For the Mongoloid appeals to all human instincts for companionship. He is cheerful, friendly, imitative, with a good memory for music and for details of situations he has experienced. A Mongoloid's life expectancy averages ten years—a decade of hopelessness, in most cases necessarily spent in a special institution.

Now it has been known for more than a dozen years that before a child is in finished form to leave his mother's womb the chromosomes of the prospective individual can be sampled and analyzed for aberrations. Dr. Fritz Fuchs, Danish-born chief of obstetrics and gynecology at Cornell University Medical College in New York, was able to pioneer such work in his native country because of the liberality of Denmark's laws governing therapeutic abortion.

The method developed by Dr. Fuchs and others is to obtain cells from the amniotic fluid, which is the stuff that every developing fetus floats in. Although the fetus derives almost all of its nourishment from rapidly pulsing blood fed from the placenta by way of the umbilical cord, the fetus before twelve weeks have passed by begins to swallow the amniotic fluid and excrete the fluid through its kidneys and bladder. In growing, the fetus sheds its skin gradually as we living persons shed ours, and other cells are dislodged from the mouth, bronchi, trachea, kidney, and bladder in the course of the swallowing and excreting. The fluid carrying all these cells must be sampled through the wall of the pregnant woman's abdomen by means of a hollow needle similar to those used to draw blood from a vein.

Where the needle enters the womb is of critical importance; if the wrong site were to be chosen, the placenta could be punctured or the fetus itself impaled. Either event could produce serious consequences.

To assure a safe choice, the exact location of the placenta and the floating head of the fetus is determined in the same way that submarines are located when afloat in sea water—that is, by sonar or echo-sounding. The method is feasible as early as the fourteenth week of pregnancy. A tiny portable gun that fires waves at very high speeds is moved across the prospective parent's abdomen in sweeps proceeding successively downward until the entire belly has been scanned. A pattern similar to that seen on a radar screen emerges. With it as a guide, the entry point of the amniocentesis needle is fixed.

After a sample of the amniotic fluid has been removed through the needle, the sample is spun in a centrifuge. The liquid part of the sample is then discarded. A pellet of cells remains. In this pellet is the knowledge we seek.

Two groups of investigators have reported varying success in culturing the cells on nutritive media they have independently developed. Their techniques, described in the medical literature, did not yield good results in our obstetrics and gynecology laboratory here at State University of New York's Downstate Medical Center in Brooklyn. So Edward J. Schutta, Tehila Kehaty, and myself have worked out a culturing method of our own and with it have obtained twenty successes in twenty-four trials. All our failures occurred where the amount of amniotic fluid used was below a certain level. The twenty successful cell cultures yielded seventeen chromosome analyses, or karyotypes. The three failures apparently were due to bacterial contamination.

Two to six weeks of growth are required before the culture is ready to be karyotyped—that is, placed on a glass laboratory slide, dried, stained, and examined microscopically to determine the chromosome pattern.

Last April, a Boston medical colleague familiar with our work referred to us a twenty-nine-year-old mother from Massachusetts who was sixteen weeks pregnant. She knew her grandfather, her mother, her brother, and herself to be balanced carriers of the D/G chromosomal translocation. That is, all four were outwardly normal and healthy, but each carried within himself only one No. 21 chromosome in its normal pairing, while the other 21 was grafted onto one of the No. 15 chromosome pair. In short, although not themselves Mongoloid, three generations of the family carried the genetic threat of Mongolism.

The young New Englander had already experienced a spontaneous abortion, borne a daughter who was also a balanced carrier of the D/G chromosomal translocation, and borne a Mongoloid son who had lived for five months. She wanted another child, and sought our assurance that it would be normal. With the support of her husband, an engineer by profession, she requested a cytogenetic diagnosis on the unborn baby.

Amniocentesis was performed after a sonar sounding on April 15. The amount of amniotic fluid obtained proved inadequate for optimum cell growth. Amniocentesis was performed again on April 29, luxuriant cell cultures were available within two weeks, and satisfactory chromosome preparations were ready for analysis on May 21. The karyotypes showed a male pattern with the D/G chromosomal translocation characteristic of Mongolism. Our hospital's abortion committee authorized a therapeutic interruption of pregnancy on the grounds that, since Mongolism was certain, failure to interrupt could subject the young mother to unjustifiable psychiatric trauma. Notice of the therapeutic abortion was posted routinely on the staff bulletin boards, and the abortion was done on May 31. Autopsy findings and palmprint and soleprint patterns were consistent with our cytogenetic diagnosis.

The young woman who volunteered for this experience recovered and returned to her New England home within forty-eight hours. She is still eager for another child if she can have a healthy one. She has requested application of amniocentesis to all future pregnancies.

This woman now has a chance for "another throw of the ovarian dice," as Dr. Berrill put it. The British medical journal, *Lancet*, last July published news of her case in the form of a letter from Schutta, Kehaty, and myself. The *Journal of the American Medical Association* has since notified us that it has accepted for publication a longer formal report of the case. So far as I know, it is the first piece of such news to appear in the medical literature anywhere. It may not be sensational news because D/G chromosomal translocations account for only 2 per cent of all Mongoloid children. But to the individual women involved, it is a promise of release from fear and guilt.

Furthermore, the potential benefits of amniocentesis and karyotyping are applicable to the much greater percentage of Mongolism caused by trisomies. In these there are forty-seven chromosomes, including three No. 21s which appear as triplets in the place of the normal 21 pair (as opposed to the pair of 21s and the 21 contained in the lopsided chromosome of the D/G Mongoloids).

Trisomies are related to aging. Human eggs spoil with time just as other eggs do. . . . Every woman's supply of eggs has been nested in her ovaries since well before she herself was born. All else being equal, she begins releasing them, at the rate of one a month (except during pregnancy and subsequent nursing), when she is about thirteen years old, and continues the process for the forty-odd years that intervene before menopause. Overall, the chance of an American woman giving birth to a Mongoloid child is one in 680. To age twenty-five, the chance is one in 2,000; after age forty-five, one in fifty.

Our laboratory has made cytogenetic diagnoses of two women who feared their pregnancies might produce Mongoloid infants. One of these women was thirty-six years old, the other thirty-seven. Amniocentesis and karyotyping showed no chromosomal aberrations.

The potential of prenatal study of fetal cells obtained by amniocentesis is far greater than we have yet been able to explore. Three broad areas are open to investigation. In the first, a smear of the fetal cells can be made immediately after the cells are collected from the amniotic fluid. The smear shows presence or absence of the sex chromatin body (a condensation of nuclear material), which only female cells possess. The sex of the unborn child can thus be identified and sex-linked hereditary diseases, such as hemophilia and muscular dystrophy, can be diagnosed in the fetus. More than ten years ago, Dr. Fuchs in Denmark demonstrated the value of the technique by screening hemophilic pregnancies and interrupting those that would have resulted in male babies. Only males actually develop hemophilia; females carry the disease without being afflicted by it.

The second field of study of cells obtained by amniocentesis is the analysis of their chromosome complement, as illustrated by the case of the young woman patient described above. Advanced maternal age can cause a number of chromosomal errors in addition to the error that results in Mongolism. Anguish for the mothers involved can be avoided in some cases by interruption of pregnancy. The number of such cases is at the moment still uncertain. The certainty is that in the present state of knowledge we cannot correct chromosomal errors. In the future, however, we may be able to correct the effect of the errors by refining our methods, by applying the principle that each effect is due to a particular enzyme and that each enzyme is ordered by a particular gene. One step in the refinement is to map the locations of the genes on the chromosomes of man, as has already been done with the mouse.

The third area of endeavor in intrauterine medicine (treatment of the fetus in the uterus) is analysis of enzymes produced by the fetal cells that are taken from the amniotic fluid. There are hereditary diseases in which deficiency of given enzymes is known in the adult. Detection of the same deficiencies in the fetal cells may permit diagnosis of diseases in the unborn baby and possibly correction of the deficiencies and thus prevention of the diseases.

For example, one of the signs of Mongolism is flaccid muscles at birth. If the body of a Mongoloid baby is laid prone on the palm of the hand, the baby's head and limbs will flop downward like those of a rag doll. The weakness of the muscles has been attributed to absence of a chemical which can be made only in the presence of a particular enzyme. According to prevailing genetic theory, this enzyme must be missing from Mongoloid cells and the absence must be related to the existence in the cells of three No. 21 chromosomes instead of the normal pair of 21s.

In an English experiment, a chemical named 5-hydroxytryptophan was administered to fourteen Mongoloid babies ranging from a few days to four months in age. Within one to seven weeks later, normal muscle tone was restored to thirteen of these babies, who became able to raise their heads, arms, and legs. Clearly, a missing something had been supplied and had counteracted at least some part of the effect of the abnormal set of three No. 21 chromosomes.

The English researchers were careful to point out that there is yet no evidence that their treatment will improve the mental development of Mongoloid babies. It is conceivable, however, that if Mongolism were diagnosed sufficiently early in the development of the fetus and if the missing chemical could be administered then, the effect on the child might be remarkable.

A great many scientists the world over are now studying enzyme deficiencies in hereditary diseases in the adult human. As their reservoir of knowledge grows, the potential of amniocentesis widens proportionately.

A major determinant of the ultimate effectiveness of intrauterine medicine will be the public attitude on abortion. At present, the laws of many states do not allow therapeutic abortion on genetic grounds. Genetic grounds are habitually construed as empirical statistical evaluations. Chromosomal analysis is not statistical but is direct and specific evidence of abnormality. As physicians, legislators, and the people come to understand the distinction, they will surely see that the law cannot be interpreted to exclude abortion based on chromosomal analysis. For a law that would compel a mother to give birth to a baby certain to be severely defective would be cruel and uncivilized.

A Chink in Our Armor

Robert E. Shank
WASHINGTON UNIVERSITY MEDICAL SCHOOL

In pregnancy, good nutrition can be a matter of life or death. And what is more, while this truism applies to pregnant women of all ages, the younger the mother, the greater the risk of poor diet.

Here is a chink in our medical armor that can be repaired.

This, briefly, is the conclusion of the Committee on Maternal Nutrition of the National Research Council. Its report, *Maternal Nutrition and the Course of Human Pregnancy*, the result of three years' study by thirteen scientists—including nine physicians—is being published this month. It provides an authoritative review of current evidence of the effect of food on the outcome of pregnancy. The report clearly shows the need for a significant change in the way physicians and others now view the pregnant woman's diet. It focuses on the need for a new approach to the dietary management of pregnancy, and suggests abandoning many current practices widely accepted as safe. Physicians, dietitians, and other health professionals will discover many practical suggestions for counseling pregnant women, prospective parents, and their families in the findings.

As Chairman of the Committee, I will try to summarize the important points of our findings, hoping that the results of our deliberations will thus

Reprinted from *Nutrition Today*, 5(2), 2–11. Copyright © 1970 Enloe, Stalvey and Associates. By permission.

become known to *Nutrition Today*'s wide audience of several hundred thousand health professionals. Everyone should avail himself of the wealth of information to be found in the complete report. (Available from the National Academy of Sciences, National Research Council, 2101 Constitution Avenue, N.W., Washington, D.C. 20418, price $7.50.)

GOSSIP THERAPY

In the most sophisticated society as well as among the most primitive tribes, gossip, old wives' tales, and ill-founded advice from physicians and others have often been the primary sources of dietary guidance for pregnant women. There are several reasons for this. Since nutrition is a very young science, it is only recently that we began to appraise the nutritive demands of the fetus. In the vacuum of this absence of scientific fact, gossip, superstition, and quaint ideas flew in—ideas that spawned faddism among professionals and laymen alike. It is hoped that we can now begin to rely less on mystery and more on fact.

It is little wonder that, for no one knows how long, pregnancy has been surrounded by mystery. Because of this, the woman has suffered all manner of proscriptions and deprivations, each calculated to shield her from the evils that might cause miscarriage or rob her body of vitality. In the absence of convincing scientific guidance, she has been the target of every fad and fancy the mind of man, aborigine or intellectual, could conjure.

The view that has been, and perhaps still is, most widely held by physicians is that, as long as the mother gets plenty of vitamins, the fetus will receive all the nourishment it needs regardless of her own nutritional status. The experience of women in Germany during World War I, who continued to give birth to viable, healthy babies despite the strictest food rationing, lent credence to this assumption. To medical educators this experience seemed to corroborate the view of Ludwig Prochownick, a German obstetrician who early in this century had contended that semistarvation of the mother was really a blessing in disguise. Keep the pregnant woman on a diet low in carbohydrates; restrict her fluid intake; and the result will be much less discomfort and difficulty for the mother at delivery time because the baby will be small and of light weight, he reasoned. This concept has been accepted and is practiced by many obstetricians today. Despite growing evidence—which, after the deliberations of the Committee on Maternal Nutrition, would seem to be overwhelming—the old argument continues to be offered that the maternal organism is somehow mysteriously endowed with an innate ability to produce a viable offspring regardless of the mother's own health or nutritional status. Anyway, it is said, the pregnant woman will instinctively act to meet the health needs of herself and her unborn infant. One argument is as fallacious as the other.

SWINGING PENDULUM

In the past thirty years, maternal nutrition has had its ups and downs. There have been times, as during World War II when food was rationed, when physicians in the United States and Canada thought it very important, and periods when what the pregnant woman ate was considered as one of those aspects of childbearing that pretty well took care of itself. Following the major advances in the science of nutrition during the period 1920–1940 when most of the vitamins were identified and their metabolic roles described, the 1940's became a decade of enthusiasm about the importance of diet in pregnancy outcome. This was followed by an era of disillusionment, even disinterest— attitudes due primarily to a series of reports in the 1950's which appeared to negate earlier claims that maternal nutrition could significantly affect the course of human pregnancy.

Now the pendulum is swinging back. The evidence, gained largely from more dispassionate appraisal of experience, indicates that maternal nutrition *is* critically important to both mother and fetus. Two things appear responsible for this development: rapidly expanding knowledge of the role of nutrition in prevention and treatment of disease; and second, realization that the numbers of stillbirths and infant deaths in the United States and Canada are considerably higher than one would expect.

The number of American women who die as a sequel to pregnancy has steadily decreased in the past three decades from 367.0 per 100,000 live births in 1940 to 83.3 in 1950 to 28.0 in 1967. This rate is more than three times as high in nonwhite as in white women, however. Proportionately, more nonwhite women bear children during adolescence and have higher parities, but these factors do not completely account for the observed differences in maternal mortality rates. In localities where mothers of both races receive comparably good maternity care, the difference is lessened. However, there is no reason to believe that fewer women and children die in pregnancy because of improved nutritional care alone. The improvement must be credited to the use of antibiotics and other forms of modern treatment. The statistics would be even better if physicians would adopt the routines for maternal nutrition now suggested.

As we have seen in so many other aspects of medical practice, when one cause of illness is overcome, another is unmasked. We are now aware of problems which appear to arise from a strange combination of malnutrition and the increasing number of younger and younger girls who become pregnant in America. Although the infant mortality rate reached a record low value of 22.4 per 1,000 live births in the United States in 1967, this rate is substantially higher than that prevailing in many other countries. This rate, which applies to the first year of life, includes babies who die during the first month of life; i.e., the first four weeks after delivery. The United States ranked thirteenth and Canada placed fourteenth in infant mortality in both 1966 and 1967. Under any circumstance, the importance of nutrition is hard to overestimate since low birth weight is now known to be associated with increased risk of neonatal death, i.e., within the first 28 days of life. Furthermore, malnutrition is one of the factors contributing to the relatively large group of infants with perinatal handicaps and congenital injuries, or who fail to grow and develop normally.

THE REASONS

Among the reasons a woman may give birth to a baby of less than normal weight, or what must now be considered as healthy weight, we can distinguish eleven causes, any one or a combination of which could be decisive. These, not in the order of importance, are: biologic immaturity (which is to say the mother is younger than seventeen), high parity, short stature, low prepregnancy weight for height, limited weight gain during pregnancy, poor nutritional status, smoking, chronic disease, certain infections, complications of pregnancy, and a history of prior reproductive loss.

In our studies, two causes of poor pregnancy outcome stand out above all others—poor nutrition and youth of the mother. Any research effort attempting to assess the relative importance of single factors, including poor nutrition, on outcome of pregnancy has been fraught with problems. And the results have been very difficult to interpret. This is true because many characteristics that thwart normal pregnancy tend to cluster in the same groups of women. For example, women in poor families are at the same time usually members of large families lacking good medical care, proper food, and education. Here we also find the greatest prevalence of infectious diseases, poor health, and bad food habits. This environment spawns the youngest mothers, who seldom grow and develop in childhood to their full genetic potential before they become pregnant. These are the young girls who enter pregnancy with suboptimal health and nutritional status. Every physician knows exceptions to this picture. While poverty is integral to this clustering of circumstances, there are, of course, women with adequate incomes who for other reasons, including the cult of slimness, approach childbearing with threatening health habits, poor health, and nutritional status which make them indistinguishable from their poorer sisters.

Why should this be so? Why should youth and suboptimal nourishment of the pregnant woman be so crucial to the outcome of this critical experience? The answer lies, so the Committee felt, in the essentials of the physiologic context of childbearing. From the first hours after fertilization, the maternal metabolic system begins a vast readjustment to efficiently provide the environment and sustenance necessary to support life and the normal growth of the fetus. Many physical and biochemical changes one sees in normal pregnancy resemble those associated with certain disease. For instance, blood volume expands, bringing with it reduction in concentrations of blood hemoglobin and plasma albumin. Amino acids may be excreted in the urine. The activity of certain enzymes in blood, such as alkaline phosphatase, increases markedly. The thyroid gland is often enlarged. Pulmonary and cardiovascular dynamics change. Edema is not infrequent. In short, clinical standards considered "normal" for the nonpregnant woman cannot always be used for the pregnant woman. The World Health Organization reminds us that

> from the standpoint of physiological function, pregnancy cannot be regarded as a process of foetal growth superimposed on the ordinary metabolism of the mother. Foetal development is accompanied by extensive changes in maternal body composition and metabolism.
>
> The (W.H.O.) Committee prefers to use the term "adjustment" rather than "adaptation" to describe the physiological changes occurring during pregnancy. Adaptation implies adjustment to an essentially undesirable situation, whereas pregnancy is neither abnormal nor undesirable. Many of the adjustments begin in early pregnancy before foetal growth is appreciable and, therefore, cannot be

interpreted as reactions to stress. Undoubtedly many of them are under hormonal control, although the precise mechanisms are poorly understood. . . .

CRUCIAL WEIGHT CHANGES

Weight gain reflects the overall physiologic consequences of pregnancy. Experience in the United States indicates that the average total weight gain in pregnancy is approximately 24 pounds, but weight gain varies greatly. Young women fed equally well tend to gain slightly more weight than older women, primigravidas more than multigravidas, and thin women more than fat women. In Western societies, the total additional calorie cost of a normal pregnancy is approximately 40,000 k calories more than that usually consumed by the same woman when not pregnant, or about 200 k calories more each day than she would usually eat. This is commensurate with total weight gain of 25 pounds.

Many observations demonstrate that malnourished girls deliver fragile babies, maternal physiology is readjusted in a fashion which would alter nutritional requirements, and women exhibit a characteristic increase in energy demand during pregnancy.

It is hardly surprising to conclude that diet during pregnancy may have important influences on the outcome. This may seem obvious now, but it was not always so. As the Committee's report points out, "One specific way in which diet during pregnancy affects the outcome of pregnancy is seen in the relationship between maternal gain in weight and the weight of infants at birth. A number of studies have shown that a strong positive association exists between the total gain in weight of the mother and the birth weight of her child. Similarly, there is an important positive association between the prepregnancy weight of the mother and the birth weight of her child. . . .

FETAL GROWTH

These conclusions are supported by studies in several species of experimental animals which have demonstrated that calorie and protein restrictions in the maternal diet profoundly affect litter size and survival, birth weight, growth patterns, and behavior of progeny. The timing and duration of dietary restriction influence the results, since fetal growth and development rates vary between species. The effects on cellular growth patterns are different between organs, and seem more extensive when the dietary restriction coincides with most rapid cell division. For example, dietary deprivation at the time of greatest rate of growth of the brain results in persistent modification and damage; deprivation at times of slower rates of cell division leads to changes which can later be corrected with improved diet. The greatest rates of cell division and of growth occur *in utero* in some species but in the postnatal period in others.

In man, birth occurs during the steepest part of the growth curve of the conceptus; in rodents, carnivores, and the pig, the event precedes maximal growth. Moreover, the relative severity of dietary restriction in animal experimentation is likely to be greater than that commonly encountered in human populations. Additional research in animals is necessary before we can achieve a sound understanding of these relationships. There is equal need for caution in extrapolating these findings to human reproduction. . . .

PREGNANCY TOXEMIAS

For years, the concept has persisted that nutrition is related in some way to the occurrence and course of toxemias of pregnancy. But little is known about the relative importance of the many etiological factors involved. Toxemia has been called "the disease of theories." Measures for prevention and treatment, including dietary procedures, have thus remained largely empirical. Lack of accepted criteria for diagnosis and absence of a suitable laboratory animal model have handicapped the study of these toxemias.

A variety of symptom complexes continues to be included under the term "toxemia." To facilitate discussions, the toxemias considered were those that could be divided into "preeclampsia" and "eclampsia." Preeclampsia was defined as an acute hypertensive disorder appearing after about the twentieth week of pregnancy, and accompanied by edema of hand and face and/or proteinuria. Eclampsia was defined as closely related to preeclampsia and, in most cases, its end result.

In the United States the maternal mortality rate from acute toxemia has dropped from 52.2 per 100,000 live births in 1940 to 6.2 in 1965. Mortality rates by states vary widely from one-third or less the national average in some states to four or five times the national average in others. The most striking association of these differences is with per capita income. The lower a state's per capita income, the higher the maternal mortality from toxemia, and vice versa. This same relation appears to hold with respect to incidence of the disease.

The relative importance of diet in the etiology of toxemia of pregnancy has been a controversial subject for many years during which calories, protein, and salt have each at one time or another been thought to be the cause of major concern. The concept of *caloric restrictions* to avoid large total weight gains and to protect against toxemia derived from the observed reduction in the incidence of toxemia in Europe during World War I, as mentioned earlier. Since the war was accompanied by a scarcity of food and pregnant women gained less, the restricted diet was considered the protective factor. During the 1920's and 1930's, caloric restriction to limit weight gain during pregnancy was widely advocated in the United States to prevent toxemia and other complications. The practice found its way into textbooks of obstetrics and has been widely followed by the medical profession—despite the fact that the practice has been subjected to little scientific scrutiny. That such caloric restriction may not be beneficial is suggested by recent university hospital studies on a large group of women who gained in excess of 30 pounds during pregnancy. Nine percent of these women developed toxemia, but 91 percent did not. Confusion has resulted from failure to distinguish between weight gained as a result of edema and that due to deposition of fat. There is no evidence that women with large total weight gain due to excessive accumulation of fat are more likely to develop toxemia than women with lesser accumulations.

The quantity of protein consumed has been held by some to influence both development of toxemia and the effectiveness of measures designed to prevent its appearance. For example, it has been widely suspected that changes in diet in the United States, particularly in the protein intake, may have contributed to the decreased national incidence of this complication. Although the proportion of total calories furnished by protein in the average diet in the United States has remained fairly constant at 11 to 13 percent, an increasing proportion has come from animal sources. The evidence is insufficient with respect to the influence of levels of protein intake of individual women to allow conclusions to be drawn concerning the influence of dietary protein levels *per se* on the development or prevention of toxemia.

Since edema is a characteristic feature of toxemia, routine salt limitation during pregnancy to avoid or reduce edema formation has gained wide acceptance in practice. Diuretics are also commonly prescribed to accomplish the same goal, often in conjunction with salt restriction. Recent experimental studies on pregnant rats demonstrated deleterious effects of salt depletion. The safety of routine salt restriction must be questioned, as well as the use of diuretics in prenatal care. The NRC report cautions against the routine use of these procedures in prenatal care.

GUIDELINES

Maternal Nutrition and the Course of Human Pregnancy contains much salient information to justify new and extended effort to utilize nutritional knowledge and services in prenatal care. The report demonstrates that reproductive efficiency is least in adolescents, the nonwhite, and those of lowest income. These are the highest-risk groups, but there are broad opportunities to improve the outcome of pregnancy for all women of all ages and strata by more careful attention to diet. Obstetricians and physicians who routinely prescribe diets restricted in calories and salt, and who feel that the routine use of diuretics is an integral part of prenatal care, are placing patients and their offspring at disadvantage and unnecessary risk.

This NRC study indicates several principles which the physician and his professional assistants will find useful in providing prenatal care which will assure the best possible outcome of pregnancy:

1. Weight gain in pregnancy should be closely monitored with the objective of achieving an average total gain of 24 pounds. This represents a gain of 1.5 to 3.0 pounds during the first trimester, followed by a gain of .8 pounds each week during the remainder of pregnancy. No scientific justification is found for routine limitations of weight gain to lesser amounts.

2. Severe restriction of calories is unphysiologic and potentially harmful to the developing fetus and the mother. Moreover, caloric limitation inevitably is accompanied by restriction of other nutrients essential for growth processes. Weight reduction of obese women should not be undertaken during pregnancy, but in interpartum periods.

3. The pattern and rate of weight gain is of particular importance. A sudden sharp increase in weight after the twentieth week of pregnancy may signal water retention and the possible onset of preeclampsia.

4. The occurrence of pregnancy in the adolescent, and girl under 17 years of age, poses special and important problems. Standardized diets which are

often used in prenatal clinics are not suited to the particular nutritional needs of the adolescent. To sustain and complete her own growth she requires a diet rich in calories, protein, and calcium. Calorie deprivation is poorly tolerated. Pregnancy, with its added nutritional requirements, demands that every effort must be made to encourage an enhanced and appropriate food intake.

5. The dietary intake and food habits of the pregnant woman should be carefully reviewed and appropriate counseling provided. Special attention should be paid to women who enter pregnancy in a poor state of nutrition and to those with poor dietary habits. Young adolescents, women who have been on slimming regimens, and those of low socioeconomic status are particularly apt to fail to meet the metabolic demands of pregnancy. When modification of the woman's usual diet is indicated during pregnancy, it should be undertaken in accordance with the principles of good nutrition. The planning or assessment of diets should be guided by the Recommended Dietary Allowances (1968) of the National Research Council.

6. The widespread practice of routinely restricting salt intake, and at the same time prescribing diuretics, is of doubtful value in preventing preeclampsia and is potentially dangerous. The routine use of diuretics without specific clinical indications is unsound and potentially harmful.

7. The provision of vitamin and mineral supplements should not be regarded as a solution for poor food habits. The supplements' cost, relative to the cost of enhancing the nutrient intake with foods, should be considered, especially in caring for pregnant women with inadequate incomes. Except for iron and folic acid, the routine augmentation with vitamin and mineral preparations is of uncertain value. When supplementation is considered necessary, the quantities of nutrients supplied should approximate the daily amounts suggested in the Recommended Dietary Allowances (1968).

8. In view of the apparent widespread incidence of nutritional anemia and the increased iron requirements of pregnancy, iron supplementation is needed during the second and third trimesters in amounts of 30 to 60 mg per day.

9. A daily supplement of .2 to .4 mg folate during pregnancy should prevent folic acid deficiency in all pregnant women.

10. In areas where the soil and water are deficient in iodine, the use of iodized salt should be encouraged.

This report is intended to call to the attention of physicians, nutritionists, and other health professionals the new emphasis on diet which pregnancy requires. Present knowledge and information indicate that the course and outcome of pregnancy can be more favorable for many women if nutritional practices are improved. A salient and not-to-be-forgotten fact is that such efforts should extend into childhood and adolescence. The woman who is likely to produce a healthy baby is one who has, through best health and nutritional practices, reached sexual maturity after completing her own growth and achieving the potentials for physical development provided by heredity.

Chapter 2

Halvar Loken

Early Infancy

Of all the species of infants, the human has farthest to go from birth to adulthood. Born in a very immature condition, he eventually becomes the most complex of creatures. In fact, if his behavior patterns were more biologically preset and determined than they are, he would not have as great possibilities for development as he does have. His brain has almost unlimited potentialities for learning and creating.

Human relationships, as well as human development, owe their variety and complexity partly to the immaturity of the human infant. If children could take off on their own like mice and lions, there would be no brothers and sisters to fight and love, no grandparents, aunts, uncles, cousins, no family at all. This immaturity was and is a necessary condition for humanity. Sometimes it is thought

71

of as a disadvantage for the infant to be able to do so little for himself at birth. Actually the infant can do everything he needs to do in order to survive and grow. Although immature, he is competent to handle the situation in which he first finds himself, provided his mother cooperates with him.

The neonatal period is used here to mean approximately the first month of extrauterine life. It has been defined in various terms, sometimes as the first week, sometimes as the period from birth until the umbilicus is healed. Although the neonatal period is short in time, it is significant because it is the beginning of life as a separate organism. Great are the changes and adaptation which take place in this brief interval.

Equipment and Functioning

An assessment of the newborn can be made immediately after birth. The usual way of evaluating his functioning is by an Apgar rating, a system of scoring the infant's heart rate, breathing effort, muscle tone, reflexes, irritability, and color. The Apgar test is very useful for predicting survival and for indicating babies who need special care [1]. Apgar scores have been shown to be correlated with intelligence, conceptual, and motor scores at age 4 [18]. More complex examinations, including routine physical examinations and elaborate batteries of tests, are also useful for assessing normality and predicting development [69].

Appearance

Neonates look strange to most people because new infants are rarely seen. Since they change quickly in looks, the normal appearance at 2 or 3 months is the one that comes to mind when most individuals think of a new baby.

The average newborn baby has a reddish, wrinkled skin which darkens when he cries. The wrinkles smooth out toward the end of the first month, as more and more fat is laid down beneath the skin. Immediately after birth the waxy vernix caseosa covers the skin for about eight hours. The large head is often elongated and bumpy, perhaps with one particularly large lump, the result of molding during birth. The head gradually resumes its normal shape, with possibly the trace of a bump or two remaining. It is quite easy to see some of the six fontanelles, the soft spots in the brain where membranes connect the bony parts of the skull. The flat, broad nose, formed of cartilage, is often pushed out of shape temporarily by the birth process.

His eyelids are puffy, making the eyes look small at first. The eyes, smoky blue for the first month or two, change gradually to their permanent color. They are large in proportion to the rest of the face, since the cranial part of the head is much more fully developed than the rest of the head. Here is an illustration of the principle of development direction: *development proceeds from anterior to posterior*.

Hair may be abundant or scanty, perhaps covering the head and scattered around the body, especially on the back. The body hair disappears and often the scalp hair too. Very often the permanent head hair is a different color from that at birth.

Size and Proportions

The average birth weight for American babies is 7½ pounds, with the average for boys about 3 ounces more than that for girls [82]. The size of babies varies with many factors, including race, climate, socioeconomic status, age and size of mother, and birth order. American Negro babies have been found to weigh, on the average, 5 ounces less than white babies at birth [49]. Information on birth weights in different socioeconomic groups suggests that the difference in birth weights between white and black is due to socioeconomic factors rather than genetic. The average birth weight for Caucasian babies is 7.50 pounds for boys, 7.44 for girls; Indian averages are 6.48 and 6.35: Indonesian figures are 6.87 and 6.72 [31]. The weight and size of a baby at birth are more strongly related to his mother's size than his father's. The fat-free weight of the newborn correlates 0.50 with the mother's fat-free weight, and 0.04 with the father's [27]. His weight is also related to the quality of environment which the mother has provided. The weight of the placenta and maternal health and nutrition are all related to birth weight [19]. If the baby's birth weight were more strongly related to his father's weight, then there would be great dangers in childbirth for a small woman married to a large man. The hereditary influence of the father makes itself felt during the catch-up period. The catch-up mechanisms allow for growth of a genetically large baby to be slowed down considerably during his last few weeks in utero and then to be speeded up during his first months after birth [31].

Body proportions, compared with those at later ages, show a large head, small trunk, and very short, undeveloped legs. The legs are bowed and drawn up, making them look even smaller than if they were stretched out.

Physiological Functioning

Respiration. The change from being a water-borne parasite to being an air-breathing, independent individual is a complex one, although one which the newborn is ready to make. An example of his fitness to adapt is that he can stand degrees of oxygen deprivation which an adult could not tolerate. The crucial change is in respiration; and this is begun as he emerges. It may take a day or two for the amniotic fluid and mucus to drain completely from the baby's breathing apparatus. Breathing is irregular, rapid, and shallow, involving the abdomen more than the chest. The neonate is often a noisy breather, wheezing and snuffling in a fashion that can be alarming to first-time parents.

Breathing reflexes are coordinated with and activated by the oxygen-carbon dioxide balance. The amount of air a baby breathes is regulated thus. Coughing, sneezing, and yawning are all reflexes with important survival value. Coughing and sneezing clear the air passages and lungs. Yawning gives a quick gulp of air when needed suddenly.

Circulation. The essential change in circulation follows immediately the change in respiration. Only a small quantity of blood goes to the lungs before birth, since it flows to the placenta to exchange products. After birth, blood is forced into the lungs, and the circulation to the placenta is cut off by the closing of the opening that leads from the fetal heart to the placenta. During fetal life, the right and left ventricles of the heart have an opening between them. Within the first week or ten days of postnatal life, the opening gradually closes. Another important change in the circulatory–respiratory combination is that the lungs expand gradually in the first two weeks. During that time, the blood includes almost twice as many blood cells per cubic millimeter as it does immediately after the lungs are fully expanded.

The heart rate decelerates during the birth process and quickly accelerates at birth. A peak heart rate of 174 beats per minute was found at two minutes after birth [81]. The heart then decelerates gradually, showing occasional periods of acceleration. Patterns of response become more stable during the first few months suggesting that important changes in control mechanisms take place during the first month of life [48]. Changes in heart rate are often used by experimenters as a means of measuring the infant's response to stimuli. Respiration is also used thus.

Digestion. The newborn changes from taking nutrients in through the placenta to taking food into the mouth and stomach. Hunger contractions and rooting, sucking and swallowing mechanisms, are present at birth. The small lower jaw and the fat pads in the cheeks are equipment for sucking. The mother's breasts supply first colostrum, a highly specialized food adapted to the newborn's needs, not available (as yet) from bottles. The breasts supply milk from the second or third day, regulating its composition and quantity to the maturity of the baby. Thus a delicately balanced nutritive relationship continues to exist between the mother and the baby after birth.

The first material evacuated from the colon is meconium, the material accumulated before birth from cellular breakdown, intestinal secretions, bile, mucus, and material swallowed with amniotic fluid. After three days, the stools assume a character which depends on the type of food, those of breast-fed babies differing noticeably from those of bottle-fed babies in appearance. Breast-fed babies usually have several bowel movements a day during the first few weeks, but after age 1, 2, or 3 months they usually change to a pattern of infrequent movements, one a day or every other day. Bottle-fed babies have one to four, or even six a day at first and later the number decreases to one or two [76]. The kidneys excrete small quantities of urine before birth. Frequency of urination increases after the second day to an average of around 20 times a day, with a wide range of individual differences.

Metabolism. The newborn has a higher metabolic rate than the adult, but lower than the preschool child's. Immediately after birth, the temperature drops 2 to 5 degrees and then rises to 98 to 99 degrees after about eight hours. Since mechanisms for maintaining a stable body temperature are immature, the neonate's temperature is unstable. Premature babies' temperatures are even more unstable than those of full-term infants. Heat loss is great through the baby's comparatively large surface, which is poorly insulated because skin and fat layers are thin. The newborn shows little diurnal change in temperature [74]. Thus he gets along best in a controlled temperature, with clothing and bedding carefully regulated to maintain a steady temperature.

Brain Function. Although all the nerve cells of the brain are present before birth, many are not mature enough to function in the newborn. Careful examination of the cells [79] suggests that no cortical function is possible at birth, although the spinal cord and the brain below the level of the cortex have mature cells. During the first month, many cells in the motor cortex mature, especially those in the areas controlling the upper trunk, back, and upper arm. By 3 months the level of maturity suggests that simple vision and hearing occur on a cortical level, but that interpretation cannot take place. Some of the research on sensory perception, reported later in this chapter, indicates that the cortex of the newborn does indeed function. In the meantime many of the motor behavior patterns of the newborn, listed below, are witness to the capacities and scope of the neural areas below the cortex.

Motor Behavior Patterns

Motor behavior—crying, sleeping, and excreting—can be observed, whereas sensory perception has to be inferred from other behavior. A list of types of neonatal motor behavior follows [16].

Eyes
1. Opens and closes lids both spontaneously and in response to stimuli.
2. Pupils widen and narrow in response to light. Narrow upon going to sleep. Widen upon waking. Widen with stimulation.
3. Following moving stimulus. Also jerky movements.
4. Oscillatory movement.
5. Coordinate, compensatory movements when head is moved quickly.
6. Coordinated movements.
7. Convergence.
8. Eye position in sleep frequently upward and divergent, as in adults.
9. Tear secretion (unusual).

Face and Mouth
1. Opens and closes mouth
2. Lips: licks, compresses, purses in response to touch.
3. Sucks.
4. Smiles.
5. Pushes material from mouth.
6. Yawns.
7. Grimaces, twisting mouth, wrinkling forehead.
8. Retracts lips, opens mouth to touch. Turns lower lip.

Throat
1. Cries. Sometimes sobs.
2. Swallows, gags to noxious stimuli or touch at back of throat.
3. Vomits.
4. Hiccoughs.
5. Coughs, sneezes.
6. Coos. Holds breath.

Head
1. Moves upward and backward when prone, especially to stimuli.
2. Turns face to side in response to touch. Turns from side to side when prone or when hungry or crying.
3. Head shudders to bitter stimuli.
4. Moves arms at random. Arms slash when crying.

Trunk
1. Arches back.

2. Twists, squirms. When head rotates, shoulders and pelvis turn in same direction.
3. Abdominal reflex in response to needle prick as stimulus.

Reproductive Organs
1. Cremasteric reflex (testes raised when inner thigh stroked).
2. Penis erects.

Foot and Leg
1. Knee jerk reflex.
2. Achilles tendon reflex.
3. Leg flexes. Plantar flexion accompanies leg flexion (reverse of adult response).
4. Leg extends in response to gentle push. May support some of weight on first day.
5. Protective reflex (if one foot or leg is stimulated, the other pushes against source of stimulation).
6. Kicking, usually during crying.
7. Stepping movements, when held upright with feet against a surface.
8. Toe usually extends when sole of foot is stroked.

Coordinate Responses
1. Resting and sleeping position: legs flexed, fists closed, upper arms extended.
2. Back arches from head to heels often during crying or when held upside down.
3. Backbone reflex (the side that is stroked or tickled bends in concave direction).
4. Tonic neck reflex or "fencing position" (head turned to the side, facing an extended arm, the other arm bent up near the head).
5. Springing position (when held upright and forward, arms extend forward and legs are brought up).
6. Stretches, shivers, trembles.
7. Startle response (Moro reflex).
8. Crying and mass or general movements.
9. Creeping movements when prone.
10. When held upright and rotated around vertical axis, arms and legs are extended in the direction of the rotation.
11. Body jerks to loud noises.*

This list illustrates the large number and broad range of motor coordinations of which the newborn is capable. Some of these responses are necessary for survival, some have no apparent immediate usefulness, and others may contribute eventually to the infant's organization of his world. As an example of the last point,

* Reprinted by permission from W. Dennis, "A Description and Classification of the Responses of the Newborn Infant," *Psychological Bulletin,* 1934, **31**, 5–22.

the antigravity reflexes might contribute to space concepts [85]. Protective reflexes include blinking to a bright light, withdrawing from painful stimuli, and shivering when cold. Some reflexes such as a startle, or Moro, reflex; the Darwinian, or grasp, reflex, and the Babkin reflex may have been useful in the history of the species, although they serve no clear purpose now. Pressure on the baby's palms produces the Babkin reflex, which consists of opening the mouth wide and turning the head toward the mid line, flexing the forearm, and closing the eyes [36].

States in Infants

The states of sleeping and waking are obviously different. There are various states of sleeping, and of waking too, all of which have significance for anyone studying the behavior of infants. Several investigators have made classifications of states, resulting in about six items, such as the following [85]: *regular sleep*, breathing smooth and even, little movement of face and body; *irregular sleep*, breathing irregular, movements of body and face, including rapid eye movements (this type of sleep, called REM for rapid eye movements, makes up a higher proportion of sleep, about 50 percent for newborns, than it does at any other age [67]); *drowsiness*, less active than in irregular sleep but more active than in regular, eyes open and close, looking glazed, eyelids heavy; *waking activity*, silent or moaning, grunting, whimpering, spurts of diffuse motor activity, face relaxed or pinched, eyes open but not shiny, skin flushed in activity, breathing irregular; *crying*, vocalizing, grimacing, diffuse motor activity, red face; *alert inactivity*, body inactive, face relaxed, eyes open, bright and shining, respirations faster and more variable than in regular sleep.

The infant's response to stimulation depends upon his state and upon the stimulus. For instance, in both kinds of sleep, infants were insensitive to touch; in alert inactivity, response to touch was increased motility; and in waking activity, touch stimuli resulted in decreased motility [85]. In studying the various sense modalities, investigators usually choose the state of alert inactivity for testing the infant's capabilities. It is in this state that he attends most to particular parts of the environment. The amount of time that 1-month-old boy babies spent in alert inactivity was correlated to length of time spent looking at pictures of faces at 3 months [53].

Babies vary in the amount of alert inactivity they show, from the moment of birth. During the first six hours, some stay awake and show intermittent visual pursuit (looking) for an hour and a half or longer; others fall into a deep sleep as soon as they are cleaned and dressed [84]. All the babies in the study increased from week to week in the amount of time spent in alert inactivity, the weekly average percent of total time being: first week 11, second 17, third 19, and fourth 21.

Relating to the World through Perception

Although physiological functions occupy most of the newborn's energy, and his first active approach to the world is a foray in search of food, some of his activity is that of taking in sensory stimuli and processing the data. The mysterious question "What is the world like to a baby?" is just as intriguing today as it was to the experimental child psychologists of the twenties and thirties. Although we still cannot tell exactly what he is feeling or experiencing, scientists are breaking

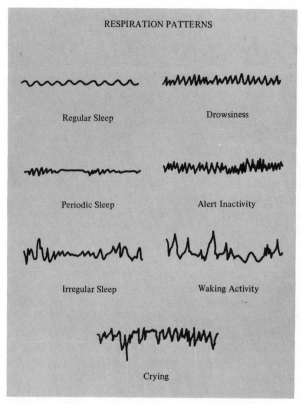

RESPIRATION PATTERNS

Regular Sleep

Drowsiness

Periodic Sleep

Alert Inactivity

Irregular Sleep

Waking Activity

Crying

Figure 2–1. Respiration patterns in the six states of early infancy.

SOURCE: Reprinted from *Psychological Issues*, 1966, **5**:1, p. 8. By Peter H. Wolff. By permission of International Universities Press, Inc. Copyright © 1966 by International Universities Press, Inc.

through this communication barrier to increased understanding of infants. Using sophisticated equipment, investigators can pinpoint what the infant is looking at and how he looks at it, measure his heart rate, breathing, brain waves, and skin conductivity, and control the conditions of stimulation. The baby emerges from this scrutiny as a creature who follows certain principles of attending, perceiving, seeking, and performing.

Tactile Senses. Skin, muscular, and vestibular (inner ear) senses are highly developed before birth, having functioned prenatally longer than the other senses. Sensations from lips, mouth, and other orifices are included in tactile sensations. The skin, being the locus where the individual is in physical contact with his environment, is the place where much interaction occurs. To name the sensations heat, cold, pressure, and pain tells a minimum about tactile experience. Animal experts and clinical experiences with infants have led to the conclusion that tactile stimulation is essential for normal development [14, 15]. Patting, caressing, cuddling, carrying, rocking, changing position, washing, drying—all these activities seem to be soothing and to promote well-being in babies. There is a connection between the skin and sympathetic nervous system [25]. Animal experiments have led to a hypothesis that early sensory stimulation of mammals affects the central nervous system, producing animals that learn better, utilize their food more efficiently, and show less reaction to stress than do average animals.

Frank [25], an inspired theorist in the field of human development, points out that the regular, rhythmic stimulation that the fetus receives from his mother's heartbeat is translated through the amniotic fluid to all of his skin. After birth the baby lying in a crib receives no such stimulation, but a baby carried by a person does, especially so if he is in skin-to-skin contact. Frank goes on to explain how tactile experience is the basis for getting meaning from other sensory experience, for personality development, and for interpersonal relationships. Sounds and sights derive their meaning initially from experiences of touch. The concept of his own body, where it stops and where the rest of the world begins, mother and other people, the objects that make up the rest of the world, are all discovered and understood first through tactile senses, with some help from vestibular senses.

Hearing. Although it has long been known that the fetus, and of course the neonate, can hear, it used to be thought that the infant's sensory world was a "buzzing, blooming confusion." Unless he showed a startle reaction—which he did to loud, sudden sounds—a baby gave no indication that one sound or another made any difference to him. Since a baby can neither understand language nor speak, it is difficult for adults to conceive of sounds that could be meaningful to an infant, and of ways in which infants' responses to sound could be observed and measured. Research is showing, however, that the neonate can make fine discriminations and that certain sounds are meaningful in his existence.

Newborn infants can distinguish small differences in pitch. In a Russian experiment [13] on learning, a baby's sucking movements were charted along with sound stimuli on a revolving drum. When a sound occurred, the sucking movements stopped, but when the sound was repeated, the baby gradually shortened the time during which he made no sucking movements. After enough repetitions of sound of one pitch, he continued to suck when it was played. When a sound of different frequency was played, the baby stopped sucking again, thus showing that he could discriminate it from the first sound. Similar experiments have used acceleration of heart rate, rather than cessation of sucking to indicate that the infant discriminates a certain tone. In one of them, a tone was sounded repeatedly until the infant stopped giving any motor response [12]. Then a note of different pitch was sounded. Many babies gave motor responses, and their heart rates increased. Figure 2-2 shows the tracings made by one infant's sucking and by the stimulating tones. On the first presentation, represented by A, the up-and-down lines indicate sucking. They stop when a tone is sounded, as shown by the second line. B shows the ninth presentation of the same tone, when the sucking lines show no interruption. C indicates reactions to a new tone, when the sucking again stops.

Different degrees of loudness of sounds stimulate different reactions. When white noise at 55, 70, 85, and 100 decibels was played to newborns, their heart rates and motor responses increased as the sound level increased [78].

The human heartbeat as a significant sound has been studied by Salk by playing a tape recording in a hospital nursery. The experimental group of newborn babies was exposed continuously to a heartbeat recording. Although there was no significant difference in food intake between these babies and the control group during the first four days of life, they differed significantly in weight gain. The experimental group averaged a gain of 40 grams, and the control group lost an average of 20 grams. Table 2-1 shows both groups' weight change in terms of birth weight.

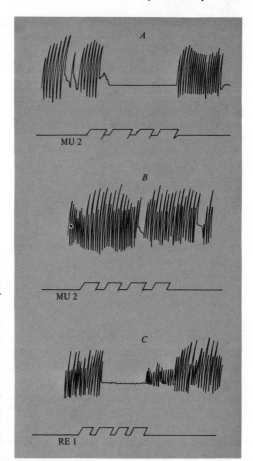

Figure 2–2. Differentiation of musical tones by a child 4 hours and 25 minutes after birth. A. Cessation of sucking when a new tone is played. B. Sucking continues during ninth playing of same tone. C. Sucking stops when another new tone is played.

SOURCE: Figure 1A, B, C from A. I. Bronstein and E. P. Petrova, "The Auditory Analyzer in Young Infants." In Y. Brackbill and G. Thompson [Eds.], *Behavior in Infancy and Early Childhood.* Copyright © 1967 by The Free Press Corporation. Reprinted by permission.

They also differed in amount of crying. During the heartbeat sounds, one or more of the nine babies in the nursery cried 38.4 percent of the time, whereas the crying lasted 59.8 percent of the time in the control situation. The author concluded that the heartbeat sound was comforting (anxiety-reducing). Since the publication of Salk's experiments, a heartbeat machine, developed in Japan, has been used in some hospital nurseries to soothe babies [43]. The wisdom of using soothing sound indiscriminately is questioned by Wolff [85], who has studied interrelationships between states and various stimuli and the organization of infant behavior as a whole. After using monotonous stimuli to produce states which looked like regular sleep, he made a provisional recommendation that, "it may be safest to assume that sleep produced or maintained by white noise is not identical with regular sleep, and that artificial devices for putting the baby to sleep may not be entirely innocuous."

Salk's interesting findings have stimulated other experimenters to see whether they could replicate his results. One study [11] showed that newborns reduced their crying when a heartbeat sound was played, but that a metronome and lullabies sung in a foreign language were just as effective as the heartbeat in soothing crying. Another experiment [66] used heartbeat at two levels of loudness

Table 2–1 Weight Changes in Newborn Babies With and Without Exposure to Heartbeat Sounds

Group	Gained Weight		Lost Weight or Did Not Change	
	NUMBER	PERCENT	NUMBER	PERCENT
102 babies exposed to heartbeat sound	71	69.6	31	30.4
102 babies not exposed to heartbeat sound	37	33.0	75	67.0

SOURCE: L. Salk [70].

(45 and 75 decibels), a regular intermittent tone at the two levels and ambient noise. The heartbeat at 75 decibels was the most effective quietener. Since rhythmic and continuous stimuli of many kinds are soothing to infants [9], it may be that the heartbeat sound owes its pacification powers to these properties. It is still possible, however, that the long prenatal experience in hearing and feeling his mother's heartbeat does indeed make it supreme as a calming rhythmic stimulus.

Another sound that may have significance for the newborn is the cry of another young infant. Although several studies have yielded conflicting evidence on response to crying, a new, carefully controlled investigation indicates that neonates do indeed cry in response to a peer's crying [73]. Tested in cribs with constant temperature and constant visual environment, 75 newborns were divided into groups that were exposed to one of these stimuli: no sound, white noise, and the tape of a 5-day-old baby crying. Crying and heart rate were recorded. Crying occurred in three times as many of the crying-tape group as in the silent control group, as Figure 2–3 shows. There was no difference between the silent control group and white noise group. When duration of crying time was measured, the babies who heard the crying tape cried significantly more than the other infants, but the silent control group did not differ significantly from the white noise group. Heart rate increases in both the white noise group and the crying-tape group exceeded those in the silent-control group. Therefore both sound conditions promoted greater arousal levels, while the crying sound stimulated crying. The experiment shows that the newborn infants responded to the vocal properties of the sound of newborn crying. In a subsequent experiment [72], infants heard recordings of their own crying. Their reactions were compared with those shown when exposed to the crying of another newborn. Their own cry seemed to be a more powerful stimulus, in terms of heart rate increases and duration of crying. It seems likely, then, that as the baby hears himself crying, he is stimulated further to crying.

Vision. Although ready to function at birth, the newborn eye has a few immaturities: an incompletely developed fovea (the part of the retina which sees color best), a short eyeball, a relatively large and spherical lens, and an incompletely developed optic nerve [75]. The immaturities result in poor fixation, focusing, and coordination of eye movements. Blinking and tear production are limited. Nevertheless, a newborn baby can fixate a light and shows a pupillary reflex. Within a few days, he follows a moving light. Brightness sensitivity develops rapidly during the first two months [17]. Fixation of objects develops during the first week or two, while following of objects develops throughout the first several weeks. It is impossible to be more specific, since the many studies of infant vision do not yield

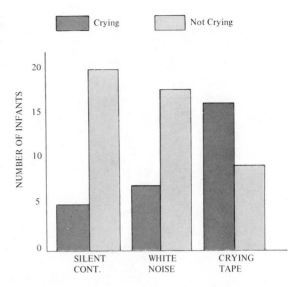

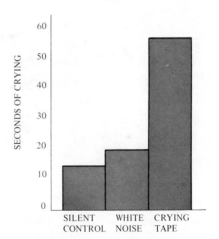

Figure 2–3. Crying of newborn infants increases when they hear a tape of an infant crying.

SOURCE: M. L. Simner and B. Reilly, "Response of the Newborn Infant to the Cry of Another Infant." Paper presented at the meeting of the Society for Research in Child Development. Santa Monica, March 28, 1969.

identical results. In one intensive study of newborns, 8 pursued a moving bright red ball within two hours of delivery [85]. After 24 hours, all 12 infants made conjugate eye movements, and by the third day all made coordinated head and eye responses. These responses took place only during a state of alert inactivity. Newborns who were sucking on pacifiers reduced their sucking rates when looking at an intermittent moving light [30].

Visual acuity, which depends on accommodation (adjusting the thickness of the lens), is limited during the first month and increases gradually. A baby can focus quite well on objects held at about 7½ inches away from his eyes but cannot accommodate to other distances [32].

Using an apparatus that makes it possible to measure how long an infant looks at either of two visual stimuli, Fantz [22] has shown that infants under two weeks of age can perceive stripes ⅛ inch wide at a distance of 9 inches, a visual angle of

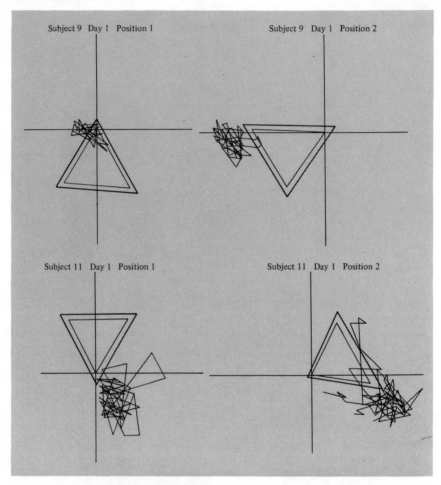

Figure 2–4. Part of the ocular orientation record for one newborn. The outer line represents a solid, black 8-inch equilateral triangle. The irregular lines are a photographic record of where the baby looked.

Source: W. Kessen, "Sucking and Looking: Two Organized Congenital Patterns of Behavior in the Human Newborn." In H. W. Stevenson, E. H. Hess, & H. L. Rheingold [Eds.], *Early Behavior*, New York: John Wiley & Sons, 1967, page 176. By permission.

slightly less than one degree. The infants looked at complex patterns, such as a checkerboard and bull's-eye, more than they looked at simple patterns, such as a square and circle. Using Fantz's method, the visual preferences and abilities of premature and newborns were studied [52]. The prematures, whose gestation age ranged from 32 to 37 weeks, had the same acuity of vision (both discriminated lines subtending a visual angle of 66 degrees). Both groups preferred patterned stimuli to plain. The prematures tended to prefer the simpler stimuli among the patterned ones. The preference for complex patterns is probably due to an unlearned tendency to pay attention to events that involve change or contrast. Newborn babies look more at moving lights than at fixed ones, and at objects with a large amount of black-white contrast than at objects of one shade. Neurological research shows the basis of the infants' tendency to look at events with contrast.

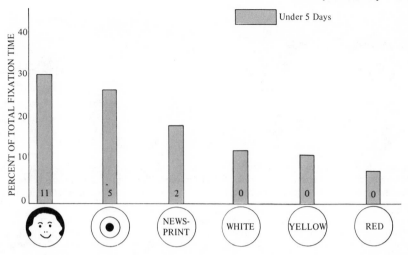

Figure 2–5. Relative visual response and number of newborn infants looking longest at representations of face, bulls'-eye, newsprint, and white and colored disks.

SOURCE: *Annals of the New York Academy of Sciences*, Vol. 118, pp. 793–814, Fig. 7, R. L. Fantz, "Visual Perception from Birth As Shown by Pattern Selectivity." In H. E. Whipple [Ed.], *New Issues in Infant Development*, © The New York Academy of Sciences, 1965. Reprinted by permission.

Such changes in stimulation of the retina produce excitement in nerve cells which could be the basis for sustained fixation [35]. When a newborn looks at a triangle, his eyes are directed at or near an angle, as can be seen in Figure 2–4. It may be that the area of greatest contrast is most attractive or there may be additional factors influencing the direction of looking [37]. Of all patterns shown, a human face elicited more interest (that is, time spent) than any, especially in the youngest babies. When given a choice between a representation of a face and a bull's-eye or between a face and oval targets with dots, stripes, or blanks, the infants looked longer at the face. It is reasonable to conclude that the newborn infant can pick out from the world a human face, the object which has more significance for his survival and well-being than anything else.

The important result of the infant's having pattern preferences is that he selects from the environment what he will take in through his senses and what he will process. He is not open to every source of stimulation in his surroundings, but exposes himself differentially to his environment. He begins to acquire knowledge from the environment with his first look [23].

Coordination of Vision and Hearing. Newborn infants can coordinate vision and hearing to a limited extent. During their first 10 minutes after birth, one baby turned her eyes in the direction of a sound. A toy cricket clicking on one side or the other elicited eye movements half of the time. Most of the eye movements were in the direction of the click [83]. A controlled study done on 64 normal newborn infants confirmed the conclusion that neonates can discriminate location of sound source [42]. Vision and hearing become better coordinated as the child learns through experience.

Taste. Taste is functional in the fetus as well as the newborn, although it seems to develop with age. Infants accept sweet solutions and tend to reject those that are salty, bitter, or sour.

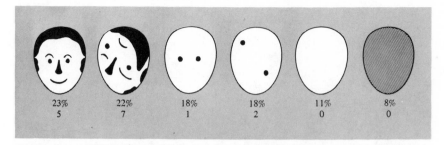

Figure 2–6. Responses of 15 infants under one week of age to stimulus targets with varying arrangements and numbers of facial features. Top figure is mean percentage of time spent looking at target. Bottom figure is number of infants looking most often at that target.

SOURCE: *Annals of the New York Academy of Sciences*, Vol. 118, pp. 793–814, Fig. 9, R. L. Fantz, "Visual Perception from Birth As Shown by Pattern Selectivity." In H. E. Whipple [Ed.], *New Issues in Infant Development*, © The New York Academy of Sciences, 1965. Reprinted by permission.

Smell. Smell has been investigated, using strong odors and measuring changes in body movements and breathing. During the first few days of life, infants showed sensitivity to chemical nasal stimuli and discrimination between different odors [44]. With repetition of an odor stimulus, the response diminished. A new odor then elicited increased response. The investigators concluded that brain action, as well as sensory organ adaptation, was involved. It would be important to discover what role, if any, smell plays in the life processes of the infant, such as the significance of odors from his mother and other people who care for him. Unfortunately, relevant research has not been done. However, it is known that man has a less developed sense of smell than have most other animals. He therefore receives less information about the environment through this sense modality than he does through sight and hearing, for instance.

Pain. Adults would like to know whether a newborn baby feels pain, and if so, what causes pain and how severe it is. Since crying and withdrawal movements are the only indication of pain an infant can give, these reactions have been studied in connection with certain kinds of stimulation. It has long been known that neonates do not cry much when circumcised, especially if given something sweet to suck during the operation. Gastrointestinal upsets, however, result in a great deal of crying. The baby seems to be more sensitive to some kinds of threats than to others and to be able to escape or avoid some more than others [54]. Early research on pain in young infants used pin pricks as stimuli, noting how many were necessary before the baby made some withdrawal response [61]. The more modern method is to use mild electric shock up to a level where a withdrawal action is observed. The stimulus can thus be measured exactly. The experiments show that pain sensitivity increases steadily during the first few days of life. Figure 2–7 shows the decrease in volts required to elicit a reaction of the toe during the first four days. A sex difference was found, as well as an age difference, with girls showing more sensitivity than boys, a result in keeping with the generally greater maturity of girls at birth [46]. Tickling has also been used to explore pain responses, since the two types of stimulation have much in common, and tickling is more acceptable ethically [85]. Newborn babies in all states of rest, responded to tickling with vigorous activity. In states of moderate activity, tickling produced moderate in-

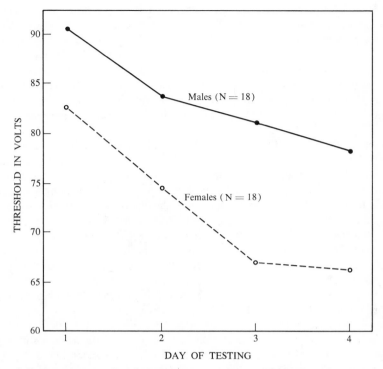

Figure 2–7. Responses to electrical stimulation during the first four days of life, showing decrease in volts required to elicit response.

SOURCE: Reproduced by permission from L. P. Lipsitt and N. Levy, "Electro-tactual Threshold in the Neonate," *Child Development*, 1959, **30**. Copyright © 1959, The Society for Research in Child Development, Inc.

creases in activity (51 percent of trials as compared with 94 percent in regular sleep). In the state of crying the infant responded with a reduction in activity as often as he did with an increase.

Temperature. Newborn babies increase their muscular activity when the temperature drops [50]. They respond to cold or warm stimuli applied to the skin [62]. While early studies had suggested that babies preferred lukewarm food, a careful investigation [34] of the use of cold formulas has caused a change in the advice given by pediatricians. Comparisons were made between a group of premature infants fed formulas at the usual lukewarm temperature. There were no significant differences in the feeding behavior, food intake, weight gain, vocal behavior, sleep patterns, or regurgitation of the two groups. Thus research indicates no reason for giving babies warm rather than cold feedings. However, there is no proof that infants cannot distinguish between warm and cold formulas.

Ways of Coping with the World

Through sensory perception, the infant takes in selected information about his environment and processes it. Lois Murphy has studied many children longitudinally (over a period of time). Careful observation has led her to consider control of stimulation a defensive coping device [54, pp. 300–301]. Within the first month, the baby selects what he is going to look at and how long he will regard it [23]. Perhaps he can do the same with other senses, such as controlling the amount of stimulation he gets from his own bodily movement. Murphy also suggests that the child's basic coping orientation takes place very early in life, most likely beginning with early experiences of success or failure in obtaining food and comfort. He is equipped to attend to certain aspects of the world. He also has some behavior patterns, ready to function at birth or soon after, with which he can shape parts of his environment to meet his own needs.

Tracking, Seeking, and Sucking. Tracking, seeking, and sucking are part of the repertory of the newborn. This behavior is sometimes called the "rooting reflex": When the cheek is touched, the infant moves his head toward the source of the touch, his mouth open. The newborn is likely to show the rooting reflex after several touches on his cheek rather than after the first stimulus [10]. When touched above the lip, the baby opens his mouth wide and moves his head from side to side. When touched on the lip, he purses his lips or pouts [63]. The first two movements are obviously useful for finding the nipple. The third may cause erection of the nipple, making it easier to grasp and suck. There are at least two components to sucking: expression and suction [37]. Expression is a lapping movement, while suction is a negative pressure, created by increasing the size of the mouth cavity. An orthodontist [6] describes the sucking movements required by a breast as being more complicated and more vigorous than those used for a bottle. In order to express the milk from the pockets behind the areola, the baby advances his lower jaw and bites. This movement, then, would add a third dimension to sucking at the breast, but not to sucking a bottle.

The sucking reflex occurs in response to anything in the mouth and, when the infant is very hungry, to stimuli to other parts of the body. Well-coordinated sucking most likely depends on a pattern of stimuli delivered to the infant's mouth. Although ordinarily the breast provides these stimuli, there are breasts that fail to supply the necessary stimuli due to some of the tissues not being sufficiently protractile [29].* In such a case, the baby is apathetic about sucking. If offered a bottle (which does go farther back in his mouth, thus stimulating the sucking reflex), he is likely to take it more enthusiastically than he does the breast. Infants vary in the strength of their sucking movements and in how well they coordinate sucking, breathing, and swallowing. While the shape of the breast has something to do with this variation, there are individual differences in newborns in efficiency of sucking. These differences were observed during the first few days of life in babies tested with standardized artificial nipples [37].

Strength of sucking varies during a feeding period and changes from one period to another, probably with intensity of hunger. The breast adapts its milk production to the length and strength of sucking on it.

Thus does the infant take an active role in finding and securing food, first by crying, then by turning toward the source of tactile stimulation, preparing the nipple to give milk, and then actively withdrawing the milk from the breast, probably stimulating the breast to give more or less. The roles of the infant and mother are completely complementary, requiring the meshing of two people's activity. The first few days of life are often crucial in establishing successful breast feeding. In

* This condition can be noticed during pregnancy. It is usually possible to correct it then.

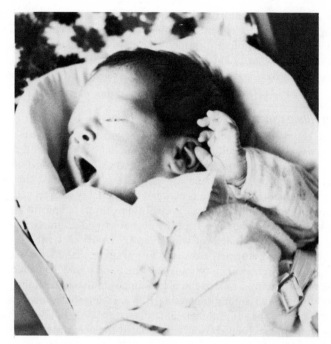

Halvar Loken

addition to failures resulting from inadequate breasts are those which arise because of the baby's having trouble breathing. Sometimes it happens that his upper lip gets pushed over his nostrils, due to the way in which he is placed at the breast. Then he has to fight for air, a frightening experience for him. After only one or two such experiences, he may reject the breast and yet eagerly accept the bottle [29]. For those babies who are in a state of alert inactivity for a period after birth, an opportunity to suck from the breast usually results in well-coordinated sucking [64, pp. 74–75].

As most people know, nonnutritive sucking is soothing to infants. Pacifiers are used widely throughout the world. A study of behavior of 4-day-old infants with pacifiers showed some interesting relationships [86]. They were tested by being tickled with a camel's hair brush during regular sleep, during regular sleep with a pacifier in the mouth but not sucking, during regular sleep while sucking a pacifier. While sucking, infants were less responsive than while not sucking. When a pacifier was in the baby's mouth but he was not sucking, he was likely to respond to the tickling with a new burst of sucking, rather than with increased motility. Apparently sucking blocks other responses.

Crying. Diffuse and crying activity are provoked by noxious stimuli from either outside or inside the infant. The state begins with soft whimpering and gentle movements, gradually changing into rhythmic crying and kicking. He enters a state where his own motility makes him more responsive to the unpleasant stimuli. The more sensitive he becomes, the more he moves and the harder he cries [85].

While the young infant cries in response to noxious stimuli such as hunger, pain, and partial body restraint, he does not do so with the intention of influencing an adult to alleviate his discomfort. Adults, however, generally interpret infant crying as meaning that the infant needs something. In the normal course of events, the mother or caretaker offers food or relief from pain or somehow removes noxious stimuli. Thus the newborn baby can effect a beneficial change in his environment through use of a behavior pattern which he had as part of his neonatal equipment.

Stable Individual Differences in Neonatal Behavior

There are certain obvious differences in babies which are nonetheless important, such as sex, weight, length, color, and hair. Common observation and research [47] show that babies differ from one another in their physiological and psychological reactions during the first days and weeks of life. Frank [26, pp. 63–70] points to the unique structural and functional individuality of every infant as being of prime concern to those who would further his healthy development. The question of basic constitutional differences is of theoretical as well as practical importance, because it is really the problem of what heredity contributes, what environment gives, and how the two interact. How much is given at birth? How fixed is it? Investigations of differences in physiological functioning and behavior, and their constancy, are beginning to fill in the blanks opposite these questions.

The amount of hand-mouth contacting is a measure that shows stable differences from one newborn to another [38]. Finger sucking, hand–face and hand–mouth contacting have been shown to be related to each other and to be significantly different from one infant to another [39]. These movements were highly correlated with total amount of motion. Mouthing (sucking, tongue movements, chewing movements) showed definite individual differences, too, but it was not related to amount of movement. Rather, mouthing was highly related to hunger.

Differences have also been found in heart rate, level of arousal, depth of sleep, tactile sensitivity and strength, oral integration (largely concerned with sucking and rooting), and similarity to fetal position [5, 65]. When 30 neonates were tested systematically with four different stimuli, and rated as to reactions, consistent individual differences were found [7]. A soft tone, a loud tone, a cold disk, and a pacifier were used to stimulate the infants. Some responded vigorously to all situations, some moderately, and others mildly. Not only were the babies different from each other in the vigor of their responses, but they tended to stay in the same position, relative to one another, from the second day of life to the fifth. Stable individual differences have been observed from birth to 4 months in irritability, sensitivity, and tension [8].

Relationships and Experiences

The meaning of his relationships and the success of his experiences depend upon *what the infant is seeking.* Much of his behavior can be explained in terms of *homeostasis,* the maintaining of physiological equilibrium in the organism. Tension is reduced and balance restored by food-seeking, sucking, and swallowing, through breathing, moving, and having baths and dry diapers. To achieve and maintain successive states of equilibrium also requires a certain level of sensory stimulation—enough but not too much of the various kinds. Equilibrium is continually being disturbed and restored on a new level. In its striving for equilibrium, the organism (either baby or adult) gives preference to some needs over others [77]. For example, a certain degree of fatigue takes precedence over a certain degree of hunger and over a certain level of desire for sensory stimulation. As equilibrium is continually disturbed and created, changes occur in the organism's structure and behavior. These changes are growth and development.

Personality is developing while the newborn is reducing his tensions and maintaining homeostasis. The sense of trust is the crucial aspect of personality growth at this time and for at least the first year of life. Erikson [21, pp. 247–251] writes of the feeling of goodness which comes when the baby is helped to cope with his environment. The world must seem like a good place to be and the people in it trustworthy when he is fed before he is overwhelmed by hunger, when he is kept at a comfortable temperature, and when he receives a satisfactory amount of sensory stimulation. As he is allowed and assisted to use his various competencies in different situations, his trust increases. In the following section, some of his relationships and experiences are examined in the light of personality development.

Feeding

The feeding of infants can be considered from many angles. The nutritional aspects are crucial to survival and growth. Through feeding, the baby builds feelings about himself, his mother, and the world. The mother, as well as the baby, is affected physically and emotionally. Culture shapes the methods of feeding available. In the United States, women make choices concerning infant feeding which they are often ill-equipped to make. The choice between breast and bottle feeding, which will affect the mother and baby throughout the first several months, must be made immediately after, if not before, birth.

Physical Aspects. Most of the world's babies begin their feeding histories at the breast. Only in highly industrialized societies has bottle feeding become a frequently used method. The United States has the dubious distinction of having the lowest breast-feeding rates in the world [56]. Only 18 percent of infants are being completely breast fed on discharge from the hospital [51]. This figure represents a decline of 20 percent in 20 years. Of babies between birth and 3 months, only 11 percent receive any breast feeding [20]. Bottle feeding is successful here because of technological sophistication in regard to making formulas that approximate human milk and presenting it under very sanitary conditions. In underdeveloped parts of the world, breast feeding is closely tied to survival and to growth. Breast feeding can make the difference between life and death or between normal and stunted development. In most of the underdeveloped areas, babies are usually wholly breast fed for at least three or four months, during which time they tend to grow very well and tend to resist disease [80]. The ability of these mothers, many of whom are poorly fed, to produce adequate supplies of good-quality milk is a surprising feature of human reproduction.

Normal lactation periods in mammals correspond to the period of rapid infant growth, when the major part of the growth of the nervous system takes place. Adequate nutrition ordinarily occurs with breast feeding during this important growth period. Animal studies show that babies suffer irreversible growth retardation, including brain deficits, when nursing mothers are seriously malnourished, and this finding suggests that humans may be similarly damaged [71]. Nutritional intake and growth were studied in 215 infants in an impoverished community in Lahore, Pakistan [58]. Fifty percent of the babies were receiving insufficient food

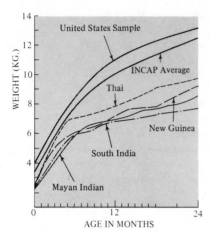

Figure 2–8. The weight curves of babies in four underdeveloped countries fall away from the average standard line just at the age when breast feeding is stopped. In two of the countries represented here, breast feeding is stopped at around 3 months. In the other two, about 6 months is the termination date.

SOURCE: M. Béhar, "Prevalence of Malnutrition Among Preschool Children of Developing Countries," in N. S. Scrimshaw and J. E. Gordon [Eds.], *Malnutrition, Learning and Behavior*. Cambridge: M.I.T. Press, 1968. Also from R. L. Jackson and H. G. Kelly, "Growth Charts for Use in Pediatric Practice," *Journal of Pediatrics*, 1945, **27**, 215–229.

during the first month of life, 77 percent by six months, and 87 percent by the end of the first year.

Even when lactating mothers in poor countries live on relatively poor diets, their babies grow better while nursing than they do after weaning, as Figure 2–8 shows. These weight curves, comparing children with an international standard, show a situation that has been demonstrated on many impoverished populations. The baby grows almost normally for the first three to six months. Then the weight curve drops off throughout the preschool years. The beginning of the depression in the weight curve corresponds with the time when breast milk becomes insufficient, and the total food supply and supplementary foods are inadequate. Although breast feeding is often prolonged into the second or third year, it does not provide enough food. Supplementary foods are usually unsuitable, insufficient, and late. Contamination from the unsanitary environment increases, immunity from the mother's milk decreases, and the baby becomes ill more and more often. Poor nutrition and disease interact with each other to depress growth [4].

In the wealthier parts of the world, where an infant's physical survival and health do not depend heavily on breast feeding, a few physical arguments in favor of breast feeding remain. Artificially fed infants differ from breast-fed infants in body composition, physiological reactions, patterns of weight gain, and resistance to disease [3]. Human milk is biochemically suited to human babies and has the added bonus of giving immunity to many diseases. Jaw development is better promoted by the complicated biting and sucking coordinations required by the breast, in contrast to the simple, relatively passive movements instigated by the bottle [6].

Nursing mothers, too, receive physical benefits. In the first few weeks after birth, the baby's sucking stimulates the uterus to contract and hence speeds its return to normal size and structure. There is evidence that nursing a baby reduces a woman's chances of ever having breast cancer [64]. Women whose breasts have too much fatty tissue are likely to find that several months of nursing improves their shape and firmness [64].

Psychological Aspects. If rooting, pursing the lips, and grasping results in breast feeding, the chain of results differs from what happens when the result is bottle feeding. The tactile sensations from breast and bottle are different, the breast being warm, more flexible, and responsive to a sucking movement which differs from the sucking required by a bottle. Taste is different, too, not only because of the differences in human and cow's milk, but because the breast gives a low concentration of fats at first and a larger amount of cream at the end. Tactile and olfactory sensations from the mother's body are likely to be more intense in breast feeding because the baby is closer to her skin.

Inability and/or unwillingness to breast-feed is widespread in western culture. Some women do not want to nurse their babies and some do not produce enough milk to sustain their babies. Still others have given up the attempt to nurse because of sore nipples. These mothers may worry about their babies' well-being or they may feel guilty about not being adequate mothers. Research into the psychological results of breast versus bottle feeding has not been definitive. One longitudinal study [33] showed that nursing had to be considered in the child's life context, an important part of which was his mother's personality. The child's sex, the mother's warmth and stability, the length of the nursing period, all had some significance for the personality development of the child. These findings, as well as common sense, raise doubt as to the wisdom of putting pressure on women to nurse their babies when they have strong feelings against it. On the other hand, many women want to nurse and fail because they do not have the right kind of instruction, encouragement, and support for their efforts. Still others would want to do so if they understood more about this elemental process and relationship. A mother's attitudes toward breast feeding and success in it are largely derived from her understanding of and feelings about the whole cycle of reproduction in human beings [56].

A movement to promote breast feeding has met with some success, especially in upper socioeconomic levels.* Many of the people who become interested in prepared childbirth and family-centered hospital care are also convinced of the benefits of breast feeding to both infant and mother. The physical pleasure and psychological well-being of the mother, resulting from breast feeding, are unknown to many women in the western world. In substituting bottles for breasts, it is important to imitate the psychological situation as well as the nutritional. In other words, holding and cuddling during feeding may be as important as getting the formula right.

Feeding As a Relationship. When working in harmony, the baby's mouth and the mother's breast together perform an act. Two people contact each other and cooperate. Bottle feeding can also be a cooperative relationship. The baby's feelings of trust and confidence are enhanced by successful use of his abilities for getting food. The mother's parental sense is nurtured and she also grows. (The parental sense or sense of generativity is one of the adult stages of personality development, during which the individual becomes involved in promoting the well-being of the next generation.)

Research on subhuman mammals shows that the development and maintenance of maternal behavior depends upon stimulation from the young. After even a brief period (a few days) of separation from their young, rats, goats, sheep, and other animals lose much of their maternal bonds with the young [68]. One study of human mothers who were separated from their babies for the first few months after birth showed that they often had trouble in establishing maternal feelings [2]. This slight research evidence, along with clinical evidence, raises the question of the effects of separating mothers and babies at birth, a practice in many hospitals.

* La Leche League.

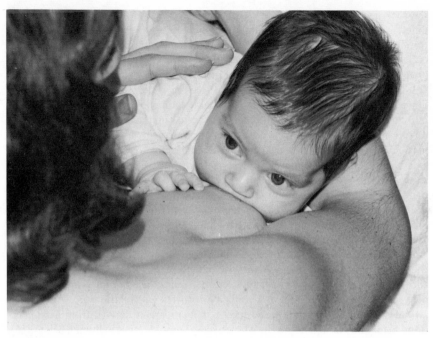

Halvar Loken

While the lying-in period is brief, it may be important for easy development of warm maternal feelings and spontaneous behavior.

Timing. If rooting, pursing the lips, grasping, sucking, and swallowing result in ingesting food, then the disequilibrium of hunger is reduced. A state of waking activity or crying changes to a quiet state of sleep or alert inactivity. The accompanying sensory stimulation, especially tactile, not only soothes the baby but promotes growth and mental organization. Such reduction of noxious stimuli occurs promptly in most non-western societies. The practice in most American hospitals is to feed babies on a 4-hour schedule, either taking them to their mothers to be breast-fed or given bottles or feeding them by bottles in the nursery. The 4-hour interval was established long ago from observations that babies' stomachs tended to empty in 4 hours and that, therefore, many babies were ready for food in approximately 4-hour intervals. The custom continues because hospitals run on schedules, and even for those who doubt the value of the 4-hour feeding plan, there is the rationalization that the lying-in period is so short that it does not matter. If homeostasis were the only goal involved, then it really would not matter. The fact that babies live and gain weight would be justification enough. However, the mother–baby relationship is involved. The early experience of the pair may be important in many ways, one of which is in determining whether feeding is by breast or bottle [29].

Family-Centered Hospital Care. A growing number of hospitals are offering care that promotes psychological health as well as physical. The 4-hour schedule takes account of neither the baby's competency in seeking and securing food nor of building competency in the mother. Nor is it concerned with the infant's states of hunger and arousal. He may be sleeping when mealtime comes; whereupon he is

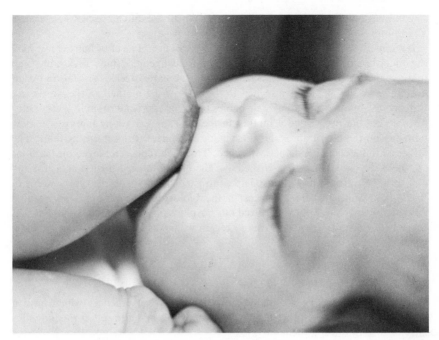

Halvar Loken

wakened and offered food. Or he may have cried, rooted, and sucked for an hour beforehand. In neither situation does he gain confidence in his ability to get food, nor in the world as a place where food is available for the seeking.

The rooming-in plan is a scheme for meeting the physical needs of baby and mother and the psychological needs of the baby, mother, and father. Developed along with prepared childbirth, *rooming-in* is an arrangment whereby the parents get well acquainted with their baby in the hospital. Although there are variations in the procedures, the essentials are thus. The baby stays in the room with his mother for a large portion of the time, in a bassinet beside her bed, or in a container that can be swung over her bed. She can pick him up and care for him if she wishes. The father, the only visitor, carefully washed and gowned, can hold his baby and care for him too. A nurse, or nurse's helper, shows the mother and father the techniques of baby care and does the care when the mother does not feel like doing it herself. When the mother wants to sleep or rest, the baby is taken into another room and cared for by the nurse. The mother is able to get to know her infant as an individual, to begin interacting with him, to find the ways of caring for him which bring most satisfactory results, and to feed him at the times which seem most appropriate. Crying has been found to stimulate a let-down reflex in the breasts of the lactating mother who is relaxed [57]. The breasts then feel heavy and ready for suckling, giving her an urge to feed the baby. The mother is likely to receive interested, informed instruction from a nurse who is skilled at helping newborn babies and their mothers to cooperate in breast feeding. With such assistance, the baby is likely to grasp the nipple in such a way that it will stimulate an adequate sucking reflex and he will avoid the pitfall of getting his nose blocked by his lip. The mother has an excellent chance to feel and be successful from the beginning.

A good beginning with breast feeding can make all the difference between success and failure.

It seems strange that America is having to rediscover a facet of baby care which the underdeveloped countries have never lost. Tribal people almost invariably keep mother and baby together, especially during the early weeks. Visiting in Asian hospitals, we saw bassinets attached to the beds of the mothers in the wards and watched the mothers handling their babies freely. In a private room in a very comfortable hospital we visited a mother in the midst of her whole family. The new baby lay on the lap of an ayah (nursemaid, not nurse) who sat on the floor. The father sat on a chair beside his wife's bed. Two older children played on the floor and held the baby when they wished to. The grandmother sat on a sofa, folding diapers. The warm family atmosphere contrasted sharply with the typical scene in the United States, where advances in the biological sciences, plus an ensuing passion for cleanliness, have sterilized our hospitals physically and psychologically. Some medical staffs are now trying to regain what was lost psychologically, while keeping the physical benefits.

Additional Aspects of Physical Care

Besides feeding, there are many different infant care practices which have a variety of results. These practices have cultural bases and also reflect the individuality of the adult using them.

Holding, Cuddling, Rocking, Changing position. Stimulation to the skin, muscles, and ear senses seems to create quiet states in the young baby, as everyone knows if he has tried these means of soothing crying. The "good feeling" which accompanies tension reduction doubtless occurs here. Crying is probably the only way in which a newborn can indicate this kind of discomfort, unless his state of waking activity also signifies it. Although he may gain some equilibrium on his own through moving his body, he does not have a very handy method of getting someone to hold him. If he cries or if his wriggles result in his being picked up, rocked, and carried, then surely he gets one more assurance that the world is a place where he can find comfort and satisfaction.

An experiment on neonates demonstrates different kinds of behavior resulting from different ways of handling infants [59]. An attempt was made to continue after birth a type of stimulation similar to prenatal stimulation. Mothers were instructed to hold the infant in fetal position, firmly wrapped in a blanket, in close contact with the mother's body. After breast feeding in this position, the mother was to rock the baby very gently. The nurses gave similar care. The control group was on regular hospital routine, with bottle feeding by the mothers. The control group cried about twice as much as the experimental group, especially when no external instigation was present. This experiment demonstrates differences in infant behavior under two different sets of circumstances, which might be characterized as mothering versus hospital routine. One of the specifics in the mothering complex, rocking, has been studied systematically in several subsequent investigations.

The effects of rocking on crying were studied in a hospital nursery [28]. An infant was chosen from the babies who were not crying and was rocked for half an hour and then observed for half an hour, while the other noncrying infants were observed for the same time. Results showed that the rocked infants cried less than the nonrocked. Another study [9] compared the soothing effects of rocking, a

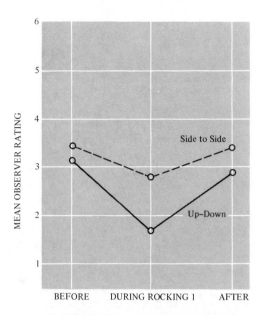

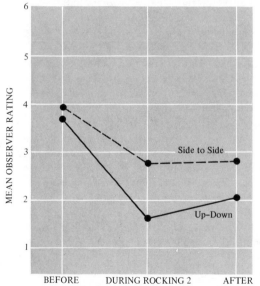

Figure 2–9. Amount of activity of young infants before, during, and after one and two sessions of horizontal and vertical rocking.

SOURCE: Reprinted by permission from D. R. Pederson, L. Champagne, and L. L. Pederson, "Relative Soothing Effects of Vertical and Horizontal Rocking." Paper presented at the biennial meeting of the Society for Research in Child Development, Santa Monica, 1969.

sweetened pacifier, a monotonous sound, and warm water. All stimuli had some quieting effect, but rocking had no more than the others. Two types of rocking were compared in a third piece of research [60]. A crib was designed to rock in either a side-to-side motion, like a cradle, or in an up-and-down direction. The infants' activity was measured and rated before, during, and after two sessions of each type of rocking. Figure 2–9 shows the results. The up-and-down rocking was more soothing than the side-to-side. Both types of rocking have a more quieting effect after the second session than after the first.

As every parent and baby-sitter knows, a crying baby can usually be soothed by picking him up and putting him to the shoulder. In studying this phenomenon, it was found that a state of alert inactivity, plus visual scanning, was induced by picking up a crying newborn and putting him to the shoulder [40]. Neither handling nor the upright position alone induced visual alertness. Since handling of young animals and tactile stimulation of human babies have been found to promote growth and development [15], it may be that one of the pathways of early stimulation is visual activation through tactile stimulation.

Touching another person involves two people. It is the simplest and most fundamental kind of relationship. Touching is communication, since two people perceive each other. The communication may well involve emotion, since along with each person's perception may go a feeling tone. By simply being the other person in a touch relationship, the baby profoundly affects his world in the form of his mother and others who care for him. The tender feelings that well up from holding a baby are the energizers of much mature adult work and development.

Although breast feeding is confined to mothers (and wet nurses), anybody can hold and cuddle a baby. A good feeling comes from meeting his needs, restoring his equilibrium, and helping him to grow. What is more, when two people touch, both get tactual stimulation, and the person who holds a baby gets a sensory and emotional satisfaction from the way his arms, chest, neck, and cheeks feel. Perhaps his own heartbeat is reflected back from the baby's body, giving mutually satisfying stimulation. It is in this situation that the newborn baby begins to build relationships with his father, grandparents, brothers, and sisters.

In most, but not all, non-western cultures, babies are frequently held close to their mothers and often sleep with them at night. Americans tend to leave the baby in his crib or playpen unless he indicates a need for care. Each culture has its own way of handling infants and supports it with theories about what is good for them. Some babies are strapped to cradleboards, others swing in hammocks, some are kept vertical, others horizontal. These different methods of handling produce different kinds and degrees of stimulation in the infants. Presumably, different kinds of development would occur in different cultures, and they do. Life and culture are too complex, however, to show a one-to-one relationship between any kind of infant care and a "piece" of adult behavior.

Bathing and Dressing. The film *Four Families* [55] shows the activities involved in the physical care of babies in four different cultures. Although the babies are older than newborns, the point is still valid that many different experiences can go under the name of "bath," and that many of those experiences symbolize a cultural attitude toward children. We (the authors) would like to report a personal cross-cultural experience which highlighted for us the different sets of sensations possible in American and Indian bathing. Laura, our 10-year-old, having fallen in love with the nightwatchman's baby, reported that Umersingh didn't like the way his mother bathed him because he always cried and kicked hard when she put him upside down on her legs, splashed water over him and rubbed him with her hand. Laura brought Umersingh home for baths in our washbasin, where he never cried, and moved his legs in the most gentle, relaxed way. "Ummy prefers American baths," she concluded. The uniformly warm temperature of our washbasin, in contrast to splashed water which cooled quickly, was probably one point in our favor. Also, having his whole body submerged must have been a more satisfying tactual stimulus than merely being wet. The buoying quality of the water, too, would give muscular stimulation. Our bath was more prolonged, with much sudsy washing, which must have felt smooth, slippery, and soothing. Even so, Umersingh might have preferred

Figure 2–10. An American mother and baby enjoy a bath together. In this family, a social bath is termed "Swedish."

Halvar Loken

the Japanese bath shown in *Four Families* if he could have compared it with American bathing. The Japanese grandmother took the baby into the bath with her, thereby adding all the tactual delights of (and to) her own skin.

Dressing symbolizes and defines attitudes toward the skin and toward activity. The kind and the amount of stimulation and activity possible depend to a large extent on how the baby is clothed. Exposed to the same conditions, a swaddled baby will not get as much stimulation as a naked baby. Swaddling has been shown to promote calmness and drowsiness, but partial swaddling produces excitement, crying, and activity which looks like outrage [85]. When the surrounding temperature is not ideal, tension reduction is achieved by adding or subtracting clothing and coverings in such a way that the infant's temperature is regulated most comfortably.

Other kinds of physical care can be pleasurably stimulating, such as massage and hair brushing, or of doubtful outcome, such as putting black around the eyes and swabbing the nose. Insofar as the baby's actions initiate care that brings tension reduction, his sense of trust probably increases.

Summary

The newborn baby is usually red, wrinkled, blue-eyed, and bumpy-headed. He has a large head, a small trunk, and very small, bowed legs. His first big adjustment is to establish breathing with his lungs. The next demand upon him is to secure food through his mouth, which he does by using a complex of reflex mechanisms. He is very limited in his ability to regulate his body temperature.

Many different motor coordinations, involving all parts of the body, can be observed in the neonate. Through crying and food-seeking, he effects environmental changes, many of which involve relationships with his mother. Mutual regulation occurs between mother and baby, especially in the realm of breast feeding, where milk supply and strength of sucking become adapted to each other. First experiences in obtaining food and comfort may be influential in patterning the ways in which the infant copes with other problems.

Sleeping and waking are differentiated into six states. External stimulation is most readily received and processed during the state of alert inactivity.

A child probably tries to maintain the level of stimulation which is optimal for him. Tactile and inner ear senses, highly developed before birth, are very important to the infant. Animal experiments show that early tactile experiences promote growth and learning. Human mothers and babies communicate to a great extent through touch. The neonate can hear, even making fine discrimination in pitch. The sound of the human heartbeat probably has significance for him. The newborn responds to visual stimuli, selecting what he regards, and showing preference for a human face and for complex patterns as compared with simple ones. Taste and smell receptors function. Pain sensitivity in the skin increases during the first few days of life. Infants vary considerably in the intensity and selectivity of their responses to stimuli.

Many or most of the neonate's efforts are directed toward maintaining and restoring states of physiological equilibrium. Growth and development occur as new states of equilibrium are achieved. Presumably, comfortable feelings and healthy personality growth accompany optimal maintenance of equilibrium. A sense of trust grows as the baby is fed, comforted, and stimulated satisfactorily and as he plays some part in bringing about these experiences. Flexible, mutually regulated feeding practices contribute to the sense of trust. Mothers and infants can be helped to establish a satisfactory feeding relationship by a rooming-in arrangement in the hospital. This plan includes expert education given by the nurses. Comfortable feelings, stimulation, and relationships are also built through other aspects of physical care, including holding, handling, dressing, and bathing.

References

1. Apgar, V. Perinatal problems and the central nervous system. In U.S. Dept. of Health, Education, and Welfare, Children's Bureau, *The child with central nervous system deficit*. Washington, D.C.: U.S. Govt. Printing Office, 1965.
2. Appel, G., & David, M. A study of mother-child interaction at thirteen months. In B. M. Foss, *Determinants of infant behavior*. Vol. III. London: Methuen, 1965, 129–147.
3. Bakwin, H. Current feeding practices for infants. *Nutrition News*, 1965, **28**:3.
4. Béhar, M. Prevalence of malnutrition among preschool children of developing countries. In N. S. Scrimshaw & J. E. Gordon (Eds.), *Malnutrition, learning and behavior*. Cambridge, Mass.: M.I.T. Press, 1967, pp. 30–41.
5. Bell, R. Q. Relations between behavior manifestations in the human neonate. *Child Devel.*, 1960, **31**, 463–478.
6. Berland, T., & Seyler, A. *Your children's teeth*. New York: Meredith, 1968.
7. Birns, B. Individual differences in human neonates' responses to stimulation. *Child Devel.*, 1965, **36**, 249–259.
8. Birns, B., Barton, S., & Bridger, W. H. Individual differences in temperamental characteristics of infants. *Trans. N.Y. Acad. Sci.*, 1969, Ser. II, **31**, 1071–1082.
9. Birns, B., Blank, M., & Bridger, W. H. The effectiveness of various soothing techniques on human neonates. *Psychosomatic Medicine*, 1966, **28**:4, Part 1, 316–322.
10. Blauvelt, H. H. Capacity of a human neonatal reflex to signal future response by present action. *Child Devel.*, 1962, **33**, 21–29.
11. Brackbill, Y., Adams, G., Crowell, D. H., & Gray, M. L. Arousal level in

neonates and older infants under continuous auditory stimulation. *J. Exper. Child Psychol.*, 1966, **4**, 178–188.

12. Bridger, W. H. Sensory habituation and discrimination in the human neonate. *Am. J. Psychiat.*, 1961, **117**, 991–996.

13. Bronstein, A. I., & Petrova, E. P. The auditory analyzer in young infants. In Y. Brackbill & G. G. Thompson (Eds.), *Behavior in infancy and early childhood.* New York: Free Press, 1967, pp. 163–172.

14. Casler, L. Maternal deprivation: A critical review of the literature. *Mono. Soc. Res. Child Devel.*, 1961, **26**:2.

15. Casler, L. The effects of extra tactile stimulation on a group of institutionalized infants. *Genet. Psychol. Mono.*, 1965, **71**, 137–175.

16. Dennis, W. A description and classification of the responses of the newborn infant. *Psychol. Bull.*, 1934, **31**, 5–22.

17. Doris, J., Casper, M., & Poresky, R. Differential brightness thresholds in infancy. *J. Exper. Child Psychol.*, 1967, **5**, 522–535.

18. Edwards, N. The relationship between physical condition immediately after birth and mental and motor performance at age four. *Genet. Psychol. Mono.*, 1968, **78**, 257–289.

19. Eichorn, D. H. Biology of gestation and infancy: Fatherland and frontier. *Merrill-Palmer Quart.*, 1968, **14**, 47–81.

20. Eppright, E. S., et al. The North Central Regional study of diets of preschool children. 3. Frequency of eating. *J. Home Econ.*, 1970, **62**, 407–410.

21. Erikson, E. H. Childhood and society. New York: Norton, 1963.

22. Fantz, R. L. The origin of form perception. *Sci. Am.*, 1961, **204**:5, 66–72.

23. Fantz, R. L. Visual perception from birth as shown by patterned selectivity. *Ann. N.Y. Acad. Sci.*, 1965, **118**, 793–814.

24. Fantz, R. L. Visual preference and experience in early infancy: A look at the hidden side of behavior development. In H. E. Stevenson, E. H. Hess, & H. L. Rheingold (Eds.), *Early behavior.* New York: Wiley, 1967, pp. 181–224.

25. Frank, L. K. Tactile communication. *Genet. Psychol. Mono.*, 1957, **56**, 209–225.

26. Frank, L. K. *The importance of infancy,* New York: Random House, 1966.

27. Garn, S. M. Genetics of normal human growth. In L. Gedda (Ed.), *De genetica medica.* Rome: Gregor Mendel Instit., 1962. Cited in Eichorn [19].

28. Gordon, T., & Foss, B. M. The role of stimulation in the delay of onset of crying in the newborn infant. *Quart. J. Exper. Psychol.*, 1966, **18**, Part 1, 79–81.

29. Gunther, M. Infant behavior at the breast. In B. M. Foss (Ed.), *Determinants of infant behavior.* Vol. I. New York: Wiley, 1961, pp. 37–44.

30. Haith, M. M. The response of the human newborn to visual movement. *J. Exper. Child Psychol.*, 1966, **3**, 235–243.

31. Harrison, G. A., Weiner, J. S., Tanner, J. M., & Barnicot, N. A. *Human biology.* New York: Oxford University Press, 1964.

32. Haynes, H., White, B. L., & Held, R. Visual accommodation in human infants. *Science*, 1965, **148**, 528–530.

33. Heinstein, M. I. Behavioral correlates of breast-bottle regimes under varying parent–infant relationships. *Mono. Soc. Res. Child Devel.*, 1963, **28**:4.

34. Holt, L. E., Jr., Davies, E. A., Hasselmeyer, E. G., & Adams, A. O. A study of premature infants fed cold formulas. *J. Pediat.*, 1962, **61**, 556–561.

35. Kagan, J. Continuity in cognitive development during the first year. *Merrill-Palmer Quart.*, 1969, **15**, 101–119.

36. Kaye, H. The conditioned Babkin reflex in human newborns. *Psychonomic Sci.*, 1965, **2**, 287–288.

37. Kessen, W. Sucking and looking: Two organized congenital patterns of behavior in the human newborn. In H. W. Stevenson, E. H. Hess, & H. L. Rheingold (Eds.), *Early behavior.* New York: Wiley, 1967, pp. 147–179.

38. Kessen, W., et al. Selection and test of response measures in the study of the human newborn. *Child Devel.*, 1961, **32**, 7–24.

39. Korner, A. F., Chuck, B., & Dontchos, S. Organismic determinants of spontaneous oral behavior in neonates. *Child Devel.*, 1968, **39**, 1145–1157.

40. Korner, A. F., & Grobstein, R. Visual alertness as related to soothing in neonates: Implications for maternal stimulation and early deprivation. *Child Devel.*, 1966, **37**, 867–876.

41. Lenard, H. G., Bernuth, H. (von), & Prechtl, H. F. R. Reflexes and their relationship to behavioral states in the newborn. *Acta Pediatrica Scandinavia*, 1968, **57**, 177–185.

42. Leventhal, A. S., & Lipsitt, L. P. Adaptation, pitch discrimination and sound localization in the neonate. *Child Devel.*, 1964, **35**, 759–767.

43. Liley, H. M. I. *Modern motherhood.* New York: Random House, 1966.

44. Lipsitt, L. P. Learning processes of newborns. *Merrill-Palmer Quart.*, 1966, **12**, 45–71.

45. Lipsitt, L. P. Learning in the human infant. In H. W. Stevenson, E. H. Hess, & H. L. Rheingold (Eds.), *Early behavior.* New York: Wiley, 1967.

46. Lipsitt, L. P., & Levy, N. Electrotactual threshold in the neonate. *Child Devel.*, 1959, **30**, 547–554.

47. Lipton, E. L., & Steinschneider, A. Studies on the psychophysiology of infancy. *Merrill-Palmer Quart.*, 1964, **10**, 102–117.

48. Lipton, E. L., Steinschneider, A., & Richmond, J. B. Autonomic function in the neonate. VII: Maturational changes in cardiac control. *Child Devel.*, 1966, **37**, 1–16.

49. Meredith, H. V. North American Negro infants: Size at birth and growth during the first postnatal year. *Human Biol.*, 1952, **24**:290.

50. Mestyan, G., & Varga, F. Chemical thermoregulation of full-term and premature newborn infants. *J. Pediat.*, 1960, **56**, 623–629.

51. Meyer, H. F. Breast feeding in the United States. *Clinical Pediat.*, 1968, **7**, 708–715.

52. Miranda, S. B. Visual-perceptual abilities and preferences of premature infants and full-term newborns. Paper presented at the meeting of the Society for Research in Child Development, Santa Monica, March 27, 1969.

53. Moss, H. A., & Robson, K. S. The relation between the amount of time infants spend at various states and the development of visual behavior. *Child Devel.*, 1970, **41**, 509–517.

54. Murphy, L. B. *The widening world of childhood.* New York: Basic Books, 1962.

55. National Film Board of Canada. *Four families.*

56. Newton, N. Pregnancy, childbirth and outcome: A review of patterns of culture and future research needs. In S. A. Richardson & A. F. Guttmacher (Eds.), Childbearing—Its social and psychological aspects. Baltimore: Williams & Wilkins, 1967.

57. Newton, N., & Newton, M. Psychologic aspects of lactation. *New England J. Medicine*, 1967, **277**, 1179–1188.

58. *New York Times.* Babies in Lahore start out hungry. October 25, 1970.

59. Ourth, L., & Brown, K. B. Inadequate mothering and disturbance in the neonatal period. *Child Devel.*, 1961, **32**, 287–295.
60. Pederson, D. R., Champagne, L., & Pederson, L. L. Relative soothing effects of vertical and horizontal rocking. Paper presented at meetings of the Society for Research in Child Development, Santa Monica, March 29, 1969.
61. Pratt, K. C. The neonate. In L. Carmichael (Ed.), *Manual of child psychology.* New York: Wiley, 1954, pp. 215–291.
62. Pratt, K. C., Nelson, A. K., & Sun, K. H. *The behavior of the newborn infant.* Ohio State University Studies, Contrib. Psychol. No. 10, 1930.
63. Prechtl, H. F. R. The directed head-turning response and allied movements of the human baby. *Behavior*, 1958, **8**, 212–242.
64. Pryor, K. *Nursing your baby.* New York: Harper & Row, 1963.
65. Richmond, J., & Lipton, E, L. Some aspects of the neurophysiology of the newborn and their implications for child development. In L. Jessner & E. Pavenstedt (Eds,), *Dynamic psychopathology in childhood.* New York: Grune & Stratton, 1959.
66. Roberts, B., & Campbell, D. Activity in newborns and the sound of a human heart. *Psychonomic Sci.*, 1967, **9**, 339–340.
67. Roffwarg, H. P., Muzio, J. N., & Dement, W. C. Ontogenetic development of the human sleep-dream cycle. *Science*, 1966, 604–617.
68. Rosenblatt, J. S. Social environmental factors affecting reproduction and offspring in human mammals. In S. A. Richardson & A. F. Guttmacher (Eds.), Childbearing—Its social and psychological aspects. Baltimore: Williams & Wilkins, 1967, 245–301.
69. Rosenblith, J. F. Prognostic value of neonatal assessment. *Child Devel.*, 1966, **37**, 623–631.
70. Salk, L. Mother's heartbeat as an imprinting stimulus. *Trans. N.Y. Acad. Sci.*, Ser. II, 1962, **24**, 753–763.
71. Sherwin, R. W. Perinatal nutrition as a developmental determinant. *Nutrition News*, 1967, **30**(4), 13–14.
72. Simner, M. L. Auditory self-stimulative feedback and reflexive crying in human infants. Paper presented at the meeting of the Eastern Psychological Association, Altantic City, April, 1970.
73. Simner, M. L., & Reilly, B. Response of the newborn infant to the cry of another infant. Paper presented at the meeting of the Society for Research in Child Development, Santa Monica, Calif., March 28, 1969.
74. Smith, C. A. *The physiology of the newborn infant.* Springfield, Ill.: Charles C Thomas, 1959.
75. Spears, W. C., & Hohle, R. H. Sensory and perceptual processes in infants. In Y. Brackbill (Ed.), *Infancy and early childhood.* New York: Free Press, 1967, pp. 49–121.
76. Spock, B. *Baby and child care.* New York: Pocket Books, 1968.
77. Stagner, R. Homeostasis, need reduction and motivation. *Merrill-Palmer Quart.*, 1961, **7**, 49–69.
78. Steinschneider, A., Lipton, E. L., & Richmond, B. Auditory sensitivity in the infant: Effect of intensity on cardiac and motor activity. *Child Devel.*, 1966, **37**, 233–252.
79. Tanner, J. M. *Education and physical growth.* London: University of London, 1961.
80. Thomson, A. M. Historical perspectives of nutrition, reproduction and growth.

In N. S. Scrimshaw & J. E. Gordon (Eds.), *Malnutrition, learning and behavior.* Cambridge, Mass.: M.I.T. Press, 1968, 17–28.

81. Vallbona, C., et al. Cardiodynamic studies in the newborn II. Regulation of heart rate. *Biologia Neonatorum*, 1963, **5**, 159–199.

82. Watson, E. H., & Lowrey, G. H. *Growth and development of children* (5th ed.). Chicago: Yearbook, 1967.

83. Wertheimer, M. Psychomotor coordination of auditory and visual perception at birth. *Science*, 1961, **134**, 1962.

84. Wolff, P. H. The development of attention in young infants. *Ann. N.Y. Acad. Sci.*, 1965, **118**, 815–830.

85. Wolff, P. H. The causes, controls and organization of behavior in the neonate. *Psychol. Issues*, 1966, **5**:1. New York: International Universities Press.

86. Wolff, P. H., & Simmons, M. A. Nonnutritive sucking and response thresholds in young infants. *Child Devel.*, 1967, **38**, 631–638.

Readings in
Early Infancy

Erik H. Erikson's discussion of basic trust provides an orientation to infancy and to the infant's family and culture. Feelings as well as thoughts are likely to be aroused by this great philosopher-analyst who makes the infant's experience and achievements so real and so important.

Growth in early infancy is very rapid, especially in small babies. James M. Tanner, a specialist in human biology, explains the birth catch-up capacity, relating it to survival value and to genetic variability. The complicated subject of breast feeding is discussed thoroughly, from the standpoint of infant and mother, by Marian Breckenridge, a nutritionist and authority on child growth, and psychologist Margaret Murphy. This treatment has particular significance for the United States, where breast feeding is little understood. We do not know of research which proves that bottle feeding, well done, is less satisfactory than beast feeding. The student who is particularly interested in this topic is advised to read a monograph* which space does not permit our including here. In it, breast feeding is examined in the context of the mother's personality, the sex of the child, the length of nursing, and other factors, which shows the complexity of the psychological aspects of infant feeding.

The research of a psychiatrist, Peter Wolff, is the basis of "State and Behavior in the Neonate." Wolff describes the six basic states in which infants live and gives physiological and psychological information about them.

* M. I. Heinstein, Behavioral correlates of breast-bottle regimes under varying parent-infant Relationships. *Mono. Soc. Res. Child Devel.*, 1963, *28*, 4.

Basic Trust vs. Basic Mistrust

Erik H. Erikson
HARVARD UNIVERSITY

The first demonstration of social trust in the baby is the ease of his feeding, the depth of his sleep, the relaxation of his bowels. The experience of a mutual regulation of his increasingly receptive capacities with the maternal techniques of provision gradually helps him to balance the discomfort caused by the immaturity of homeostasis with which he was born. In his gradually increasing waking hours he finds that more and more adventures of the senses arouse a feeling of familiarity, of having coincided with a feeling of inner goodness. Forms of comfort, and people associated with them, become as familiar as the gnawing discomfort of the bowels. The infant's first social achievement, then, is his willingness to let the mother out of sight without undue anxiety or rage, because she has become an inner certainty as well as an outer predictability. Such consistency, continuity, and sameness of experience provide a rudimentary sense of ego identity which depends, I think, on the recognition that there is an inner population of remembered and anticipated sensations and images which are firmly correlated with the outer population of familiar and predictable things and people.

What we here call trust coincides with what Therese Benedek has called confidence. If I prefer the word "trust," it is because there is more naïveté and more mutuality in it: an infant can be said to be trusting where it would go too far to say that he has confidence. The general state of trust, furthermore, implies not only that one has learned to rely on the sameness and continuity of the outer providers, but also that one may trust oneself and the capacity of one's own organs to cope with urges; and that one is able to consider oneself trustworthy enough so that the providers will not need to be on guard lest they be nipped.

The constant tasting and testing of the relationship between inside and outside meets its crucial test during the rages of the biting stage, when the teeth cause pain from within and when outer friends either prove of no avail or withdraw from the only action which promises relief: biting. Not that teething itself seems to cause all the dire consequences sometimes ascribed to it. As outlined earlier, the infant now is driven to "grasp" more, but he is apt to find desired presences elusive: nipple and breast, and the mother's focused attention and care. Teething seems to have a prototypal significance and may well be the model for the masochistic tendency to assure cruel comfort by enjoying one's hurt whenever one is unable to prevent a significant loss.

In psychopathology the absence of basic trust can best be studied in infantile schizophrenia, while lifelong underlying weakness of such trust is apparent in adult personalities in whom withdrawal into schizoid and depressive states is habitual. The re-establishment of a state of trust has been found to be the basic requirement for therapy in these cases. For no matter what conditions may have caused a psychotic break, the bizarreness and withdrawal in the behavior of many very sick individuals hides an attempt to recover social mutuality by a testing of the borderlines between senses and physical reality, between words and social meanings.

Psychoanalysis assumes the early process of differentiation between inside and outside to be the origin of projection and introjection which remain some of our deepest and most dangerous defense mechanisms. In introjection we feel and act as if an outer goodness had become an inner certainty. In projection, we experience an inner harm as an outer one: we endow significant people with the evil which actually is in us. These two mechanisms, then, projection and introjection, are assumed to be modeled after whatever goes on in infants when they would like to externalize pain and internalize pleasure, an intent which must yield to the testimony of the maturing senses and ultimately of reason. These mechanisms are, more or less normally, reinstated in acute crises of love, trust, and faith in adulthood and can characterize irrational attitudes toward adversaries and enemies in masses of "mature" individuals.

The firm establishment of enduring patterns for the solution of the nuclear conflict of basic trust versus basic mistrust in mere existence is the first task of the ego, and thus first of all a task for maternal care. But let it be said here that the amount of trust derived from earliest infantile experience does not seem to depend on absolute quantities of food or demonstrations of love, but rather on the quality of the maternal relationship. Mothers create a sense of trust in their children by that kind of administration which in its quality combines sensitive care of the baby's individual needs and a firm sense of personal trustworthiness within the trusted framework of their culture's life style. This forms the basis in the child for a sense of identity which will later combine a sense of being "all right," of being oneself, and of becoming what other people trust one will become. There are, therefore (within certain limits previously defined as the "musts" of child care), few frustrations in either this or the following stages which the growing child cannot endure if the frustration leads to the ever-renewed experience of greater sameness and stronger continuity of development, toward a final integration of the individual life cycle with some meaningful wider belongingness. Parents must not only have certain ways of guiding by prohibition and permission; they must also be able to represent to the child a deep, an almost somatic conviction that there is a meaning to what they are doing. Ultimately, children become neurotic not from frustrations, but from the lack or loss of societal meaning in these frustrations.

But even under the most favorable circumstances, this stage seems to introduce into psychic life (and become prototypical for) a sense of inner division and universal nostalgia for a paradise forfeited. It is against this powerful combination of a sense of having been deprived, of having been divided, and of having been abandoned—that basic trust must maintain itself throughout life.

Each successive stage and crisis has a special relation to one of the basic elements of society, and this for the simple reason that the human life cycle and man's institutions have evolved together. In this chapter we can do little more than mention, after the description of each stage, what basic element of social organization is related to it. This relation is twofold: man brings to these institutions the remnants of his infantile mentality and his youthful fervor, and he receives from them—as long as they manage to maintain their actuality—a reinforcement of his infantile gains.

The parental faith which supports the trust emerging in the newborn, has throughout history sought its institutional safeguard (and, on occasion, found its greatest enemy) in organized religion. Trust born of care is, in fact, the touchstone of the *actuality* of a given religion. All religions have in common the periodical childlike surrender to a Provider or providers who dispense earthly fortune as well as spiritual health; some demonstration of man's smallness by way of reduced posture and humble gesture; the admission in prayer and song of misdeeds, of misthoughts, and of evil intentions; fervent appeal for inner unification by divine guidance; and finally, the insight that individual trust must become a common faith, individual mistrust a commonly formulated evil, while the individual's restoration must become part of the ritual practice of many, and must become a sign of trustworthiness in the community.[1] We have illustrated how tribes dealing with one segment of nature develop a collective magic which seems to treat the Supernatural Providers of food and fortune as if they were angry and must be appeased by prayer and self-torture. Primitive religions, the most primitive layer in all religions, and the religious layer in each individual, abound with efforts at atonement which try to make up for vague deeds against a maternal matrix and try to restore faith in the goodness of one's strivings and in the kindness of the powers of the universe.

Each society and each age must find the institutionalized form of reverence which derives vitality from its world-image—from predestination to indeterminacy. The clinician can only observe that many are proud to be without religion whose children cannot afford their being without it. On the other hand, there are many who seem to derive a vital faith from social action or scientific pursuit. And again, there are many who profess faith, yet in practice breathe mistrust both of life and man.

[1] This is the communal and psychosocial side of religion. Its often paradoxical relation to the spirituality of the individual is a matter not to be treated briefly and in passing (see *Young Man Luther*). (E.H.E.)

The Birth Catch-Up

James M. Tanner
INSTITUTE OF CHILD HEALTH, LONDON

This capacity to catch up in growth seems to be used normally around the time of birth in man. There is evidence that the growth rate of the foetus at least in weight slows down during the last four weeks of pregnancy, as illustrated in Figure 1. The prenatal values are calculated from McKeown and Record's (2) data on birthweights of live children born after a shorter gestation than average. In using them we are assuming that these early-delivered children's weights are the same as the weights of foetuses of the same age as yet still in the uterus; in other words that amongst healthy singletons the early-born are not specially big or small children for their gestational age. Such an assumption may be challenged. But there is good evidence also of a catch-up occurring after birth, particularly in small babies. Figure 2, taken from the Ministry of Health (3) partially longitudinal survey of some 17 thousand babies shows this

Reprinted from "The Regulation of Human Growth," *Child Development*, *34*, 828–830. Copyright © 1963 by the Society for Research in Child Development, Inc. By permission.

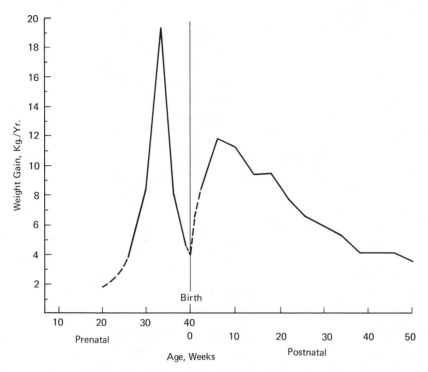

FIGURE 1. *Velocity of growth in weight of singleton children. Prenatal curve is derived from data of McKeown and Record (2) on birthweights of live-born children delivered before 40 weeks of gestation. Postnatal data from Ministry of Health (3) mixed longitudinal data (their Table VII). Dotted line shows estimate of velocity immediately before and after birth, showing catch-up.*

well. Babies below the average weight gained more than the others, thus reducing the range of weight in the whole group. The catch-up finishes by about 5 months in these data and is distinctly more marked in boys than in girls (see Ministry of Health [3], Figure III). Thus there is a negative correlation between birthweight and weight gain from birth to 3 months or from birth to 6 months of the order of about −.15 (7). The negative correlation is still present, though lower, by the time 1 year is reached. Norval, Kennedy, and Berkson (4) give figures for the correlation of birthweight with the birth-to-1-year increment of −.15 in boys and −.05 in girls. The catch-up occurs also in length, indeed probably to a greater extent than in weight. Simmons and Todd (6) found it in the longitudinal data of the Brush Foundation and in 1938 remarked that "of particular interest are the negative coefficients between birth length and the birth to one year increment in length (boys −.46, girls −.01) and of the three month length with the three month to one year increment in length (boys −.20, girls −.05). It appears that during the first post-natal year our short babies gain in length more than our long babies and that this reversal occurs to a greater extent in the male than in the female" (6, p. 126). Thomson (8) found correlations of the order of −.4 in both sexes between birth length and the length increment from birth to 6 months, in some four and a

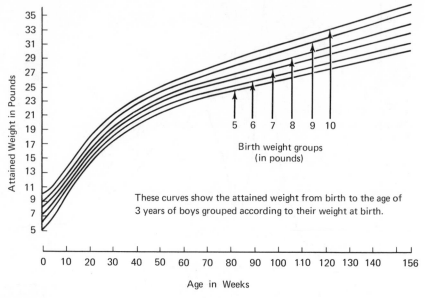

FIGURE 2.   *Attained weight from birth to age 3 of boys grouped according to birthweight. From Ministry of Health (3).*

half thousand babies in Edinburgh. By 1 year the correlation had somewhat dropped, but was still appreciable (average correlation −.35).

The catch-up mechanism at birth is of much genetical importance. It seems to be the chief means by which variability in adult size is maintained in the population. Most of the adult size variability is established by 2 years after birth, since by then the individual's adult size is to a large extent fixed (presuming adequate environmental conditions). The correlation coefficients between length of child at 2 years and length of the same child when adult is nearly .8; it approaches .7 even at age 1. (Genetical differences in the time and intensity of the adolescent spurt account for the remainder of the adult variability.) Thus there would be many genetically large children developing in the uteri of small mothers and constituting a problem at the time of birth, unless selection for assortative mating were very strong, a solution which would produce other genetically undesirable effects. The problem is solved by birth size being controlled almost entirely by uterine factors (5), the correlation of birth length and adult length being only about .2. The catch-up after birth does the rest. Note that this is a true regulatory problem, for the form of Figure 2 makes it clear that only some of the small babies catch up. A proportion of them need little or no catch-up to reach and continue on their natural growth curves, since they are genetically small; it is those aimed, so to speak, at large-ness who catch up on to their proper track. The same phenomenon appears particularly clearly in cattle, where the size at birth of a calf born to a small-breed mother mated with a large-breed father is considerably smaller than a calf of large-breed mother and small-breed father. The two calves grow at different rates after birth so that by the time adult size is reached there is no longer any difference (1). . . .

References

1. DICKINSON, A. G. Some genetic implications of maternal effects: an hypothesis of mammalian growth. *J. agric. Sci.*, 1960, 54, 379–390.
2. McKEOWN, T., and RECORD, R. G. Observations on foetal growth in multiple pregnancy in man. *J. Endocrin.*, 1952, 8, 386–401.
3. Ministry of Health. Standards of normal weight in infancy. *Min. Hlth. Rep. Publ. Hlth. No. 99*, London: H.M.S.O., 1959.
4. NORVAL, M. A., KENNEDY, R. L. J., and BERKSON, J. Biometric studies of the growth of children of Rochester, Minnesota. The first year of life. *Hum. Biol.*, 1951, 23, 274–301.
5. PENROSE, L. S. *Recent advances in human genetics*. London: Churchill, 1961.
6. SIMMONS, K., and TODD, T. W. Growth of well children: analysis of stature and weight, 3 months to 13 years. *Growth*, 1938, 2, 93–134.
7. THOMSON, J. Observations on weight gain in infants. *Arch. Dis. Childh.*, 1955, 30, 322–327.
8. THOMSON, J. Infant growth. *Arch. Dis. Childh.*, 1956, 31, 382–389.

The Infant's First Food

Marian E. Breckenridge
LATE OF THE MERRILL-PALMER INSTITUTE

Margaret N. Murphy
PURDUE UNIVERSITY

THE INFANT'S FIRST FOOD

One of the adjustments the infant makes at birth is a change in the manner of nourishment. He now ingests appropriate food, namely, milk, orally through sucking, digests it and absorbs the necessary nutrients. A vital part of this adjustment is becoming accustomed to the feeding situation, that first intimate mother-child relation through which he obtains his food. In this situation both mother and child can gradually establish a satisfying venture which not only provides the infant with food, but also can be the beginning of a close relation between mother and child (Bakwin, 1964). The infant is believed to derive a sense of security and of belonging in this relation from the warmth of the mother's body and from the comfort of being held. These are different variables from those of the feeding process itself (Guthrie, 1967).

Reprinted from *Growth and Development of the Young Child*. Philadelphia: W. B. Saunders Company, 1969, pp. 180–189. Copyright © 1969 by W. B. Saunders Company. By permission.

During the first few days the infant becomes proficient in finding the nipple and sucking, and the mother becomes adjusted to the pull on the nipple. At this time the nursing period may be limited to five to ten minutes to allow the mother time to adjust to the pull on the nipples and to help to prevent them from becoming sore. A short nursing time seems to satisfy the infant. During this transition period, colostrum is secreted by the mammary glands. This secretion is admirably adapted to the needs of the newborn. It contains less fat and more protein, ash and vitamin A than does milk secreted later when lactation is completely established. The colostrum period varies with individual women from one to five days. During the next five days the composition changes gradually to that of mature milk. Most authors agree that the principal changes from colostrum to mature milk are completed by the tenth day (Committee on Nutrition, 1960).

When the infant absorbs and digests breast milk or its substitute, he begins the third stage in his progress toward maturation of the nutriture. Human milk, if the supply is adequate, provides the essential nutrients for the early months except vitamin D. The adequacy of vitamins other than D depends upon the mother's diet. The amount of breast milk the infant receives depends on the ability of the mother to synthesize milk and the demands he makes in sucking. The usual amount is about 1 pint after the first week or two, and this increases to about 1 quart a day in the fifth month (Toverud, Stearns and Macy, 1950). The amount he needs at a feeding can be determined by the infant if he is fed when he is hungry (as indicated by rooting, sucking or crying) and permitted to nurse until he is satisfied. He will not necessarily take the same amount at each feeding.

Some infants have a sharp satiety reaction (Bakwin, 1964); when they are satisfied, further attempts at feeding are actively resisted. In others, satiety appears gradually and is preceded by playfulness toward the end of feeding. Bakwin pointed out that some infants do not seem to know when they have had enough food. These infants regurgitate and vomit frequently. Recognition of satiety was indicated as being especially difficult in infants with small appetites.

If the infant is not breast fed, a formula to meet his needs should be prescribed by a physician. Both the nutritional and emotional needs of the infant can be met in bottle-feeding. Standardized interviews with mothers of five-year-old children (Sears, Maccoby and Levin, 1957) showed that the early feeding experience, whether breast or bottle, had no consistent effect upon later behavior such as aggression in the home, "considerable" or "high" conscience, dependency, severe feeding problems, bed-wetting at age five or strong emotional reaction to toilet training. The authors point out that feeding as well as other experiences affect the child, but the effects are specific to each child.

The self-regulation type of feeding program can be followed with bottle-fed infants. One mother, whose baby was bottle-fed and varied his intake at different feedings, met the problem by dividing the milk unevenly among the bottles for the day. This baby was taking 35 ounces. She distributed this in two bottles of 6 ounces, three of 5 ounces, and two of 4 ounces. She found that the baby, after having been asleep, wanted to eat several times at $1\frac{1}{2}$- to 2-hour intervals and so took less at those times. When she anticipated that he would sleep four or five hours after a feeding, she gave him 6 ounces. Thus she was able to satisfy the baby without waste of formula or keeping him waiting in the middle of a feeding in order to warm another bottle.

LACTATION

Lactation consists of two processes: secretion and "let-down" or flow of milk. Secretion is strikingly increased after the birth of the infant and appears to be caused by a change in the balance of endocrines. The exact mechanisms have not been fully agreed upon (Turner, 1966). The inhibitory action of ovarian hormones is reduced, while the stimulating action of prolactin of the posterior pituitary gland is increased. Hormones of the thyroid and of the adrenal cortex also act in controlling lactation. The "let-down," or flow of milk, is effected by a complex psychosomatic mechanism by which, it is believed, sensory stimuli associated with suckling excite nerves of an afferent arc to the midbrain, which in turn acts to release the posterior pituitary hormone, oxytocin (Linzell, 1959; Lloyd, 1962).

The processes of lactation are influenced by a number of biologic, emotional and social factors which interact one with another. Heredity, size and anatomic structure of the breast (which has a strong hereditary component), food and environmental conditions such as the balance of rest and activity, which takes into account the amount and intensity of work, will affect lactation.

The potentiality for both the quantity of milk and the length of time lactation continues under normal conditions is inherent in the mother (Macy et al., 1930). Various conditions will determine how much of that potential will be utilized; one is the demand by the baby. A hungry baby nursing vigorously, as is likely to be the case of an infant on a self-regulatory schedule, is an aid to lactation. Illingworth and Stone (1952) found that 80 per cent of babies on self-demand feeding in Jessup Hospital for Women in Sheffield, England, were fully breast fed at one month, compared with 65 per cent of those on schedule. This difference was significant.

Food is another factor. Nutrition for lactation begins before the birth of the baby. A study in Australia (Woodhill et al., 1955) indicates a consistent correlation between the duration of lactation and the level of maternal diet before and during pregnancy. After the birth of the infant certain nutrient intakes should be increased above those during pregnancy in order to supply the nutrients required for the elaboration of milk. According to the Recommended Allowances of the Food and Nutrition Board (National Academy of Sciences—National Research Council, 1964), diet during lactation is increased over that of pregnancy about one half in calories, protein, calcium and vitamin A and about one third in thiamine, riboflavin and ascorbic acid. These additions to an adequate diet during the latter half of pregnancy will provide sufficient energy and nutrients (1) to maintain the mother's body and to meet her energy needs, and (2) to provide the essentials for milk and the activity of the mammary glands. The nursing mother will probably find that she desires the additional food. The need for extra calcium, riboflavin, vitamin A and protein indicates a liberal intake of milk. At least 1 quart a day is advisable. Liberal amounts of fruits and vegetables, including citrus fruits, are also indicated. Other foods providing protein and calories can be chosen according to the mother's needs and preferences. Vitamin D can be supplied by fortified milk or a concentrate. . . .

Physical rest and relaxation are also essential for successful lactation. The flow of milk can be stimulated or inhibited by the emotional state. A mother who dislikes breast feeding, is indifferent to it or has mixed feelings about it, or who is tense from concern about the care of the infant or feels uncomfortable about the nursing situation or is under some emotional strain is less likely to be successful than one who begins the experience with desire and determination to nurse her infant, who is calm and enjoying the experience (Call, 1959; Egli et al., 1961, Newton and Newton, 1950b).

The society in which a woman lives may influence her feelings about breast feeding and her willingness or hesitation to try it. The practice of breast feeding is closely bound to the culture of a society. In the United States the prevailing fashion for some time has been to feed infants by the bottle. This was shown in a survey (Meyer, 1958) in which 21 per cent of mothers were breast feeding their babies when they left the hospital, compared with 38 per cent in an earlier survey (Bain, 1948). American mothers nurse their infants less often and for a shorter time than do women in Europe, Asia or Africa. The practice of most European mothers falls between that of mothers in American and the Eastern countries (Aitken and Hytten, 1960),

The decline of breast feeding seems to accompany increasing sophistication of a community (Jelliffe, 1962). Salber et al. (1959) commented that lactation is certain to be affected when woman's role in society is not clearly defined and there is conflict between her ambitions and her biological make-up.

In spite of the low incidence of breast feeding among mothers in the United States, there is a slight revival among women of the middle and upper social classes (Salber et al., 1958, 1959; Yankhauer et al., 1958). Education seems to be an influencing factor. From a sample of mothers in the Boston area, Salber and Feinlieb (1966) found that only 22 per cent of the total group breast-fed, but that 70 per cent of those married to students, 40 per cent of those in the upper social class and only 14 per cent in the lower social class breast-fed. This difference between social classes in breast-feeding practices, which is the reverse of an earlier period, has also been reported in England (Douglas, 1950).

Many women, especially those having their first baby, will profit by some assistance in understanding the process of lactation and by suggestions of ways it can be promoted. A woman can learn that the reflex which releases milk from the breast is stimulated by the sucking of the infant and by associations with the nursing situation (sight of the baby, time for feeding, breast preparations for feeding) and inhibited by pain and distraction. The following suggestions for aiding this reflex to function, as offered by Newton and Newton (1950a), include (1) feeding the baby when he is hungry to afford more vigorous nursing; (2) no supplementary bottle if possible; (3) avoiding pain, emotional conflict and embarrassment; (4) conditioning the reflex by the use of pleasant stimuli, e.g., favorite food or music preceding nursing, nursing in the same quiet place, stroking the breast with clean tissue, or manual expression of a little milk.

A woman needs guidance while lactation is being established. She may need help in the techniques of nursing. The techniques necessary for successful management have been demonstrated by Barnes et al. (1953) and Waller (1946). Mothers sometimes become concerned because milk is slow to come after delivery. The child may receive almost no milk for the first few days. The mother needs to understand that his needs at this time are small. It is not until the fifth day that transitional or mature milk begins to flow. This may be a crucial time for the mother, since she may be leaving the hospital to return home on the fifth day, before lactation has become firmly established. At this time she faces the responsibilities of the care of the infant and of the home. Unless she has some assistance during this transitional period, lactation may suffer because of fatigue and anxieties. Some knowledge of what to expect in the behavior of the infant and some opportunity to care for babies before the birth of her own may strengthen her confidence in her ability to care for her child. Also, the provision of opportunities for her to become acquainted with her baby in the hospital so that he is no stranger when they arrive home may help. Jackson et al. (1956) found a significantly longer period of breast feeding (up to seven months) among mothers who had rooming-in, and thus had their babies with them, than among mothers whose babies were kept in the nursery. The husband can also be of assistance by giving support to the mother and seeing that she is relieved of some of the household responsibilities.

Although most women are able to breast-feed their babies, some cannot. For those who cannot there is ample evidence that babies can thrive on bottle feedings modified to approximate the composition of human milk. A good bottle feeding is preferable to inadequate breast feeding. Also these mothers can give their babies the essential mothering during feeding time and at other times of the day. No mother should feel inadequate or have any sense of self-reproach because of inability to nurse her child.

VARIATION IN QUANTITY OF MILK SECRETED   As lactation proceeds, the quantity of milk secreted from day to day and from week to week may vary considerably (Macy et al., 1931). The gradual increase in milk flow is evidently peculiar not only to the individual, but also to the particular lactation period. The average daily output of milk in three women from the sixth week through the fourteenth month of lactation was 2602 cc in one lactation period and 3134 cc in another period in the same subject, 2366 cc for one lactation period in another subject, and 1419 cc for the third subject (Macy and co-workers, 1931). These women produced especially large quantities of milk. The total quantity of breast milk produced during a lactation period was found to depend not only on the women's immediate capacity to produce, but also on the demands placed on the mammary glands and on the duration of the lactation period. The investigators showed that, if augmented milk production is to be secured, the milk should be removed from the breast at regular intervals and as completely as possible. These observations confirm the belief that excessive and heavy work tends to depress maximum output of milk and also that nervous factors such as excitement, fear and anxiety lessen the flow, and that severe shock may cause complete cessation.

DIFFERENCES BETWEEN BREAST AND BOTTLE
FEEDING

There is wide agreement that breast feeding is preferable to bottle feeding,
but most infants in this country are bottle-fed (Bakwin, 1964; Maternal and
Child Health and Food and Nutrition Sections, 1966). This section presents the
similarities and differences of human and cow's milk and the progress of infants
receiving each.

When comparing the *content of human and cow's milk* and their relative
value in promoting health and growth of an infant, it must be remembered that
infants are generally fed not whole cow's milk, but formulas in which the cow's

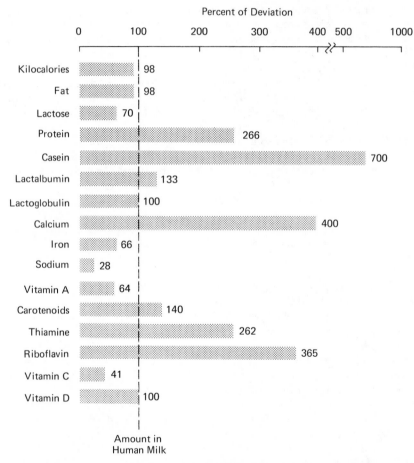

FIGURE 1.   *Relative amounts of various nutrients in human and cow's milk.* [Based on
data from *Composition of Human Milk*, National Research Council Publication No. 254,
Washington, D.C., 1953, National Research Council. (H. A. Guthrie: *Introductory
Nutrition.* St. Louis, C. V. Mosby Company, 1967, p. 334.)]

milk is adapted by dilution, addition of carbohydrates, and treatment to soften the protein curd. When comparison of the progress of infants fed the two milks is made, it is important to note the composition of the formula. Grouping all bottle-fed infants as receiving the same food introduces an error which could lead to misinterpretations of observations.

Infants fed breast milk or cow's milk receive, ounce for ounce, different amounts and proportions of certain nutrients (Committee on Nutrition, 1960; Guthrie, 1967; Macy, Kelley and Sloan, 1950) (Fig. 1). Cow's milk contains about three times as much protein as human milk; the proteins of each milk have essentially the same biologic value (György, 1961) and similar ability to promote nitrogen retention (Fomon, 1960). The protein of cow's milk forms a heavy curd in the stomach, whereas human milk, having less casein and more lactalbumin, forms a finely divided, flocculent mass which is easily digested. Milk mixtures used in bottle feeding are treated, however, so that the protein curd is also soft, small and digestible. Cow's milk also contains about four times as much calcium and six times as much phosphorus as human milk. These and some other constituents, when absorbed in excess of bodily needs, must be excreted. Young infants excrete more water with them, since the kidney's function of concentrating urine is immature in the early months (Smith, 1959). When young infants are fed cow's milk in relatively large proportions, the resulting increase in certain minerals and the metabolic products of proteins to be excreted may tax the water reserve, whereas the breast-fed baby is not subjected to this strain (György, 1961).

Human milk contains three to four times more of the essential fatty acids (Williams, 1961). The significance of this difference is not known. Human milk is about one-third richer in iron than cow's milk. Dietary iron is apparently not utilized during the first four or five months (Smith et al., 1955). After this age the difference in iron of the two milks would be important if the infant were not fed other foods rich in iron.

Human milk is also about one-third richer in vitamin A and more than twice as rich in vitamin C. A quart of human milk contains about 41 mg. of vitamin C (Williams, 1961); a cow's milk formula prepared by boiling and diluting may contain almost none (Stevenson, 1947). Human milk, if the mother's diet is adequate in vitamin C, meets the recommended allowance for vitamin C, but a cow's milk formula falls far short of it. The niacin content of breast milk is about twice that of cow's milk, but both milks are a poor source of this vitamin, though a good source of tryptophan, precursor of niacin, which compensates for the relatively small amounts of niacin. Cow's milk is more than twice as high in thiamine. But when thiamine in human milk is compared with the amount an infant receives in bottle feeding, the amounts are similar, owing primarily to the loss of thiamine in the sterilization process. The riboflavin content of cow's milk is more than three times that in human milk, but the relative utilization of the two milks is not known (National Academy of Sciences—National Research Council, 1964). Cow's milk also is about five times richer in vitamin B_{12} and about four times richer in B_6. The amount in human milk appears to be ample, however. The water-soluble vitamins C and B in breast milk vary with the mother's diet, since these vitamins are not stored. Neither human nor cow's milk contains significant amounts of vitamin D.

The feces of breast-fed infants are acid in reaction; those of bottle-fed infants are neutral or alkaline. György (1961) stated that there is a prevalence of *Lactobacillus bifidus* in the intestinal flora of breast-fed infants and that these bacteria and the acidity in the intestine may be beneficial through the suppression of pathogenic or otherwise harmful bacteria. Human milk contains a fiftyfold greater supply of a factor which stimulates the growth of *L. bifidus* than cow's milk (Williams, 1961).

Weight and weight gains have been used chiefly in the *comparison of growth* of infants who have been breast-fed or bottle-fed. In the United States (Gross and Moses, 1956; Paiva, 1953), the United Kingdom (Levin et al., 1959; Stewart and Westropp, 1953; Thomson, 1955) and Sweden (Mellander et al., 1960) breast-fed infants gain about the same in weight or slightly more than bottle-fed infants from birth to one month or to three or four months. From three or four months on the gains are greater for the artificially fed. When the whole six-month period or the first year is considered, the bottle-fed infants' gains exceed those of the breast-fed. Aitken and Hytten (1960) remarked that the ability of bottle-fed infants to gain almost as well or equally well as the breast-fed in the early months and better in the later months implies a high standard of artificial feeding and hygiene and possibly other environmental conditions. In less favorable conditions results differ, as indicated by studies in a Stockholm children's home (Gyllenswärd, 1960) where the infants breast-fed for at least six months gained more than those bottle-fed, and in Singapore, where Millis (1956), comparing gains in weight of infants breast-fed for only twelve weeks and those breast-fed for more than twenty-four weeks, found that only in the well-to-do Chinese families was the first-year gain greater for infants weaned early.

Progress in weight is not the only criterion a physician uses in evaluating the feeding program of an infant. Gross and Moses (1956) commented that "it would be particularly undesirable to use weight gain alone as a measure of breast feeding." Just what measures physicians use which cause them to advocate breast feeding are not clearly defined. Jackson et al. (1964), studying 599 American infants through six months of age, used at least four length and weight measurements: one at birth, one at six months, and the others at intervals of not less than one month. They found that infants fed various cow's milk formulas and vitamin supplements grew at about the same rate as infants fed human milk with or without vitamin supplements.

Little information about skeletal development of breast- and bottle-fed infants is available. Stewart and Westropp (1953) noted no difference in skeletal maturity at one year. Mellander et al. (1960) observed that girls, but not boys, who were weaned early had significantly more ossification centers at seven or eight months than those weaned late.

Comparison of the incidence of disease in breast- and bottle-fed infants can easily be complicated by environmental conditions under which the infant is fed. The value of breast feeding as a protection against disease is greater in less developed countries (Welbourn, 1958) and in less favored economic classes (Aldrich, 1947) where lack of knowledge and facilities militates against carrying out adequate health measures, or where supervision of the infant's feeding by physicians and nurses is not available. A study of American Indians showed that

95 per cent of infants with severe diarrhea in a group requiring hospitalization were bottle-fed, although only 30 per cent of the infants in the area were being bottle-fed (Maternal and Child Health and Food and Nutrition Section, 1966). Stevenson (1947) found that in a series of carefully supervised infants who were given complements of vitamins considered adequate, there was no significant increase in the incidence of gastrointestinal and other infections in the bottle-fed group. Aitken and Hytten (1960) concluded that "it would appear that under modern standards of hygiene bottle-fed infants suffer no higher overall incidence of infections throughout infancy than breast-fed infants."

Breast-fed infants may have some advantages, however. Stevenson (1947) found that breast-fed babies had significantly fewer respiratory infections during the second half of the first year than those bottle-fed. Stewart and Westropp (1953) found that although the incidence of gastrointestinal and other infections in infancy was not related to the length of breast feeding, it was rare for an infant to have a gastrointestinal infection while receiving breast milk solely. Douglas (1950) found that the difference between breast-fed and bottle-fed infants was not in the number of infections, but in the timing of them. Bottle-fed infants had their peak of incidence earlier than breast-fed infants. The younger the child, the more immature he is and perhaps less well equipped to cope with infections. Whether these differences between breast- and bottle-fed infants can be attributed to qualities in the milk or to conditions associated with the feeding procedure remains to be ascertained.

The existence of viral antibodies in human milk has been known for some time (Valquist, 1958). These antibodies have been considered relatively unimportant in the immune system of the human infant because the quantity is usually low and the absorption slight (Smith, 1959). Recent studies (Gonzaga et al., 1963, Warren et al., 1964; Review, 1965) indicate that breast-fed infants are more resistant to infection with poliomyelitis virus. This was attributed to the inhibition of virus replication within the intestinal tract by the antibodies in human milk. The incidence of measles has also been reported to be lower in breast-fed than in bottle-fed infants (Review, 1958). These findings raise the question whether antibodies in human milk may not have some immunologic value and offer some degree of immunity to intestinal infections during early infancy.

The feeding of breast milk virtually eliminates the possibility of a milk allergy. Heiner et al. (1964) reported that clinical sensitivity to cow's milk occurs in 0.3 to 7 per cent of all infants. During the first few months these infants become hyperallergic to proteins of cow's milk. The sensitivity ranges from immediate, anaphylactoid reactions to markedly delayed reactions from chronic low-grade gastrointestinal blood loss. Milk-induced hypochromic microcytic anemia is the best example of the latter.

There are certain psychological components in breast and bottle feeding. Psychologically, both infant and mother gain something in the nursing situation. The infant gains comfort in his close physical contact with another person. He may profit indirectly by the effect of nursing upon the mother. There is some feeling that the greatest psychological advantage accrues to the mother who feels that she is involved in a unique relation with the child and is fulfilling her true maternal role (Guthrie, 1967). Spock (1950) suggested that breast feeding gives a woman confidence in herself as a mother and that as a result she is more relaxed and effective in her relations with and care of her child.

The bottle-fed infant need not be deprived of close mother-child contacts. Such contacts can be provided in a bottle-feeding situation.

Mothers have various reasons for not breast feeding their infants. Sometimes they are unable to nurse their infants because they cannot produce sufficient milk to satisfy the infant's needs. For many mothers the freedom and flexibility of social life that bottle feeding allows are an important consideration in the choice of the type of feeding. Among fifty-five mothers who had had a satisfying breast-feeding experience, the loss and restriction of their social life were considered disadvantages by twenty-nine of them (Guthrie, 1967). Some mothers cannot breast-feed because they must work; still others may have strong feelings against it (Sears, Maccoby and Levin, 1957). In this event, even if the mother could nurse her infant, the experience would satisfy neither mother nor child. In any case, the mother should have no sense of inadequacy or self-reproach (Levine, 1951).

Although knowledge of the excretion of drugs in milk is limited, nearly all products ingested by the mother are believed to be excreted in her milk in some form. Knowles (1965) recommends curtailment of unnecessary medication during lactation, but does not discourage breast feeding.

Bibliography

AITKEN, F. C., and HYTTEN, F. E. 1960. Infant feeding: comparison of breast and artificial feeding. *Nutrition Abst. and Rev.*, *30*:341–371.

ALDRICH, C. A., 1947. Advisability of breast feeding. *J.A.M.A.*, *135*:915–916.

BAIN, K. 1948. The incidence of breast feeding in hospitals in the United States. *Pediatrics*, *2*:313–320.

BAKWIN, H. 1964. Feeding programs for infants. *Fed. Proc.*, *23*:66–68.

BARNES, G. R., Jr., et al. 1953. Management of breast feeding. *J.A.M.A.*, *151*:192–199.

CALL, J. D. 1959. Emotional factors favoring successful breast feeding of infants. *J. Pediat.*, *55*:485–496.

Committee on Nutrition. 1960. Composition of milks. *Pediatrics*, *26*:1039–1047.

DOUGLAS, J. W. B. 1950. The extent of breast feeding in Great Britain in 1946, with special reference to health and survival of children. *J. Obst. Gynaec. Brit. Emp.*, *57*:335–361.

EGLI, G. E., et al. 1961. The influence of the number of breast feedings on milk production. *Pediatrics*, *27*:314–317.

FOMON, S. J., YOUNOSZAI, M. K., and THOMAS, L. N. 1966. Influence of Vitamin D on linear growth of normal full-term infants. *J. Nutrition*, *88*:345–350.

GONZAGA, A. J., WARREN, R. J., and ROBBINS, F. C. 1963. Attenuated poliovirus infections in infants fed colostrum from poliomyelitis immune cows. *Pediatrics*, *32*:1039–1045.

GROSS, R. T., and MOSES, L. E. 1956. Weight gains in the first four weeks of infancy: A comparison of three diets. *Pediatrics*, *18*:362–368.

GUTHRIE, H. A. 1967. *Introductory Nutrition*. St. Louis, C. V. Mosby Company.

GYLLENSWÄRD, C. 1960. Reported in F. C. Aitken and F. E. Hytten: Infant feeding: comparison of breast and artificial feeding. *Nutrition Abst. & Rev.*, *30*:341–371.

GYÖRGY, P. 1961. Orientation in infant feeding. *Proc. 5th International Congress of Nutrition*. Fed. Proc. 20 Part III: 169–176.

HEINER, D. C., WILSON, J. F., and LAHEY, M. E. 1964. Sensitivity to cow's milk. *J.A.M.A.*, *189*:563–567.

ILLINGWORTH, R. S., and STONE, D. G. H. 1952. Self-demand feeding in a maternity unit. *Lancet*, *262*:683–687.

JACKSON, E. B., et al. 1956. Statistical report on incidence and duration of breast feeding in relation to personal-social and hospital maternity factors. *Pediatrics*, *17*:700–715.

JACKSON, R. L., WESTERFIELD, R., FLYNN, M. A., KIMBALL, E. R., and LEWIS, R. B. 1964. Growth of "well-born" American infants fed human and cow's milk. *Pediatrics*, *33*:642–652.

JELLIFFE, D. B. 1962. Culture, social changes and infant feeding. Current trends in tropical regions. *Am J. Clin. Nutrition*, *10*:19–45.

KNOWLES, J. A. 1965. Excretion of drugs in milk. A review. *J. Pediat.*, *66*:1068–1082.

LEVIN, B., et al. 1959. Weight Gains, Serum Protein Levels and Health of Breast Fed and Artificially Fed Infants. *Med. Res. Council Spec. Rep.* Ser. No. 296. London, Her Majesty's Stationary Office.

LEVINE, M. 1951. A modern concept of breast feeding. *J. Pediat.*, *38*:472–475.

LINZELL, J. L. 1959. Physiology of the mammary glands. *Physiol. Rev.*, *39*:534–576.

LLOYD, C. W. 1962. The Ovaries. Chap. 7 in R. H. Williams (Ed.): *Textbook of Endocrinology*. 3rd ed. Philadelphia, W. B. Saunders Company.

MACY, I. G., et al., 1930. Human milk flow. *Am. J. Dis. Child.*, *39*:1186–1204.

MACY, I. G., et al. 1931. Human milk studies. *Am. J. Dis. Child.*, *42*:569–589.

MACY, I. G., KELLEY, H., and SLOAN, R. 1950. Composition of Milks. Bulletin No. 119. Washington, D.C., National Academy of Science—National Research Council.

Maternal and Child Health and Food and Nutrition Section 1966. Economy in nutrition and feeding of infants. *Am. J. Pub. Health*, *56*:1756–1784.

MELLANDER, O., et al. 1960. Reported in The Nornbotten Study. *Nutrition Rev.*, *18*:6–8.

MEYER, H. F. 1958. Breast feeding in the U.S.: extent and possible trend. *Pediatrics*, *22*:116–121.

MILLIS, J. 1956. The influence of breast feeding on weight gain in infants in the first year. *J. Pediat.*, *48*:770–775.

National Academy of Sciences—National Research Council. 1964. Recommended Dietary Allowances. Report of the Food and Nutrition Board. Revised 1964. Publication 1146. Washington, D.C., National Academy of Sciences—National Research Council.

NEWTON, N. R. and NEWTON, M. 1950a. Relation of let-down reflex to ability to breast feed. *Pediatrics*, *5*:726–733.

———, 1950b. Relationship of ability to breast feed and maternal attitudes toward breast feeding. *Pediatrics*, *5*:869–875.

PAIVA, S. L. 1953. Pattern of growth of selected groups of breast fed infants in Iowa City. *Pediatrics*, *11*:38–47.

Review. 1958. The role of breast-feeding in immunity. *Nutrition Rev.*, *16*:261–263.

Review. 1965. Breast-feeding and polio susceptibility. *Nutrition Rev.*, *23*:131–133.

SALBER, E. J., et al. 1958. Patterns of breast feeding. I. Factors affecting the frequency of breast feeding and reasons for weaning. *N. Eng. J. Med.*, *259*:707–713.

SALBER, E. J., et al. 1959. Patterns of breast feeding in a family health clinic. II. Duration of feeding and reasons for weaning. *N. Eng. J. Med.*, *260*:310–315.

SALBER, E. J., and FERNLEIB, M. 1966. Breast-feeding in Boston. *Pediatrics*, *37*:299–303.

SEARS, R. R., MACCOBY, E., and LEVIN, H. 1957. Patterns of Child Rearing. New York, Harper and Row.

SMITH, C. A. 1959. Physiology of the Newborn Infant, 3rd ed. Springfield, Ill., Charles C Thomas.

SMITH, C. A., et al. 1955. Persistence and utilization of maternal iron for blood formation during infancy. *J. Clin. Invest.*, *34* : 1391–1402.

SPOCK, B. 1950. Round table discussion on present day attitudes toward breast feeding. (Smith, C. A., Chairman) *Pediatrics*, *6* : 656–659.

STEVENSON, S. S. 1947. Adequacy of artificial feeding in infancy. *J. Pediat.*, *31* : 616–630.

STEWART, A., and WESTROPP, C. 1953. Breast-feeding in the Oxford Child Health Survey. 2. Comparison of bottle-fed and breast-fed babies. *Brit. Med. J.* *2* : 305–308.

THOMSON, J. 1955. Observations on weight gain in infants. *Arch. Dis. Childhood, 30* : 322–327.

TOVERUD, K. U., STEARNS, G., and MACY, I. G. 1950. Maternal Nutrition and Child Health; Interpretative Review. Bulletin No. 123, Washington, D.C. National Academy of Science—National Research Council.

TURNER, C. D. 1966. *General Endocrinology.* 4th ed. Philadelphia, W. B. Saunders Company.

VALQUIST, B. 1958. The transfer of antibodies from mother to offspring. *Advances Pediat.*, *10* : 305–310.

WALLER, H. 1946. The early failure of breast feeding; clinical study of its causes and their prevention. *Arch. Dis. Child.*, *21* : 1–12.

WARREN, R. J., LEPOW, M. L., BARTSCH, G. E., and ROBBIN, F. C. 1964. The relationship of maternal antibody, breast feeding, and age to the susceptibility of newborn infants to infection with attenuated polioviruses. *Pediatrics, 34* : 4–13.

WELBOURN, H. F. 1958. Bottle feeding: A problem of civilization. *J. Trop. Pediat.*, *3* : 157–170.

WILLIAMS, H. H. 1961. Differences between cow's and human milk. *J.A.M.A.*, *175*: 104–107.

WOODHILL, L. M., et al. 1955. Nutrition studies of pregnant Australian women. Part II. Maternal diet and the duration of lactation. *Am. J. Obst. & Gynec.*, *70* : 997–1003.

YANKHAUER, A., et al. 1958. Social stratification and health practices in child-bearing and child-rearing. *Am. J. Pub. Health*, *48* : 448–463.

State and Behavior in the Neonate

Peter H. Wolff

HARVARD UNIVERSITY, MEDICAL SCHOOL

The following excerpt is part of Wolff's discussion of the results of his study of neonates. The "raw data" that he mentions in the first sentence are his reports of observations of behavior made during the babies' four days in the hospital following birth, for a total of twenty-four hours of observation. Some of the behavior was spontaneous; some was the result of stimuli systematically applied by Wolff. During the observations the babies were in various "states." The description of these states is the content of the excerpt.

Reprinted from "The causes, controls and organization of behavior in the newborn," *Psychological Issues*, 1966, *5*: 1, 80–86. By Peter H. Wolff. By permission of International Universities Press, Inc. Copyright 1966 by International Universities Press, Inc.

The state concept was useful for grouping the raw data and interpreting the results, but it was never precisely defined. At times it referred to a quantitative continuum in levels of excitation, at other times to unconnected descriptive categories identified by discontinuous criteria such as the appearance of the eyes and the pattern of vocalization. By the first definition, state might have been equated with level of reticular activation, and in this sense called *arousal state*. Properly, however, "arousal" refers to a functional change rather than to a stable condition or a state. Moreover, "arousal" would have been inappropriate since the term implies some knowledge about the functional status of the nervous system, but no electroencephalographic recordings were used in this study for independent corroboration. According to the second definition, the concept of state was meant to imply *stable structures of the whole* which in practice were identified by selected behavioral indices, but signified a semistable organization of action patterns.

Terminological difficulties in defining state are not entirely of my own making, and come up in all infant studies which take heed of the great variability and instability of infantile response patterns. I would like to propose that both conceptions of "state" are meaningful and both can be useful at different levels of discourse as long as the distinction between, and the functional interdependence of, the two dimensions are kept in mind.

The theoretical limitations of state as an arousal continuum in isolation from organismic considerations become evident when we compare highly aroused "colicky" infants with infants who are frantic because they have been teased by repeated presentation and withdrawal of the nipple, or infants who cry because they are hungry with infants who cry because they are left alone. On the electroencephalogram these infants might all show the same degree of arousal, but behaviorally they would be clearly differentiated according to their motor activity and their selective responses to environmental intervention. The limitations of state as an arousal continuum become even clearer in the case of older individuals, for example, who may be excited for a great variety of physical and psychological reasons that cannot be adequately categorized on a quantitative continuum.

Since both dimensions of state are nevertheless important in the study of infant development, I will first review the findings in terms of the arousal dimension in order to tie them in with findings reported by others, and then interpret the results in terms of state as a "structure of the whole," in order to put them into a developmental framework for more extensive studies.

REGULAR SLEEP

Regular sleep may now be defined as a state which obtains when internal or external stimulations are absent or subliminal; when, with the exception of spontaneous discharges, motor activity is minimal; and when thresholds to sensory stimulations are high. I have assumed that this combination of factors fosters a disposition of neural activity in low-frequency, high-amplitude pulses which instigate periodic motor discharges. Intense external or visceral stimuli can break into regular sleep at any time, but the infant is usually immune to mild arousal stimuli during regular sleep until an inherent cycling biological clock alters the state automatically. At that point the infant becomes more susceptible to both internal and external stimulations.

Sleep induced by white noise is a special state, probably analogous to but certainly not identical with regular sleep. The onset of continuous white noise may elicit a transient arousal but the infant rapidly habituates to the stimulus, and, depending on his previous history, either goes back to sleep or gradually goes into a state analogous to regular sleep. While exposed to white noise, the infant is less susceptible to external stimulation than during natural sleep, presumably because white noise raises the threshold to external stimulations. When random noise is turned off the infant may revert to a higher arousal state—thus the disturbing effects of visceral stimuli are suppressed by the white noise. Finally, the noise may redistribute spontaneous discharge behaviors—thus white noise damps the trigger effect of physiological stimuli.

Regular sleep was classified as the low point on the arousal continuum, or as the condition when the infant is least susceptible to external stimulations. Jouvet has described a phase of sleep in animals which appears to be more profound than synchronous sleep, and which is called "rhombencephalic," or "activated," or "paradoxical" because it can be induced by the experimental stimulation of brain-stem centers, and because the organism shows intermittent twitching movements and irregular respirations although the thresholds to external stimulations are higher than during synchronous sleep (Jouvet et al., 1959, Jouvet, 1963). It has also been called "archisleep" because it is the prevalent form in premature infants and newborn kittens (Parmalee et al., 1964).

Since respirations were my only defining criterion for depth of sleep, I could not distinguish what I have called irregular, and assumed to be light, sleep from what Jouvet calls profound desynchronized sleep, and therefore cannot assess the implications of Jouvet's findings for sleep in the full-term human neonate.

IRREGULAR SLEEP

One probable cause for the transition from regular to irregular sleep was the intrusion of intense external or visceral stimulations; since no systematic experiments were conducted to convert regular to irregular sleep by external stimulation, my only evidence for the disruptive effects of extrinsic stimulation is the observation that the ratio of regular to irregular sleep becomes smaller as the time for feeding comes closer.

Another mechanism for the transition from regular to irregular sleep was inferred from the retrospective analysis of sleep records which indicated that the cycles of alternating deep and light sleep described by Aserinsky and Kleitman (1955) are present at birth, and that even the powerful sleep-inducing effects of white noise do not override these cycles.

As the infant passes from regular to irregular sleep he becomes more susceptible to pre-existing visceral or external stimulation. Disturbing stimuli which were subthreshold during regular sleep now become sufficient to initiate diffuse motor activity; the sensory feedback from this activity in turn raises the level of reticular activation, further reduces sensory thresholds to external stimulation, and desynchronizes autochthonous neural pulses so that spontaneous discharges are rare.

DROWSINESS

Drowsiness is a "paradoxical" state in which the infant is almost immobile yet sensitive to external stimuli, while the incidence of spontaneous discharges is high at certain times, low at others.

According to the stated assumptions, a combination of immobility, regular respirations, and absence of focused attention (which by analogy from electroencephalographic studies on adults might be expected to desynchronize large-amplitude pulses) should predispose the organism to paroxysmal discharges during drowsiness, but spontaneous discharges in drowsiness were frequent only at the time of falling asleep. At least in some respects, therefore, drowsiness while falling asleep and while waking up are not identical conditions, even though the infant's clinical appearance may be the same. The observed difference raises a larger question: whether it is ever sufficient to define the organism's state according to static criteria alone or whether one must also consider the sequence of steps leading to the state in question as one of its defining properties. The infant who is alert-inactive after a period of drowsiness may well behave in quite a different manner from the baby who becomes alert-inactive after a period of crying. Comparisons of this kind were not made in the present study but deserve further attention, since they add the temporal to the spatial dimension in our conceptions about the hierarchic integration of states.

ALERT INACTIVITY

Although Kleitman (1963) modified his original genetic theory of sleep and wakefulness (Kleitman, 1939) to assimilate the neurophysiological findings of the intervening period, his classification of the sleep-waking continuum remains the only one based on ontogenetic principles. Rejecting the conception of a biological instinct for sleep (as well as other partial explanations), Kleitman proposed that a *wakefulness of necessity* provoked by disturbing internal or external stimulations is the only form of wakefulness in the infant and that as soon as the disturbing stimuli are removed the infant returns to sleep. Sleep is considered as the ontogenetically "basic" condition on which a voluntary waking state is superimposed in the course of cortical maturation.

Stating a contrary point of view, I proposed (Wolff, 1965) that the full-term infant may be awake for brief periods even while he is free from distressing internal or external stimuli. Naturalistic observations indicate that newborn infants are alert and inactive for limited periods of time after all controllable visceral and external irritations have been alleviated by the mother, and that the first developmental increases in the duration of alertness occur *after* the infant has been fed, diapered, and burped—in other words, after all distressing circumstances under the mother's control have been eliminated.

What then "causes" the newborn infant to be alert and inactive? There is now evidence to support the assertion that newborn infants can selectively attend to their immediate environment for brief periods of time (Fantz, 1958, 1961; Wolff, 1959; B. L. White, 1963; Wolff and White, 1965; Salapatek and Kessen, 1965). It is also possible to maintain the infant in a state of alert inactivity by focusing his attention on a specific visual task, but the state evaporates as soon as the "interesting spectacle" is removed, while the drowsy or fussy baby can be repeatedly brought back to a state of alert inactivity by environmental distractions which have no peremptory qualities since the infant has a "choice" of responding or not responding (Wolff, 1965). Periods of alert inactivity induced in this way last for a considerably longer time (10–40 minutes) than the "orienting investigatory reflex" (Sokolov, 1963; Berlyne, 1960), and cannot be considered homologues of such a "reflex."

This is not to say that the infant intends to wake in order to act, as might be the case for an adult who wakes up by habit or because he has a job to do. The need to function (Piaget, 1936), the driving force of manipulatory or exploratory behavior (Harlow, Blazek, and McClearn, 1956), or competence motivation (R. W. White, 1963) can hardly be invoked as mechanisms for arousal from sleep in the infant. But once the infant wakes to the point of drowsiness for other reasons, a provocative or "interesting" environment may initiate and then maintain the quiet alert state. The greater the number of pathways for attending to the environment, and the more diverse the structures for organizing the perceived events, the longer we would expect the infant to remain awake and attentive. In this way we could account for the finding that discontinuous jumps in total time of alertness occur at those points in motor development when the infant acquires new ways of exploring his environment and of expanding his range of "interesting spectacles," for example with the inception of hand-eye coordination or turning over (see B. L. White, 1963).

The proposed arousal continuum can now be extended to include the alert states: inherent biological clocks as well as visceral or external stimulations contribute to the transition from regular to irregular sleep; once the infant is in light sleep he becomes more sensitive to stimulations which have been subliminal during regular sleep. Depending on the intensity of such stimuli he may remain in irregular sleep and eventually return to regular sleep, or he may become drowsy. When the eyes open while he is still drowsy, his attention may be drawn to novelties in the environment and direct his action to objects. The act of attending itself will desynchronize large-amplitude pulses and inhibit spontaneous discharge even while the infant is immobile and breathing regularly, and as long as he is occupied with directed motor actions, diffuse activity is inhibited. Sooner or later the intensity of visceral stimulations breaks through, and then neither the influx of nonspecific external excitations (e.g., visual and tactile events that do not draw the infant's attention) nor the attending to external events will be sufficient to keep diffuse motility in check.

WAKING ACTIVITY AND CRYING

The conditions of heightened arousal classified here as waking activity and crying, can be described in terms of the concepts already at our disposal. When internal or external stimuli are sufficiently intense to overcome the "defensive" aspects of attending, a cycle is set in motion which only fatigue or the mother's intervention will interrupt: diffuse activity provoked by noxious stimuli presumably increases the level of reticular activation and further sensitizes the organism to the offending stimuli; the infant enters a state in which motility itself promotes his response to noxious stimulation, and the more sensitive he becomes, the more vigorously he struggles. Such a cycle may be compared to the tantrum of a young child, or the hysterical attack of an adult, both of which seem to feed themselves once the person has given way to motility.

The cycle starts with soft whimpering and gentle movements, and these gradually lengthen to become a rhythmical pattern of crying and kicking. If allowed to persist they eventually break down into uncoordinated thrashing and spasmodic screeching, flooding the infant with proprioceptive and tactile stimuli to which he cannot habituate since their intensity and locus varies constantly. A high influx of nonspecific but variable stimulations renders him insensitive to those additional "test" stimuli which might have evoked a noticeable response during sleep, drowsiness, or alert inactivity.

While the primary causes of heightened arousal that interrupt the stable state of alert inactivity in the neonate are probably physical and physiological stimulations, the borderline between physical and psychological causes at this stage is indistinct. During the early days after birth, stimulations of some "psychological" significance which are not painful in the physiological sense can provoke excitement and crying. For example, infants respond with outrage to partial body restraint (e.g., when they are "badly" swaddled), but with calmness and drowsiness to total body restraint or "good" swaddling; even well-fed infants react with excitement and crying when a pacifier is repeatedly offered and taken away. Global "psychological" provocations therefore act side by side with physiological distress and physical pain as sufficient causes of heightened arousal and must be included among the instigations of high arousal states in the neonate.

References

ASERINSKY, E., and KLEITMAN, N. (1955). A Motility Cycle in Sleeping Infants as Manifested by Ocular and Gross Body Activity. *J. Applied Physiol.* 8 : 11–19.

BERLYNE, D. E. (1960). *Conflict, Arousal and Curiosity.* New York: McGraw-Hill.

FANTZ, R. L. (1958). Pattern Vision in Young Infants. *Psychological Reports* 8 : 43–47.

———(1961). The Origin of Form Perception, *Scientific American, 204* : 66–72.

HARLOW, H. F., BLAZEK, W. C., and McCLEARN, G. E. (1956). Manipulatory Motivation in the Infant Rhesus Monkey. *J. Comp. Physiol. Psychol.*, 49 : 444–448.

JOUVET, M., MICHEL, F., and COURJON, J. (1959). Sur un Stade d'Activité Électrique Cérébrale Rapide au Cours du Sommeil Physiologique. *C. F. Soc. Biol.*, 1953 : 1024.

———(1963). The Rhombencephalis Phase of Sleep. In *Brain Mechanisms*, Vol. 1, ed. G. Moruzzi, A. Fessard, and H. H. Jasper. New York: Elsevier, pp. 406–424.

KLEITMAN, N. (1939). *Sleep and Wakefulness.* Chicago: University of Chicago Press.

———(1963). *Sleep and Wakefulness*, 2nd. edition, revised and enlarged. Chicago: University of Chicago Press.

PARMALEE, A. H., AKIYAMA, Y., WENNER, W., and FLESCHER, J. (1964). Activated Sleep in Premature Infants. Address to Assoc. Psychophysiol. Study of Sleep, March.

PIAGET, J. (1936). *The Origins of Intelligence*. New York: International Universities Press, 1952.

SALAPATEK, P., and KESSEN, W. (1965). Visual Scanning of Triangles by the Human Newborn. Paper presented at the Eastern Psychological Association Meetings, April.

SOKOLOV, Y. N. (1963). *Perception and the Conditioned Reflex*. New York: Macmillan.

WHITE, B. L. (1963). The Development of Perception During the First Six months of Life. Address to the American Association for the Advancement of Science, Cleveland, Ohio, December.

WHITE, R. W. (1963). Ego and Reality in Psychoanalytic Theory. *Psychological Issues, III* (3). New York: International Universities Press.

WOLFF, P. H. (1959). Observations on Newborn Infants. *Psychosom. Med., 21*:110–118.

——(1965). The Development of Attention in Young Infants. *Ann. N.Y. Acad. Sci. 118*:815–830.

——and WHITE, B. L. (1965). Visual Pursuit and Attention in Young Infants. *J. Amer. Acad. Child Psychiat., 4*:473–484.

Chapter 3

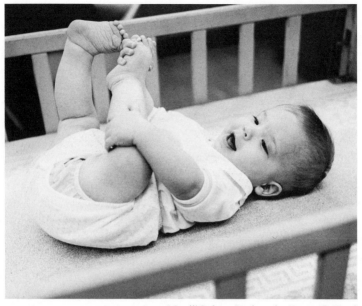

Merrill-Palmer Institute by Donna J. Harris

Emerging Resources for Coping
with the World

The drama of the first two years of life involves the change from horizontal to vertical, from sedentary creature to runner, from crybaby to speaker, from vast dependency to a large measure of autonomy. The changes are comparable to the changes from prenatal to postnatal life, and much more visible and comprehensible. Although the newborn comes equipped for maintaining his body processes, his behavior is largely subcortical, controlled by lower brain centers and not those basic to thinking and consciousness. As the cerebral cortex matures, behavior rapidly becomes more complex and flexible. Reflex activity is suppressed and/or integrated into larger coordinations that have some conscious control. For example, the area of the motor cortex controlling the arms matures before the area that controls the legs. At 3 or 4 weeks, the legs are at their peak of making reflex crawling movements, while the arms, inhibited by cortical control, do not make many reflex movements. The interpretation and use of sensory perception is thought to follow the order of maturing of the cerebral cortex, with vision more advanced

127

than hearing during infancy. Active, like all living creatures, and with powers emerging, like all developing creatures, the infant deals more and more effectively with the world, the people in it and himself.

Directions in Personality Development

Infancy encompasses the first critical period in personality growth and part of the second. The development of the sense of trust comes first, laying the groundwork for a feeling of security throughout life. The development of a sense of autonomy is central to personality growth from about $1\frac{1}{2}$ to $3\frac{1}{2}$ or 4 years of age. Most of the infant's behavior and experiences can be understood in the light of these two achievements in personality development [25, pp. 247–254].

Trust

Successful growth during the first year results in a well-established sense of trust. Begun with the first experience of securing food and skin stimulation, the growth of trust continues through experiences with things, other people, and the self. The good feelings from tension reduction, repeated consistently in good physical care, make the baby confident that he will be fed when hungry, dried when wet, rocked when restless, and stimulated when bored. He is confident also that he can do something toward initiating these satisfying experiences.

People, largely mother, are part of the good-feeling experiences and come to stand for the whole. Thus the 4-month baby, crying from hunger, stops crying and even smiles when he sees his mother or hears her footsteps, trusting that she will feed him.

Appreciation of the permanence of objects is a basic ingredient of the sense of trust. Through his interactions with the world during his first year and a half, the baby comes to know that things exist even when he is not perceiving them. As will be described in greater detail later in the chapter, the first 18 months is the sensori-motor period, in Piaget's series of stages. The two essential achievements of this period are a realization of the permanence of objects and the organization and control of his movements in space. These two achievements go along together. As the baby controls the movements of his body, he deals with the objects of the world, seeing and feeling them, noticing them as they appear and disappear, understanding that events can take place when he is not watching. He comes to trust the world to have certain kinds of order in it, to be dependable. He also comes to know his own powers and how to use them, a beginning of the sense of autonomy.

Establishing trust also involves learning that mother (and others) exists even when she cannot be seen, and that she will come again and again. The game of peekaboo dramatizes mother's disappearance and reappearance. In playing it, the infant lives and relives the frightening situation which has a happy ending, enjoying it throughout the months when trust is growing as he learns that mother continues to exist apart from him. His sense of self begins perhaps from this knowledge and certainly grows as he explores his own body. Fingering his hand and watching it move yield one complex of sensations; fingering the blanket gives another. Reaching, grasping, securing, releasing, touching, mouthing—all tell him what is himself, what are other things and what he can do, or what he can trust his body to do with the world. As a good feeling goes along with the accumulation of knowledge of his body, his power, the objects outside himself, and other people, then the sense of trust grows. Mistrust arises from discomfort, disappointment, anxiety, inability to explore, discriminate, and cope with the world.*

Autonomy

In the beginning or early months of the second year, the baby who trusts himself and the world is ready to concentrate on the next stage in personality growth, the development of autonomy. Able to move himself from one place to another, able to pick up, manipulate and reject toys, able to say a few words, able to feed himself some foods, able to "hang on" for a while when he feels the urge to eliminate, he has many choices to make. He feels autonomous as he makes choices freely and wholeheartedly. He gets the feeling "What I do is all right" and a companion feeling, "There are many things that I can either do or not do."

Me do is the keynote phrase of the age from 18 months to 2½. Everyone knows how determined 2-year-olds are to do things in their own ways at their own times. The doing and the choosing are the means of growth, for these are the ways in which toddlers test themselves, other people, and the world in order to establish themselves as creatures who function independently and adequately.

Choosing involves taking or leaving, holding on to or letting go. When the child discovers, through active testing, that there are many situations in which he can choose and live comfortably with his choice, then he feels good about himself. He can decide whether to take a proffered hand or not, whether to play with the truck or the bunny, whether to have a second serving of applesauce or not, whether to sit on grandma's lap or stand on his feet. He also needs restrictions that are clear and firm, in order to prevent him from making choices that are beyond him. Frustration and consequent anger are frequent even in older infants who are guided with skill and understanding. Temper outbursts increase in the latter part of infancy, as the child tests himself to find out what he can do and tests his parents and his world to find out what they will let him do. Each successful encounter and choice adds to his sense of autonomy. Shame and doubt arise when disaster follows choice-making and also when the child is not allowed to make enough choices. Shame, doubt, and inadequacy (lack of autonomy) lead to extremes of behavior—rebellion or oversubmissiveness, hurling or hanging on tight.†

In longitudinal studies of children, the beginnings of autonomous behavior have been seen even in early infancy, especially in the ways in which infants defended themselves from unwanted experiences [74, pp. 226–227, 302]. Babies differed in how often and how vigorously they protested over feeding, rejected foods and ended the meal. They differed in ways of rejecting stimulation and being moved. For instance, some babies of 3 or 4 months stiffened their back and legs when adults

---

* The period of development of trust is the *oral stage* in psychoanalytic theory. The mouth is the site of the most important experiences, feeding and the love relationship associated with feeding. Pain from teething is associated with biting and cruel, harsh experiences. In many psychoanalytic writings the skin senses and other senses, too, are greatly overshadowed by the significance of the mouth.
† The period of autonomy is the anal stage in psychoanalytic theory. The central problem is dramatized by the idea of the anal sphincters which open or shut, hanging on or letting go. Depending on the child's experiences with bowel control and control by other people, his personality takes on characteristics like suspicion or confidence, stinginess or generosity, doubt and shame, or autonomy and adequacy.

were performing unwelcome procedures, while others relaxed and went limp. The first reaction resembled taking a stand, even before the child could literally stand up, whereas the second was more like passive resistance. As soon as infants can move around, some will crawl, pull, or stretch to get away from an unpleasant situation, and others will push the adult away, kick, fight, or protest against him.

Infants in the study were shown to differ in how much stimulation they accepted and sought and in how they reduced unwelcome stimulation. Some children were hyperalert to sights and sounds, and others seemed to shut out many of them. Thus while the peak age for concern with autonomy is between 18 months and 3 or 4 years, some attempts at autonomous behavior occur much earlier.

Physical and Motor Development

Development and change are rapid during the first two years of life. This period, as well as the preschool years, is a time when illness is relatively frequent, and careful physical care is consequently very worthwhile.

After the first month, more or less, a baby really looks like a baby, like babies in ads and photograph albums, like other babies in the neighborhood—chubby, skin pink and white, golden, brown, or whatever it is destined to be, bumps smoothed out, and nose in shape. New coarser hair comes in during infancy, replacing the fine black hair of the newborn (if he had it) and showing more and more the color it is going to be. Compared with an older child, a baby has a large forehead, large eyes, small nose, small chin, and plump cheeks. His hands and feet are chubby and his abdomen round; his delicate skin looks soft and fragile.

Babies differ in appearance, from one to another; the older they are, the more obvious the differences. They differ, of course, in coloring, facial features, amount and type of hair, height, and weight. They feel different, too. Firm muscles and good muscle tone give a solid impression, in contrast to the softness of slacker muscles or abundant fat. The baby's reactions to being held also add to the impression, according to whether the infant holds himself erect, pushes away or yields to the arms which hold him.

Proportions and Measurements

Changes in shape and proportion continue along the lines charted prenatally, the head regions being most developed, the trunk and legs beginning to catch up, the center of gravity high in the trunk but descending. Birth weight is doubled by 4 or 5 months and tripled at 1 year. Height is doubled by about 4 years. Thus the child starts life as a slender neonate, fills out to a round, plump infant during the first year, and then in the second year, he again becomes more slender, continuing this trend into middle childhood. A ratio useful for diagnosing malnutrition is that of head to thorax. After 6 months of age, the thorax is larger than the head in normal children. The difference in circumference between thorax and head increases with age. When a child is growing inadequately, his weight deficit is related to the difference between head and thorax [21]. Height and weight percentile tables (Tables 3–1 through 3–4) can be used to compare a baby with others the same age and sex. These tables are based on repeated measurements of more than 100 white, normally healthy infants of each sex, living in Boston. Height was measured with the infant lying on his back. This table can be used to tell how many children (of

Table 3–1 Height Percentile Table for Boys from Birth through Age 2

Age				Length in Inches			
	3%	10%	25%	50%	75%	90%	97%
Birth	18¼	19	19½	20	20½	21	21½
1 mo.	19¾	20¼	20¾	21¼	22	22¼	23¾
2 mo.	21	21½	22	22½	23	23½	24
3 mo.	22½	22¾	24¼	23¾	24¼	24¾	25
4 mo.	23½	23¾	24¼	24¾	25¼	25¾	26
5 mo.	24¼	24½	25	25½	26	26½	27
6 mo.	24¾	25¼	25¾	26	26¾	27¼	27¾
7 mo.	25½	26	26¼	26¾	27¼	28	28½
8 mo.	26	26½	27	27½	28	28¾	29¼
9 mo.	26½	27	27½	28	28¾	29¼	30
10 mo.	27	27½	28	28½	29¼	29¾	30½
11 mo.	27½	28	28½	29	29¾	30¼	31
12 mo.	28	28½	29	29½	30¼	30¾	31½
13 mo.	28½	29	29½	30	30¾	31¼	32
14 mo.	29	29½	30	30½	31¼	31¾	32½
15 mo.	29¼	29¾	30¼	31	31½	32	33
16 mo.	29¾	30¼	30¾	31½	32	32½	33½
17 mo.	30¼	30½	31¼	31¾	32½	33	34
18 mo.	30½	31	31½	32¼	33	33½	34½
19 mo.	31	31½	32	32¾	33¼	34	35¼
20 mo.	31¼	31¾	32½	33	33¾	34½	35½
21 mo.	31½	32	32¾	33¼	34	34¾	36
22 mo.	32	32½	33	33¾	34½	35	36½
23 mo.	32¼	32¾	33½	34	34¾	35½	36¾
24 mo.	32½	33	33¾	34½	35¼	36	37¼

SOURCE: From *Growth and Development of Children*, 5th edition, by Ernest H. Watson and George H. Lowrey. Copyright © 1967, Year Book Medical Publishers, Inc., Chicago. Used by permission of Year Book Medical Publishers.

the type sampled by this study) out of 100 will be longer or shorter, heavier or lighter than any given baby. For example, Becky, at 6 months, weighs 17 pounds and measures 27¼ inches. The table shows that she is above the 97th percentile in height (length) and slightly below the 75th percentile in weight. Taller than 97 baby girls in 100, she is a very tall girl. In spite of her chubby face and rounded abdomen, the table tells that as to weight, she is average, since 24 in 100 exceed her in weight and no more than 2 exceed her in height.

Height–weight tables which give only averages have little use for the individual, although they are useful for comparing groups. Percentile tables, such as those shown here, give more information than mere averages. However, they take no account of body build nor do they consider heredity. The ideal weight for a short-legged, long-trunked child such as an Aleutian Islander would obviously be greater than for a white American of the same age. The expected height for the child of tall parents is greater than for the child of short parents. For example, for white Ohio sons of short parents, the average length at 1 year was 29 inches, at 2, 33.6; for sons of tall parents, the 1-year length was 30.5 inches and at 2, 35.0 [31].

Skinfold thickness is a measurement useful for detecting suboptimal nutrition in large groups of children, as in national surveys [54]. Accurate scales may not be

Table 3-2 Height percentile Table for Girls from Birth through Age 2

Age	Length in Inches						
	3%	10%	25%	50%	75%	90%	97%
Birth	18½	18¾	19¼	19¾	20	20½	21
1 mo.	19¾	20¼	20½	21	21½	22	22½
2 mo.	21	21½	21¾	22¼	23	23¼	23¾
3 mo.	22	22½	22¾	23½	24	24¼	24¾
4 mo.	22¾	23¼	23¾	24¼	24¾	25¼	25¾
5 mo.	23½	24	24½	25	25½	26	26½
6 mo.	24	24½	25	25¾	26¼	26¾	27
7 mo.	24½	25¼	25¾	26¼	27	27½	27¾
8 mo.	25¼	25¾	26¼	27	27½	28	28½
9 mo.	25¾	26½	27	27½	28¼	28¾	29¼
10 mo.	26¼	27	27½	28	28¾	29¼	29¾
11 mo.	26¾	27¼	28	28½	29¼	29¾	30½
12 mo.	27	27¾	28½	29¼	30	30¼	31
13 mo.	27½	28¼	29	29½	30¼	30¾	31½
14 mo.	28	28½	29½	30	30¾	31¼	32
15 mo.	28¼	29	29¾	30½	31¼	31¾	32½
16 mo.	28¾	29½	30¼	31	31¾	32¼	33
17 mo.	29	29¾	30¾	31¼	32¼	32¾	33½
18 mo.	29½	30¼	31	31¾	32½	33¼	34
19 mo.	30	30½	31½	32¼	33	33¾	34½
20 mo.	30¼	31	32	32½	33½	34¼	35
21 mo.	30½	31¼	32¼	33	33¾	34¾	35½
22 mo.	31	31¾	32¾	33¼	34¼	35¼	36
23 mo.	31¼	32	33	33¾	34½	35½	36¼
24 mo.	31½	32¼	33¼	34	35	35¾	36¾

SOURCE: From *Growth and Development of Children*, 5th edition, by Ernest H. Watson and George H. Lowrey. Copyright © 1967, Year Book Medical Publishers, Inc., Chicago. Used by permission of Year Book Medical Publishers.

available for weighing and exact ages may not be known. Exact age is not necessary when skinfold measurements are used between 1 and 5 years of age. Children with protein–calorie malnutrition were usually below the third percentile and almost always below the tenth.

Illnesses

Respiratory infections are the most frequent type of physical difficulty for American children, with gastrointestinal upsets second in frequency [103]. Figure 3–1 shows the number of occurrences of various kinds of illnesses in a group of 134 American children between birth and 2 years of age. For over half the children in the world, however, the greatest physical threat is from malnutrition, especially protein malnutrition [56]. And while protein malnutrition contributes to the high death rate in underdeveloped countries, the majority of afflicted children survive, impaired physically and often mentally [17]. Growth in height and weight of well-nourished children slows down in the latter half of the first year. At the same time, the rate of muscle growth increases. Also at this age, the baby is getting a smaller proportion of his calories from milk. For each unit of body weight, the 6-months-

Table 3–3 Weight Percentile Table for Boys from Birth through Age 2

	Weight in Pounds						
Age	3%	10%	25%	50%	75%	90%	97%
Birth	5¾	6¼	7	7½	8¼	9	10
1 mo.	7½	8½	9	10	10½	11½	13
2 mo.	9	10	10½	11½	12	13¼	14¾
3 mo.	10½	11	11¾	12½	13½	14½	16¼
4 mo.	11¾	12½	13¼	14	15	16¼	18
5 mo.	13	13¾	14¼	15	16½	17¾	19½
6 mo.	14	14¾	15½	16¾	18	19¼	20¾
7 mo.	15	15¾	16¾	18	19	20¾	22¼
8 mo.	15¾	16¾	17¾	19	20½	22	23½
9 mo.	16½	17¾	18¾	20	21½	23	24½
10 mo.	17¼	18¼	19½	20¾	22½	23¾	25¼
11 mo.	18	18¾	20¼	21½	23¼	24½	26¼
12 mo.	18½	19½	20¾	22¼	23¾	25½	27¼
13 mo.	19	20	21¼	22¾	24½	26	27¾
14 mo.	19½	20½	22	23¼	25	26½	28½
15 mo.	19¾	21	22½	23¾	25½	27¼	29½
16 mo.	20¼	21½	23	24¼	26	27¾	30¼
17 mo.	20¾	21¾	23½	24¾	26½	28½	31
18 mo.	21	22¼	23¾	25¼	27	29	31½
19 mo.	21½	22¾	24¼	25¾	27½	29½	32¼
20 mo.	22	23¼	24¾	26	28	30	33
21 mo.	22¼	23½	25	26½	28½	30½	33½
22 mo.	22½	24	25½	26¾	28¾	31	34
23 mo.	23	24¼	26	27¼	29¼	31½	34½
24 mo.	23¼	24¾	26¼	27¾	29¾	32	35

Source: From *Growth and Development of Children*, 5th edition, by Ernest H. Watson and George H. Lowrey. Copyright © 1967, Year Book Medical Publishers, Inc., Chicago. Used by permission of Year Book Medical Publishers.

old baby needs about twice as many calories and five times as much high quality protein as an adult needs. The 2-year-old needs about 70 percent more calories and three times as much protein as an adult [12]. If the infant is living in poverty, his protein is drastically cut as he is weaned onto inadequate foods. At an international conference on nutrition, one of the leaders [56] said,

> for every small child anywhere in the world, of any race or ethnic heritage, of any social or economic background, it is nutritionally now or never. This is particularly so for each newborn infant in city or farm, in desert or jungle, for every day of his first two years of life. Some will make it. Many will not. "Too little" and "too late" may indeed be forever.

Nutrition and Disease. Marasmus and kwashiorkor are two severe diseases due to malnutrition. *Marasmus* is a wasting away of body tissues. When suffering from marasmus, an infant is grossly underweight, with atrophy of muscles and subcutaneous fat but with no clinical edema [49]. Marasmus is caused by undernutrition, resulting from insufficient food or from not utilizing food. A severe emotional disturbance can cause the child not to eat or to be unable to utilize food adequately. A longitudinal study of children with *marasmus* was done in Chile, where a recent decline in breast feeding has produced some severe malnutrition in

134 Infants

Table 3–4 Weight Percentile Table for Girls from Birth through Age 2

Age	Weight in Pounds						
	3%	10%	25%	50%	75%	90%	97%
Birth	5¾	6¼	7	7½	8	8½	9½
1 mo.	7	8	8½	9¾	10¼	11	11¾
2 mo.	8¼	9½	10¼	11	11¾	12½	13½
3 mo.	9½	10¾	11½	12¼	13	13¾	14¾
4 mo.	10¾	12	12¾	13¾	14½	15½	16½
5 mo.	11¾	13	13¾	14¾	16	17	18¼
6 mo.	12¾	14	14¾	15¾	17¼	18½	19¾
7 mo.	13½	15	16	17	18½	20	21¼
8 mo.	14¼	15¾	16¾	18	19½	21¼	22½
9 mo.	14¾	16¼	17½	18¾	20¼	22	23½
10 mo.	15½	17	18¼	19¾	21¼	23	24¾
11 mo.	16	17½	19	20½	22	23¾	25¾
12 mo.	16½	18	19½	21	22½	24½	26½
13 mo.	17	18½	20¼	21¾	23¼	25¼	27½
14 mo.	17½	19	20¾	22¼	23¾	25¾	28
15 mo.	18	19½	21¼	22¾	24½	26½	28¾
16 mo.	18½	20	21¾	23¼	25	27	29½
17 mo.	18¾	20½	22¼	23¾	25½	27½	30
18 mo.	19¼	21	22½	24¼	26	28	30¾
19 mo.	19½	21½	23	25	26½	28¾	31¼
20 mo.	20	21¾	23½	25½	27	29¼	32
21 mo.	20¼	22¼	23¾	25¾	27½	29¾	32½
22 mo.	20¾	22¾	24¼	26¼	28	30½	33
23 mo.	21¼	23	24¾	26¾	28½	31	33¾
24 mo.	21½	23½	25¼	27	29¼	31¾	34½

SOURCE: From *Growth and Development of Children*, 5th edition, by Ernest H. Watson and George H. Lowrey. Copyright © 1967, Year Book Medical Publishers, Inc., Chicago. Used by permission of Year Book Medical Publishers.

early infancy [72]. These babies were admitted to the hospital at ages 3 to 11 months, with acute marasmus which had begun at some time between 1 and 5 months. Most of them weighed little more than they did at birth. They were treated to recovery and sent home with a steady and adequate supply of milk. At ages 3 to 6 years, all were clinically normal, with height far below average (lower than the third percentile) for Chilean children. Legs were short. Weights were all above the third percentile, many close to the fiftieth percentile. Thus weights were above normal for heights and some children looked obese. Head circumferences were below normal.

Kwashiorkor occurs most often in 1- to 4-year-olds whose diets are very low in proteins while being not so low in total calories [49]. The biochemical changes in the body are quite different in the two diseases, kwashiorkor having more lasting effects after the acute stage is alleviated. Symptoms of kwashiorkor are swelling of face, legs, and abdomen due to water retention, growth retardation, wasting of muscles with some fat retained, apathy, or whimpering. The hair may be reddish and thin and the skin coarse, spotted, or with a rash or lesions. Liver damage and brain damage are likely to occur [65, pp. 216–223]. Full-blown kwashiorkor and marasmus represent only a small part of the worldwide picture of child malnutri-

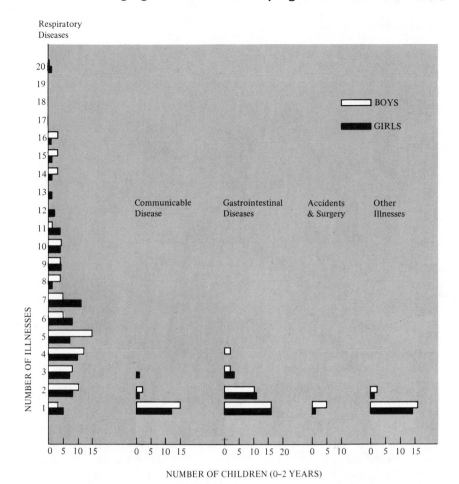

Figure 3–1. In 134 children between birth and 2 years, numbers of illnesses and accidents are shown. Respiratory infections are by far the greatest cause of illness in infancy.

SOURCE: I. Valadian, H. C. Stuart, and R. B. Reed, "Studies of Illnesses of Children Followed from Birth to Eighteen Years," *Monographs of The Society for Research in Child Development,* **26**:3.

tion. "Protein–calorie malnutrition is like a huge undersea mountain, a small fraction visible above the surface, while the great bulk is submerged and unseen" [93, p. 42]. All over the world, including the United States of America, poor children are suffering from insufficient protein, often along with insufficient calories. Their physical and mental growth and health are being depressed now and for the future.

A recent nutritional survey of low-income areas in Texas, Louisiana, and parts of New York and Kentucky gives some data on nutrition and disease [88]. The children between 1 year and 3 years old were considerably below the average height of children in the United States. Three times the expected number were below the sixteenth percentile of the Iowa Growth Chart. Figure 3–2 gives an idea of how these children compared with the average in height. The authors reported to a Senate

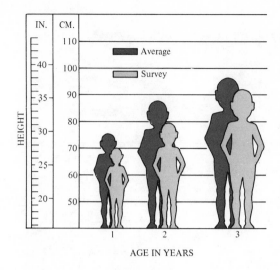

Figure 3–2. Average height of boys one-to-three in National Nutrition Survey compared with American averages.

SOURCE: Reprinted by permission from A. E. Schaefer and O. C. Johnson, "Are We Well Fed?" *Nutrition Today*, 4:1, 2–11. Copyright © 1969, Enloe, Stalvey and Associates.

committee; "... we found every kind of malnutrition that any of us has seen in similar studies in Central America, Africa and Asia. It is just as prevalent in these areas as it is in many of the remote countries" [88]. The clinical findings included seven cases of severe kwashiorkor and marasmus.

Malnourished children are more likely than well-nourished to suffer all sorts of infections and to have more severe cases. Infections add to the state of malnutrition by depressing the appetite and requiring mobilization of nitrogen and other essential nutrients [92]. After the period of stress is over, during convalescence, the normal course of events is the returning of the nutrients to the tissue from which they were drawn, but this process requires extra proteins and vitamins, the very elements most lacking in the diets of the poor. The baby who started an illness as malnourished, then, is in a worse state of nutrition when the infection subsides and is ready to pick up another infection, for which his resistance is even lower. Malnutrition depresses the body's manufacture of antibodies. Growth is slowed down, since the nutrients it requires are insufficient.

At the time of weaning from the breast, or the time when the mother's milk becomes inadequate, supplementation with poor quality, unsanitary food introduces disease organisms causing infections, diarrhea, and parasite infestations. Widened social contact introduce viral diseases such as measles and other childhood diseases. Pneumonia is a frequent complication of measles.

Poverty and Disease. Poverty makes for poor hygiene which spreads disease. In Asia and Africa, drinking boiled water greatly reduces one's chances of contracting amebic dysentery, typhoid, and many more diseases, but the ordinary family does not have facilities for boiling and storing water, nor do they believe it would be worthwhile to do so. The weanling baby receives an inadequate diet not only because the family diet is inadequate but also because his mother believes that a watered gruel is good for him because it looks like milk, that eggs and meat are too strong for him, or that coconut milk will make him stupid. Illiteracy and ignorance of the mother are important influences on the baby's health and growth. Figure 3–3 summarizes the interaction of malnutrition, disease, their causes, and results.

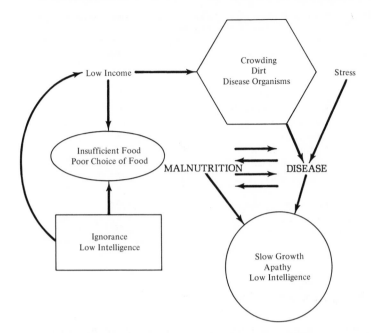

Figure 3–3. Interlocking causes and results of malnutrition and disease.

Injuries

As soon as the baby can creep, he needs increased care in protecting him from accidents. When he walks and climbs, potential danger is much greater. Accidents to toddlers are discussed in Smart and Smart, *Preschool Children* (Macmillan, 1973), along with accidents at older preschool ages. In Chapter 4 (see also *Preschool Children*) we shall consider a kind of injury which is taking on new proportions in America: the damage that parents do intentionally to their own children.

Teething

Almost as obvious as children's increase in height and weight is the appearance of teeth. A baby's toothless grin, the single tooth of a slightly older baby, the gaps left in the row of teeth between the shedding of the first incisors and the coming of the permanent incisors—these are familiar landmarks in development. The timing of tooth eruption differs considerably (more than 10 percent) when Chinese, whites, blacks, Amerinds, East Indians, and Eskimos are compared [32]. The least favored groups seem to have the most advanced eruption times.

Growth studies of American children have shown a low, positive correlation between skeletal development and dental development [32]. The correlation is too small to be useful in predicting maturity.

At birth the crowns of the 20 deciduous (baby) teeth are partially calcified. It will be 7 months or more before one of them appears. Table 3–5 shows average, early, and late timing of eruption of the deciduous teeth.

Genetic factors are important in determining eruption time, size, shape, and discrepancies in number of teeth [105, pp. 386–387]. Environmental influences on health and development of teeth will be discussed later in relation to the school-age child.

Table 3–5 Ages (in months) for Early, Average, and Late Eruption of Deciduous Teeth

	Early	Average	Late
Percentiles	10	50	90
Lower central incisor	5	7.8	11
Upper central incisor	6	9.6	12
Lower lateral incisor	7	11.5	15
Upper lateral incisor	7	12.4	18
Lower 1st molar	10	15.1	20
Upper 1st molar	10	15.7	20
Lower cuspid	11	18.2	24
Upper cuspid	11	18.3	24
Lower 2d molar	13	26.0	31
Upper 2d molar	13	26.2	31

SOURCE: Data from S. L. Horowitz and E. H. Hixon, *The Nature of Orthodontic Diagnosis.* St. Louis: C. V. Mosby, 1966.

Establishing Regularity of Basic Processes

The body must stay within certain physical and chemical limits if it is to stay alive. In order to function optimally, it must stay within narrower limits. Homeostasis, the maintenance of steady states within these limits, is accomplished by integrated control of the nervous and endocrine systems. During the first 3 or 4 months of life, the mechanisms of homeostasis become more and more efficient. The baby settles down to an easier, more automatic supporting of life processes, his energies freed for a wider variety of activities.

Temperature regulation is one of the vital homeostatic processes. A certain constancy has to be kept in spite of heat loss and heat production. The baby regulates his temperature more adequately after the neonatal period than he does in the beginning. For example, the sweat glands become active at about a month of age. Even with temperature regulation improving, infants and young children are still highly susceptible to temperature fluctuation. Bodily temperature is likely to shoot up with active exercise, crying, emotional upset, or rise in surrounding temperature [9, p. 133]. Bodily temperature responds readily to chilling. Infants and young children, when suffering from infections, usually show higher temperatures than do older children. Table 3–6 shows the average temperature throughout infancy and childhood. Note that while the average temperature at 3 months is 99.4, about one third of babies this age have temperatures above 100.2 or below 98.6. At 6 months, two thirds of infants have temperatures between 100.1 and 98.9. The corresponding range at 1 year is 100.2 to 99.2. Thus average temperature and individual variations decrease as the infant grows into childhood. Individual differences continue to exist, though, and it is important to realize that an occasional child may have an unusually high (or low) temperature which is normal for *him* [105].

Heat production increases with age throughout the growth period. The younger the child, the more he is likely to vary from the average and also to vary with himself from time to time [55]. The larger the body, of course, the greater the absolute amount of heat produced. Taken in terms of heat production per unit of body

Table 3–6 Average Body Temperature of Infants and Children

Age	Temperature		Standard Deviation	
	F.	C.	F.	C.
3 months	99.4	37.5	0.8	0.4
6 months	99.5	37.5	0.6	0.3
1 year	99.7	37.7	0.5	0.2
3 years	99.0	37.2	0.5	0.2
5 years	98.6	37.0	0.5	0.2
7 years	98.3	36.8	0.5	0.2
9 years	98.1	36.7	0.5	0.2
11 years	98.0	36.7	0.5	0.2
13 years	97.8	36.6	0.5	0.2

SOURCE: From *Growth and Development of Children*, 5th edition, by Ernest H. Watson and George H. Lowrey. Copyright © 1967, Year Book Medical Publishers, Inc., Chicago. Used by permission of Year Book Medical Publishers.

weight, however, the 6-month baby produces more heat than anybody. Heat production builds up from birth to 6 months and then tapers off to adulthood.

Considering what is known about temperature in children, it can be seen that good care includes protection against extremes of temperature and supervision which helps the child to regulate his own temperature. During about the first year a room temperature between 68° and 72° is recommended [9, pp. 133–134]. When the baby can run around, 65° to 68° is a good temperature for him. Adequate clothing helps to keep temperature at an optimal level while also providing flexibility. Since infants and young children produce such large amounts of heat, they are likely to become overheated through active play or when wearing heavy clothing. They will show discomfort by a flushed face, perspiration, and perhaps irritability.

Respiration changes considerably during the first year. The rate slows down to about half what it was at birth. After 1 year, it continues to become slower. Breathing becomes deeper, too. At birth, the diaphragm does practically all of the work in breathing. The chest gradually comes into play during infancy, but thoracic breathing is not well established until the end of the preschool period [105]. A young baby's breathing sounds harsh, irregular, and shallow. Gradually his breathing becomes more regular and less noisy as he changes toward thoracic breathing, as his chest grows, and as the tissues covering his chest thicken and insulate the sounds.

The timing of eating, sleeping, and eliminating becomes regularized. By 3 or 4 months, even the baby who has made his own schedule (fed when hungry, allowed to sleep until he wakens) eats and sleeps at fairly predictable times. The newborn sleeps 16 or 17 hours a day, nearly all of the time when he is not eating and receiving care [76]. From age 1 month to 3 months, the infant stays awake for longer periods, shortening the average number of hours of sleep to 15. From this time until 6 months, he gradually stays awake more in the daytime and sleeps longer at night. During the second year, most babies sleep through the night and take one or two naps during the day. Some time during this year, the second nap tends to drop out, with one nap continued until age 4 or 5 years.

Development takes place in the quality of sleep as well as in the total quantity. Sleep occurs in cycles that include two different kinds of sleep, active and quiet.

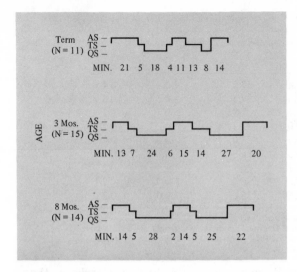

Figure 3–4. Changes in length of sleep cycles and changes in relation of active to quiet sleep.

SOURCE: Reprinted by permission from E. Stern, A. H. Parmelee, Y. Akiyama, M. A. Schultz, and W. H. Wenner, "Sleep Cycle Characteristics in Infants," *Pediatrics*, **43**, Figure 1, p. 67, Copyright © 1969 American Academy of Pediatrics.

Active sleep, sometimes called primitive sleep, is characterized by irregular respiration and heart rate, many small body movements, and bursts of eye movements [97]. Primitive sleep is triggered by the reticular system in the midbrain and does not involve the cortex. Quiet sleep, in contrast, is a highly controlled state which involves the cortex as well as lower brain structures. In quiet sleep, breathing and heartbeat are regular, and there are neither body movements nor eye movements. The proportion of a sleep cycle spent in quiet sleep increases as the baby matures. At birth quiet sleep was found to be 37 percent of a cycle, at 3 months 49 percent, and at 8 months 56 percent [97]. This progression indicates the maturation of higher brain structures. Figure 3–4 shows typical sleep cycles at birth, 3 months, and 8 months. Note the lengthening of the quiet phase. The illustration also shows the lengthening of the total sleep cycle. In this study, the total cycle increased from an average of 47.0 minutes at birth to 50.3 at 8 months. (The sleep cycle in adults is about 90 minutes.)

As eating and sleeping become regularized, bowel movements also tend to do so. By 6 months, one or two stools a day are most usual. Wide individual differences occur, however. About half of 2-year-olds have bowel movements at predictable times, and half are unpredictable [87].

Feeding Behavior

Feeding is one of the essential ways in which a baby deals with his world. In describing an individual, a family, a culture, or even homo sapiens, it is important to tell what food is used, how it is obtained, and how it is prepared. Foods become endowed with meanings and even become symbols, ways of communicating. (Rice is an almost universal fertility symbol at weddings, coconuts mean good luck in India, wine is a Christian symbol for blood.) The culture into which an infant is born is organized to offer him certain foods in certain ways with certain meanings attached. Within the opportunities and limits he encounters, he develops ways of obtaining food and eating it, as well as ways of thinking and feeling about food. The quantity and quality of food available set limits on the growth of his body, including his nervous system, and this, in turn, sets limits on his intelligence.

Ellen S. Smart

Figure 3–5. The sense of autonomy is enhanced as Becky feeds herself.

In *Feeding Behavior of Infants,* Gesell and Ilg [36] devote a section to the history of nursing implements and techniques. They show pictures of artificial baby feeders, including the Roman clay boat, the French cow's horn, the English bubbly pot and pap boat, metal nipples, chamois nipples, and modern glass and rubber equipment. They tell of such practices as pigeon feeding, in which the mother or nurse chewed food before putting it in the baby's mouth, and of soothing teething discomfort with hare's brain or dog's milk. When faced with these historic practices or with some of the customs reported by modern anthropologists, one is struck by the adaptability of infants' feeding behavior.

By the end of the second year, the baby can chew well and can use the basic implements and utensils—cup, spoon, and plate. He can seek and find food and obtain and reject it through the use of words. *All gone, more, drink,* and similar expressions are powerful symbols through which he can control many important events.

Nursing. The meshing of roles of mother and infant is a powerful argument for the value of breast feeding. As the previous chapter has shown, the newborn baby's reflex activity is adequate for finding the nipple, stimulating it, and withdrawing milk. The mother's reactions and the baby's can mutually regulate each other, the baby taking what he needs, the mother supplying it. Nevertheless, the majority of American and European babies are fed by bottle. Under conditions of optimal sanitation which are easy for prosperous Westerners to achieve, bottle feeding is safe and convenient, although expensive.

Weaning. Emerging resources include new ways of eating. Instead of getting all of his food as liquids which he sucks, the baby learns to bite and chew solids and to drink liquids from a cup. This particular changeover is called weaning. Weaning is also used sometimes to mean any gradual change from immature to mature behavior. In all contexts, weaning usually involves some pushing and encouraging of the child toward more mature behavior. Since an older baby can hold his bottle and carry it with him, he can enjoy his sucking and his autonomy at the same time, whereas with breast feeding, the growing desire for independence may make him accept cup feeding more readily. The timing and techniques of weaning are related to personality development of the child and to cultural prescriptions. Americans are advised by their authorities to wean gradually. The Children's Bureau, The Child Study Association, and Dr. Spock, all recommend gradual substitution of the cup for the bottle or breast. In addition to being gradual, the mother is usually warned that the baby needs extra loving and attention when he is being asked to give up a familiar way of eating. Americans usually wean babies during the first year. The Children's Bureau says, "Take your time with weaning. Breast-fed babies can be weaned directly and gradually to a cup after about 6 months old. Bottle-fed babies usually like to suck the bottle a little longer" [16].

The stress on gradualness and gentleness is consistent with what is known about personality development during the first year. While developing his sense of trust, it is most helpful for the baby to be assured that the world and the people in it can be trusted. Traumatic experiences and major readjustments to life are injurious to the sense of trust and hence to the establishment of the foundations of a healthy personality.

An example of another cultural setting shows how weaning can be crucial to the sense of autonomy, rather than to the sense of trust, when weaning occurs at a time when the sense of autonomy is growing rapidly. A group of Zulu babies were studied before, during, and after weaning, which occurred between 15 and 24 months, at the average age of 19 months [3]. The day of weaning was a serious event, fixed months ahead. Bitter juice of the aloe was put on the mother's breast while the child watched and then the breast was offered to him throughout the day. A charm was put around his neck, to help him in various ways. On the day of weaning, all but one baby refused the breast after the first encounter with the aloe juice. Behavior changes followed a definite pattern of disintegration, followed by integration on a higher level. During the first two hours, the toddlers became more negativistic, aggressive, and fretful. They sucked their fingers and other objects. Some performed stereotyped actions. After the first day, relationships changed with everyone in the home. With their mothers, they first alternated attacking and ignoring, then tried to gain attention by illness, clinging, fretting and crying, and finally paid little attention to their mothers, showing no anger and behaving with increasing independence. Sudden increases in mature behavior included helping with housework, imitating others, using new words, talking more distinctly, leaving home more often, and showing hospitality. Children also became more aggressive and mischievous, spilling water, playing with fire, and wasting food. Eating patterns changed, with preferences for adult food and greatly increased appetite.

These behavior changes can be seen as contributing to a growing sense of autonomy. Normal development during the second year, especially the latter half of the second year, involves establishing oneself as a separate individual. All of these six changes in behavior indicate increased independence, power in decision making, differentiation, and reorganization. The weaning experience apparently precipitated the second stage of personality growth. Thus the method of sudden weaning, conducted differently and timed differently, had a very different result from weaning conducted American-style. Both methods of weaning can be seen to be functional in regard to the stage of personality growth during which they are conducted.

Self-Regulation of Diet in Infancy. Of great practical significance is the question of how competent the child is to select the quantity and quality of his food. "Does the baby know how much he ought to eat?" and "Does the baby know what is good for him?" are questions which have long been debated by parents, doctors, nurses, and teachers of young children. The classic experiment of Clara Davis [18, 19] gives information as to choices infants can make under a certain set of conditions. Davis took a group of newly weaned babies and gave them complete freedom to choose their diets from a variety of simple, natural, unmixed, unseasoned foods, including fruits, vegetables, milk, eggs, meat, whole-grain cereals, salt, and cod liver oil. At first a baby tended to sample all of the food on his tray, but later on, he was likely to settle down to a smaller selection of foods. Sometimes an infant would go on a "jag" and eat five eggs at a sitting or drink a large amount of cod liver oil. No child suffered a digestive upset from such a spree. At the end of the experiment, all subjects had grown well, were in good health, and some in better nutritional condition than at the beginning. An analysis of their 36,000 meals showed that the infants had balanced their diets perfectly. Davis [20] paints a vivid word picture of the babies:

> Before meals hands and faces are washed and when the dietitian comes in and says, "The trays are ready," all who can walk join in an eager rush to the dining room, the nurses carrying the others. Bibs are tied on and, as the trays are brought in, the smaller babies often show their eagerness for food by jumping up and down in their chairs, and trying to reach the trays before they are set down on the tables. Yet, once started, they eat with an evident absence of strain, without hurry and without dallying and with poise and complete satisfaction, knowing that they may have all they want of everything. Sometimes they fall asleep while eating as their eyes close like nursing babies. This almost pagan joy of eating reminds one of young animals or the accounts of the eating of primitive peoples. Since they feed themselves with their hands the babies rapidly become independent, and by the time they are fifteen or sixteen months old the nurses' functions are reduced to moving dishes that the child cannot reach and seeing that empty ones are refilled, so that one nurse seated between their tables can attend to two infants. From the age of twenty months on all the babies thus far have been able not only to feed themselves entirely, but to rearrange their dishes on the tray to suit themselves and to hold up empty ones to attract attention when they wish them refilled. These older ones have only waitress service, no nurse sitting beside them. When a baby is through eating, he gets down or is helped down and leaves the dining room whether the others have finished or not.*

Thus research showed that human beings, at least as infants, have the ability to choose a balanced diet from a wide variety of simple, nutritious foods and to eat the amounts they need for adequate growth and maintenance. Even though Davis first reported her research in 1928, it is still misinterpreted quite often. For example, the mother of a crib-chewer declared that it was all right for her baby to eat wood and paint, because Davis had shown that babies could eat whatever they chose! It is impossible and absurd to try to reproduce Davis's experiment at home. What mother can provide cafeteria service while keeping her toddler away from all contact with candy, soft drinks, ice cream, and other snack foods, as well as the dishes she prepares for the other members of the family who like stew, salad, and pie? Davis's contribution was to show that infants of about a year of age can be very autonomous in choosing what to eat, how much to eat, and how to eat it. The possibility that children have good nutrition while being autonomous in the selection of foods requires not only that they be allowed their selections but also

* From C. M. Davis, "Self-Selection of Food by Children," Copyright May 1935, The American Journal of Nursing Company. Reprinted from *American Journal of Nursing*, May 1935.

that all of the choices available to them be foods that are nutritionally valuable in themselves. Chocolate bars and lollipops, pies and doughnuts, were not on Davis's menus.

What happens at mealtime is significant not only for physical growth but for personality development too. Trust grows as the baby learns he can count on satisfying meals turning up as he feels a need for food. Early autonomous activity includes the defensive actions of dribbling, drooling, not accepting, not swallowing, compulsive repetitious acts, using substitute oral comfort, such as sucking fingers, blanket, or pacifier [74, p. 305]. Seeking, finding, and taking in food are positive kinds of autonomous acts.

Locomotion

The baby's world expands and stimulation increases greatly when he learns to move from one place to another. Much maturation and learning go on before the infant actually creeps, crawls, or hitches.

Growth of the parts of the brain concerned with locomotion is indicated as the baby progresses through the locomotor sequence. The cerebellum, concerned largely with balance and posture, grows slowly during the first few months and rapidly in size and complexity between 6 and 18 months [34]. The sequence of motor development is shown in the silhouettes presented in Figure 3–6. Here is shown progression from fetal position to walking—in 15 months.

The locomotion of the first year is creeping, of the second year, walking. Each of these patterns of moving can be traced from early beginnings. Considering creeping, you can see its beginning in the early attempts to raise the head when the baby is in prone position. Most babies do this momentarily at 1 month or 2 months, gradually lifting their heads higher and for longer periods of time. Although some babies actually make progress by crawling during their first weeks, this reflexlike movement fades out, leaving infants stationary until they develop the more purposive kind of creeping movements. Although maturation plays a major role in the achievement of creeping, anyone who watches a baby go through the final stages before creeping notices a great deal of effort trial and error. For instance, the *swimming stage* is one in which the baby perches on his abdomen, does a completely ineffectual frog kick, and moves his arms at cross purposes as often as not [94]. Any progress at this point is likely to be backward and slight. Shortly afterward comes a stage when babies try out a variety of methods, such as using the stomach as a pivot, hitching by means of head and feet, shoulders and feet, or buttocks and hand, making a bridge by standing on toes and hands and scooting backward. Although some infants retain idiosyncratic ways of creeping, most do it in the usual style, which is shown in Figure 3–6.

Basic to walking are holding the head and shoulders erect, sitting, making stepping movements, and standing. Even in the first three months, most infants resist with their feet when held in standing position. Gradually more and more of the baby's weight is borne by his feet. Stepping movements (while held) begin in what looks like dancing, standing on the toes, lifting one foot and then the other and putting both feet down in the same place. Later come putting one foot down ahead of the other, and bouncing. Before they can pull themselves up into standing position, most babies can stand onto helping hands or to the rail of a playpen. Some children, however, learn to pull up before they can remain standing [35, p. 39].

Figure 3–6. The sequence of motor development, with ages at which the average baby achieves each coordination.

SOURCE: Reprinted by permission from M. M. Shirley, *The First Two Years: A Study of Twenty-Five Babies.* Vol. II: *Intellectual Development,* Copyright © University of Minnesota, Minneapolis, 1933.

Most children learn to walk during the first three months of the second year. Parents often think that their baby really could walk if he would, since he gets around so quickly and easily with one hand held or with just one hand on a piece of furniture. The stage of cruising or walking with help seems to be a period of perfecting walking skills and gaining confidence before setting out independently. Walking is unsteady at first, gradually improving with maturing and practice. Maturation includes a change in proportions and posture, as well as neuromuscular development. The toddler has short legs, a long trunk, large head and abdomen, and consequently a center of gravity high in his trunk. In order to balance himself better, he spreads his feet, walking on a broad base. As his proportions change toward those of childhood, he can afford to place his feet closer together. By the second half of the second year, he can run, covering territory at least twice as fast.

Locomotion includes climbing, too, which looks much like creeping, but begins in the second year, usually in the first three months. Climbing further enlarges the infant's scope of activities, giving him the run of all the floors of his home and access to the sofa, chairs, tabletops, cupboards, drawers.

Because the world expands so enormously with sitting, creeping, walking, running, and climbing, there are a multitude of opportunities for the sense of autonomy to grow. So many choices to make! So many ways in which to test oneself! So many avenues to discovery of powers and limits on powers! It can be very heady or even overwhelming.

Group Differences in Motor Development. Whenever motor differences between white and black American infants have been noted in the research literature, the black babies have been advanced in comparison with the whites. A group of black children in New Haven, tested over their first two years of life, showed definite acceleration on the motor section of the Gesell developmental test [57]. Bayley's infant scale of motor development was given to 1409 babies between 1 month and 15 months, in 12 cities representing most of the areas of the United States [5]. Forty-two percent of these babies were black. White and black averages, compared for each month, showed higher values for blacks at every level except 15 months. The differences were highest in the early months, becoming nonsignificant at 1 year. Another investigator [104] divided groups of black and white babies into low, middle, and high socioeconomic groups and tested them at age 12, 24, and 36 weeks on Gesell developmental schedules. She found all black groups superior in motor development at age 12 weeks but at 36 weeks only the black high socio-economic group was superior. Although this author argues against a genetic factor being responsible for the superiority, the genetic explanation is possible. Thirty-six weeks corresponds with the time when Bayley's black and white groups were narrowing the difference between them. The superiority maintained by only the high socioeconomic group could be due to excellent environmental conditions strengthening a genetic superiority which was in the process of leveling out.

African babies have been reported to show extremely advanced motor development. Working under the World Health Organization, Geber [33] tested over 300 babies in Uganda. She found them to be consistently advanced in psychomotor functions, as compared with European and American babies. This finding has been confirmed by other observers of African babies [1, 5, 26]. The acceleration in development is greatest at birth, then gradually decreases. From the first day, the children could hold their heads steady when drawn into sitting position, an achievement of the European child at about 6 weeks. The average Uganda baby sat alone at age 4 months and walked at 10. Some individuals achieved these coordinations earlier. Language, problem solving, and personal–social development were likewise two or three months advanced over European standards. Since the babies were born developmentally accelerated, the reason for their condition must be in something that happened before birth. Geber suggests that the reason for the infant acceleration is the way in which pregnancy is conducted. She describes it thus:

> The arrival of a baby is always looked forward to with great pleasure (sterility is thought to be a calamity) and is not a source of anxiety for the future. The mother is in no way upset by her pregnancy and is active up to the moment of delivery. The unborn child is the chief object of her life, especially as she believes that any other interest may have an adverse affect on him [33, p. 194].

Careful studies of infants in widely separated parts of the world have yielded results similar to Geber's although not as pronounced. Newborn babies in Guatemala were 3 to 5 weeks above American Gesell norms in psychomotor functions and over 1 week ahead in adaptive behavior [17]. The same author reports that in six rural communities in Mexico and Guatemala, infants' superiority on the Gesell test declined from birth until 18 months, when they reached levels below those of European and American babies. Indian research has yielded the same results, using the Bayley infant tests in a longitudinal study of 278 babies [77]. At 1 month of age, the Indian babies were extremely advanced in motor tests and moderately advanced in mental tests. Their superiority declined steadily throughout the first year. A similar report comes from Israel, on groups of home-reared and kibbutz-reared infants who were given Bayley tests throughout the first 27 months [59]. Both groups were superior to American babies from age 1 month to 4 months. Between age 5 months and 15 months, the differences were not significant, although Israeli averages were above the Americans.

The Mexican investigator, searching for an explanation of the superiority of newborns in various parts of the world, suggests that conditions of life in pre-industrial communities may produce fetal environments which result in precocious neonates [17]. He names two possible contributors: the relation of the mother to heavy labor and her high status because of being pregnant. A recent finding with animals suggests an explanation yet to be tested with human beings [42]. Puppies raised on a low protein diet or born from mothers on low protein showed precocious development, along with a high tolerance for glucose. Their later development was retarded. It remains to be seen whether human infants show high glucose tolerance plus precocity after having been deprived of adequate protein prenatally and immediately after birth.

Eye–Hand Coordination and Manipulation

Through the use of his hands, the baby reaches out into the world, finds out about it and changes it. He cannot interact much with his hands until he can sit up, although he does make a beginning in the early weeks. The first three months is a time of contacting objects with eyes more than with hands, following moving objects in several directions. The grasping reflex, present at birth, is strong for the first three months and loses its automatic quality before the first half year. At first the grasping reflex consists of grasping anything that is placed against the palm. Gradually the child becomes able to grasp objects that he touches with his hand, first in a fumbling way and then more and more deftly. At the same time that he is starting to grasp what his hand contacts, around the end of the first three months, he also looks at his hands and glances at the objects he holds [34].

Photographs from Halverson's classic study [41] of the development of reaching and grasping show how grasping changes from a primitive sequence of palm and fingers to a precise coordination of thumb and forefinger. As can be seen in Figure 3–7, coordination of thumb and forefinger occurs when a baby picks up a pellet or a crumb.

In a description of the sequence of development in eye–hand coordination, the principle of differentiation and integration stands out. Early grasping is an all-out event, with both arms active and the whole body straining. On the Gesell test [35], 12 weeks intervene between this kind of approach and a one-handed grasp. Transferring objects from one hand to another comes at the same time as one-handed grasp. Here is the beginning of the differentiation that is basic to human manipulation. One hand does one thing while the other does something else, and the two are integrated, working toward one goal. In the course of differentiation and

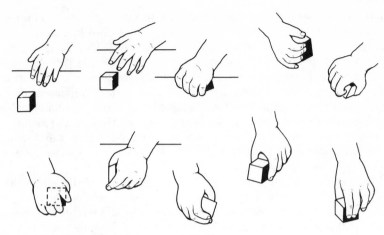

Figure 3–7. Stages in the development of grasping.

SOURCE: Reprinted by permission from H. M. Halverson, "An Experimental Study of Prehension in Infants by Means of Systematic Cinema Records," *Genetic Psychology Monograph*, **10**, 107–286. Copyright © 1931, The Journal Press.

integration one hand becomes the preferred hand, to be used as the leader in manipulation. The baby gains in the ability to use objects and to use more than one object at a time. Here are the early stages of man's ability to use tools. You can see him as an infant, hitting a cube against a cup, choosing between bottle and pellet, considering the details of a ball and using a pencil on a paper.

Gesell's normative sequences of eye–hand coordination, like his other sequences of behavioral development, show what the average, middle-class American child does at successive ages. Piaget, too, is interested in the actions of eyes and hands, but in terms of the development of intelligence.

Based on observations of his own infants' interactions with objects, Piaget described sequences of schemas involving eyes and hands. He also pointed out that "the construction of reality" takes place by means of these activities [80]. Through grasping and looking, the infant interacts with the world to develop mental structures or schemas that give rise to new behavior. More is said about Piaget's theories of development in the following section of the book. Many recent studies have been focused on the stages and processes of the development of the concept of object [90]. A study of the development of schemas used in relating to objects [102] is of particular interest here, where we are concerned with eye–hand coordination. Results on 84 infants showed certain clusters of reactions characterizing each level of development. As a baby grew older, his earlier reactions did not disappear, but became less prominent by being integrated into higher-level reactions or used very specifically. The schemas involving eyes and/or hand coordination were holding, mouthing, visual inspection, hitting, shaking, examining, differentiated schemas, and letting go. Their characteristics are

Holding: When an object is placed in the hand of an infant over 1 month old, he holds it for 30 seconds or more. He neither looks at it nor brings it to his face, nor does he seem to notice when he drops it. Through the use of this schema, he gets some tactual experience with objects.

Mouthing: The infant brings the object in his hand to his mouth or tries to do so, as shown by opening and closing his mouth. All infants in the study showed mouthing at 2 months. This schema is very prominent in early interactions with objects but later tends to drop out, as far as play materials are concerned.

Visual Inspection: In the beginning stages of this schema, the baby catches glimpses of objects as he brings them to his mouth. Gradually he holds objects in view for longer periods of time and looks at them intently. All infants did visual inspection at three months. This schema does not drop out but becomes integrated into higher level examining.

Hitting: An up-and-down motion of the arm is the basis of several hitting schemas, which most infants showed by age 4 months and all by 7 months. The most frequently seen one was hitting an object on a surface. There is also the schema of waving an object, which is like hitting but the object does not touch a surface. Patting is another variation. If hitting results in sounds, then the schema serves to establish coordination between hand movements and sound perception.

Shaking: Moving the arm from side to side is similar to hitting and occurs at about the same time, by age 5 months in most babies, and by age 10 in all observed. At first shaking is indiscriminate but soon is applied mainly to objects that make a noise.

Examining: This is a complex schema, including looking, turning, poking, feeling, manipulating. Whereas in earlier stages, the schemas of holding, visual inspection and hitting were used for themselves, the emphasis here is on interaction with the object. Schemas are used according to how they affect the object. Most infants used examining by age 6 months, all by 10.

Differentiated schemas: After he begins examining, the baby develops a cluster of new schemas which include tearing, pulling, crumpling, squeezing, rubbing, sliding, and pushing. He applies these schemas appropriately to different objects. Most babies used differentiated schemas by age 7 months, all by 10.

Letting go: Dropping becomes possible when the baby can let go at will. He uses dropping for finding out how things fall and what noises they make when they land. At 8 months most infants dropped objects purposefully, at 9 months all did. Throwing develops one to two months after dropping, permitting observation of trajectories, speeds, and perceptual transformations and coordinating this information with muscular sensations of greater and less effort.

A concept of object implies that the child knows that the object continues to exist after it disappears from his view. When he hunts for an object after it has been placed behind a screen, he shows that he has some notion of its permanence. Examining behavior increases during the period just before the child is able to solve the problem of finding the hidden object [90].

Attention

In the previous chapter, the neonate's attention to certain stimuli was noted. The state of alert inactivity was found to be the condition in which the young infant attends most readily to visual stimuli. Infants select certain stimuli to attend to and pay attention for longer periods to some than to others. Movement and contour, or dark–light contrast, are some of the determinants of visual attention in young infants. Attention has been studied by measuring how long an infant looks at a stimulus and/or monitoring his heart rate, which decelerates as he attends [62].

STIMULUS	DEGREE OF FACENESS	AMOUNT OF DETAIL	% FIXATION TIME
	1	3	.33
	2	1	.28
	3	4	.19
	4	2	.20

Figure 3–8. Stimuli used to test responses to resemblance to the human face and to complexity, with rank orders on the two dimensions and fixation times.

Source: Reprinted by permission from R. A. Haaf and R. Q. Bell, "A Facial Dimension in Visual Discrimination," *Child Development*, **3-8**, Figure 1, p. 895. Copyright © 1967, The Society for Research in Child Development, Inc.

One-year-olds showed preference for complex auditory stimuli by responding for a longer time when lever-pushing resulted in a chime than they did when it resulted in a bell sounding [96].

Determinants of Visual Attention. Complex patterns are consistently preferred (as measured by looking time) over plain surfaces by both newborn and older infants [27]. This preference, which seems to be innate, is highly functional for the baby in getting to know and understand the world around him, in learning to recognize objects, places, and people, and in creeping without bumping into things or falling off edges. At the normal time for learning to creep, for instance, the baby stays away from a surface pattern which indicates a dropoff, even though that pattern is only a simulation of an edge. The early preference for the human face may begin from preference for pattern and complexity. However, the face may derive attractiveness by being the first object which the baby experiences as being influenced by his own activities. Infants show excitement and pleasure when they realize that they can make something happen [106].

Response to "faceness" or similarity to a face, was pitted against a dimension of complexity in an ingenious experiment using the drawings shown in Figure 3–8. The drawing at the top, which is the one most like a real face, received the most visual attention from 4-month-old boys [40]. The real face ranks third in amount of detail, or complexity. The most complex stimulus, which is second in faceness, ranks second in amount of regard accorded it, whereas the second most complex drawing ranks last.

The baby's tendency to look at another person's eyes is consistent with a strong preference for the bull's-eye pattern, which is preferred to stripes from the age of 2 months [28]. Infants in the third month looked eight times as long at the bull's-eye as at the stripes. Further preference experiments showed babies choosing bull's-eye and circular patterns over lattice patterns equated to the circular arrays in length of contour, number, and size of elements, area, light reflectance, and contrast.

Faces and facelike stimuli have been explored in many studies with infants. By 2 months of age, a solid object is preferred over a flat one, by 3 months, a textured sphere over a textured disc and a solid head model over an outline form. In order to see whether familiarity had something to do with choosing facelike stimuli, a nursing bottle containing milk was paired with the round and oval objects. The bottle received less attention than the other stimuli from infants 2 to 5 months old, nor did it evoke more response before feeding time than after [28].

Stimuli that are almost like real faces, but not quite, are powerful attractors of attention. This phenomenon has been explored by using drawings or photographs of faces with scrambled features and blanked-out features. At 6 months infants looked longer at the realistic faces, but after that age they showed increasing preference for the distorted faces [51]. The authors theorize that while the infant is developing a schema (an inner representation) of an object, that object is very attractive. After he has a well-developed schema, through which he easily recognizes the objects it represents, he is attracted to novelty, or deviations from his schema.

The effect of changes in stimulation on the attention paid by infants to visually presented objects was investigated in a study that used mobiles that were progressively more different than one of standard design [99]. The babies were between 4 and 5 months old. At home, for three weeks, they were all shown the same mobile for half an hour a day. They were presumed to have developed a schema of the mobile. In the laboratory each of seven groups was shown a mobile which was related to the standard mobile in a controlled way. Those infants who were shown a moderately discrepant mobile in the laboratory looked longer at it than those infants who were shown a minimally or maximally discrepant one. They paid attention to novelty, if the new stimulus was not too different from the one for which they had a schema.

Reasons for a long fixation time are not all the same. By studying other responses which go along with the long fixation, it has been found that normal faces received more smiling and greater cardiac deceleration than did distorted faces, although fixation times did not differ [51]. Thus the infant may look for a long time because he enjoys the sight, as with a familiar face, or because he is trying to reduce the uncertainty (to assimilate or accommodate) in the case of the distorted face, which is close to his face schema but different enough to not fit.

The effect of uncertainty on attending behavior was studied by varying the location of the stimulus rather than the stimulus itself [15]. A game of peekaboo with two groups of infants aged 5 to 10 months and 12 to 19 months was played under three degrees of uncertainty. One third saw the face which played peekaboo always appear in the same spot, one third had the face alternating from side to

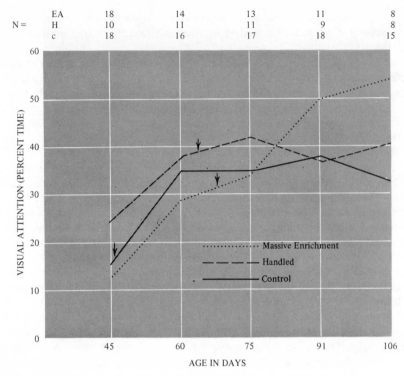

Figure 3–9. Percent of observation time during which three groups of infants showed visual attention.

SOURCE: B. L. White and R. Held, "Plasticity of Sensorimotor Development in the Human Infant." In J. Hellmuth [Ed.], *Exceptional Infant: The Normal Infant*, Vol. I. 1967, New York, Brunner/Mazel, Inc. By permission.

side, and the remainder had random presentations. The extent to which both age groups persisted in playing the game varied with the amount of uncertainty involved. In other words, the alternating face evoked more persistence than the face in the same place, and the random appearances received more attention than the alternating.

Individual Differences. Attentiveness varies between individual babies [40, 61]. The highly attentive infant tends to remain highly attentive, at least throughout the first year, as long as the stimuli given are interesting and relative to his age level [61]. Sex differences in attentiveness have also been found. At 6 and 13 months of age, girls attended longer to visual stimuli and preferred more novel sounds than did boys [52].

One source of individual differences in visual attentiveness has been found in the amount and variety of experience available to the young infant [109]. (Visual attention was defined as a state in which the eyes are more than half open and the direction of gaze shifting at least once every 30 seconds.) The subjects were physically normal institution babies, half of whom were given 20 minutes of extra daily handling. These babies were significantly more visually attentive than the controls. A second experimental group received "massive enrichment" which included 20 minutes of extra handling, placement in prone position, removal of crib bumpers which interfered with seeing ward activities and addition of stabiles, printed sheets and bumpers instead of plain. As Figure 3–9 shows, visual attention was first slower in the enrichment group but at about a month after the experiment started, at age 75 days, the enrichment group increased sharply in visual attention, as compared with the handled and control groups.

Intellectual Development

The infant experiences people, objects, and himself as he interacts with his environment. He explores through his sensory and motor resources, making some changes in the objects and people he contacts, changing himself as he receives sensory data and processes them. He communicates with people, rapidly improving his techniques for doing so. As he refines his methods of communicating, he is also developing a tool of thinking.

Cognition

Cognoscere, Latin for "to know," gives rise to the term *cognition*, one of man's most human activities. By *cognition* is meant the individual's becoming acquainted with the world and the objects in it, including himself. He comes to understand relationships between objects and between himself and the world, by taking in information through his senses and processing it and acting on it. While cognition is of great practical use from day to day and from moment to moment, man cognizes just for fun in addition to cognizing for necessity. The toddler's flow of "Wazzat?" the curiosity of the preschool child, the drive of the research scientist—all reflect a certain amount of wanting to know for the sake of knowing. Cognition goes on during most of what is called play in infancy. While using all of his resources for dealing with the world, the infant is also cognizing and developing cognitively.

Sensorimotor Intelligence, According to Piaget. Intelligence is a process of organization which extends the biological organization of the body [79, p. 407]. Intelligence includes adaptive thinking and actions. The child constructs his intelligence through his own efforts, beginning with what is genetically given. Piaget calls sensorimotor intelligence practical intelligence, since it has no words at its service for use in thinking and problem solving: "... in place of words and concepts it uses percepts and movements organized into 'action schemata'"* [80]. The mental structures, or intellectual abilities, which the child builds during the sensorimotor stage are what he needs for constructing and reconstructing objects.

The achievement of the infancy stage in cognition is to come to know one's immediate environment as permanent objects and background, separate from oneself. *Permanent* means that the object (bottle, mother, rattle, and such) continues to exist even though it is moved, hidden, or placed in a new relationship with other objects (such as mother in a party-going hat). All the parts of an object (such as the nipple on a bottle) must be known to exist even when they cannot be seen.

Understanding some facts about movement is a part of coming to know permanent objects. A child has to find out that when an object is moved, it can be put back again, that when it turns around, it can be turned in the other direction,

---

* In his writings Piaget used *schemata* as the plural of the word *schema*. We follow the practice of most American writers and use *schemas* as the plural.

Halvar Loken

that when an object is moved away, he can reach it by a path other than the one taken by the object, in fact by many different paths.

Starting with the resources he has for dealing with the world, the baby uses them to develop new patterns of action. For example, he integrates schemas of mouthing, holding, and looking (see pages 148–149). The result is an examining schema. Using this method of exploration many times with toys, bottles, clothing, and other objects, the infant makes progress toward the conviction that objects are permanent. Other behavior patterns, involving seeing, smelling, tasting, hearing, touching, and manipulating, are used in getting knowledge of the world. Locomotion, moving from place to place, gives the baby chances to map out the space in which he lives, getting to truly cognize it and himself as an object in space.

As experience with reality shows his existing resources to be inadequate or insufficient, the baby develops new schemas through accommodation or improvements in what he has. When the child falls only slightly short of being adequate to cope with an experience, his feeling tone is pleasant and interesting. Growth is stimulated. When he is very inadequate in dealing with the experience, the child is frightened and tries to withdraw [43].

Piaget has described six substages of the period of sensorimotor intelligence,* the period during which the infant establishes basic knowledge of the world. Piaget is not concerned with the exact ages at which children reach the successive stage of intelligence. He is interested in *how* rather than *when*, and in which structures are invariably built before certain other structures. The substages of sensorimotor intelligence are:

I. *Simple Reflexive Action.* The schemas of the neonatal period include the reflex movements described in Chapter 2 and a general mass activity. The perceptual abilities described in Chapter 2 are also schemas of the early sensorimotor period.

* This account follows Flavell [29, pp. 85–121].

During this stage, various abilities, such as the sucking reflexes, improve and consolidate. The baby can neither reach for an object nor search for it. There is no indication that he cognizes objects as separate parts of the environment or as distinct from himself.

II. *Primary Circular Reactions.* Neonatal behavior patterns begin to change through maturation and experience. The baby learns to bring his hand to his mouth and to suck on it, most likely his thumb. He touches his hands together and fingers them, looks at his hands and at objects grasped by his hands. Objects grasped by the hands are carried to the mouth. He looks at an object making a noise. He does not know what he can cause and what takes place independent of his own actions.

III. *Secondary Circular Reactions.* The baby develops ways of prolonging interesting events. When a change in the environment results from his actions, he is likely to repeat those actions. He reaches for the toy suspended from his crib, hits it, watches it move and hits it again.

He still does not search for an object that has disappeared, suggesting that he still does not conceive of it as existing permanently. However, if all but a small part of an object is covered, as when his bottle sticks out from under his blanket, he recognizes it and can recover it. If an object is made to disappear slowly, he follows it with his eyes and continues the movement of his eyes in the direction in which the object went. If, however, it is jerked away, or quickly screened, he does not look for it. One of Piaget's experiments with his son, Laurent, showed that the baby did not even miss the bottle when it was hidden quickly. Just before a feeding time, when Laurent was hungry, Piaget showed him his bottle, whereupon Laurent cried. Piaget quickly hid the bottle and Laurent stopped crying. This sequence was repeated several times. When Laurent could see a small portion of the bottle, he cried harder than ever [78, p. 30].

Another interesting aspect of substage III, evident in Laurent's behavior, was failure to realize the existence of the nipple if it did not show. When he saw a small portion of the bottle but not the nipple, he tried to suck the bottle itself, but when the nipple was visible, he turned the bottle around so that he could suck the nipple. Thus he cognized the bottle as a suckable object, but unless he could see the nipple, he did not deal with the bottle as an object with a specialized suckable portion. Thus in this stage, objects are becoming endowed with permanence, but the process is not complete.

IV. *Coordination of Secondary Schemas.* Secondary circular reactions become coordinated with each other to form more complex schemas. The new schemas are used definitely as means to ends. This is the earliest age at which the baby shows intention in a definite and unmistakable way. For example, hitting is not just for the sake of hitting, but in order to grasp a new object. Piaget tells how Laurent, at 9½ months, pushed his father's hand and at the same time pulled on the toy which Piaget was holding [79, p. 219].

There is true searching for a vanished object, although still not complete appreciation of the object's permanence. Piaget describes how his daughter Jacqueline searched for a toy parrot. First, Piaget covered it with his hand. Jacqueline raised his hand and grasped the parrot. Piaget slowly took the toy away from her, hid it under a rug and put his hand on her lap, on the spot where the parrot had first been. Jacqueline raised his hand and looked under it for the parrot. This process was repeated three times [78, p. 51].

V. *Tertiary Circular Reactions.* Instead of merely prolonging or reproducing interesting events, the baby tries to produce new events. He experiments to see what will happen. He appears definitely curious, looking for new experience.

Now the baby looks for a vanished object in the place where it disappeared instead of in the place where he last found it. He demonstrates increased understanding of movements of objects by following a trajectory and looking at its end and by throwing something in back of himself and turning around in the other direction to look for it.

Throwing and dropping toys are common kinds of play at this age, as the infant examines movements of objects, disappearance, and reappearance, building his understanding of the permanence of objects. Piaget watched Laurent using various methods of letting a tin can fall from his hands and then dropping a chunk of bread first as a whole and then in the form of crumbs. Later Laurent dropped toys from different positions.

VI. *Invention of New Means through Mental Combinations.* Instead of having to go through a series of sensorimotor explorations and trials, the child can find solutions mentally. He begins this stage by representing objects and actions to himself. Probably the first kind of representing is to act it out. Piaget's daughter, Lucienne, illustrated this behavior when she was trying to get a little chain out of a match box. She looked at the small opening, not knowing how to open it wider, then opened and shut her mouth several times, each time opening it wider [78, pp. 337–338]. After a few quiet moments, she used a new technique to open the box with her finger. Lucienne's opening of her own mouth was a symbolic act, representing the opening of the box, which she desired. This stage, in coping with problems, is midway between trying out solutions in action and thinking them out. When problems are solved by thinking, without any action, the child is representing objects and actions to himself by symbols which are entirely within. He thinks of ways of acting and tries them out by thinking. He can think of objects which are not present, of past events, and of events which might happen.

The toddler shows his new powers by imitation and pretending and insightful problem solving. When he imitates a past event, he shows that he has a mental image of it. When he pretends, he uses a mental image of a behavior pattern to act out that pattern in a new situation. Feeding a doll, he uses his mental image of his mother's behavior, acting it out at his little table. The achievement of imitation, pretending, and insightful problem solving marks the completion of the stage of sensorimotor development. As with all the stages outlined by Piaget, the average age for beginning and ending a stage is not placed exactly but approximately. The sensorimotor stage, according to Piaget, ends at around 18 months. Gesell [35, p. 71] places imitation and pretending at 2 years, which is probably closer to the age at which most children achieve these feats.*

Ordering and classifying, cognitive behavior which develops noticeably during the next stage of intellectual development, can be observed in its very beginnings during infancy. Gesell mentions the 1-year-old's sequential play with cubes as being a preliminary to ordering and counting, and his looking at a round hole while holding a matching block as being incipient perception of geometric form [35, p. 65]. Between 12 and 24 months, infants will do some selective ordering and group-

---

* Piaget's observations on sensorimotor activity were on his own children, who were most likely advanced in development. The importance of Piaget's work lies in his revealing the ways in which intelligence grows. Gesell contributed information on norms.

ing when presented with an array of two different kinds of objects, such as four clay balls with four yellow cubes [86]. Selective ordering and grouping activity increased with age between 12 and 24 months.

Knowing the Self. Only a small beginning in self-cognition can be made in infancy, but it is essential. To know reality means to know that you are an object distinct from other objects, including background and people. One of man's unique features is the ability to stand off and look at himself, himself as an individual and himself as related to the rest of the world.

Although one may recognize a human being as an organism-in-a-field, as an individual intimately bound up with and interacting with his environment, the common definition of a baby's or a man's boundary is his skin. For most practical purposes, he stops where his skin stops. When a baby fingers his hands, bites his toes, lets his hand fall on his chest, when he watches these actions with his eyes, feels them with both hands, with mouth and toes, with chest and hand, he is coming to know his body. He is cognizing his body, or building an inner image of it. The sensations which come from within, largely gastrointestinal, add to the image. At first, the baby probably does not make a distinction between his own body and his mother's. Psychoanalysts say that gradually he realizes their separateness as he experiences wanting the breast and not getting it. There are additional experiences of separation from the mother—being alone instead of seeing her, feeling the tactile pleasure of her arms and face and hearing her voice. These separations also define his being from his mother's.

The body image surely grows in clarity as the infant finds out which events in the world are caused by him and which are not. In fact, the two are reciprocal. It is only around 4 months of age that the baby seems to make a dim connection between one of his actions and an event, such as hitting the cradle gym and seeing it swing. He gradually cognizes the interaction of his body with the rest of the world and as he does, he knows his body better.

Parents' Contribution to Development of Sensorimotor Intelligence. Parents provide two essential parts of the world of children's learning, the home base and the field to explore. Shortly before he is able to move around on his own, the infant becomes attached to important people, especially his mother. (The process of attachment is described in the following chapter.) When separated from people to whom he is attached, or threatened with separation, the baby makes efforts to regain contact or nearness, crying, reaching, leaning, looking, and if possible, pursuing. These efforts, attachment behavior, preclude exploratory behavior. When, on the other hand, the mother is present or nearby and available, the baby is free to explore. Studies on both monkeys and humans show clearly that the mother's presence facilitates exploration of the environment. Locomotion, manipulation, and visual exploration were studied in an experimental situation involving 56 one-year-old babies and mothers [2]. Figure 3–10 shows the frequency of these three kinds of exploratory behavior in a series of situations. Episode 1, not shown, consisted of the mother carrying the baby into the room, ushered in by a person who then departed. The room contained two adult chairs, a child's chair, and toys. In Episode 2, the mother put the baby down on the floor and sat down on her chair. Babies showed a high degree of locomotion, manipulation, and visual exploration. In Episode 3, a stranger entered, sat quietly, conversed with the mother, gradually approached the baby and showed him a toy. Note the sharp decrease in exploratory behavior with the entrance of the stranger. In Episode 4, the mother

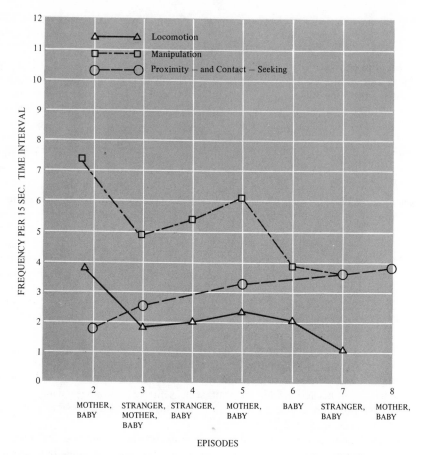

Figure 3–10. Babies' exploratory and proximity- and contact-seeking behavior under different conditions of mother presence.

SOURCE: Adapted from Mary D. S. Ainsworth and Silvia M. Bell, "Attachment, Exploration and Separation: Illustrated by the Behavior of One-Year-Olds in a Strange Situation," *Child Development*, 1970, **41**, 49–67.

departs and attachment behavior (crying and searching) increase, while exploratory behavior remains depressed. In Episode 5, the mother returns and tries to get the baby to explore more. Visual and manual exploration do pick up significantly, although locomotion does not. The mother then departs again and Episode 6 shows further decline of exploration. Crying, which is negatively correlated with exploration ($r = -0.67$), increases. The stranger returns, and Episode 7 shows the lowest levels of exploration. Reunion with the mother, in Episode 8, involves heightened proximity-seeking. The experiment demonstrates the supportive function of the mother (or attachment object) in providing a base from which her baby can examine the world by looking, handling, and moving through space. Through these activities, the infant obtains stimulation necessary for his sensorimotor development.

The second type of contribution made by the mother and other caring people is direct stimulation, and an environment offering optimal stimulation. A mother picks up her baby, cuddles, pats, strokes and kisses him, murmurs words of baby talk, and sings a lullaby to him. Giving him a great rich field of perception: touch sensations on the skin of his body and head; muscle sensations as his muscles are pressed by his mother's hands and as he moves himself; inner ear stimulation as his head swings up from a horizontal to vertical orientation and the balance mechanisms operate; a completely different visual world, full of varied objects instead of walls and ceiling; for his hands to feel, his mother's clothing, her firm shoulder, soft neck and hair; against his cheek, her warm cheek and lips; her voice to listen to. His cognition, his knowing of the world, proceeds through sensory experiences, these and others. Picking him up is only one small act among the many educational acts his mother performs. She props him up, too, so that he can see the world from this angle. He looks at his hands, at toys his mother puts in his lap, at his hands contacting the toys. Babies of 3 or 4 months who have had normal opportunities (for American culture) strain to sit up and show by their pleasure in being propped that this is welcome experience. A frequent change of position prevents fatigue and enriches the sensory field. Here is one place where resident grandparents and older brothers and sisters can add to a baby's education, since mothers often have many duties in addition to baby teaching, and many fathers are absent all day.

When sitting and examining schemas are sufficiently developed, the normally experienced infant enthusiastically accepts and examines all objects that come his way. For example, here is part of a half hour's observation of an 11-month-old baby.

> George pulled himself to his feet and stood watching his mother for a few minutes. He moved around the rail of the playpen by putting one foot out to the side and bringing the other up to it. . . . He squealed, tried to hurry and fell down. . . .
> Mrs. MacIntyre gave George a cardboard box with a ball in it. George pounced on the ball and dropped it . . . he crept after it and then put it back in the box. He took it out, dropped it, crept after it, and so on, going through the whole process four times. He sat and watched the adults for a minute. Then he picked up a stuffed cat by the tail. His fingers slipped up and down the tail. He squeezed the cat and touched the fur. He poked its eyes and pulled the whiskers. A red ribbon and bell around the cat's neck came in for a share of fingering and pulling. George dropped the cat and pulled himself up.
> George sat down and picked a string of brightly colored beads out of his toy basket. He looked at several of the beads and poked at them with his finger. He shook the string and put it round his neck. Then he tried to get it off by pulling down. The beads worked down over his arm. George roared until his mother pulled them off. He put them on again immediately. . . .
> George beat on the saucepan and lid with the spoon, gnawed the spoon, put the lid on the saucepan with a bang, removed the lid. He thumped the pan on the lid and the lid on the pan, put the spoon in the pan and the lid on his head. He put the ball in the saucepan [95, pp. 122–123].

Thus a baby sought and found many sensations. Visual sensations were combined with touch, giving varieties of shape, texture, size, and color. Touch sensations came from his hands, lips, gums, tongue, knees, feet, and buttocks. He elicited sounds. Active as George was, he could not have experienced such a wealth of sensations had the toys and play materials not been present in his environment. Due to his mother's planning, management, and constant care, he had the wherewithal to educate himself.

Several studies have demonstrated the importance of sensory stimulation during the sensorimotor period. Both the amount of stimulation and quality of stimulation provided by the mother are related to the baby's motor and mental status [111]. By *quality* is meant the appropriateness of the stimulation to the child as an individual and to his developmental level. A study done in infant welfare clinics in England, where 90 percent of young children are served by such clinics, related babies' sensory and motor development to their mothers' ways of caring for them [8]. The infants who received maximum stimulation were furthest ahead on the tests of sensory and motor achievement.

Deprivation of Sensorimotor Experience. A dramatic study of sensorimotor stimulation was done by comparing two groups of infants in Lebanon. The effect of sensorimotor experience on IQ was demonstrated by a comparison between subjects from a well-baby clinic and a group from a creche where babies were kept in cribs with covered sides [23]. The latter could see nobody but the caretakers, and those only rarely. Bottles were propped for feeding. Caretakers picked the babies up only for physical care. Words and caresses were very rare. When tested on the Cattell Infant Scale, the clinic group had an average IQ of 102; the creche group, 68. The institution babies had had practically none of the experiences which would give them a fair chance on the test. The test requires that babies over 2 months be held on an adult's lap for many of the items. The creche babies had not sat on laps, and therefore had not had the sensory perceptions and the consequent cognitive development that stem from lapsitting. Such restricted children would not have a fair chance in real-life situations, either. A study of babies in institutions in Iran is concerned with the development of motor coordination under conditions of deprivation [22]. In Institution I, where the infants lay in cribs with covered sides, they remained in the cribs until they were able to pull themselves to sitting, when they were placed on pieces of linoleum on the stone floor. There were no toys. Bottles were propped in the beds. Baths were given on alternate days. The control group was from Institution III, where babies were held in arms while fed, placed prone, propped to sit, put in playpens on the floor and given plenty of toys. Both groups were tested on five motor items.

Table 3–7 shows their achievements. Children in Institution III were much superior to those in Institution I, although the former did not equal the performance of home-reared children. Although all normal American home-reared children sit alone by 9 months and nearly all walk alone by 2 years, among the children in Institution I less than half could sit alone before age 2 years. Only 8 percent could walk before age 3 years.

Children in Institution I were thus severely retarded in motor development. They also showed differences in mode of locomotion. Almost all who could progress did it by scooting, whereas those in Institution III progressed by creeping. The author reasons that the babies scooted because they had never been placed in positions where creeping and preparation for creeping were possible. They rarely, if ever, rolled from supine to prone in their cribs because the cribs were very small and the mattresses soft. In contrast, a child in Institution III, often prone in bed and on the floor, could raise his head, push with his arms, raise his chest, pull his arms and legs beneath his body and thus practice creeping. Thus delayed walking, as well as delayed creeping, can result from denying a child the prone position. The child who creeps can go to the playpen rail or a piece of furniture and pull himself to his knees. He may walk on his knees. Soon he pulls himself to his feet. He then is

Table 3–7 Motor Achievements of Babies in Two Contrasting
Institutions in Iran

Institution	Percent of Group Passing Each Test			
	I	I	III	III
N	50	40	20	31
Age Range	1.0–1.9	2.0–2.9	1.0–1.9	2.0–2.9
Sit alone	42	95	90	100
Creep or scoot	14	75	75	100
Stand holding	4	45	70	100
Walk holding	2	40	60	100
Walk alone	0	8	15	94

SOURCE: Reprinted by permission from W. Dennis, "Causes of Retardation Among Institutional Children: Iran," *Journal of Genetic Psychology*, **96**, 46–60. Copyright © 1960, The Journal Press.

in a position to practice walking while hanging on, and this he does, in the normative sequence for Americans, for two or three months.

The data assembled by a number of investigators have been summarized to show that rate of intellectual growth is influenced in infancy by the number of new objects and events experienced. The more varied the experiences the child has coped with, the more the child seeks new experiences [44, pp. 148–149]. That is, the more curious he becomes. Thus children who have had few toys and other stimulation become apathetic, as do institutional children who have had limited space and opportunities to explore.

Infants born into a culture of poverty in America and in poor countries all over the world are likely to have inadequate sensory and motor opportunities, as well as many other environmental restrictions. Near our home in India was a water tank where washermen and washerwomen worked. Their babies and young children sat on the ground nearby with nothing in their hands, perhaps hearing the repeated whack-whack of the clothes on the rocks. In the center of town, women sat on the sidewalks selling fruit, baskets, or sticks for cleaning teeth. Babies lay or sat beside them, hearing the noises of the street, but again, with nothing in their hands and rarely, if ever, a word directed to them. Once we saw a yearling putting pieces of broken pottery into one of the clay pots his mother was selling. He had found the only play materials that would ever come his way on the Delhi sidewalk. What would happen to his sensorimotor experience after he had exhausted the possibilities of the pots and fragments of pot? Many American infants, too, have few encounters with objects of varying size, shape, texture, color, and temperature, few chances to look, hold, squeeze, suck, bite, taste, smell, hear, examine, climb onto, crawl under, push, pull, drag, ride, swing, jump, float, and splash.

Compensatory Education for Infants. Project Head Start was an attempt to compensate for deficiencies shown by many poor children in the early grades at school, sensorimotor experience being only one of the areas in which these children had been deprived. While enriching and compensating at 4 and 5 years of age was helpful, it was not enough. Head Start was too late. Intervention by 18 months is recommended for deprived children, both rural and urban [24]. Educational programs for infants are now under way. They will be described more fully in the next chapter, since relationships with people are very much involved. Rich sensorimotor experience is basic in all of these programs, however. Whether the babies are cared for in groups, as in the Children's Center in Syracuse, N.Y. [13], or taught by tutors in the home, as in programs at the University of Illinois [75] and the National Institute of Mental Health in Washington [89], or taught by mothers who have received special parent education, as at the University of Florida [38], infants are given a variety of toys, materials, and sensorimotor experiences suited to their level of development. Results reported from infant education studies are positive, in terms of measured cognitive gain. In Syracuse, the mean gain in developmental quotient was 5.6 points after 7.5 months [13]. The Washington project, using measures at intervals from 14 months to 36 months, showed steadily increasing differences in mean scores between the experimental and control groups. Of special interest here are the highly significant differences on a perceptual test at 3 years [101]. The Florida project, using the Griffiths Mental Development Scale on the babies' first birthdays, reported significant superiority of the experimental group in general IQ, hearing, speech, and eye and hand coordination [38]. The Illinois project reported significant gains after one year of home tutoring, in IQ as measured by the Stanford-Binet, and significant differences between experimental and control groups on conceptual tests [75].

Communication

Communication gradually takes on a conscious and purposeful quality, overlaid upon the subcortical feeling and tactual experiences and behavior displays of the newborn. The baby cuddles and snuggles in ways that spell love and affection to adults. Perhaps to the baby it means simply a good feeling or a feeling of warmth and closeness. It is a relationship which a baby can choose or reject, since even during the first half of the first year, he will sometimes snuggle close, relaxing and melting his body to conform with the adult's while at other times he will stiffen and push his body upright. During the second year, to cuddle or not to cuddle is a choice that the baby prefers to make. While he wants and needs loving arms and a hospitable lap, it is important to him to take it or leave it according to how he feels at the moment. He cries and shoves the gushing auntie who snatches him up to hug and kiss him at an inappropriate time, communicating to her clearly.

Stroking, patting, and hugging develop out of early cuddling. Kissing probably comes from the pursing reflex of feeding. During his first two years, the baby takes into himself the acts of love he has experienced, the gestures by which his family have symbolized their love for him. He gives them back, and the expression of love becomes more of a true communication.

Children in the second year often communicate purposefully with their hands, pulling another person to show him something, pushing him away, putting a hand over a mouth that is saying what the child does not want to hear, pointing at food, toys, and wet pants. Such language of the hands can be very effective in transferring ideas, even without a single word. Insofar as they achieve what the baby wants, these methods of communicating are, to him, adequate ways of coping with the world.

Vocal communication begins with crying, which has a variety of patterns in the neonate [110]. Spectrograph analysis has shown the basic cry of the newborn to consist of a characteristic rhythm of cry, rest, inspiration, rest. Adults usually interpret the basic cry as meaning hunger, although Wolff says it has no causal relationship with hunger. Variations from the basic rhythm are commonly identi-fied as the "mad" or angry cry, the pain cry, and the frustration cry. There is also a typical cry of a brain-damaged baby, more shrill and piercing than a normal cry. Mothers usually respond differently to cries, especially experienced mothers. They are likely to be tolerantly amused after answering a "mad" cry and disturbed when they hear a pain cry.

Bell and Ainsworth [7] have analyzed the relationship between infants' crying and maternal responsiveness during the first year of life. In general, the more re-sponsive the mother, the less often the baby cried and the shorter his periods of crying. Babies who cried little and whose crying decreased during the year had mothers who were more responsive than did babies who cried a great deal and whose crying increased. Babies who decreased in crying and who had responsive mothers were more likely than their opposites to communicate through channels other than crying.

Not crying at 1 month is a passive reaction to frustration; it is correlated with passivity at 1 year, shown both by crying, at that age, and by apparently waiting to be carried over a barrier [61]. Crying, or the tendency to cry, remains in everyone's repertory of communication as a way of showing distress.

Language. The great human invention, spoken language, is of vast significance as a method of communication. "The child may begin as a parrot, imitating what others say, but he will end as a poet, able to say things that have not been said before but which will be grammatical and meaningful in his community" [11]. The human baby, unlike all other babies, has innate capacities for understanding and producing speech. Some investigators suggest that the human brain has a genetically given predisposition to develop a set of special structures which generate language [69]. The language generator must include information-processing pro-cedures which are activated by exposure to speech. The language generator can respond to any language, and of course the language to which the child is exposed determines what he will understand and speak. At birth the infant vocalizes and responds to sounds. He interacts with his environment through his genetically given organs of speech and brain structures to understand and produce language. Language comprehension can be built up without producing speech at the same time. Since deaf and blind children learn to speak, neither hearing nor seeing is essential for language learning. Some sort of interaction with a speech community, however, is necessary. Maturation of the nervous system, the respiratory system, and the organs of eating are also basic to language development. In fact, language is in-timately related to all the maturation and learning that take place in the child.

Beginnings of Speech. The amount of vocalizing by an infant is influenced by various factors, some of which were investigated in boy and girl babies between 7 days and 14 days of age and again at 85–95 days [50]. As can be seen by Figure 3–11 the amount of vocalization varied considerably with the state of the infant, at both 10 days and 90 days of age. The infants were most vocal in the active awake state, defined as eyes open and sustained movement involving more than one limb. The passive awake and drowsy states included considerably less vocalization, even less than the state of active sleep. There is a sequence in the sounds that all babies make, and considerable regularity in the ages at which they are produced [45, 46, 48]. The first noncrying sounds are vowels. During the first 2 months about four vowel sounds are heard in noncrying vocalization. The earliest vowels are those made in the front part of the mouth. A new vowel sound appears about

164 Infants

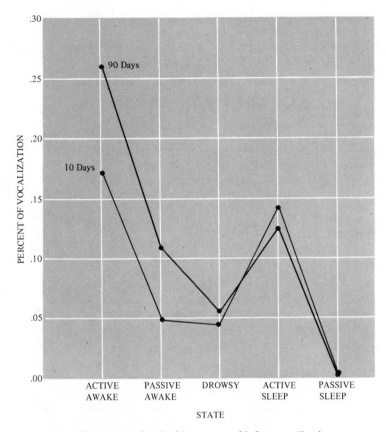

Figure 3–11. Age and state associated with amount of infant vocalizations.

SOURCE: Reprinted by permission from S. J. Jones and H. A. Moss, "Age, State and Maternal Behavior Associated with Infant Vocalizations." Paper presented at the meeting of the Society for Research in Child Development, Santa Monica, March 29, 1969.

every two months during the first year. The first consonant, *H*, is associated with gasping and crying. The early consonants are those made in the back of the throat, and the labials and dentals are the last to come.

The sounds made at the earliest stages of development are based on movements similar to those used in sucking and swallowing. It is only after breathing and eating and physiological equilibrium are established that the infant coos and plays vocally. Progress in language seems to be associated with postural development, too. "Talking back," or responding vocally to a human face and/or voice, first occurs at 2 or 3 months, the time when the baby holds his head erect. Since it is well-known that babies will talk more when a person responds to their vocalizing, one study focused on different types of social stimulation, to see which is most effective [91]. Three-months-old babies were compared as to amount of vocalizing after their utterances were reinforced by an adult talking, smiling, or rubbing the baby's abdomen, or by combinations of these adult behaviors. Results showed all reinforcing conditions to be effective for increasing infant vocalizing. A variety of adult action will increase vocalizing in babies.

The early sounds made by infants have been classified into discomfort cries and

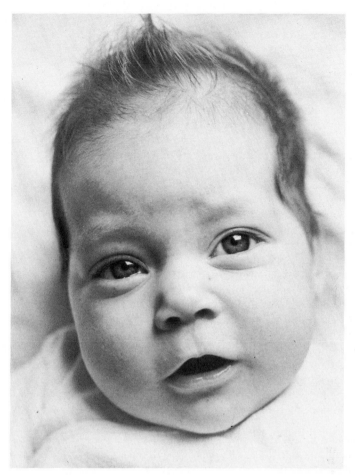

Halvar Loken

comfort sounds, in an attempt to show how language has biological roots [64]. Both types of sounds are, of course, expressive. Discomfort cries, which begin immediately after birth, at first consist of front, narrow vowels, frequently shrill and nasalized, resulting from tension in the whole body including the face. In the second stage of discomfort cries, consonants like *w*, *l*, and *h* are added. The third stage of discomfort cries includes *m* and *n* sounds. Comfort sounds occur in a relaxed state, starting after discomfort cries have begun. The first stage of comfort sounds are vowel-like and indistinct, developing into *a*, *o*, *u*. Back consonants, such as *g*, *k*, *r*, are added in the second stage and front consonants, *p*, *b*, *m*, *t*, *d*, *n*, in the third stage. The almost-universal use of *mama* or *nana* for mother or nurse might be accounted for by the fact that if the hungry baby makes anticipatory sucking movements while giving a nasalized discomfort cry, the result is mama or nana. *Papa* might be explained as the result of vocalizing in a state of relaxation [64].

Babbling is a series of repetitive sounds, uttered in a state of contentment and relaxation. In contrast to expressive sounds of comfort and discomfort, babbling seems to be done for its own sake. The baby seems to be playing with sounds. It may be the time when the baby practices the phonemes (smallest units of sound) typical of his family's language and when he minimizes or drops the phonemes not used by that language [83]. The greatest number of phonemes are produced between ages 8 and 12 months. The peak for repetition of sounds is at 12 months. Some of the American infant's babbling sounds like words to the adults near him. American parents respond in a special way to *tata* and *dada*, for instance, but not to *geegee* or *lili*. Thus the older infant practices sounds he hears spoken around him and also receives reinforcement (reward) when he chances to utter sounds that resemble real words. In the early months, however, at least the first three, all babies make the same sounds whether they hear normal human speech or not, as shown by a comparison of sounds made by infants of deaf and hearing parents [60]. This is not to say that they cannot tell the differences between different kinds of sounds, however, but to point out that they make a variety of sounds spontaneously.

Other events connected with the mouth are probably of great importance in language development. It is during the time that the teeth are erupting, 6 to 28 months, that the labial and dental sounds are established. The connection with early sucking and swallowing has been mentioned. Spoon and cup feeding and swallowing solids are associated with the babbling period. At 10 months, most infants handle solids well, eating a variety of them and chewing some chopped foods. At this time also, considerable vocalizing occurs in the feeding situation [68].

Expressive jargon, a kind of speech used in the middle of the second year, is not communication in the sense of expressing ideas through words. The youngster sounds as though he were really talking, but none of it makes sense because there are no real words in it, rather like double-talk. There are rhythm rises and falls and feeling in the sounds. Expressive jargon is probably an expression of feeling for the child, perhaps of ideas, and it may be intended as a contact with another person.

Beginnings in Use of Words. Parents are likely to record the baby's first word as an important milestone, although it may be hard to tell whether the word is used with real meaning. Children have been known to say meaningful first words as early as 7 months, as did the little girl who commented "buh" each time the hourly bus thundered past her house. The median time for uttering the first word is about 11 months, for children of middle-upper socioeconomic families [66]. Two words are the most common vocabulary at 12 months. The year-old baby covers a lot of territory under his own powers of locomotion, whether it be creeping, or walking with support, or even independent walking. A rush of new experiences stimulates the learning of new words. A single word at this point stands for a whole experience, often an emotionally toned one. "CAR" might mean, "Here we are, going for a ride in the car, seeing the wide world and having such an exciting time together." At 16 months, Becky's word, "Ow" meant, "This particular object is out of place, or inappropriately arranged. I am not going to continue with my play until you make everything right." Single words can also be commands, requests, names, and actions. The one-word sentence is the usual mode of expression from about 12 to 18 months, when the baby begins to combine words [66]. The first combinations may be functionally one-word utterances, such as *allgone* or *whazzat*? While the average vocabulary increases slowly between 12 and 18 months, it picks up quickly during the following six months. Most babies start to combine words during this time when they are adding words rapidly. The early two-word sentence usually consists of a noun and a verb or predicate word, such as *Daddy allgone*. Words are usually put together in the right order, although the sentences are not complete and words are omitted. The words which give the essential meaning are the ones used first. One reason for this may be that those are the words stressed by adults, just as when children try to repeat words that are too long and difficult, they reproduce the stressed syllables, such as '*raffe* for *giraffe*' [10, p. 219].

Understanding of Language. Communication is a reciprocal process; language must be understood as well as spoken. The understanding of what other people say occurs before the ability to express oneself in words, as you can see in yourself by the many words which you understand yet never use in speech. The child as a talker has been studied more than the child as a listener because it is more difficult to detect what he hears than what he says. Recent studies have shown, however, that infants under a year of age make fine discriminations in listening to speech Infants between 20 and 24 weeks of age showed that they perceived a difference between *bah* and *gah* when their heart rates changed upon presentation of *bah* after becoming habituated to *gah* [71]. When tapes of the mother's voice and of distortions of the mother's voice were presented to infants of 3, 6, and 9 months, the infants showed through quieting and crying behavior that they discriminated the difference [100]. Another study [107] found 6-month-olds adapting their production of vowels and consonants to differing numbers of vowels and consonants played to them on tapes. When boys between 11 and 15 months of age were given opportunities to choose which recorded sounds they would hear, these infants showed definite preferences which changed from time to time [30]. Operating a machine attached to the playpen, the infants could choose between the mother's voice, a stranger's voice, music, and between different types of vocalized sounds. The subjects showed that they could tell the difference and they preferred some to others, such as the mother's voice over simple music.

Understanding of words is ordinarily shown between 9 and 12 months when babies respond and adjust to such words as *no* and *bye-bye*. An occasional infant shows comprehension of words earlier, as did the little girl of 6 months who would open her mouth when her mother said *peaches* after keeping it firmly shut on presentation of squash with the word *squash*. *No, bye-bye*, and *peaches* are not merely sounds but indicators of situations which have important meaning for the baby.

Autonomy and Language. The ability to communicate with language must surely facilitate the sense of autonomy. For instance, saying "drink" can produce water at one's lips or "out" can transform the whole environment from indoors to outdoors. The extension of the child's powers and control is enormous. As it dawns upon him that everything has a name, that verbal symbols exist and that he can use them, he must have a surge of satisfaction over his expanded powers. One can imagine next a push to discover just how much he can do with these symbols, words, in both understanding and controlling the world and the people in it, including himself.

The End of Infancy. By the end of the sensorimotor period, the child has gone about as far as a creature can go without true language. Here is where other animals stop in their mental development, but man takes a great leap forward. *Words come to stand for things and actions.* Instead of having to go through sensory and motor acts, words can be manipulated in a twinkling. One doesn't even have to be where the problem is. He can think and talk about things which are remote in time and space. *The world is expanded and differentiated* as words come to stand for parts of experience which were formerly embedded in a larger experience. (Knowing *red*, he can pick out things that are red.) *Words are combined.* Here is what makes man's speech truly different from the utterances of birds and animals. He can combine words in ways which he has not even heard before, to mean something which has the same meaning for his listener. No wonder that, for many students of human nature, this intellectual leap marks the end of infancy, since it transforms the individual into a very different kind or person.

Parents' Contribution to Language Development. Language education is another activity which goes on spontaneously for normal infants in normal homes, with the mother taking the lead as teacher. The mother and others ordinarily talk to the baby in affectionate tones while they are feeding, bathing, changing diapers, picking up, cuddling, and otherwise taking care of the baby. There is also the conversation of the household which forms a background and punctuation marks in an infant's experience.

Students of human nature have long pondered on how infants learn to speak. Imitation and reinforcement of meaningful sounds by parents are understandable enough as contributing to the learning of language, but they do not explain why the child tries to imitate. The structure of the organs of speech and spontaneous exercising of them in vocal play are also understandable as part of the process. Research on language and personality disorders has led to an appreciation of the mother's essential role in language development. Slowness in starting to talk, defective articulation, and stuttering are all associated with certain kinds of disturbed parent–child relationships [67, 68].

Several studies shed light on the process of learning to talk, showing how it is related to the infant's experiences in the family. Infants vocalized more when adults smiled at them than when they looked with solemn faces at the babies [85]. A psychologist noted that his 10-weeks-old infant made an average of 4 sounds per 3-minute period under ordinary circumstances. When the father said "Hello" every 10 seconds, the baby averaged 18 sounds per 3-minute period [63]. An experiment on influencing sound production used subjects of lower socioeconomic status between 13 and 30 months of age [47]. Their parents were given picture-story books and encouraged to read to the toddlers. At the end of the experimental period, the stimulated children were producing significantly more sounds than a control group. Several investigations have shown the language development of infants in institutions to be below normal. One such study [81] found speech development the most retarded of the four Gesell areas, which are described on page 169. Production was more retarded than comprehension. Sound production was beginning to be deficient in the second month and no words were spoken at 1 year. Another study [84] conducted in an institution compared the behavior of babies who had many caretakers with that of babies who were cared for by only one person. From 6 to 8 months of age, the experimental infants had the attentive care of one person for seven and a half hours a day. They became more socially responsive than babies on the regular routine. At 18 months of age, after they had settled down in adoptive homes, the infants were tested again. The only significant difference between experimental and control groups was that the former vocalized more. The "quality of stimulation," mentioned before [111] as significant, probably operated here. One caretaker would be more likely than many caretakers to offer stimuli appropriate to the child as an individual.

These studies offer convincing proof that the infant's early experience with people's talking have definite effects on his own language behavior. One theory suggests that sounds become associated with mother and with the experiences of comfort and stimulation which her presence brings [73]. As the baby hears himself make a sound like mother makes, he feels comforted and happy, just as he does in her presence. Thus he stimulates himself to make more noises like mother makes. "Words are reproduced if and only if they are first made to sound good in the context of affectionate care and attention." This theory has been borne out by a study in which the sound production of infants was shown to be related to the warmth and amount of vocalization of their mothers [82]. On visits to the infants' homes, records were made of their sound production, including crying as well as cooing. Correlations between infant vocalization and mother vocalization and between infant vocalization and mother warmth increased with age.

The early stages of learning to talk are deeply emotional as well as intellectual and motor. Language is embedded in the total mass of experience, affected by a multitude of factors. None of the studies mentioned above explains *why* children begin to talk.

Measuring Infant Intelligence

Many tests of infant behavior are available. Three widely used tests are the Gesell Developmental Test [35], Bayley's Scales of Infant Development [6], and the Cattell Infant Intelligence Scale [14]. Uzgiris and Hunt's ordinal scales, based on Piaget's delineation of stages of sensorimotor development, constitute an instrument which is used for research in infant development [102].

The Gesell tests consist of four categories of items—motor, adaptive, language, and personal–social behavior—arranged at age levels according to where the average child showed the behavior pattern. In testing an infant, his behavior in each area can be matched to a normative level, giving his developmental age in motor, adaptive, language, and personal–social behavior. Conflicting conclusions have been drawn from studies on the predictive value of the Gesell tests. Some studies have shown little or no correlation between Gesell scores and later intelligence test scores [98]. Other investigators have found the Gesell tests to predict later behavior very well, as in a study which found significant correlation with an intelligence test (WISC) at 10 years [4]. The tests are also helpful in detecting and diagnosing neurological abnormalities.

The Bayley Scales of Infant Development consist of a motor scale and a mental scale, derived from repeated examinations of 1409 infants in 12 research centers scattered throughout the United States [70]. Norms are given for each half-month level. The Bayley scales have been used in several different parts of the world, since they provide a method for comparing different populations of infants. Bayley mental scale data from Israeli infants have been factor analyzed into different scales, the names of which suggest the main functions included in them: eye–hand, manipulation, object–relation, imitation–comprehension, vocalization–social contact, and active vocabulary [58]. The items of the first two scales can be classified as belonging to Piaget's third stage of sensorimotor development, the third scale to Piaget's fourth stage. All three first scales are similar to Gesell's Adaptive Behavior.

The Cattell Scale was developed as a downward extension of the Stanford–Binet test of Intelligence. Like the Stanford-Binet, it provides a mental age score, which can be converted into an intelligence quotient. The scale, given at 8 months, showed significant low correlations with IQ at 7 years for white and black girls and for white boys, but not for black boys [37]. When the Bayley Scale was given at 20 months to a sample of children drawn from a whole community in Hawaii, it was a good predictor of IQ at age 10 [108]. Combined with a pediatrician's appraisals, the tests served even better. Problems in school achievement could be expected when Cattell IQ and pediatricians' ratings were low. There seems to be little doubt that clinicians can use Gesell and Cattell tests to predict retarded, average, and advanced development.

Summary

The sense of trust grows as the baby has successful experiences in seeking and finding food, comfort, and stimulation, as he gains more and more control of his body, and as he comes to realize that certain regularities and permanencies exist in the world. He develops trust in his mother and in other key people as they repeatedly interact satisfactorily with him.

The sense of autonomy grows quickly during the second year, as the baby realizes his power as a maker of choices. He knows himself as a person who can decide which action to take, to do or not to do, to hold on or to let go. Healthy personality growth results not only from experiencing himself as choosing, but upon an accompanying conviction that what he does is generally all right and acceptable. The negative feelings typical of this stage are doubt and shame, feelings which occur when the child has too few opportunities for choosing and also when his choices are disastrous.

Physical development is rapid during infancy, with changes occurring in appearance and proportions. The deciduous teeth erupt. The basic physiological processes of respiration and temperature control become regularized, along with the timing of eating, sleeping, and elimination. Feeding behavior matures as the infant learns to hold his food, to sit up, to drink from a cup, to chew, and to control situations by talking. Although no specific technique of feeding has been shown to have definite results, the emotional context of feeding is significant. Weaning, the substitution of cup for breast or bottle, can be conducted and timed in various ways. When offered a wide variety of simple foods, year-old babies choose adequate diets. Many of the infant's autonomous acts occur in feeding situations.

Progress in locomotion takes place in a regular sequence of achievements. Creeping is perfected during the first year, walking during the second. The sense of autonomy grows as the child gains upright position and as he becomes more and more mobile, enlarging the scope of his interactions and his possibilities for choice making. Manipulation also develops through a regular sequence, increasing the baby's competence in exploring his environment, changing it, and understanding it.

Attention is determined by certain properties of stimuli and by the infant's maturity and experience. Movement, contour, and complexity are attractive to young infants. Faces are especially compelling. When objects are becoming familiar (the child is building a schema or inner representation), they are very attractive. When the object *is* familiar (the schema is well developed), novelty, in the form of a variation from the schema, is preferred.

Cognition is the activity of coming to know and understand. Cognitive development takes place in a sequence which stretches throughout infancy, childhood, and adolescence. The infant first interacts with his environment through reflex patterns. Then he adapts and combines these patterns to enlarge his repertory. He comes to realize that objects and people continue to exist even when he cannot see them. He experiments, trying out different kinds of actions in order to see their results. Finally, he imitates and pretends, representing objects and actions to himself mentally. As he cognizes the environment, he also comes to know himself more clearly, as an object which is distinct from the rest of the world. He also realizes his mother as a creature distinct from himself and from everything else. Cognitive development is promoted by a mother and other members of the family who offer the baby a rich variety of experiences.

The acquisition of language extends the child's powers, encouraging growth of the sense of autonomy. The baby discovers that words stand for objects and actions, and that everything has a name. Language learning takes place in the context of family communication, the baby experiencing other people talking to each other as well as direct interaction with his mother and others. The process is deeply emotional as well as cognitive and motor.

The Gesell, the Cattell, and the Bayley tests of infant behavior can be used to distinguish between retarded, average, and advanced development. Combined with other kinds of data they can also be used to predict later intellectual development.

References

1. Ainsworth, M. D. S. Personal communication to the authors. April, 1963.
2. Ainsworth, M. D. S., & Bell, S. M. Attachment, exploration and separation: Illustrated by the behavior of one-year olds in a strange situation. *Child Devel.*, 1970, **41**, 49–67.
3. Albino, R. C., & Thompson, V. J. The effects of sudden weaning on Zulu children. In W. Dennis (Ed.). *Readings in child psychology.* Englewood Cliffs, N.J.: Prentice-Hall, 1963, pp. 128–148.
4. Ames, L. B. Predictive value of infant behavior examinations. In B. Staub & J. Hellmuth (Eds.), *Exceptional infant.* Vol. I: *The normal infant.* Seattle: Special Child Publications, 1967, pp. 207–239.
5. Bayley, N. Comparisons of mental and motor test scores for ages 1–15 months by sex, birth order, race, geographic location and education of parents. *Child Devel.*, 1965, **36**, 379–411.
6. Bayley, N. *Bayley's scales of infant development.* New York: Psychological Corporation, 1968.
7. Bell, S. M., & Ainsworth, M. D. S. Infant crying and maternal responsiveness: Reinforcement reassessed. Paper presented at the meeting of the Eastern Psychological Association, Atlantic City, June, 1970.
8. Blank, M. Some maternal influences on infants' rates of sensorimotor development. Paper presented at the meeting of the Society for Research in Child Development, Berkeley, April 12, 1963.
9. Breckenridge, M. E., & Murphy, M. N. *Growth and development of the young child* (8th ed.). Philadelphia: Saunders, 1969.
10. Brown, R. *Social psychology.* New York: Free Press, 1965.
11. Brown, R., & Berko, J. Word association and the acquisition of grammar. *Child Devel.*, 1960, **31**, 1–14.

12. Calder, R. Food supplementation for prevention of malnutrition in the pre-school child. In National Research Council, *Preschool child malnutrition: Primary deterrent to human progress.* Washington: National Academy of Sciences, 1966.

13. Caldwell, B. M., & Richmond, J. B. The children's center in Syracuse, New York. In C. A. Chandler et al, *Early child care.* New York: Atherton, 1968, pp. 326–358.

14. Cattell, P. *The measurement of intelligence of infants.* New York: Psychological Corporation, 1940.

15. Charlesworth, W. R. Persistence of orienting and attending behavior in infants as a function of stimulus-locus uncertainty. *Child Devel.,* 1966, **37,** 473–491.

16. Children's Bureau. *Your baby's first year.* Washington, D.C.: U.S. Govt. Printing Office, 1962.

17. Cravioto, J. Nutritional deficiencies and mental performance in childhood. In D. C. Glass (Ed.), *Environmental influences.* New York: Rockefeller University Press and Russell Sage Foundation, 1968.

18. Davis, C. M. Self-selection of diet by newly weaned infants. *Am. J. Dis. Child.,* 1928, **39,** 651–679.

19. Davis, C. M. Self-selection of diets. *The Trained Nurse and Hospital Review,* 1931, **86**:5. Cited in C. A. Aldrich & M. M. Aldrich, *Feeding our old-fashioned children.* New York: Macmillan, 1941.

20. Davis, C. M. Self-selection of food by children. *Am. J. Nursing,* 1935, **35,** 403–410.

21. Dean, R. F. Effects of malnutrition, especially of slight degree, on the growth of young children. *Courrier,* 1965, **15,** 73–83.

22. Dennis, W. Causes of retardation among institutional children: Iran. *J. Genet. Psychol.,* 1960, **96,** 46–60.

23. Dennis, W., & Najarian, P. Infant development under environmental handicap. *Psychol. Mono.,* 1957, **71,** 1–13.

24. Edwards, E. P. Kindergarten is too late. *Sat. Rev.,* 1968, June 15, 68–70, 76–79.

25. Erikson, E. H. *Childhood and society.* New York: Norton, 1963.

26. Falade, S. Le développement psychomotor du jeune *African* originaire du Sénégal au cours de sa première année. Paris: Foulon, 1955. Cited in Geber [33].

27. Fantz, R. L. Visual perception from birth as shown by pattern selectivity. *Ann. N.Y. Acad. Sci.,* 1965, **118,** 793–814.

28. Fantz, R. L., & Nevis, S. Pattern preferences and perceptual-cognitive development in early infancy. *Merrill–Palmer Quart.,* 1967, **13,** 77–108.

29. Flavell, J. H. *The developmental psychology of Jean Piaget.* Princeton, N.J.: Van Nostrand, 1963.

30. Friedlander, B. Z. The effect of speaker identity, voice inflection, vocabulary, and message redundancy on infants' selection of vocal reinforcement. *J. Exper. Child Psychol.,* 1968, **6,** 443–459.

31. Garn, S. M. The applicability of North American growth standards in developing countries. *Canad. Med. Assoc. J.,* 1965, **93,** 914–919.

32. Garn, S. M., Lewis, A. B., & Kerewsky, R. S. Genetic, nutritional and maturational correlates of dental development. *J. Dent. Res.,* 1964, **44,** 228–242.

33. Geber, M. The psychomotor development of African children in the first year and the influence of maternal behavior. *J. Soc. Psychol.*, 1958, **47**, 185–195.
34. Gesell, A., et al. *The first five years of life.* New York: Harper, 1940.
35. Gesell, A., & Amatruda, C. *Developmental diagnosis.* New York: Hoeber, 1951.
36. Gesell, A., & Ilg, F. *Feeding behavior of infants.* Philadelphia: Lippincott, 1937.
37. Goffeney, B., Henderson, N. B., & Butler, B. V. Negro–white, male–female 8-month developmental scores compared with 7-year WISC and Bender Test Scores. *Child Devel.*, 1971 (in press).
38. Gordon, I. J. Stimulation via parent education. *Children*, 1969, **16**, 57–59.
39. Griffiths, R. *The abilities of babies.* New York: McGraw-Hill, 1954.
40. Haaf, R. A., & Bell, R. Q. A facial dimension in visual discrimination by human infants. *Child Devel.*, 1967, **38**, 893–899.
41. Halverson, H. M. An experimental study of prehension in infants by means of systematic cinema records. *Genet. Psychol. Mono.*, 1931, **10**, 107–286.
42. Heard, C. R. C., & Turner, M. R. Glucose tolerance and related factors in dogs fed diets of suboptimal protein value. *Diabetes*, 1967, **16**, 96.
43. Hunt, J. McV. Experience and the development of motivation: Some reinterpretations. *Child Devel.*, 1960, **31**, 498–504.
44. Hunt, J. McV. *Intelligence and experience.* New York: Ronald, 1961.
45. Irwin, O. C. Infant speech: equations for consonant–vowel ratio. *J. Speech Dis.*, 1946, **11**, 177–180.
46. Irwin, O. C. Infant speech: Vowel and consonant frequency. *J. Speech Dis.*, 1946, **11**, 123–125.
47. Irwin, O. C. Infant speech: Effect of systematic reading of stories. *J. Speech Hear. Res.*, 1960, **3**, 187–190.
48. Irwin, O. C., & Chen, H. P. Infant speech: Vowel and consonant types. *J. Speech Dis.*, 1946, **11**, 27–29.
49. Jackson, R. L. Effect of malnutrition on growth of the preschool child. In National Research Council, *Preschool child malnutrition: Primary deterrent to human progress.* Washington: National Academy of Sciences, 1966.
50. Jones, S. J., & Moss, H. A. Age, state and maternal behavior associated with infant vocalizations. Paper presented at the meeting of the Society for Research in Child Development, Santa Monica, Calif., March 29, 1969.
51. Kagan, J., Henker, B. A., Hen-tov, A., Levine, J., & Lewis, M. Infants' differential reactions to familiar and distorted faces. *Child Devel.*, 1966, **37**, 519–532.
52. Kagan, J., & Lewis, M. Studies of attention in the human infant. *Merrill-Palmer Quart.*, 1965, **11**, 95–127.
53. Karelitz, S., Fisichelli, V. R., Costa, J., Karelitz, R., & Rosenfeld, L. Relation of crying activity in early infancy to speech and intellectual development at age three years. *Child Devel.*, 1964, **35**, 769–777.
54. Keet, M. P., Hansen, J. D. L., & Truswell, A. S. Are skinfold measurements of value in the assessment of suboptimal nutrition in young children? *Pediat.*, 1970, **45**, 965–972.
55. Kelley, V. C., & Bosma, J. F. Basal metabolism in infants and children. In I. McQuarrie (Ed.), *Brennemann's practice of pediatrics.* Vol. I. Hagerstown, Md.: W. F. Prior, 1957.

56. Keppel, F. Food for thought. In N. S. Scrimshaw & J. E. Gordon, *Malnutrition, learning and behavior*. Cambridge, Mass.: M.I.T. Press, 1968, pp. 4–9.
57. Knoblock, H., & Pasamanick, B. Further observations on the behavioral development of Negro children. *J. Genet. Psychol.*, 1953, **83**, 137–157.
58. Kohen-Raz, R. Scalogram analysis of some developmental sequences of infant behavior as measured by the Bayley Infant Scale of Mental Development. *Genet. Psychol. Mono.*, 1967, **76**, 3–21.
59. Kohen-Raz, R. Mental and motor development of kibbutz, institutionalized, and home-reared infants in Israel. *Child Devel.*, 1968, **39**, 489–504.
60. Lenneberg, E. H., Rebelsky, F. G., & Nichols, I. A. The vocalizations of infants born to deaf and to hearing parents. *Human Devel.*, 1956, **8**, 23–37.
61. Lewis, M. The meaning of a response, or why researchers in infant behavior should be oriental metaphysicians. *Merrill-Palmer Quart.*, 1967, **13**, 7–18.
62. Lewis, M., Kagan, J., Campbell, H., & Kalafat, J. The cardiac response as a correlate of attention in infants. *Child Devel.*, 1966, **37**, 63–71.
63. Lewis, M. M. *How children learn to speak*. New York: Basic Books, 1959.
64. Lewis, M. M. *Language, thought, and personality in infancy and childhood*. New York: Basic Books, 1963.
65. Lowenberg, M. E., et al. *Food and man*. New York: Wiley, 1968.
66. McCarthy, D. Language development in children. In L. Carmichael (Ed.), *Manual of child psychology* (2nd ed.). New York: Wiley, 1954, pp. 492–630.
67. McCarthy, D. Language disorders and parent–child relationships. *J. Speech Dis.*, 1954, **19**, 514–523.
68. McCarthy, D. Language development. In N. E. Wood (Ed.), Language development and language disorders: A compendium of lectures. *Mono. Soc. Res. Child. Devel.*, 1960, **25**:3, 5–14.
69. McNeill, D. Developmental psycholinguistics. In F. Smith and G. A. Miller (Eds.), *The genesis of language: a psycholinguistic approach*. Cambridge, Mass.: M.I.T. Press, 1966.
70. Mendelson, M. A. Interdisciplinary approach to the study of the exceptional infant: A large scale research project. In B. Staub & J. Hellmuth (Eds.), *Exceptional infant*. Vol. I: *The normal infant*. Seattle: Special Child Publications, 1967, pp. 15–38.
71. Moffitt, A. R. Speech perception by 20–24 week-old infants. Paper presented at the meeting of the Society for Research in Child Development, Santa Monica, Calif., March 29, 1969.
72. Mönckeberg, F. Effect of early marasmic malnutrition on subsequent physical and psychological development. In N. S. Scrimshaw & J. E. Gordon (Eds.), *Malnutrition, learning and behavior*. Cambridge, Mass.: M.I.T. Press, 1968, pp. 269–278.
73. Mowrer, O. H. Hearing and speaking: An analysis of language learning. *J. Speech Dis.*, 1958, **23**, 143–151.
74. Murphy, L. B. *The widening world of childhood*. New York: Basic Books, 1962.
75. Painter, G. The effect of a structured tutorial program on the cognitive and language development of culturally disadvantaged infants. *Merrill-Palmer Quart.*, 1969, **15**, 279–294.
76. Parmelee, A. H., Schultz, H. R., & Disbrow, M. A. Sleep patterns of the newborn. *J. Pediat.*, 1961, **58**, 241–250.

77. Phatak, P., et al. (Eds.) Motor and mental growth of Indian babies of 1 month to 35 months. Unpublished Research Report No. 1. Baroda, India: Department of Child Development, University of Baroda.
78. Piaget, J. *The construction of reality in the child.* New York: Basic Books, 1954.
79. Piaget, J. *The origins of intelligence in children.* New York: Norton, 1963.
80. Piaget, J. *Six psychological studies.* New York: Random House, 1967.
81. Provence, S., & Lipton, R. C. *Infants in institutions.* New York: International Universities Press, 1962.
82. Rebelsky, F. G., Nichols, I. A., & Lenneberg, E. H. A study of infant vocalization. Paper presented at the meeting of the Society for Research in Child Development, April 12, 1963.
83. Rebelsky, F. G., Starr, R. H., & Luria, Z. *Language development: The first four years.* In Y. Brackbill (Ed.), *Infancy and early childhood.* New York: Free Press, 1967.
84. Rheingold, H., & Bayley, N. The later effects of an experimental modification of mothering. *Child Devel.,* 1959, **30**, 363–372.
85. Rheingold, H., Gerwitz, J. L., & Ross, H. W. Social conditioning of vocalizations in the infant. *J. Comp. Physiol. Psychol.,* 1959, **52**, 68–73.
86. Ricciuti, H. N. Object grouping and selective ordering behavior in infants 12 to 24 months old. *Merrill-Palmer Quart.,* 1965, **11**, 129–148.
87. Roberts, K. E., & Schoelkopf, J. A. Eating, sleeping, and elimination: Practices of a group of two and a half year old children. *Am. J. Dis. Child.,* 1951, **82**, 121–152.
88. Schaefer, A. E., & Johnson, O. C. Are we well fed? The search for the answer. *Nutrition Today,* 1969, **41**, 2–11.
89. Schaefer, E. S. A home tutoring program. *Children,* 1969, **16**, 59–61.
90. Schofield, L., & Uzgiris, I. C. Examining behavior and the concept of object. Paper presented at the meeting of the Society for Research in Child Development, Santa Monica, Calif., March 29, 1969.
91. Schwartz, A., Rosenberg, D., & Brackbill, Y. An analysis of the components of social reinforcement of infant vocalization. Paper presented at the meeting of the Society for Research in Child Development, Santa Monica, Calif., March 29, 1969.
92. Scrimshaw, N. S. The effect of the interaction of nutrition and infection on the preschool child. In National Academy of Sciences, *Preschool child malnutrition: Deterrent to human progress.* Washington, D.C.: National Research Council, 1966, pp. 63–73.
93. Scrimshaw, N. S., & Gordon, J. E. *Malnutrition, learning and behavior.* Cambridge, Mass.: M.I.T. Press, 1968.
94. Shirley, M. *The first two years: A study of twenty-five children.* Vol. I: *Postural and locomotor development.* Monograph Series, 7. Minneapolis: University of Minnesota, Institute of Child Welfare, 1933.
95. Smart, M. S., & Smart, R. C. *Living and learning with children.* Boston: Houghton Mifflin, 1961.
96. Smith, S. S. The effect of stimuli of different modalities as reinforcers of lever-pushing by young children. Unpublished Ph.D. thesis. University of Vermont, 1970.
97. Stern, E., et al. Sleep cycle characteristics in infants. *Pediat.,* 1969, **43**, 65–70.

98. Stott, L. H., & Ball, R. S. Infant and preschool mental tests: Review and evaluation. *Mono. Soc. Res. Child Devel.*, 1965, **30**:3.

99. Super, C. M., Kagan, J., Morrison, F. J., Haith, M. M., & Weiffenbach, J. Discrepancy and attention in the 5-month infant. Unpublished manuscript. Harvard University, 1970.

100. Turnure, C. Response to voice of mother and stranger by babies in their first year. Paper presented at the meeting of the Society for Research in Child Development, Santa Monica, Calif., March 29, 1969.

101. U.S. Department of Health, Education, and Welfare. *Infant education research project Washington, D.C.* Superintendent of Documents, U.S. Govt. Printing Office, Washington, D.C., 1969.

102. Uzgiris, I. C. Ordinality in the development of schemas for relating to objects. In B. Staub & J. Hellmuth (Eds.), *Exceptional infant*. Vol. I: *The normal infant*. Seattle: Special Child Publications, 1967, pp. 315–348.

103. Valadian, I., Stuart, H. C., & Reed, R. B. Studies of illnesses of children followed from birth to eighteen years. *Mono. Soc. Res. Child. Devel.*, 1961, **26**:3.

104. Walters, C. E. Comparative development of Negro and white infants. *J. Genet. Psychol.*, 1967, **110**, 243–251.

105. Watson, E. H., & Lowrey, G. H. *Growth and development of children* (5th ed.). Chicago: Year Book, 1967.

106. Watson, J. S., & Ramey, C. T. Reactions to response-contingent stimulation in early infancy. Paper presented at the meeting of the Society for Research in Child Development. Santa Monica, Calif., March, 1969.

107. Webster, R. L. Selective suppression of infants' vocal responses by classes of phonemic stimulation. *Devel. Psychol.*, 1969, **1**, 410–414.

108. Werner, E. E., Honzik, M. P., & Smith, R. S. Prediction of intelligence and achievement at ten years from twenty months pediatric and psychologic examinations. *Child Devel.*, 1968, **39**, 1063–1075.

109. White, B. L., & Held, R. Plasticity of sensorimotor development in the human infant. In B. Staub & J. Hellmuth (Eds.), *Exceptional Infant*. Vol. I. Seattle: Special Child Publications, 1967, pp. 425–442.

110. Wolff, P. H. The natural history of crying and other vocalizations in early infancy. In B. M. Foss (Ed.), *Determinants of infant behavior:* IV. London: Methuen, 1969, pp. 81–109.

111. Yarrow, L. J., Rubenstein, J. L. & Pedersen, F. A. Dimensions of early stimulation: Differential effects on infant development. Paper presented at the meeting of the Society for Research in Child Development. Minneapolis, Minn., April 4, 1971.

Readings in
Emerging Resources for
Coping with the World

American values with regard to children are compared with Soviet values by the first author, psychologist David Rosenhan. He maintains that the Soviets are eager to have their infants and children develop just as fast as they can. Americans, on the other hand, are concerned with health, and although they believe that the child should be allowed to grow at his own rate, they have some ambivalence about precocity. The Soviets believe more strongly in environmental influence than do Americans. The reader can judge for himself how closely the next article is consistent with the American values described by Dr. Rosenhan.

The focus of an article by Lois B. Murphy, well known for her research on personality development and her long-standing concern for the well-being of children, is on what young children need for optimal development. Dr. Murphy summarizes and clarifies what is known about meeting children's needs and what needs to be learned through research.

The synchronization between motor development and language development is shown in an excerpt from Biological Foundations of Language, *by Eric Lenneberg. His emphasis on maturation as a basis for speech and other learning makes an interesting contrast to the Soviet beliefs described by Dr. Rosenhan. Lenneberg's chart of developmental milestones is very impressive.*

Preface to *Soviet Preschool Education*

David Rosenhan
SWARTHMORE COLLEGE

Not long ago, but long after I had completed my formal undergraduate and graduate training, I attended a seminar that proved to be one of the strangest and most stimulating in my career. Entitled: "What shall the values in

American education be?'', it was convened by William Kessen of Yale University for more than thirty people, all deeply committed to quality education through their disciplines, mainly psychology and education. Kessen made only one stipulation at the outset: that it would be a true seminar in that he would neither prime the meeting with his own ideas nor otherwise goad the participants to action, but would rather listen for the ideas that came from them.

A strange seminar indeed. Forty-five minutes passed, as I recall, in absolute silence, punctuated only by an occasional self-conscious giggle, enshrouded by anxious glances as one member looked to his peer for salvation from intellectual helplessness. The seminar terminated silently, profoundly. We went our ways.

What was it that sealed our mouths, fogged our wits? Lord knows we cared, for the issue of values goes right to the heart of educational programs, curricula and goals. We who were the planners, preachers and implementers in American education, had nothing to say about the premises that underlay our work. Sad, indeed. Was it that we feared to speak openly lest we offend the sensibilities of an illustrious colleague? Was it that the present turmoil in American education has shaken our values to the roots, to such a degree that the entire matter needs to be reconsidered and that the first approach to reconsideration is silence? Was it, perhaps, that no value consensus can be arrived at in a democracy such as our own that stresses individualism and the right of each man to have his own values? Was it, worst of all, that we had no values, that we traveled the American educational scene by the pragmatic seat of our pants, that we were carpenters rather than creators, implementers and not ideators?

This seminar (for it was truly that) was discussed heatedly for months to come. We never did answer these questions, nor did we finally come up with an educational Magna Carta upon which all could agree. We were, however, brought in that silence more poignantly than by words to examine the central issue of education: What shall our values be?

Our Soviet counterparts apparently have none of our problems in this regard. *Soviet Preschool Education: Teacher's Commentary* not only communicates clearly and in considerable detail the ways and means of proper education for children aged two months through seven years, but also the philosophies that should guide that education. I will not dilute your pleasure by describing at length those values here: they are amply and well interspersed among the educational instructions that are found in the volume. There are, however, tacit value metaphors hidden beneath the explicit philosophies and it will serve us some considerable gain to explicate some of these. Two that are most striking are what I would call the values of *precocity* and *intentional environmentalism*. They are, in many ways, overlapping categories and they emerge as forceful premises on the Soviet educational scene. Let us examine them in quite some detail.

It will surprise you, I am sure, as you peruse the first thirty pages of this volume, to find that the Soviets teach everything as early as they can. At four months, the rudiments of vocalization and sound discrimination are introduced: at eight months, the beginnings of toilet training. Play itself is ordered and designed to the child's capacity with a view to serving as the basis for what will come later. At one year of age, a full educational program is in swing: Esthetics—yes, esthetics!—through music appreciation; speech training;

neatness and toilet training; obedience and self-control; active stimulation of interest in the environment—these and many others constitute the core curriculum for infants. It is a sensible program, tailored to the infant's capacities with considerable leeway given to individual differences. But its most striking hallmark is its emphasis on precocity: that which will be learned inevitably ought to be learned early.

It is not automatically evident why earlier is better, and extreme precocity best. Perhaps for the Soviets it is simply a matter of insurance. Soviet preschools, by our standards, seem understaffed and overworked (teachers and their assistants put in a twelve hour day with only a 30 minute break). A mandate for precocity may serve to assure society that Soviet children will be functioning as they should be functioning when the appropriate time arrives. A more interesting view, however, holds that the Soviet imagination, like our own, is captured by the notion that precocity augurs future achievement, that the earlier we start the further we go. On this matter, the evidence is ambiguous at best, and the measure of that ambiguity is amply reflected in our own society. On the one hand, we do have a vigorous nursery school movement and a Headstart program (albeit one whose merit and future are, at this writing, clouded). There is, moreover, a privately held norm of precocity, especially in the middle class, that permits us to take great pleasure in the child who walks, talks or tumbles before these are expected, and encourages us to teach him at home before he is taught in school.

Yet we are ambivalent about the virtues of precocity; this is seen mainly in the laissez-faire theories of development that are tacitly and overtly held in our public school systems. In these theories cognitive development is linked to age and physical development, these latter held to be immutable, and therefore cognitive development immutable also. Such thinking is buttressed from several sources. First are the normative studies, such as by Gesell and Ilg, which dominate the common mind such that it thinks only of that which is ordinarily achieved and turns away from that which is potentially achievable. Second are the oversimplified views of Piagetian psychology which see cognitive growth as a naturally unfolding process that cannot be hastened. Finally, there is fear, most evident in the writings of Dr. Spock, that appears to originate in the presumed fragility of the child and leads us to feel that in attempting anything we may attempt too much, and by attempting too much the child might be harmed. (Not to speak of parental aspiration: better not to aspire than to risk failure.) The sum of the matter is that while we take joy on the occasion of precocity, we are hesitant to facilitate it, and herein lies our first tacit value contrast with the Soviets.

The norm of precocity is linked in Soviet thinking to intentional environmentalism. This is to say that on the question of the relative contribution of nature and nurture to cognitive social and personality development, they opt strongly for nurture. But nurture is not a random thing: environments don't simply happen. They are created, willy-nilly, or intentionally, by those who live in them. The Soviets prefer to intentionally create their environments, to leave as little as possible to chance happening. One senses throughout this volume that they have not only a fair image of the kind of person they would have at each stage of development, but also of the manner in which he might be created. Correctly or incorrectly, they believe that for a child to be sociable, he needs to spend his infancy in a crib with other infants: for him to have an appreciation of music at eight years, he needs to be systematically exposed to melody at age eight months; for language to blossom, its elements need to be inculcated early. Toilet training, speech, moral behavior, muscular development, independence, curiosity, cognition and conformity are all analyzed into their elemental components, graded for their difficulty, and systematically fed to the child just as early as possible.

The American system, by contrast, is more casual. Of course, we have no nurseries for our infants: until they are three years old (and commonly until five), our children are raised at home. That fact alone guarantees a greater diversity of child-rearing approaches, if only because there are no systematic social controls and mothers are not usually professionally-trained infant teachers. These facts notwithstanding, there *are* manuals for mothers, one of the most widely used being Spock's *Baby and Child Care*. And even taking into consideration that Spock speaks to parents and this volume to teachers, the diversity of approach is remarkable. Confronted by a child whose development is irregular in some respects, the Soviet teacher is urged to concentrate on the weaknesses with a view to bringing them up to par. Compare this to Spock's advice to the American mother confronted with the same dilemma: "Enjoy him as he is . . . that's how he'll grow up best . . . enjoy your child for what he is . . . and forget about the qualities he doesn't have." (pp. 43–44) Indeed, the very notion of facilitating or encouraging development, particularly in a formal way during the early years, is anathema, the mark of an overly pushy parent. Hear Spock again: "A child becomes interested in dressing dolls properly, coloring carefully, playing trains realistically, each at a certain stage of his development. You can't hurry him. When you try, you only make him feel incompetent. This does more harm than good . . . let *him* show *you* how [to play]." (pp. 306–307) Compare this now to the Russian mandate, here in connection with language development: "Every moment in which the nurse and her assistant are in close contact with the child must be utilized: during care, feeding, independent games and outdoor play. . . . Name objects at the moment children seem to take a particular interest in them; name actions and movements while the child is performing them. . . . Develop in the child the ability to imitate sounds and words used by adults and create the necessary conditions to stimulate the children to pronounce various sounds as often as possible." (p. 48) Clearly the Soviet approach is one of active intervention, while ours is mainly one of appreciative watching.

Perhaps the critical difference between the Soviet approach and ours lies herein: that we are concerned to avoid pathology and they to promote development; that our manual for child-rearing is authored by a physician whose main concern is to interpret and prevent illness and harm (. . . "and when you try, you only make him feel incompetent. This does more harm than good.") while theirs is compiled by educators whose central mission is the promotion of talent (. . . "Create the necessary conditions to stimulate the child . . ."). My own judgment and that of many of my colleagues is increasingly on the side of educational intervention from the earliest years. Much as the absence of vice is no guarantor of virtue, the absence of illness in no way signifies the maximal development of educational potential. If we believe (and the scientific evidence is now too large to ignore) that early experience is critical for subsequent development, we may need to become intentional environmentalists ourselves, leaving development not to fortuitous chance (too many children are under-privileged in that regard), not even to avoidance of injury, but to the careful and orderly elaboration of ability.

There is a close and sensible relationship between the practices recommended in this book and psychological theory and practice. Not that *all* psychological research is translated into practice, nor that only matters that have been clearly researched are recommended. Far from it: scientific psychology and scientific education are not so advanced that we can rely on them fully, but neither are they so retarded that they can teach us nothing. This volume, you will find, is a delightful blend of good sense and good science.

Take language development as a case in point. The common view, strongly buttressed by many normative studies, holds that language "develops": that at a certain age, the infant babbles "da-da," that somewhat later he acquires a more descriptive word or two, that by age two his vocabulary is larger, and by four, larger still. A moment's reflection, however, reminds us that language does not "develop," certainly not as second-year molars develop. It is acquired, learned, by exposure to speakers. And exposure to speakers is by no means equal for all children, as recent explorations into the language of under-privileged children have dramatically demonstrated. And if the child actively *learns* language (rather than passively developing it), language should be *teachable*, with better methods or with worse. The Soviets offer some concrete suggestions for language education.

For the infant, the words we speak have no meaning unless they are associated with things he somehow knows. Otherwise, words are quickly assimilated into the noisy and meaningless surroundings. Language teaching begins, reasonably enough, with precise pairing of familiar things with words. (Even before that, by training vocalization and sound discrimination.) "Mommy has arrived," the nurse says to the five-month-old. "Let's go to Mommy." By nine months the nurse is pointing to familiar toys and naming them; hiding the toy and asking the infant to find it; giving commands ("bring me the rattle"). Subsequently, a program for naming actions and abstractions is implemented and finally, as the child approaches the time to learn reading and writing (about seven years old), consciousness of phonics and word structure is developed. The stress is not only on active teaching, but on *programmatic* teaching of language, such that the steps constitute a sensible progression from the simple to the complex.

Readers familiar with the works of Vygotsky or Piaget, or the more recent efforts of Roger Brown, George Miller and John Flavell, will easily understand the relations between language and thought, and abstract learning itself. Some of the relevant research in this area is, in fact, presented in Volume I of *Soviet Preschool Education*. Clearly, the simple message of all research in this area is that language is too important a matter for its acquisition to be left to chance or passive "development." The foundations of thought and facilitators of interpersonal relationship must be taught actively, sensibly, relentlessly.

Neither is moral development left to the accident of growing up, to chance learning. Concern for others, moral judgment and behavior, thoughtfulness, respect and courtesy are taught, again at early ages. There will be some disagreement about how far moral education can proceed at age three, but clearly the rudiments are inculcated then, to be developed later. The Soviet program is specific about how this is done. Not by preachments alone, but by *actions* performed by adults jointly with children. Adults influence children by their behavior, by their personal approach to other people around them, toward traditions, and toward the homeland. Such personal moral qualities as humility, modesty, truthfulness, diligence, sociability, goodwill, cooperativeness, thoughtfulness and cheerfulness form the foundation of a child's moral being. The evaluation and development of these qualities is aided by the example set by the teacher, by the consistent and fair attitude she maintains towards all the children of the group. Many of the techniques recommended here are supported by and consistent with research findings that have been available both in America and abroad. Many other techniques seem to be based more on good sense, or at least on good intentions, and will require further verification.

The matter of verification is critical for those who would propose educational procedures as for those who would borrow them. If education is too important a matter to be left to chance, it is also too important to be left to good intentions, however well those seem founded in common sense. What is critical is what works, and how and why it works. For determining these there are no easy substitutes for research. One cannot really assess from these volumes the degree to which a substantial research effort in education is ongoing in the Soviet Union. Clearly some progress is being made, as is evident in Volume I: how much and how successful are the questions. In any event, for those who would utilize these promising Soviet techniques for the solution of educational problems elsewhere, the message is clear and urgent: a program of evaluation, no less substantial in commitment and fiscal magnitude than that of the educational program itself, is required.

There is not, to my knowledge, a manual quite like this one presently available. For older children there is, of course, Marie Montessori's *The Montessori Method*, which describes her work in the *Casa dei Bambini* in the slums of Rome. Even earlier, there is the writing of Pestalozzi, who apparently greatly influenced Soviet thinking on education, and of Froebel. Readers familiar with those writings will immediately sense important commonalities and differences. All of these writers, along with authors of these volumes, hold that development is an unfolding process, and that education consists simply of not hindering that process, and of providing the child with precisely what it requires from the environment at each stage of development. There are differences in view about what the environment needs to supply and how it should do so. Montessori, you will recall, opts for structure, carefully designing all manner of educational apparatus to the presumed needs of the children. This volume suggests no special equipment, relying rather on what society naturally provides: a ball, a doll, a flower. Soviet conceptualization, on the other hand, stresses a matter that is considerably muted, if it is present at all, in these other writings: the critical importance of a warm teacher-child relationship. Throughout this volume where the Soviets criticize their teachers, it is entirely for neglect and abuse of this relationship: for their rudeness, their ordinary tendency to make invidious comparisons between children, their confusion of curiosity with disobedience, their failure to sustain a loving, caring relationship. It is no small mission that they assign their teachers, to retain and encourage that which is personal and facilitating midst that which is systematically required and anomic. It does us well to recall, as we revise our own curricula for young children, that care precedes technique, that positive regard is a necessary ingredient for intellectual maturation.

If there has been a central message in education during the past century, it is that the child is father to the man, that what is acquired early determines in good measure what will be learned later. How early is "early"? For us, education in kindergarten begins around age five. Is that early enough? Perhaps it is for privileged children, though I doubt it. But it is patently not early enough for underprivileged ones for whom enrichment programs such as Headstart now begin at age three, and even at this age show no real pattern of merit. Clearly we shall have to begin earlier, for the underprivileged as perhaps for the privileged, at home or in formal institutions. For such a program. *Soviet Preschool Education* is unique and will provide an excellent first approximation for a general program.

Children Under Three: Finding Ways to Stimulate Development*

Lois Barclay Murphy
MENNINGER FOUNDATION

I. ISSUES IN RESEARCH

Since the beginning of World War II, the U.S. gross national product (GNP)—the aggregate of its agricultural and industrial output—has steadily increased. Unfortunately, the Nation has not proportionately increased its resources for protecting its human products. Neglect of prenatal care, birth defects, nutritional needs, and appropriate infant care lies behind our poor standing among the nations in infant mortality rates—13 highly developed nations have reported rates lower than the United States.[1] It also underlies much of the distorted development of children as reflected in mental retardation, delinquency, and mental illness. This neglect has been paralleled by the

Reprinted from *Children*, 1969, *6*, 46–51. By permission.

* The observations on which this article is based were made during work under two grants from the Public Health Service—MH10421 to the Children's Hospital of the District of Columbia and 5 R12 MH9236–02 to the Menninger Foundation, Topeka, Kans.
[1] United Nations, Department of Economic and Social Affairs, Statistical Office: Demographic yearbook, 1966. United Nations, N.Y. 1967.

country's failure to provide employment for the thousands of workers abandoned by employers as technology has superseded human labor on farms, in mines, and in factories.

As a result of such neglect of human needs, today large numbers of children throughout the Nation are unable to make use of the learning opportunities provided by the schools. Discouraged, depressed, undernourished parents become apathetic and so rear their children for passive tolerance of frustration rather than for active mastery of a skill. Too many children in lower socio-economic groups do not learn to learn; their speech, concepts, experience, and drive to achieve are inadequate for learning. Their normal aggression is not directed into socially constructive channels, and they have little help in dealing with emotional problems, which arise more often among the disadvantaged than among other segments of the population.[2] In the past decade, however, many pressures—the space race, a personal concern about retardation on the part of persons in high office, and research reporting school failure among millions of poor children, white, black, and Mexican-American—have brought about efforts to do something about their faltering intellectual development.

The first response was legislation to provide some Federal aid to the schools, but this could do little to help the child who arrived at kindergarten or the first grade with an irreversible intellectual handicap. Then came Project Head Start to ready the preschool child for school and also some exhilarating experiments in the cognitive stimulation of preschool children, sometimes reinforced by candy rewards. But it was discovered that "Head Start was too late" and candy was not enough. Some children's IQ's did increase as they participated in these experiments, but their scores tended to lapse back again or even to get lower after they entered school. As this tendency became apparent, there came a push for cognitive stimulation of babies, based on the research efforts of learning theorists. Some of these theorists, however, were operating from their own conceptual islands, ignoring the forces of drive, motivation, affective response, constitutional factors, individual personality, and subculture values that could thwart or attenuate the effects of learning techniques and gastric rewards. Nevertheless, some cognitive stimulators even asserted that the prevention of delinquency, emotional disturbance, and a negative self-image could all be achieved through early cognitive stimulation.

Meantime, other forces were at work. The stultifying and distorting effects of sterile institutional life on children without families had led to the widespread avoidance of institutional care. Foster families were to provide the nearest equivalent to a natural family for the children who had no "real" mother or father, or no adequate parents. In some cases this goal was achieved. But in the large cities, the limited space in most families' homes and the many parentless, neglected, or mistreated children defeated efforts to find foster homes for all who needed them; moreover, the stress experienced by families who attempted to bring up foster children in a crowded urban setting led in many instances to shifts from one home to another,[3] which defeated the aim of a stable family life for these children. After a series of acceptances and rejections,

[2] Srole, L., et al.: Mental health in the metropolis. McGraw-Hill, New York, N.Y. 1962.
[3] Mass, H. S.; Engler, R. E., Jr.: Children in need of parents. Columbia University press, New York, N.Y. 1959.

many children became disturbed and alienated and as a result they had difficulties in school and the community.

In response to these problems, the pendulum has swung back to a revived interest in group care, at least in the form of supplementary care during the day. This interest has become more intense as a result of the view that mothers who passively receive public assistance might better go to work and let their children be cared for in adequate day-care centers. Because of the simultaneous concern about school failures, the thinking about day care has tended to focus on cognitive stimulation, as if this were the only need to be met.

Most of the discussion of cognitive stimulation has been oriented toward children from 3 to 5 years old, but in the past 5 years children under 3 have also begun to receive attention. Under the impression that "Head Start is too late," research workers have been exploring the effects of cognitive stimulation on babies.

AN UNDERLYING ERROR   One major error underlies many failures to provide for adequate development: the notion that "We have *the* answer." There was a time when the central concern of administrators of child-care programs was to prevent infection; they thought that if the children were kept clean they would grow well. At other times, "the" answer was thought to be good nutrition, or fresh air, or activity, or freedom. And now it is cognitive stimulation. But disappointments have followed each one-track attempt to follow "the" one important prescription, as Skeels,[4] Spitz,[5] and others have shown in studying clean, but sterile, institutions. We now know that institutionalized children who are merely kept clean and well fed lack most of the ingredients for healthy personality, social, and cognitive development; and that these lacks contribute to varying degrees and kinds of deficiency and distortion—mental retardation, social inadequacy, disorganized behavior, delinquency, failure to grow, and at worst marasmus and death.

In Israeli kibbutzim and in the best day-care centers in the United States, the multiple needs of the child are met: warm, mothering caretakers provide stimulation, space for activity, time for free play, response to the child's efforts, along with lots of fresh air and good food—and a chance to experience joy. It seems paradoxical that so many recent investigators are again following a single track—cognitive stimulation through specific teaching programs—and overlooking many other aspects of development, despite evidence that nutrition, activity, emotions, and human relationships affect a child's learning.

Moreover, in many instances the idea of what learning is has been shaped by a narrow range of concepts such as vocabulary, memory, reasoning, and comprehension and by Piaget's insights regarding the child's development of time and space concepts and the conservation of objects. But the growth of a child's mind involves many cognitive functions (including complex sensory-motor and coping efforts) not measured in intelligence tests. These include, for example: differentiation between the familiar and the strange; the process of

[4] Skeels, Harold M.: Effects of adoption on children from institutions. *Children*, January–February 1965.
[5] Spitz, René: Hospitalism—an inquiry into the genesis of psychiatric conditions in early childhood. *In* The psychoanalytic study of the child, vol. I. International Universities Press, New York, N.Y. 1945.

familiarization (visual and auditory examination, manual manipulation, and so forth); movement-in-space problems; combining objects; solving problems requiring manipulation; use of tools, such as the door knob, screen hook, faucet knob; self-dressing—pulling off and putting on socks; finding or creating substitutes; and clarification of relationships and experience by rehearsing them in fantasy.

Ability to do such things develops in children who are growing up in an environment where they are exposed to a variety of objects, challenges, and opportunities to use their minds and bodies and can observe the everyday problem solving of their parents and brothers and sisters. As with all aspects of mental development, development of these skills needs the support of varied experience.

CRITERIA FOR EVALUATION   How then shall we formulate what is needed to foster good physical, emotional, social, and cognitive development? And what criteria should guide research for evaluating programs for children under 3?

Here I list seven basic areas to consider in evaluating proposals for early child care:

1. *Adequate nutrition*—proteins, vitamins, minerals, and other nutrients required for the physical development of the child. In many parts of the world, where infants receive insufficient protein and other nutrients, the mortality rates among children are high. A large proportion of those who manage to live are malnourished, vulnerable to infection, and retarded. Similar conditions are reported to exist among infants and small children in "hunger areas" of the United States.

2. *Ability to deal with the baby in distress.* How to handle the baby who has poor digestion, colic, diarrhea or constipation, or susceptibility to infection is still inadequately understood by many child-care workers. That there are *emotional and mental consequences of distress in early infancy* is even less appreciated. Such babies need help with gastrointestinal and other aspects of basic functioning. Marked or prolonged infantile distress, or both, can contribute to anxiety, hostile reactions, withdrawal, and disturbances of perception and cognition.

3. *Stimulation designed to meet the infants' needs, tolerance level, and capacity for enjoyment* at different stages of sensory-motor development, emotional response, and resources for self-management. What is too much for one infant may not be enough for another. The kind and amount of stimulation provided each infant have to be based on intelligent observations made by his mother or mother-surrogate. Sensitive mothers report such observations as: "He likes bright colors"; "He minds soft noises more than loud ones"; "His bath has to be just the right temperature"; or "He can sleep in the midst of noise." One baby likes to be jounced vigorously while another likes gentle, rhythmic rocking. Visual, auditory, kinesthetic, rhythmic stimulation are each important. The proper amount of stimulation implies both protection from excessive or overwhelming stimuli, which the baby cannot manage or which disrupt his functioning, and provision of enough stimulation of satisfying kinds to encourage response.

4. *Talking to the baby.* This provides important support for the baby's own vocalizing efforts that are a precursor of language.

5. *Opportunities for exercise of emerging sensory-motor functions,* through handling toys and other objects. Such activities as touching, feeling, banging, throwing, or combining teach the baby the qualities of things and also help him develop awareness of himself, the different parts of his body and what he can do. Being played with by older children and adults helps him become accustomed to different people, to distinguish his mother or caretaker from others, and to develop flexibility in responding to and interacting with others. In addition, the adult's or older child's delight, pride, and surprise at the baby's reaction provide an important feedback to the infant and, by enhancing the importance to him of his own achievements, stimulate further efforts on his part.

6. *Encouragement of the baby's efforts* to make himself comfortable, amuse himself, feed himself, and master new skills. Such efforts can help the baby develop independence and an ability to cope with problems.

7. *Continuity in a few basic, warm relationships,* as with a mother, father, brothers, sisters, and other relatives. Such continuity contributes to the development of a stable core of self, a sense of being valued, a capacity for dependable relationships, a sense of trust, and identification with motherly and fatherly adults.

INTERRELATED FACTORS   The child's emotional and affective development seems to go hand in hand with his social responsiveness. And, according to studies made among children of higher socioeconomic status, relationships also exist between social behavior and the level of language development.[6] Both superior language development and superior social and emotional development have been found to reflect the quality of family interaction. Some studies of family life that describe conversation between parents and children at mealtimes suggest that the higher level of verbal exchange found in middle- and upper-middle-class families is an integral part of the social atmosphere in families that enjoy their children and communicate with them regularly. In such families, the social and emotional interaction itself provides cognitive stimulation and contributes substantially to language development as well as to the development of perception and other cognitive faculties. Our studies at the Menninger Foundation found positive correlations between the mother's talking to the baby and the baby's vocalization, as well as between the baby's vocalization and his later IQ.[7] These findings probably reflect the mother's affective response to communication initiated by the baby as well as the baby's response to the mother.

It is astonishing that in current efforts to stimulate the intellectual development of deprived children, so little detailed analysis has been made of the day-to-day communication between parents and children in well-functioning families as compared with parent-child communication in depressed families of any specific socioeconomic, racial, or other subcultural group. Aspects of

[6] Murphy, G.; Murphy, L. B.; Newcomb, T. M.: Experimental social psychology. Harper & Row, New York, N.Y. 1937.
[7] Murphy, L. B.; Moriarty, A. M.: Development, vulnerability, and resilience. In preparation.

cognition stimulated by such communication also need to be studied. There is no lack of research methods. For example, Barker and Wright have provided detailed, moment-by-moment records of a child's life through one day:[8] Escalona and Leitch have provided even more detailed records on infants;[9] Leon Yarrow and his team have recorded in detail a baby's response to environment.[10]

Much recent research on cognitive development as such and ways of stimulating it in young children has been carried out without a sufficiently broad orientation to the total context of mental development. The procedure of some investigators might be compared to that of a man who in order to fly to Samoa equipped himself with the best airplane and took off with a plan to fly southwest without studying all the relevant factors such as headwinds, tailwinds, climatic variations at different longitudes and latitudes, or visual landmarks. The need is for a full analysis of the *total* development context in which learning takes place, both in formal stimulation situations (which always include factors not mentioned in the records) and within families of various socioeconomic backgrounds.

SOME QUESTIONS   A host of questions cry for answers: What was the atmosphere in the learning situation in which marked success occurred as compared with the situation that produced only limited success? Did the first situation involve a day-care teacher who enjoyed children and made their daily experiences happier, more fun, and thereby, perhaps, more stimulating? Is it possible that some caretakers who take a personal interest in each child evoke in the child a deeper identification with the teacher and a deeper investment in the learning process? Do some children through identification with the teacher or through other as yet unrecognized processes acquire a "drive to learn" that furthers their progress?

The lack of curiosity and drive to explore, of capacity for organization, planning, and creativity, and of the resourcefulness that these traits utilize and develop has been characteristic of many children in Head Start programs. A child needs such tendencies and capacities to clarify potential uses of his cognitive resources and to find new satisfactions in putting them to work in interesting ways. But the roots of such cognitive activity have not been adequately studied. Could it be that the relative emptiness and monotony of the environment in economically deprived homes automatically prevent the child from making comparisons, finding interesting similarities and differences, organizing experiences in exciting new ways, or trying to make an increasingly detailed and expanding "cognitive map," as children in middle-class homes must do to cope with the variety of experiences in their richer environment?

There is an urgent need to compare the effects of different experimental methods with the effects of the methods used in good "traditional" nursery schools as described in the literature.[11,12] Such a comparison, ideally, would

[8] Barker, R.; Wright, H.: One boy's day. Harper & Row, New York, N.Y. 1951.
[9] Escalona, S. R.: Leitch, M. E., et al.: Earliest phases of personality development. Child Research Monograph No. 17, 1953.
[10] Yarrow, Leon: Conceptualizing the early environment. *In* Early child care (Laura L. Dittmann, ed.). Atherton Press, New York, N.Y. 1968.
[11] Beyer, E.: Teaching young children. Pegasus Press, New York, N.Y. 1968.
[12] Read, K.: The nursery school. W. B. Saunders Co., Philadelphia, Pa. 1966.

involve a careful, comprehensive analysis of the cognitive aspects of all the activities of children in nursery school. An analysis of this kind would require fresh study of the complex processes through which the child integrates and reconstructs his observations of objects, parts of the environment, and adult roles and rehearses for future activity. These mental processes and others are involved in activities typical of good nursery school programs—for example, block construction, puzzle-solving, painting and drawing, storytelling and description of discoveries by the child, and group imaginative play. Cognitive aspects of social experience should also be studied. Such processes as learning to take turns, to work together on joint tasks, to explain feelings of anger instead of beating up or biting the offender, to plan a joint block-building project all involve cognitive efforts of varying degrees of complexity of understanding, verbal skill, sequential ideation, organization of objects and people, and useful fantasy.

Complex preschool activities like these have significance for many aspects of development in the young child, among others: (a) putting cognitive skills to work in activity the child cares a great deal about; (b) developing skills, insight, and values important as foundations for socialization; and (c) enhancing the sense of autonomy, the capacity to cope with varied life situations, and the drive to continue in the social use of cognitive resources. The child becomes self-propelling in his cognitive, affective, and social use of the environment. These beginnings imply possible next steps in research, which are foreshadowed in the discriminating reports of Herbert Zimiles.[13]

INDIVIDUAL DIFFERENCES   Another point needs emphasis. Most results of experiments in cognitive stimulation have been reported in terms of averages or means on the assumption that the only adequate measurement of change is a summary of the change in a group as a whole. Such a statistical approach has been sharply criticized by some of the world's most outstanding statisticians. One of these, C. R. Rao,[14] urges that subgroups be looked at separately to avoid the confusion of results when two contrary tendencies are represented in the same group. For instance, when we find that in a given group the level of cognitive functioning has decreased in some children and dramatically increased in others, we need to consider the factors behind these opposite responses. What was going on in the lives of those children whose level of functioning has decreased? Did the child become ill? Was there some severe trauma at home? Was the child disturbed by separation from home and mother? Did the child have special needs that were not met? Similarly we need to learn more about the children who made the greatest progress. Were these the children whom the teacher particularly appreciated or enjoyed, tuned in with, or felt she understood?

In other words, we need to consider the individual physiological, social, and emotional context of both negative and positive changes in cognitive

13 Zimiles, Herbert: An analysis of current issues in the evaluation of educational programs. *In* The disadvantaged child, vol. 2 (J. Hellmuth, ed.). Special Child Publications, Seattle, Wash. 1969.
14 U.S. Department of Health, Education, and Welfare, National Institute of Mental Health: Proceedings of a conference on classification in psychiatry and psychopathology, Chevy Chase, Md., 1965, p. 559.

development. At the same time we need more study of the differences in individual children's responses to whatever is offered or withheld—differences in what evokes interest and drive as contrasted with withdrawal, in vulnerability to deprivation, separation, and strangeness, and in capacity to cope with the stresses of life.

Research on the early years, then, must ask: What physical, emotional, and cognitive support does each child need for optimal all-round development?

A project that will attempt to answer these questions is just getting underway at the Children's Hospital of the District of Columbia. It is aimed at demonstrating the advantages for infants and young children of group care in settings that emphasize warm relationships and careful attention to the individual needs of each child. Still in a pilot stage, the project is designed on the theory that only comprehensive support for the infant's physical, mental, and personality development will be adequate.

The project will attempt to provide the baby with a foundation for developing a strong healthy body and emotional stability, a trusting but independent outlook, curiosity and drive to learn, responsiveness to and considerateness of other people, and a capacity for participating in social endeavors. In one group each child's mother or mother substitute will receive help closely related to the needs of her child in the belief that if the gains from a good beginning are to be maintained, the child's mother must be helped to understand his needs and to use the community resources to strengthen her family life. She will also receive training and education that will develop her own potentialities, confidence, and determination to further support her children's development. The program is bound to be expensive, but its potentialities are great, especially since attention to each child's individual maturational tempo, areas of sensitivity, and range of interest is rarely included in experimental programs. . . .

The Regularity of Onset of Speech and Language

Eric H. Lenneberg
HARVARD UNIVERSITY, MEDICAL SCHOOL

The onset of speech consists of a gradual unfolding of capacities; it is a series of generally well-circumscribed events which take place between the second and third year of life. Certain important speech milestones are reached in a fixed sequence and at a relatively constant chronological age. Just as impressive as the age constancy is the remarkable synchronization of speech milestones with motor-developmental milestones, summarized in Table 1.

Reprinted from *Biological Foundations of Language.* Copyright © 1967 by John Wiley & Sons, Inc. By permission. Pp. 127–135.

TABLE 1.

Developmental Milestones in Motor and Language Development

AT THE COMPLETION OF:	MOTOR DEVELOPMENT	VOCALIZATION AND LANGUAGE
12 weeks	Supports head when in prone position; weight is on elbows; hands mostly open; no grasp reflex.	Markedly less crying than at 8 weeks; when talked to and nodded at, smiles, followed by squealing-gurgling sounds usually called *cooing*, which is vowel-like in character and pitch-modulated; sustains cooing for 15–20 seconds
16 weeks	Plays with a rattle placed in his hands (by shaking it and staring at it), head self-supported; tonic neck reflex subsiding.	Responds to human sounds more definitely; turns head; eyes seem to search for speaker; occasionally some chuckling sounds
20 weeks	Sits with props	The vowel-like cooing sounds begin to be interspersed with more consonantal-sounds; labial fricatives, spirants and nasals are common; acoustically, all vocalizations are very different from the sounds of the mature language of the environment
6 months	Sitting: bends forward and uses hands for support; can bear weight when put into standing position, but cannot yet stand with holding on; reaching: unilateral; grasp: no thumb apposition yet; releases cube when given another	Cooing changing into babbling resembling one-syllable utterances; neither vowels nor consonants have very fixed recurrences; most common utterances sound somewhat like ma, mu, da, or di
8 months	Stands holding on; grasps with thumb apposition; picks up pellet with thumb and finger tips	Reduplication (or more continuous repetitions) becomes frequent; intonation patterns become distinct; utterances can signal emphasis and emotions
10 months	Creeps efficiently; takes side-steps, holding on; pulls to standing position	Vocalizations are mixed with sound-play such as gurgling or bubble-blowing; appears to wish to imitate sounds, but the imitations are never quite

(*continued*)

TABLE 1 *Continued*

AT THE COMPLETION OF:	MOTOR DEVELOPMENT	VOCALIZATION AND LANGUAGE
		successful; beginning to differentiate between words heard by making differential adjustment
12 months	Walks when held by one hand; walks on feet and hands—knees in air; mouthing of objects almost stopped; seats self on floor	Identical sound sequences are replicated with higher relative frequency of occurrence and words (mamma or dadda) are emerging; definite signs of understanding some words and simple commands (show me your eyes)
18 months	Grasp, prehension and release fully developed; gait stiff, propulsive and precipitated; sits on child's chair with only fair aim; creeps downstairs backwards; has difficulty building tower of 3 cubes	Has a definite repertoire of words —more than three, but less than fifty; still much babbling but now of several syllables with intricate intonation pattern; no attempt at communicating information and no frustration for not being understood; words may include items such as thank you or come here, but there is little ability to join any of the lexical items into spontaneous two-item phrases; understanding is progressing rapidly
24 months	Runs, but falls in sudden turns; can quickly alternate between sitting and stance; walks stairs up or down, one foot forward only	Vocabulary of more than 50 items (some children seem to be able to name everything in environment); begins spontaneously to join vocabulary items into two-word phrases; all phrases appear to be own creations; definite increase in communicative behavior and interest in language
30 months	Jumps up into air with both feet; stands on one foot for about two seconds; takes few steps on tip-toe; jumps from chair; good hand and finger coordination; can move digits independently; manipulation	Fastest increase in vocabulary with many new additions every day; no babbling at all; utterances have communicative intent; frustrated if not understood by adults; utterances consist of at least two

TABLE 1 *Continued*

AT THE COMPLETION OF:	MOTOR DEVELOPMENT	VOCALIZATION AND LANGUAGE
	of objects much improved; builds tower of six cubes	words, many have three or even five words; sentences and phrases have characteristic child grammar, that is, they are rarely verbatim repetitions of an adult utterance; intelligibility is not very good yet, though there is great variation among children; seems to understand everything that is said to him
3 years	Tiptoes three yards; runs smoothly with acceleration and deceleration; negotiates sharp and fast curves without difficulty; walks stairs by alternating feet; jumps 12 inches; can operate tricycle	Vocabulary of some 1000 words; about 80% of utterances are intelligible even to strangers; grammatical complexity of utterances is roughly that of colloquial adult language, although mistakes still occur
4 years	Jumps over rope; hops on right foot; catches ball in arms; walks line	Language is well-established; deviations from the adult norm tend to be more in style than in grammar

The temporal interlocking of speech milestones and motor milestones is not a logical necessity. There are reasons to believe that the onset of language is not simply the consequence of motor control. The development of language is quite independent of articulatory skills (Lenneberg, 1962); and the perfection of articulation cannot be predicted simply on the basis of general motor development. There are certain indications for the existence of a peculiar, language-specific maturational schedule. Many children have learned a word or two before they start to toddle, and thus must be assumed to possess a sufficient degree of motor skill to articulate, however primitive; yet the expansion of their vocabulary is still an extremely slow process. Why could they not rapidly increase their lexicon with "sloppy" sound-symbols much the way a child with a cleft palate does at age three? Similarly, parents' inability to train their children at this stage to join the words *daddy* and *by-by* into a single utterance cannot be explained on the grounds of motor incompetence, because at the same age children babble for periods as long as the duration of a sentence. In fact, the babbled "sentence" may be produced complete with intonation patterns. The retarding factor for language acquisition here must be a psychological one, or perhaps better, a cognitive one and not mechanical skill. About age three manual skills show improved coordination over earlier periods, but dexterity is still very immature on an absolute scale. Speech, which requires infinitely precise and swift movements of tongue and lips, all well-coordinated with laryngeal and respiratory motor systems, is all but fully developed when most other mechanical skills are far below their levels of future accomplishment. The evolvement of various motor skills and motor coordinations also has specific maturational histories; but the specific history for speech control stands apart dramatically from histories of finger and hand control.

The independence of language development from motor coordination is also underscored by the priority of language comprehension over language production. Ordinarily the former precedes the latter by a matter of a few months (especially between the ages of 18 to 36 months). In certain cases this gap may be magnified by many years (Lenneberg, 1964). Careful and detailed investigations of the development of understanding by itself have been undertaken only in more recent years (Brown and Bellugi, 1964; Ervin, 1964; Ervin and Miller, 1963). The evidence collected so far leaves little doubt that there is also an orderly and constant progression in this aspect of language development.

The development of children with various abnormalities provides the most convincing demonstration that the onset of language is regulated by a maturational process, much the way the onset of gait is dependent upon such a process, but at the same time the language-maturational process is independent of motor-skeletal maturation. In hypotonic children, for instance, the musculature in general is weak, and tendon reflexes are less active than normal. Hypotonia may be an isolated phenomenon that is quickly outgrown or a sign of a disease such as muscular atrophy, which would have unfortunate effects on the child's future motor development. Whatever the cause, the muscular development alone may be lagging behind other developmental aspects and thus disarrange the normal intercalation of the various processes. Here, then, speech and language emerge at their usual time while motor development lags behind.

On the other hand, there are some children with normal intelligence and normal skeletal and motor development whose speech development alone is markedly delayed. We are not referring here to children who never learn to speak adequately because of acquired or congenital abnormalities in the brain, but rather of those who are simply late speakers, who do not begin to speak in phrases until after age four, who have no neurological or psychiatric symptoms which can explain the delay, and whose environment appears to be adequate. The incidence of such cases is small (less than one in a hundred), but their very existence underscores the independence of language-maturational processes from other processes.

There are also conditions that affect all developmental processes simultaneously. These are diseases in which growth and maturation are retarded or stunted through a variety of factors (for instance, of an endocrine nature as in hypothyroidism); or retardation may be due to an intracellular abnormality such as the chromosomal disorder causing mongolism. In these cases all processes suffer alike, resulting in general "stretching" of the developmental time scale, but leaving the intercalation of motor and speech milestones intact (Lenneberg, Nichols, and Rosenberger, 1964). The preservation of synchrony between motor and speech or language milestones in cases of general retardation is, I believe, the most cogent evidence that language acquisition is regulated by maturational phenomena.

The evidence presented rules out the possibility of a direct, causal relationship between motor and speech development. Normally, growth and maturation proceed at characteristic rates for each developmental aspect. In the absence of specific retardations affecting skills or organs differentially, a picture of consistency evolves such as represented in Table 1 or in the many accounts of normal human development (McGraw, 1963; Gesell and Amatruda, 1947).

The use of the word *skill* brings out another interesting aspect of the emergence of speech. With proper training probably everybody could attain some proficiency in such diverse skills as roller-skating, sketching, or piano playing. However, there are also vast individual differences in native endowment and considerable variation with respect to the age at which training is most effective. Perfection can rarely be expected before the teens. The establishment of speech and language is quite different; a much larger number of individuals show equal aptitude, absence of the skill is rare, and onset and fluency occur much earlier, with no particular training required.

Nevertheless, individual differences in time of onset and reaching of various milestones exist and must be accounted for. The rate of development is not constant during the formative years, and there may be transient slowing in the rate of maturation, with subsequent hastening. This is hardly surprising in view of the complex interrelation of intrinsic and extrinsic factors that affect development. Nevertheless, there is a remarkable degree of regularity in the emergence of language. Figure 1 illustrates the regularity in the attainment of three major language-developmental levels and Figure 2 illustrates the sudden increase in vocabulary size, particularly around the third birthday.

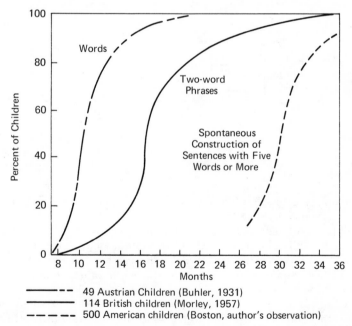

FIGURE 1.   *Emergence of various developmental milestones in the acquisition of language*

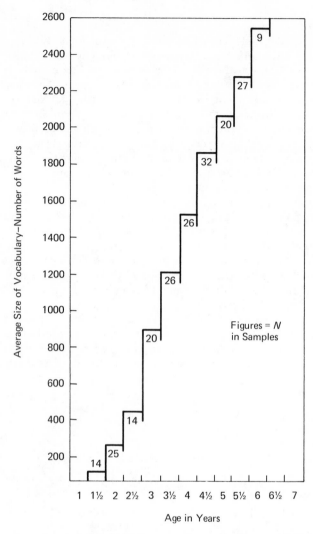

F I G U R E 2.   *Average vocabulary size of ten samples of children at various ages.* (Data based on Smith, 1926.)

In a survey of 500 middle and lower-class children in the Boston area, examined in connection with an epidemiological study, we found that nine out of ten children had acquired all of the following verbal skills by the time they reached their 39th month; ability to name most objects in the home, fair intelligibility, ability to comprehend spoken instructions, spontaneous utterance of syntactically complex sentences and spontaneity in oral communication. The field observations were made in the child's home by specially trained social workers who worked with a screening test and a schedule of questions. Any child who was found or suspected to fall short of these standards was referred by the social worker, to my office where he was examined by a speech therapist, an audiologist, and by myself. Fifty-four children were thus referred and found to fall into the classifications shown in Table 2.

T A B L E 2.

Distribution of Causes for Failing Language Screening Test
(Given to 500 children at about the third birthday)

	NUMBER
(1) Uncooperative child but, upon more intense examination, apparently normal speech development (health good, environment adequate)	7
(2) Poor articulation, but otherwise normal onset of language milestones (health good, environment adequate)	29
(3) Various types of speech defects associated with psychiatric conditions	9
(4) Speech defects associated with other behavioral disorders due to gross environmental abnormalities	2
(5) Speech defects associated with central nervous system disease	3
(6) Delayed onset of speech, unexplained (health good, environment adequate)	4

Differences in age at onset becomes much less dramatic if we scrutinize these statistics. Of 486 children who were free from nervous or mental disease and were raised in an adequate environment (all children in the sample except those of groups 3, 4, and 5) only 33 (less than 7%) were below the norm of attainment. . . .

References

BROWN, R. W. and BELLUGI, U. (1964), Three processes in the child's acquisition of syntax, in *New Directions in the Study of Language*, E. H. Lenneberg (ed.), M.I.T. Press, Cambridge, Massachusetts.

BÜHLER, C. (1931), *Kindheit und Jugend* (3rd ed.) Hirzel, Leipzig.

ERVIN, S. M. (1964), Imitation and structural change in children's language, in *New Directions in the Study of Language*, E. H. Lenneberg (ed.), M.I.T. Press, Cambridge, Mass.

——— and MILLER, W. R. (1963), Language development, *Child Psychology*, 62nd Yearbook, National Society for the Study of Education. Univ. of Chicago Press, Chicago, Ill.

GESELL, A. and AMATRUDA, C. S. (1947), *Developmental Diagnosis; normal and abnormal child development, clinical methods and pediatric applications* (2nd ed.), Hoeber, New York.

LENNEBERG, E. H. (1962), Understanding language without ability to speak: a case report, *J. abnorm. soc. Psychol.* **65**:419–425.

——— (1964), Speech as a motor skill with special reference to nonaphasic disorders, in *The Acquisition of Language*, Monograph of the Society for Research in Child Development. U. Bellugi and R. Brown (eds.), Serial No. 92, Vol. 29, No. 1.

———, NICHOLS, I. A., and ROSENBERGER, E. F. (1964), Primitive stages of language development in mongolism, in *Disorders of Communication Vol. XLII: Research Publications*, A.R.N.M.D. Williams and Wilkins, Baltimore, Maryland.

McGraw, M. B. (1963), *The Neuromuscular Maturation of the Human Infant*. Hafner, New York.

Morley, M. (1957), *The Development and Disorders of Speech in Childhood*. Livingstone, London.

Smith, M. E. (1926), An investigation of the development of the sentence and the extent of vocabulary in young children, *Univ. Iowa Stud. Child Welfare*, Vol. 3, No. 5.

Chapter 4

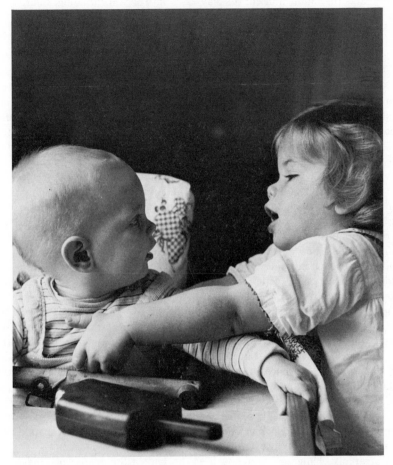

Robert J. Izzo

Relationships with People

The baby is active in building relationships with people, just as he is active in the world of things. His very arrival causes changes in the world, especially in the people responsible for his care. Their interaction with each other and with him is the basis of social, emotional, and personality development. The baby's family is already anchored in a cultural framework that will direct and limit all of their interactions. The values and attitudes that influence parental behavior are understandable in their cultural context [50]. Before discussing actual parent–child relationships, this chapter will deal with some of the influences on relationships that come from different sources.

The Social Environment

Three main types of influences are basic to the building of a baby's relationships with people and hence to his social and emotional development. The culture, the family, and the infant himself, all play essential roles in initiating, limiting and guiding interactions.

Culture

Culture influences the infant by drawing the outlines of his parents and structuring his relationships with other people, especially relatives. This function is mentioned first because of the importance of parents to babies. It is only one small aspect of culture, however, and all those other aspects also influence the infant. The language he hears determines what he will speak and to a large extent, how he will think. The food he receives affects not only his preferences but his life and growth. His house, furniture, clothing, grooming equipment, and medicine all bear relation to his health, posture, activity, and attitudes. Toys, art, and music are vital in his cognitive and emotional life. Even the more distant aspects of culture, like government and law, have important effects on infants. For instance, what support does the government give to poor families in the way of nutrition, housing, family planning, and day care of young children? How well do the laws protect children whose parents abuse them?

Ideals of behavior are pictures of how roles *ought* to be performed. What is a good husband? A good wife? A good child? A good employer? Sometimes a culture presents a detailed word picture of an ideal, as did Judaism in Proverbs and Hinduism in the Laws of Manu. Ideals of child-rearing techniques are part of a culture which determine the parental role and the roles of other people concerned with children. These ideals state "right" punishment, rewards, regulations, and other methods of influence. In a simple, stable society most parents treat their children in the ways that they themselves were treated as children, and these ways coincide rather well with the ideals. Ideal patterns are expressed in the folklore and art. To spank or not to spank, to wean early or late, to toilet-train or to let the child train himself—these and similar questions are not really questions to parents who live in an unchanging culture.

In a rapidly changing culture, such as the United States, parents and grandparents often conflict over child care. Parents cannot rely comfortably on custom to give them definite directions on child rearing, since many different and changing directions are available. The same is true of other changing societies, which include a fair share of the world. When actual behavior differs widely from the ideal pattern, then conflict and confusion result.

Ideals for child rearing come in profuse variety in the United States as influenced by social class, ethnicity, region, religion, and other factors. Some attempts have been made to clarify the ideal role through pamphlets, books, and articles giving advice to mothers. Although the publications of the Children's Bureau do not carry religious authority, as do the Book of Proverbs, the Laws of Manu, and the Koran, they do reflect the ideals of the culture. One investigator [88] studied nine editions of the Children's Bureau publication *Infant Care*, spanning about 40 years. She found progressive changes in recommendations for parents, especially in the degree of severity with which the good mother was supposed to cope with various kinds of behavior in her infant. Changes in delineation of the mother's role stemmed from changes in conceptions of baby nature, in fact, of human nature. In 1914 the good mother was urged to be vigilant and relentless in her battle against the child's sinful nature, stamping out thumb-sucking and masturbation. In the thirties the mother must not permit the baby to dominate her. During the forties the mother was advised to be nonchalant in distracting her baby from thumb-sucking and masturbation, since he would be almost equally interested in toys and exploration. Since the fifties there has been no appreciable change in professionals' advice on guidance, as typified by the Children's Bureau and Dr. Spock [40]. Gentleness, gradualism, and a generally permissive attitude toward infants are recommended. An occasional magazine article, however, suggests that parents be more strict. For example, a recent article in *Baby Talk* magazine was titled "Best to start disciplining early" and advocated gently but firmly spanking the 7-months-old baby who cries when he is put to bed [4].

In both Israel and the Soviet Union, social upheaval has led to conscious formulation of child-rearing ideals designed to develop a new culture. In both cases, the child-rearing methods are planned to strengthen devotion to the state and ability to serve it. Since women are workers as well as mothers, they spend considerable time away from their children, and the care provided is planned with certain purposes in mind.

While the *kibbutzim* include only 4 percent of the Israelis, they represent conscious ideals and offer rich opportunities for the study of child development in a planned society. Ideals basic to the child care methods are equality of individuals, including equality between men and women, and deep peer attachment stemming from full participation in the common enterprise [9, p. 25]. Therefore from early infancy, children live apart from their parents in peer groups where they help one another and satisfy one another's emotional needs, learning cooperation rather than competition, and minimizing dependence on parents. Thus they are educated and prepared for the collective way of life [60].

In Moscow 50 percent of children under 2 are enrolled in nurseries, although the figure is only 10 percent for the whole country [18]. The demand for nursery placement far exceeds the supply. The babies are taught by specific methods worked out and described by educational and medical authorities. Children are supposed to develop as fast as possible, to learn at the earliest teachable moment, a value that contrasts with the American notion of letting them grow at their own rate [71]. The Russian teaching methods were carefully designed to promote behavior and values consistent with Communist ideals. Infants are put in groups into large playpens where they are taught to share toys, to help each other, and to play together. Self-reliance and self-control are taught early, since a proper attitude toward work is a major goal. Children learn to supervise one another and to accept supervision. Since the family is subordinate to the state, it is logical that professional educators should know more than parents about what is best for children. Educators work with parents to make sure that they bring up their children correctly and to integrate the child's total education. Bronfenbrenner, a Russian-speaking American psychologist and keen observer of the Russian scene, reports this comment from a Russian who visited in an American day-care center: "I wouldn't have believed it," he said, "if I hadn't seen it with my own eyes. There were four children sitting at a table, just as in our nurseries. But each one was doing something different. What's more, I watched them for a whole ten minutes, and not once did any child help another one. They didn't even talk to each other. Each one was busy in his own activity. You really are a nation of individualists" [18].

Social Class : A Cultural Influence

   Differences between middle-class and working-class behavior have been studied extensively for several decades. More recently, researchers have turned their attention to differences between the very poor and the other socioeconomic levels. Very little research has been done on upper-class behavior [21]. An accumulation of evidence indicates real but often small differences in the way children are brought up in the middle class, as contrasted with the working class. Middle-class parents tend to be warmer, to use more love-oriented discipline, and to be more permissive as to demands for attention from the child, sex behavior, orderliness, aggression, bedtime, and obedience. Working-class parents use more physical punishment, shouting and ridicule, and they tend to be more restrictive [6]. Observations of middle-class and working-class mothers interacting with young children have shown the former being warmer and more stimulating while encouraging the child to be autonomous and to find satisfaction through his own efforts [15]. The working-class mothers were more passive with their children and placed more emphasis on control through rewards and punishments.

   The same kinds of differences between middle- and working-class parental behavior have been found in several different cultures. A sample of Greek mothers showed the middle-class group to be more warm and permissive with young children than were the peasant and lower-class urban groups [63]. Similar class differences were found for Italian mothers in a cross-culture study done in Turin and Washington [62]. In a study comparison of the attitudes of German and American mothers, samples in both countries were divided into upper, middle, and lower classes [65]. In both samples, lower-class mothers were most controlling (least permissive), middle-class mothers were next, and upper-class mothers least controlling in regard to their children.

   In the United States there is evidence that class differences have changed over time [16]. Before World War II, working-class mothers, in contrast to middle-class mothers, did more breast feeding and more self-demand feeding, weaned children later, and toilet-trained them more leniently. After World War II these trends were reversed, probably due to the middle-class mothers' being in closer touch with the advice of experts and more readily influenced by it. The changes which took place in the concepts of child nature were transmitted faster to middle-class mothers than to working-class mothers by pediatricians, the Children's Bureau, magazine writers, and other parent educators. Middle-class, working-class differences in child training are diminishing [16]. Two sets of observations of mothers with children done 20 years apart show lower-class mothers to be more coercive with their children than middle-class mothers. This research also indicates a progressive change over time in which the general trend is for mothers to be less coercive [84]. Not only do differences between middle- and working-class behaviors tend to be small, but the range of behavior patterns in each class is relatively large [21]. Thus, for example, while more working-class mothers use physical punishment than do middle-class mothers, we might find that Mrs. Carpenter reasons gently with her Danny while Mrs. Lawyer spanks her Jimmy often.

IQ during the first two years of life is not related to socioeconomic level in those studies where birth complications, malnutrition, and poor health are ruled out. Most, but not all, studies indicate that by the end of the third year children from poor families tend to lag behind the average on measures of intelligence [38]. When the 8-month IQs of over 3000 infants were compared with their IQs at 4 years, a downward trend was noted. More dramatic, however, was the status of infants who tested low at 8 months [87]. When tested at 4 years of age, children who had been retarded infants were seven times more likely to have IQs below 79 if they came from poor families than they were if they came from middle-income families. Thus poorly developed infants suffer more damage from a poor environment than do well-developed infants.

Family

The infant's family translates the broad culture into a unique specific family culture that the baby experiences directly. The ideals, goals, beliefs, and customs of his family affect the way in which the baby is received and cared for. Suppose he is a fourth child born to a family where every child is a welcome gift from God. In contrast, suppose he is a fourth child born to a family where two children are considered the ideal number. Consider a family that holds that a baby is born wicked and must be trained to be good; that the infant must learn early who is boss; that crying exercises the lungs. Then consider a family that holds that infants have a right to happiness and that children cannot learn anything until they reach the age of reason, at 6 or 7.

Family customs are important in the experience of infants. Many rural Dutch babies ride in boxes on their parents' bicycles, enjoying the stimulation of sun and wind, getting the feel of balancing, watching the Van Gogh-like landscape change before their eyes. Many English babies loll and crawl on the green grass of Kensington Gardens, watching the swans and the fountains, accompanied by parents, brothers, and sisters who play and relax. Indian babies who live in joint families have constant companionship and immediate attention to their cries. Others, who live in small families, are left alone or inadequately tended by small children for long periods when their mothers must carry water.

In these ways, and in other ways, does the family determine the experience of its babies. Cognitive, emotional, and social growth are thus influenced.

The composition and stage of development of the family, of course, affect a baby [27]. For example, it is well known that the first-born carries a different burden from subsequent babies and that, in fact, each order of birth has its own assets and liabilities. The arrangement of sexes affects each child. Being a member of a boy and girl pair is different from being a member of a like-sexed pair. An older boy with a younger girl is different from a younger boy with an older girl. Being a twin is different from being a singleton. It makes a further difference which kind of twin you are, a monozygotic or dyzygotic, like-sex or unlike, and which sex [51].

Family to most American readers means parents and children, but even in America millions of children live in families which are otherwise. A parent is absent, a grandparent is present, or other relatives are present. The composition of the family can make a big difference in the amount of stimulation a baby receives. Many people in the house, especially children, make for noise, excitement, handling, play, and variety of contacts. When there are several or many adults present in the household, children are more likely to be continually controlled but less likely to be treated harshly than if parents are the only adults present [27]. The number of children is an important family dimension with meaning for all members. Child-rearing methods of parents of many children are different from those of parents of a few. Every added child complicates the network of human relationships and calls for a redistribution of space, goods, and services. Too many children strain the material and emotional resources of the parents. An excessive number of children for one family may not be the same as too many for another family.

Stages of development refer to a way of looking at family life as cyclic. Each stage has its own characteristics. A typical way of naming the stages is (1) beginning, (2) childbearing, (3) preschool, (4) school-age, (5) teen-age, (6) launching, (7) middle-age, (8) old age, and (9) broken.

It is possible for a baby to be born to a mother when the family is in any one of the stages from (2) to (6) or (7). Infants born in the early stages come to families oriented toward living with babies. Home, furnishings, schedules, menus, and pace are suited to young children. Those who come later are likely to be swept into activities appropriate for older children or teen-agers, such as camping trips and Scout meetings, or perhaps they will be left out frequently as the family goes off to meetings and parties and engages in conversation too mature for the youngest.

Emotional climate is a summary term for all the feelings that exist in the home. Love and tenderness are known to be essential ingredients for healthy growth. Affectional interchange in the family has been found to be correlated with test performance of babies at 6 months of age [91]. A longitudinal study at Berkeley yields some correlations between family situations during the first two years of life and intelligence scores in childhood and adolescence [49]. Parental compatibility and lack of conflict over discipline and cultural standards correlated with girls' intelligence throughout childhood and adolescence. Closeness of mother and son during infancy was positively related to the son's test performances between 8 and 18 years. Father's friendliness to the infant daughter was predictive of her intelligence between 7 and 18. Mothers who were energetic, tense, and concerned with their young children, probably responding very carefully to their needs, were more likely than lethargic mothers to have children with high IQs in childhood and adolescence.

The basic factors in emotional climate are the parents' satisfaction with marriage and family living, and their personality maturity in regard to taking on parent roles. Relationships with their own parents also influence the mother and father, since they themselves are children as well as parents. Not only do the parents act in the light of their past experiences as children, but they are affected by present and changing relationships with their own parents. Furthermore, parents react emotionally to such strains as money troubles and inadequate housing. Big crises and joys and small irritations and pleasures all register in the emotional climate of the home, from which the baby receives stimuli.

Mother's Characteristics

The mother's behavior with the baby is of course a very important set of influences on him, since she controls so much of what happens to him. Some of her responses are determined by what the baby is and does, as will be discussed in the following sections. Other sources for her behavior are wide and varied. Many studies [1, 3, 8, 81, 86, 91, 93] reveal the influence of mother behavior on infant behavior, suggesting that the personal characteristics of mothers have definite consequences in the form of infant development.

The Harvard Preschool Project [86] began studying competence in children who were seen as coping in superior ways with the situations they met from day to day. When the investigators came to realize that competence was well developed in some children by 3 years, they set out to discover how the contributing abilities were built during the first 3 years of life. Although the project is not yet completed, the researchers have tentatively identified different types of mothers who were more or less successful in raising competent children. They are

1. *The competent mother.* She interacts more with the child than does the average mother, initiating some interactions and letting the child initiate some. She is verbal, teaching spontaneously and in terms of cause and effect. Using rational discipline, she often gives choices. She rewards cognitive achievement and mastery while accepting and enjoying the child at his stage of development. She understands his preverbal behavior. She often takes part in role playing with the child.
2. *The mother who almost makes it.* Although she enjoys and accepts the child, she often cannot understand his preverbal cues. She initiates less interaction and less teaching than the competent mother.
3. *The overwhelmed mother.* She often ignores the child. While she gives some evidence of enjoyment, she does little understanding, instructing, or rewarding. Often she is in a low socioeconomic level and has many children. Life is too hard.
4. *The rigid, controlling mother.* A careful household schedule includes placing the child in a play area for certain times. This mother has almost no interaction with the child, as though she does not like him, is not involved, or does not understand his stage of development.
5. *The smothering mother.* She initiates many interactions, responding to every cue and teaching him for hours. She interferes with his activities and rewards him for doing cognitive tasks.

The competent mother, of course, seems to be an important source of competence in her child. The study has so far shown that "confident, competent mothers who are accepting of their role and enjoy and approve of their children seem to produce well-developed children. None of the mothers of poorly developed children could be described in that way." Another finding was that the quality of mother–child interaction is more important than the quantity.

The related functioning of mothers and 1-year-olds was studied at the University of Syracuse [81], using factor analysis of ratings made on the mothers' and infants' behavior and personalities and on the babies' mental and motor development. Since the babies in this study were younger than most of the Harvard subjects, maternal behavior would be expected to differ. However, similarities can be seen in the description of the Harvard competent mother and the Syracuse mother who is high in factor 2, a cluster of behaviors which reads like a description of ideal mother–infant interaction. This type of mother is very loving, shown by frequent happy, affectionate talking, tenderness, sensuousness in handling the baby, play,

Table 4-1 Mother–Infant Interaction Factor Summary

	Factor								
	2	1	3	8	7	6	9	4	5
Mother's needs	Emotional, involvement	Warm, supportive, organized, dependent, anxious	Achievement oriented, high drive, good-humored, extroverted, friendly	Exhibitionistic, involved	Anxious	Avoidance of physical contact or stimulation	Self-centered, disorganized, low frustration tolerance	Disorganized, low frustration tolerance, abasive	Permissive, warm, supportive, good-humored, abasive
Mother's behavior	Loving, emotionally involved, high vocal and visual contact, skilful care	Involved, high visual contact, high play, exhibitionistic with baby	Exhibitionistic with baby	Vigilant, warm physical contact, overtly maternal	Solicitous, emotionally involved, high rate of response and physical contact	Vigilant, enjoys baby	High play, indifferent to baby's health, overconfident		Solicitous exhibitionism
Baby's needs and behavior	Accelerated development	Lovingness and involvement with mother	Achievement oriented, energetic attempts to dominate mother	Environmentally responsive, sensual	Responsive to comforting, comfortable, attractive, active, low mental age	Good-humored, advanced development, achievement oriented, high drive, fearless, avoidance of physical contact	Impulsive, changeable	Hostile to mother, excitable, self-centered	Good-humored and nurturant toward mother
Composite factor description	Involved mothers with accelerated infants	Symbiotic mother-child affective rapport	Parallel active and social achievement orientation	Maternal display behavior with infant sensuality	Slow infants with solicitous and concerned mothers	Mutual maintenance of distance with accelerated infant development and drive	Unwarranted maternal satisfaction with disorganized interaction	Maternal, self-criticism reinforced by demanding and hostile infant behavior	Exhibitionistic indulgence with happy child response

SOURCE: Reprinted by permission from George G. Stern et al., "A Factor Analytic Study of the Mother–Infant Dyad," *Child Development*, **40**, Table 7, p. 178. Copyright © 1969, The Society for Research in Child Development, Inc.

empathy, attentiveness, enjoyment, and visual contact. The outstanding characteristic of babies belonging to these mothers is accelerated motor and mental development.

The opposite extreme of mother type noted in the Syracuse study was the one characterized by factor 9. This mother was self-centered, disorganized, capricious, overconfident, indifferent, and with low tolerance for frustration. These mothers tend to treat their infants like dolls, playing with them without regard for the baby's needs, feelings, or well-being even though they maintain high visual contact. Infants of such mothers tended to be capricious, lacking in purpose and plan. The interaction between mother and child was disorganized and yet the mother seemed to be satisfied with it. Since space does not permit descriptions of mothers typifying all nine factors plus the resulting interactions, the summary table is reproduced as Table 4–1, for the student who is interested in pursuing this topic.

Father's Characteristics

Fathers are very important to the development of sex role orientation, especially of boys and particularly during the first four years of life [10, 11]. Fathers may be just as important to baby girls as to baby boys, but because research in this area has focused so largely on boys, the significance of fathers to girls has not been emphasized. The main result of research is proof that the father's presence in the home makes a difference to psychosexual development. Fathers' ways of interacting with infants have not been explored very much, but we know that their interaction is important and that it is different from that of mothers.

Father's verbal interaction was studied in ten father–baby pairs [66]. Twenty-four-hour tape recordings were made every two weeks for three months. One striking result of the analysis was the small amount of time spent by the fathers in interaction with their infants, an average daily frequency of 2.7. The average number of seconds spent each day was 37.7. The father who averaged the most interaction spent only about ten minutes per day talking with his baby. Fathers were different from mothers in their ways of interacting, as shown by comparing results of this study with research on mothers. Fathers talked less often and for shorter periods. Fathers decreased their vocalizations during the first 3 months, while mothers increased theirs. Although the number of cases was very small for comparing sexes, it was noted that fathers of (2-week-old) girl babies talked to them more than fathers of boys that age, but when the infants were 12 weeks old, fathers of boys talked more. This shift is the reverse of what has been observed in mothers of girls compared with mothers of boys. Further studies, dealing with physical interaction, are needed to supplement these findings on verbalization.

Infant's Characteristics

The baby himself plays a big part in determining the course of relationships with people. Some of his effects are obvious, others subtle. The uniqueness of each infant can be appreciated by considering the interplay of appearance, sex, and temperament, which are only some of the categories under which human beings can be described.

Appearance. Looks can make a difference in how a baby is accepted and regarded. Although this statement is more in the realm of common belief than scientific fact, it is important if true. Not only is the matter of beauty or good looks involved here, but of an appearance that suggests something significant to the parents: a family resemblance causing pride or the expectation that the new baby will act like Uncle Joe or like his big brother; fragility, including delicate handling, or sturdiness, inciting rough play; a characteristic thought to predict a personality trait, such as red hair indicating temper or a weak chin indicating weak character.

Sex. According to whether the newborn is a boy or a girl, the baby is immediately placed in some categories and removed from others. The infant's sex determines many of the feelings, attitudes, and actions of people. Cultures and families vary widely in the ways in which they interpret and value sex roles. The Shah of Iran divorced a wife he loved (or so the newspapers said) because she bore him no sons, even though she produced daughters. His duty to perpetuate his line, for the good of his country, was a value above and beyond love for his wife. Imagine the welcome a son would receive in such a family and the disappointment that would mount with the birth of each daughter! Followers of religions like Hinduism and Confucianism want sons in order to carry out religious duties toward ancestors and to assure their own religious fulfillment. Therefore the birth of the first son is an occasion of boundless joy and relief from anxiety. Sons are less essential in the West than in Asia. Some Americans prefer daughters. Religion and property are not involved, and daughters are considered easier to bring up. Americans may try not to form a sex preference before a baby is born, realizing that it makes for better relationships to be happy with their offspring no matter which sex it is.

Adults treat boy and girl babies differently. An obvious reason for differential treatment is that adults have different expectations of boys and girls and that they are beginning to teach sex role. Research on both human and monkey infants, however, indicates biological influences also at work, in the form of the infant's own characteristics. Animal research, especially on primates, often gives useful leads for research on humans. Data from several studies at the University of Wisconsin Primate Laboratory have shown differences between interactions of mother monkeys with male infants and mother monkeys with female infants [57]. In the first 3 months of life, males did more mouthing, cuffing, slapping, clasping, and pulling the fur of the mothers, and as they got older, this behavior increased. As the females got older, they decreased in clasping and body contact and increased in cooing and exploration with their eyes, mouth, and hands. The mothers of female infants embraced and restrained them more, withdrew from them less, and groomed them more. Mothers of male infants played with them more and tended to be more aggressive and rejecting. The author concluded that the mothers protected the females more, encouraging them to maintain close attachments, while the males were pushed into independence and wide contacts with the other members of the troop. Thus we see the infant's own characteristics playing a part in development of interactions. Turning to the human scene, boy and girl babies can be seen exerting different influences on their mothers during the first 3 months of life [58]. Boys slept less and cried more and were more irritable than girls. Mothers held boys more than girls, about 27 minutes longer during an 8-hour period at 3 months, for example. As well as being more irritable, males seemed to respond less satisfactorily to mothers' efforts to console them. The data indicated that mothers responded more readily to girls' cries, since they had been more successful in quieting girls.

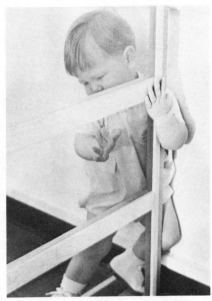

Courtesy Michael Lewis

Figure 4–1. Sex differences in response to a frustrating barrier. The baby girl stands and cries; the baby boy tries to get around the barrier.

Two samples of babies examined at 6 and 13 months showed sex differences in their toy preferences, responses to frustration, and interactions with their mothers. At 13 months, each baby was placed in an observation room with toys [37]. The mother, who sat on a chair in the corner of the room, was told to watch the baby's play and to respond as she wished. The floor of the room was divided into 12 squares, permitting recording of the child's position for each 15 seconds of time. When removed from their mothers' laps girls were more reluctant to leave and more often returned immediately. When playing, they stayed closer to their mothers. Girls spent more time touching their mothers, looking at them, and vocalizing to them than did boys. When a barrier was placed between the infant and the mother, with the toys on the mother's side, sex differences in response to stress were seen. Figure 4–1 illustrates the typical difference between boys and girls. Boys were more likely to try to get around the barrier, girls to stand in the middle crying and motioning for help from the mother. Differences in play were seen, also. Girls sat more and spent more time with blocks, pegboard, dog and cat (the only toys with faces). Boys were more active and played more with the mallet, lawn-mower, and nontoys, such as the doorknob and electric outlets. Girls used more fine muscle coordination while boys used more large muscles and were more vigorous. Figure 4–2 illustrates typical sex differences in choice of toys and play behavior. Data on mother–infant interaction at 6 months showed the mothers touched girls more than boys. When related to the baby's behavior at 13 months, there was a direct relationship between mothers touching boys at 6 months and boys touching mothers at 13 months. That is, the mothers who did the most touching at 6 months had sons who did the most touching at 13 months. For girls,

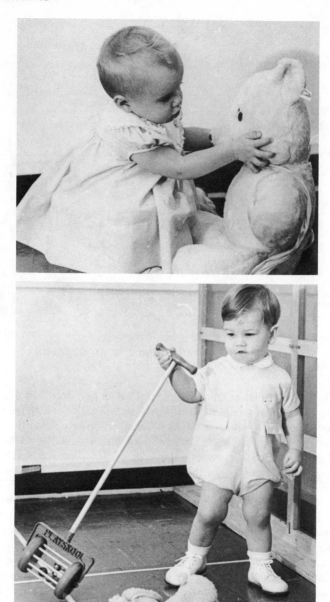

Courtesy Michael Lewis

Figure 4–2. Sex differences in choice of toys and play activity. The baby girl sits and plays with the soft, cuddly animal; the baby boy is active with a mechanical toy.

the picture was different. A medium amount of touching by the mother was correlated with a medium amount of touching by the daughter, but mothers who did little or much touching were likely to have daughters who touched them a great deal. Corroboration of mothers' differential treatment is found in observations at beaches, where mothers touched girl babies more than boy babies [28] and in a description of mothers in the feeding situation [59, pp. 346–347]. "Come and get it" typified the attitude toward boys, who were permitted considerable autonomy in establishing their own rhythms and in starting and stopping. "Mother knows best" was the key to the prevalent attitude toward girls, indicating that they were supposed to conform and fit into the mother's way of doing. Mothers tended to hover over girls, to fiddle with their clothing, and to give them a great deal more tactile stimulation than boys received. Given less opportunity to move, to explore and to choose, restricted in expression and yet stimulated, girls must discharge more emotion inward. Here could be a contribution to feminine passivity and masculine activity. From data on infant–mother interaction, it seems that masculine and feminine behavior patterns are built from certain early experiences of the infant which are the results of his own spontaneous behavior shaping the behavior of his parents who are also influenced by cultural and personal notions of sex-appropriate behavior.

Temperament. Behavioral style, or temperament, varies from one child to another. Certain qualities have been defined at 2 or 3 months of age and at subsequent ages throughout childhood through observations of 136 children and interviews with their parents [25]. Nine categories of reactivity emerged: *Activity level*, motility during feeding, bathing, handling, play, and proportion of active and inactive states; *rhythmicity*, or biological regularity, in relation to sleep-waking, hunger, and elimination; *approach-withdrawal*, the type of response to new objects or situations; *adaptability*, or ease of modifying behavior in response to changed situations; *intensity of reaction*, level of vigor of response; *threshold of responsiveness*, intensity of stimulation needed to provoke a response; *quality of mood*, the proportion of happy, friendly, pleased behavior to fussing, crying, and unfriendly behavior; *distractibility*, readiness to be diverted from ongoing activity by a new stimulus; *attention span* and *persistence*, the time that a child stays with an activity and the strength with which he maintains it in the face of obstacles.

Differing combinations of these categories of reactivity produce children who are different from each other. Although every child is unique, there are recurring types and generalizations about them that can be made. The most usual type shows high rhythmicity, positive approach to new situations, adaptability to change, positive moods, and mild to moderate thresholds of responsiveness. This type is called "the easy child." Such an infant usually fits easily into his family, developing regular sleeping and feeding schedules, accepting new foods, new situations, and strangers. Parents and, later, teachers, are usually very much pleased with an "easy child."

"The difficult child" is his opposite number, being irregular in biological functions, negative and withdrawing from new experiences, having slow adaptability and intense reactions. About 10 percent of the children studied were thus [26]. Mothers find such babies difficult to care for and threatening to their feelings of competence, and families are often upset by their fussing, crying, temper tantrums, and protests. These infants need unusually firm, patient, consistent, tolerant handling. When parents are able to meet these needs, the infants usually learn the rules of social living and function energetically and well. When parents cannot give the needed sort of guidance, behavior problems are likely to develop.

Another type is the "slow-to-warm-up" child, who quietly withdraws from new situations and adapts slowly. This kind of baby needs patience, encouragement, and protection from pressure. The "very persistent" type of child becomes extremely absorbed in an activity and resists efforts to divert him. If adults interfere arbitrarily with what he is doing, he is likely to become very angry.

Behavior of the baby has an immediate and continuing impact [7]. From a study of the first 6 months of life and the relation between the mother's behavior and the infant's, this story illustrates how different temperaments call forth different responses from the family [91]. Two boy babies of the same age were placed in one foster home. Jack was passive and quiet, slept a great deal, showed little initiative and little response to social approaches. George was vigorous and active, showing much initiative and response. By 7 weeks of age, there was a difference in the way the foster mother referred to the babies. George was "George" and Jack was "the other one." By 3 months, the mother complained openly that "the other one" slept too much and did nothing. The whole family wanted to feed George. Nobody wanted to feed Jack. Jack's bottle was propped more often than George's. George was often found in the middle of a family activity, while Jack stayed in the playpen, apart from the general stream of action. With two infants the same age and same sex in the same family at the same time, it is apparent that to an unknown degree the difference in their care and experience was initiated by the babies themselves.

The relationships of the baby with his family depend upon all the people involved and how their personalities fit together. It is conceivable that another mother would have preferred Jack to George, a mother who wanted a quiet baby with little initiative and vigor. Certainly, adults vary in how much they approve of characteristics such as ease and vigor in expression of needs and self-assertion in response to coercion.

Correlates of Mother Love

Maternal warmth and affection was found to be positively correlated with development in the Cattell Infant Intelligence scale in a longitudinal study of infants in low-income families [21]. The strength of the mother's love was defined, measured, and correlated with infant behavior in a longitudinal study done at the University of California [73]. Using the data from many observations and ratings of maternal behavior, a factor analysis showed the existence of two dimensions of behavior, autonomy–control and love–hostility. Although the first did not show clear relationships to infant behavior, the second did. Tests that tapped the mother's feeling of love and hostility could predict, to a very small degree, the baby's behavior. In other words, small, significant correlations were found between certain maternal measures and certain infant measures. One of the mothers' rating scales which tapped hostility, for example, used these questions: Does she often comment on how much extra work or trouble the child is? Does she tend to overlook the needs of the child? Babies were rated on seven point scales on these characteristics: degree of strangeness, shy to unreserved; activity, inactive to vigorous; speed of movements, slow to rapid; responsiveness to persons, slight to marked; amount of positive behavior; irritability, or tendency to be sensitive to and react to stimulation; emotional tone, unhappy to happy. Mothers' love behavior was found positively related to babies' happiness, positive behavior and calmness, especially between 10 and 36 months. Correlational studies such as this one tell nothing about whether the mother's love caused the babies' happiness or if the babies' being happy and behaving positively caused the mothers to love them.

Although an educated guess would be that the reaction was reciprocal, the results do not permit a definite conclusion.

Social–Emotional Development

Social behavior is behavior involving interaction with another person. Social development means progressive changes in behavior patterns used in social interaction. Although all experiences have feeling or affective aspects, some social interactions entail much more affect than others. The affective side of transactions with the environment is basic to social relationships, but so is perception basic. The infant's responses to other people depend upon what he perceives in his environment, how he feels about it, and what he is able to do. As he adapts to his world by changing both the world and himself, he organizes his affective system, as well as his motor and cognitive systems.

Emotional behavior is behavior that shows some sort of change from the characteristic level or mode of response, plus some physiological change and an affective state of pleasure or displeasure [69]. Emotional development refers to progressive changes in emotional behavior. The newborn is generally thought to express only excitement, a general, undifferentiated active state. Bridges' classic study on emotional development of infants resulted in a description of more and more specific emotions being differentiated out of the primary state of excitement. Her theory, represented diagrammatically in Figure 4–3, illustrates one of the principles of development stated in Chapter 5, that development proceeds through differentiation and integration. The diagram shows the emotions of distress and delight, representing all negative and positive affective tones, being differentiated out of general excitement in the early weeks of life. Excitement, distress, and delight continue in the infant's emotional repertory while the negative emotions of fear, anger, and disgust and the positive ones of elation and affection are added. This rough outline of emotional development has served as a foundation to many of the detailed studies that have been done since then. Of special interest today is the research on attachment: the bond between two people, particularly the attachment of infant and mother. Although a great deal is known about infant–mother relationships, information on fathers', siblings', and grandparents' relationships with babies is scarce indeed. Related to attachment, the development and control of fear and the development of curiosity are foci of current research.

Love and Attachment

Hardest to define, impossible to agree upon, *love*, for our present purposes, means delight in being with, desire to be with, and desire for contact and response from, another person. Perhaps we should add to this list the budding of a desire to give to the other person, not just for the purpose of eliciting a response. Probably this dimension of love is noticeable toward the end of infancy.

Because *love* has so many different meanings, it is fruitful to use more precise terms rather than the word *love* in discussing the love between a baby, his family, and friends. In employing the more exact terminology, we indicate no callousness toward that mysterious emotional relationship, but rather a warm interest in understanding it better.

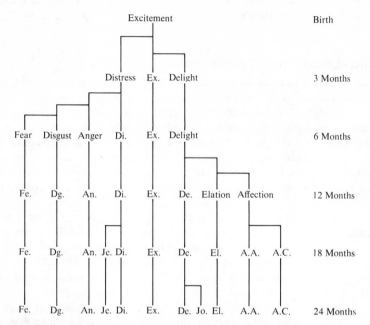

Figure 4–3. Bridges' schematic representation of the differentiation of emotion from general excitement in the newborn to 11 types of emotion at 2 years. *Key:* A.A. = Affection for adults, A.C. = Affection for children, An. = Anger, De. = Delight, Dg. = Disgust, Di. = Distress, El. = Elation, Ex. = Excitement, Fe. = Fear, Je. = Jealousy, Jo. = Joy.

SOURCE: Reprinted by permission from K. M. B. Bridges, "Emotional Development in Early Infancy," *Child Development*, 3, 324–341. Copyright © 1932, The Society for Research in Child Development, Inc.

Attachment. An attachment is an ongoing condition of an individual through which he seeks proximity to and contact with another person [2]. Human attachment behavior includes approaching, embracing, smiling, and calling. Animal babies, as well as human babies, seek the proximity of certain members of their own species, and each species has characteristic attachment behavior patterns. The bond is created as the baby exercises the behavior patterns basic to attachment and specific to his species. The time required for establishing the attachment differs with the species and the pertinent behaviors. Geese become attached in no more than 2 hours, perhaps a few minutes, through their inborn tendency to follow the first moving, sound-emitting object they see. Herd animals' babies are on their feet a few minutes after birth, following their mothers and forming attachments within the first 2 or 3 days. Primates take a little longer. Clinging seems to be the most important attachment behavior of monkeys, who require 10 days or 2 weeks to form their bonds. Chimpanzees take about 2 months and human babies 5 or 6 months. Human beings, born very helpless and with a long infancy to live through, require extensive and long-continued protection. They are born with the means for instigating the necessary care and for evoking it, not only from the principal caretaker (mother), but from the father, the rest of the family, and other human beings. A long infancy makes possible a long time for adapting and learning, hence the development of very complex behavior and wide individual variations. The genetic code provides for the beginnings and growth of exploratory behavior in coordination with attachment behavior. The child is protected while he learns.

Bowlby [14, pp. 326–327], a pioneer in the study of attachment, points out that in the second quarter of the first year, an infant is ready to make his first attachment to a specific person. After the first 6 months, an infant can still do so, but the older he grows, the more difficult it is to make his first attachment, and if he has not done so by the second year, the difficulties are very great. An established attachment is vulnerable for several years after the first birthday. These facts illustrate the principle of *critical periods in development* which is discussed in Chapter 5.

Development of Attachment Behavior. Like many other babies, the human newborn elicits his mother's attention and care when he cries. His crying is a spontaneous expression of distress, and her response is an anxious feeling that she seeks to relieve by stopping his crying. Thus crying fulfills the criterion for attachment behavior in that it brings the pair into proximity or contact. Sucking also brings the two together and causes pleasant sensations in both mother and baby. The human baby also does an approximation of clinging, although he cannot hang on unaided. He grasps what is put into his hands, which means that when he is held to the shoulder, he may grasp the clothing, skin, or hair of the adult. His body snuggles or bends to fit the body on which it rests. These kinds of contact evoke pleasure in the mother—in fact, in most people.

Looking also contributes to attachment. The newborn has a built-in tendency to look at stimuli that move and that have light–dark contrast. Since a face has both attractions, babies look readily at faces, particularly at the eyes, which have a concentration of both contrast and movement. By 3 weeks of age, a live human face elicited more excitement than did a moving drawing of a face [79]. All of the babies in this experiment showed excitement at the human face while actively scanning it, by general limb movements, head movements, and a variety of mouth movements. By 5 to 7 weeks, mouth and head movements declined as part of the excitatory pattern, while smiling and soft cooing increased. Looking and grasping become integrated into nursing behavior, the infant scanning his mother's face and fingering her person while he sucks.

Smiling occurs readily at the sight of a human face by the time the baby is 5 or 6 weeks old. The smile is a very important form of human behavior, having universal meaning of friendliness and cutting across language barriers between adults. Thus, when the infant smiles regularly at his mother and other people, it serves as attachment behavior, bringing people close to him, keeping them with him, and eliciting friendly social behavior in the form of smiles. Cooing and babbling, which often accompany smiling, tie the bonds between baby and others in much the same way that smiling does. Baby babbles. Mother babbles back, nodding and smiling, all quite spontaneously. They scan each other's faces and fixate on each other's eyes.

Familiar objects seem to be pleasurable as the baby recognizes them. He develops schemas or some sort of internal representations with which he can match perceptual experiences. Most likely his mother's face is one of his early schemas. During Piaget's stage of secondary circular reactions, which lasts from about 4 to 8 months, the baby tries to make interesting sights last or to regain perceptual contact with familiar objects. When he succeeds he shows pleasure by smiling, and when he does not he may cry.

Following and approaching are attachment behavior in that they bring the pair closer together or into contact. Until he can crawl or creep, the infant cannot follow bodily, but he can follow with his eyes. The distance receptors, eyes and ears, are also active in the process of making and keeping contact with the object of attachment.

Signs of Growing Attachment. A crucial step in the development of social relationships is to distinguish between people and inanimate objects. Observations of infants' responses in home settings indicated that 65 percent of babies made this distinction by 1 month of age. All did by 5 months. Recognition of the mother, indicated by showing excitement and approach movements to her but not to strangers, was exhibited by some infants as early as 1 month, by 81 percent at 3 months, and by all babies at 5 months [92]. By 3 months of age, babies will smile more to reinforcements (saying "Hi, Baby," smiling and lightly touching his chest) offered by the mother than to the same reinforcements offered by a stranger [83]. Even though he apparently perceives a difference between his mother and other people, however, he will smile at strangers and, in fact, smiles at everyone who approaches him until he is around 6 months of age. Then he becomes more selective, smiling at familiar people and most of all to his mother and to other people to whom he is becoming attached. Confidence in the mother, as shown by signs of expecting her to soothe or comfort, was shown in half of babies studied at 3 months and in 75 percent of the babies at 5 months [92].

Continuing to build the bonds of love, the baby vocalizes selectively, "talking" more to his attachment object. Another sign of beginning attachment which occurs as smiling becomes selective, or possibly before, is differential crying. The baby cries when held by someone other than his mother and stops when she takes him. The next step is to watch the object of attachment, as when the baby keeps his mother in view even though he is in someone else's arms. Then comes a definite indication of attachment, crying when the specific person leaves and not crying when other people do. Figure 4–4 shows the intensity with which infants at various ages protested being left by anybody and by attachment objects. The curve for "indiscriminate attachment" shows that babies as young as 2 months may protest when social stimulation is withdrawn but that it takes a maturity of 7 or 8 months to cry for attention from specific individuals. Other indications of attachment include clinging, scrambling over the mother and exploring her person, burying his face in her lap, following the attachment object as soon as he can creep, lifting arms, clapping hands, and crowing in greeting [1]. Attachment behavior is not confined to close physical contacts. Vision and hearing, vocalizing and gestures, are used for keeping and making contact as the infant widens the environment in which he operates. As sensorimotor competency increases, the baby can allow his mother to go farther away, since he is able to contact his attachment objects over a wider area.

Varieties of Attachments. Attachment has been studied longitudinally in 60 babies, focusing on the infant's protest at being separated from the objects of attachment [75] and the strength of his crying or whimpering at the ending of a contact between him and the other person. The situations were everyday, ordinary occurrences, such as being left alone in a room, being left in his pram (this was a British study) outside a store, and being put down from arms or lap. Using these criteria, it was found that half of the specific attachments, including attachments to the mother, occurred most often between 25 and 32 weeks. A few occurred earlier and the rest later, between 32 and 78 weeks. Individuals showed variation from time to time in strength of protest over separation. Interesting stimulation made separation much more tolerable, as shown by the frequent acceptance of the mother's

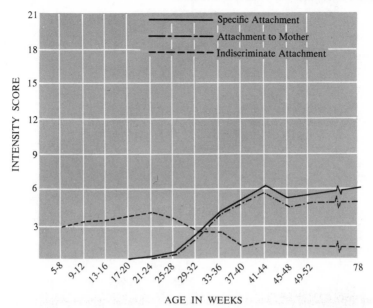

AGE IN WEEKS

Figure 4–4. Development of infants' attachments to the mother, to other persons, and to people-in-general, shown in terms of strength of protest at being left.

SOURCE: Reprinted by permission from H. R. Schaffer and P. E. Emerson, "The Development of Social Attachments in Infancy," *Monographs of The Society for Research in Child Development*, **29**:3. Copyright © 1964, The Society for Research in Child Development, Inc.

absence when she parked the pram outside the shop, on a busy street, in contrast to the protest which occurred on being left alone in bed. Figure 4–5 shows the difference between these two situations. Pain, illness, fatigue, and fear led to intense protest and strong seeking of the mother's presence. When the attachment object returned from an absence, the infant was more demanding of attention, as when the father came in after work. A temporary change in social stimulation, such as the visit of an attentive relative, also brought increased demands on the mother after the period of extra stimulation had ended, but this demand was only temporary.

Often, but not always, the infant becomes attached to one person before he forms attachments to several. Often, but not always, the first person is his mother. Table 4–2 shows the objects of attachment at various ages. It will be noted that the mother soon comes to share the baby's affections with the father, grandparents, siblings, relatives, and friends. The number of attachments depended largely on number of available people. Mere presence was not enough. Babies tended to become attached to people who offered interesting stimulation.

Strongly attached infants were found to have mothers who responded quickly to their indications of need [75]. Subsequent studies have focused on the quality of attachment and behavior of mothers, finding that babies tend to show clear-cut, unambivalent attachment to mothers who are very perceptive, responsive, and eager to gratify them in the feeding situation and socially [8]. The type of attachment which develops under these circumstances is associated with early development of a schema of person permanence, followed by development of a schema of

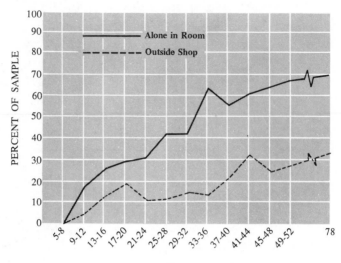

AGE IN WEEKS

Figure 4–5. Percent of babies protesting being left alone in room, contrasted with percent protesting being left alone outside a shop. Interesting stimulation makes separation from attachment object much more acceptable.

SOURCE: Adapted from H. R. Schaffer and P. E. Emerson, "The Development of Social Attachments in Infancy," *Monographs of The Society for Research in Child Development,* **29**:3. Copyright © 1964, The Society for Research in Child Development, Inc. Used by permission.

the permanence of objects which is also early [8]. In colloquial terms, a loving, competent mother is likely to have a baby who loves her and whose sensorimotor intelligence progresses rapidly.

Exploratory Behavior. As soon as he is able to do so, the baby separates himself briefly from his mother by crawling away to explore and play. The human baby seems to be the only mammalian infant who leaves his mother just as soon as he can move himself, but then he is the only creature who spends 6 or 7 months interacting with the world in a sedentary condition. Separations, however, do not mean detachment. He is still attached, but the bond is elastic and can be maintained through seeing, hearing, calling, and smiling, with only periodic physical contact. When he is playing, he is not looking at or calling to his mother constantly, but only occasionally. The mother or other attachment object serves as a secure base from which the infant can venture forth as an explorer, returning either bodily, visually, or auditorily as he needs reassurance.

The relationship between attachment and exploratory behavior was first studied by Harlow [42] with his baby monkeys who had become attached to wire, cloth-covered mothers. When placed alone in a strange room, the little monkey cowered, crouched, rocked, sucked, and clutched his own body. With the surrogate mother there, the baby clung to her, ventured forth to explore the objects in the room, clung again and explored again, as though he neutralized his fear by contacting her, and derived continued reassurance by seeing her in the room. Later studies on chimpanzees showed a relation between clinging and calming the baby from high levels of arousal resulting from strange situations or separations from companions. After clinging, the little chimp would return to playing and exploring [54].

Table 4–2 Identity of Attachment Objects : Percentage of Subjects Forming Specific Attachments According to Identity of Object at Successive Age Period

Identity of Object	Lunar Month Following Age at Onset in First Year						18 Months (CA)
	1ST	2ND	3RD	4TH	5TH	6TH	
Mother (sole object)	65	53	32	50	47	17	5
Mother (joint object)	30	35	54	43	50	77	76
Father (sole object)	3	9	7	2	0	5	4
Father (joint object)	27	23	42	29	44	59	71
Grandparent (sole object)	2	0	0	0	0	0	0
Grandparent (joint object)	9	12	14	12	10	29	45
Other relative (sole object)	0	0	0	0	0	0	2
Other relative (joint object)	5	5	5	14	10	18	16
Friend or neighbor (sole object)	0	0	2	0	0	0	0
Friend or neighbor (joint object)	3	7	7	9	3	12	26
Sibling (sole object)	0	0	0	0	0	0	2
Sibling (joint object)	2	5	7	7	7	12	22
Other child (sole object)	0	0	0	0	0	0	0
Other child (joint object)	3	5	14	7	3	12	14

SOURCE: Reprinted by permission from H. R. Schaffer and P. E. Emerson, "The Development of Social Attachments in Infancy," *Monographs of The Society for Research in Child Development*, **29**:3, Table 8. Copyright © 1964, The Society for Research in Child Development, Inc.

Studies on human babies have shown a similar articulation between attachment and exploratory behavior. The usual plan is for observers, sitting behind a one-way vision screen, to record the actions of babies and mothers in space that is marked off to facilitate accurate measuring of distance. A study of 1-year-old infants was conducted in a setting of seven consecutive 3-minute episodes [3]. The mother entered the room, which had a supply of toys, sat down, put the baby down, and did nothing unless the baby sought her attention. A stranger entered, sat quietly, then approached the baby with a toy. The mother left the room. If the baby was not active with toys, the stranger tried to interest him in them. If he cried, she tried to comfort him. The mother returned, the stranger departed, and as soon as the baby was settled in play, the mother again left. The baby was alone for 3 minutes until the stranger reappeared, behaving as she did before. Then the mother came back. Results showed the largest amount of exploratory behavior, as seen in locomotion, manipulation, and looking, occurring in the beginning of the observation, when the baby was alone with his mother. When the stranger entered, exploration decreased and remained on a low level until the mother returned from her absence. Exploration picked up somewhat, but when the mother left, it dropped again and remained depressed. Proximity- and contact-seeking behaviors increased throughout the experiment. When left alone 37 percent of the babies cried little and searched strongly, 20 percent cried desperately but searched weakly or not at all, and 32 percent both cried and searched. As might be expected, crying and exploration were negatively correlated (-0.67 for crying and manipulation). Figure 4–6 shows the amounts of crying and exploratory manipulation throughout the experiment. Other experiments have shown that although infants showed marked distress and almost no locomotion when placed alone in a room, reactions were entirely different when they were permitted to enter an unfamiliar empty room on their own initiative [68]. The latter infants were placed on the floor in front of their mothers in a

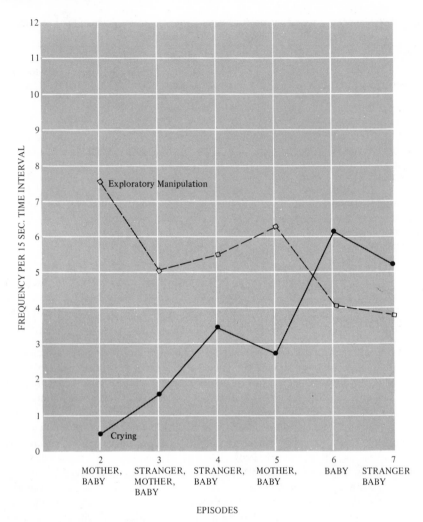

Figure 4–6. Amounts of crying and exploratory behavior of 1-year-olds under conditions of mother present and mother absent.

SOURCE: Adapted from M. D. S. Ainsworth and S. M. Bell, "Attachment, Exploration and Separation: Illustrated by the Behavior of One-Year-Olds in a Strange Situation," *Child Development*, **41**, 49–67.

small room adjoining the large room. Whether the large room contained a toy or not, all the infants left their mothers and went into the other room, with no sign of distress. All returned to their mothers and most reentered the large room, some several times. Their behavior illustrates using the mother as a secure base for exploration. These experiments offer strong evidence that attachment behavior and exploratory behavior are in dynamic balance in young children and that both kinds of behavior are related to the mother's presence [3].

Exploratory behavior varies from one infant to another. The quality of temperament called *approach-withdrawal* (see page 211) can be observed as early as 2 or 3 months of age. A tendency to approach new situations rather than to withdraw from them would facilitate exploratory behavior. The baby's social experience in addition to his relations with his mother also affects his exploratory behavior. Since so many research studies have focused on the mother–infant relationship and so few on the infant's additional social life, a study of exploratory behavior of first-born and later born infants is especially interesting [29]. The subjects were a group of 12 first-born babies, and 6 whose next siblings were 6 or more years older and a matched group of 18 whose next siblings were no more than 5 years older. When tested with new, attractive toys, the first-born and widely spaced babies paused much longer before picking up the toy than did the later-borns and showed greater variability in the length of the pause. Later-borns made more responses to the toys, laughed and smiled more, and initiated more play with the examiner. Interviews with the mothers confirmed the expectation that preschool siblings would play often with the baby and that mothers tended to protect first-borns from close contact with others. Most likely the first-borns and widely spaced babies were more fearful and therefore less exploratory than infants who interacted freely with young siblings.

Separation and Reunion. The experiments mentioned above have shown that the usual immediate response to involuntary separation from the mother is crying and searching by infants of about 1 year of age. When the mother returns, physical contact usually restores the child's equilibrium. About half of the infants showed angry, resisting behavior when their mothers returned after the second absence [3]. The infants who scored high in contact-resisting behavior tended to be the same ones who scored high in contact-maintaining behavior. This finding suggested that the babies felt much ambivalence, wanting to be close to mother and yet feeling angry at her. The short samples of behavior shown in the experimental situation are consistent with behavior seen in real-life situations involving longer separations of mothers and attached young children.

Bowlby [12, 13, 14] has investigated attachment, separation, and long-term separations in hospitals. When the child between about 8 months and 3 years is first left by his mother, he is likely to cry and protest, showing acute distress and trying to find and regain the mother. The initial phase gives way to despair, when the child is very quiet. Then comes a more active phase when he pays more attention to the environment and interacts with people and things. When children go home after short hospital separations, they often show angry, contact-resisting behavior along with proximity-seeking [46]. Clinging and whining are also very common after hospital separations. It is easy to see how all of these reactions to reunion would be annoying and disturbing to mothers and how they might rebuff or punish the irritating child. A rebuff, however, tends only to intensify the child's attachment behavior [3]. Observations on animal behavior show similar relationships in infant monkeys, who cling all the harder to "heartless mothers" who ignore, reject, or hurt them [44]. When a child persists in clinging, whining and/or angry, aggressive behavior following a separation, recovery is more likely if his mother gives him extra opportunities for the proximity and contacts he is seeking [3].

Separation and reunion are dramatized in the game of peekaboo, which delights children between about 3 months and 4 years of age. It has been suggested that peekaboo symbolizes being and nonbeing, or being alive and being dead [55]. The game is of ancient origin and widespread throughout the world. Some parents have reported that they or their baby invented it. One way of playing it is to put a light cloth over the baby's face, saying "Where's Baby?" He then flails his arms and removes the cloth, revealing wide eyes scanning anxiously until they meet the mother's or father's, whereupon the parent says "Peekaboo" and laughs, and the baby laughs and wriggles with delight. While dramatic play is ordinarily thought of as dominating the years between 3 and 7, peekaboo surely is an instance of playing out a crucial, fearful experience that recurs in the life of the infant. The happy ending of reunion with the loved one is reassuring, suggesting not only that Mother is sure to come back, but that Baby has some control over his fate.

Peer Relationships. Since babies in the United States do not often come together in groups, there has not been much American observation of peer interaction in infancy. A few studies have shown that babies did indeed interact with each other, from about 5 months onward. Conflict over toys seemed to be at a peak between 9 and 14 months, with personal aggression increasing with age. Cooperation in play was observed at about 9 months, increased with age and increased considerably at 19 months [41]. Although Americans have not conducted many group care projects with infants, the Soviets and Israelis have had considerable experience with young children in groups. In the yasli-sad of the U.S.S.R., the children are cared for and educated from the age of 2 months to 7 years. Among the objectives of the yasli-sad are fostering friendship and mutual assistance between peers, teaching children to relate good-naturedly to children their own age, to help anyone in need, and to be friendly in work and play [24]. An American observer [18] reports that this teaching is begun in the first year of life when babies are placed in groups in large playpens. The playpens are raised off the floor at heights that permit adults to interact face-to-face with the infants. The youngest babies, who are lying down, are at the highest level. When they can crawl and pull up, the playpens are lowered to maintain face-to-face position with the caretakers. Educators stress making learning situations happy. The teacher is to prevent the types of conflicts which arise among babies if they gather in one place and get in each other's way. The instructress must also watch to see that negative relations do not occur because of one trying to take a toy away from another. During the second year, the children are not expected to play together for long periods, but when together, they imitate and help each other and they are expected not to take toys from each other and not to interfere with each other [24]. Thus do Soviet educators prepare children from the first year of life to live in a collective society.

In another collective society, the kibbutzim of Israel, infants likewise begin early to orient to their peers. Although practices vary somewhat from one kibbutz to another, the descriptions of one observer [9] will give an idea of some of the ways in which infants relate to each other in such settings. The children sleep, eat, and play in the kibbutz, going to their parents' rooms for visits and having their parents visit them. From the first days of life, a baby is in a room with others his age and he sees them more than he sees his parents or siblings. He is never alone. From the time he can crawl, he spends waking time in a large playpen with his age-mates. When the babies can walk, they are together in fenced play yards. Since the caretakers are busy with housework as well as child care, they interfere little with the children's play. In learning to adjust to one another, the babies crawl over each other and push each other down occasionally. They also comfort others in distress and pick up the ones who get pushed over. Helpfulness is much more apparent than any efforts to dominate. "The children are comrades, not competitors" [9, p. 89]. By the time they are toddlers, they have learned much about how to fend for themselves in the group and how to find satisfaction there. They have made a strong beginning in establishing group relations that are their main source of emotional security and orientation.

The long-term results of close peer relationships in infancy have been exposed to careful scientific scrutiny in monkeys [45] but not in man. Harlow had demonstrated that monkeys brought up with surrogate but inanimate mothers grew up to be abnormal. He also found that babies raised with normal mothers but without the company of other babies showed later behavior abnormalities, as far as sex and play were concerned. In order to analyze contributions of mothering and of peer companionship to normal development, he tried raising babies with surrogate mothers, giving them daily time in a playroom with their peers. Although they did not play as much with peers during their first year as did infants with real mothers, these monkeys developed normal play patterns and normal social-sex behavior in their second year.

Nobody knows whether seriously deprived human infants would get a comparable beneficial result from playing together. The same situation could not even occur for humans, even if such experimentation were possible, since they are still immobile at the age (or even at the comparable point in the life span) when little monkeys are racing, chasing, climbing, swinging, scuffling, and playfully biting each other.

It is not feasible to experiment with human beings in such a way as to show a relationship between mother–infant experience and adult sexual behavior. Animal experiments give hints, guides, and suggestions but not blueprints on human behavior mechanisms. Harlow's experiments on monkey infant–infant relationships suggest that the peer relationships of young human beings may be extremely valuable and important in assuring normal growth and in compensating for some deprivation in other areas of life. As for discovering the age at which peer play would have maximum benefits or where its absence would be most serious, the monkey experiments are of little help. Research indicates that preschool social play can help children to recover intellectually from early deprivation [30]. What is more, a "natural experiment" during World War II showed that preschool children could become strongly attached to one another and dependent on one another for emotional satisfaction, in the absence of permanent adults in their world [34]. The group consisted of six children whose parents had been killed or separated by the Nazis during their first year of life (mostly during the first 6 months). They were cared for in a restricted ward in a concentration camp, with changing caretakers, and after liberation, had five or six sets of caretakers. When studied at ages 3 and 4, they were a closely knit, cooperative, affectionate group of children with only tenuous relationships to adults.

Fear

Everyone knows how fear feels—stomach turning over, heart racing, mouth dry, skin perspiring, thoughts concentrated on how to get away from the situation in which one is. When infants show distress through crying and apparent attempts to withdraw, adults usually conclude that the children are afraid. When the baby is old enough to cling and to seek proximity to his mother, these behaviors, along with crying and withdrawing, are probably universal indications to adults that young children are afraid.

Fear behavior is neither rigid nor automatic. The physiological basis for fear reactions is inherited, but its expression is an interaction with the environment. Possible reactions are those that facilitate withdrawal from dangers the young are likely to encounter: strangers, heights, excessive stimulation. As the section on attachment behavior has shown, attachment and fear are articulated in ways that promote survival of the infant and that permit exploration and growth. When a strange person, object, or situation causes distress and withdrawal, contact through clinging, touching, or even looking at a loved person restores the baby's equilibrium in such a way that he can approach and explore. Loss of support, pain, loud noises, and other intense stimuli also cause distress reactions which look like fear and which can usually be alleviated by holding the baby close. Individual differences in temperament make for more intense reactions in some infants and less in others. Some can be comforted more easily than others.

A group of infants between 2 and 23 months were examined in a series of fear-provoking situations and other tests, and their mothers were interviewed [72]. Fears of loud noises, masks, a Jack-in-the-box, and a mechanical dog were correlated and showed more intensity in younger and older infants than in those in the middle of the age range. The babies who indicated most fear in these situations of intense stimulation and strange objects tended to be the "cuddliest" babies, or to show highest need for physical contact. This result is consistent with the observation that clinging seems to allay fear. Fear of falling was tested on a visual cliff, a platform of strong glass with a textured pattern under it. Half of the patterned surface is directly under the glass and the other half far below it, giving the visual illusion of a dropoff, halfway across the platform. The fear of crossing the visual cliff increased with age, from 6 months onward. Noncreepers showed different reactions to the two sides of the cliff when placed on its edge, but no fear reactions. Even when pulled across the cliff, they had no fear reactions. Creepers showed some fear, and walkers more fear. Below 10 months of age, the babies did more tactile than visual exploration but after that age, visual exploration increased and tactile decreased. By 5 or 6 months most of the infants could distinguish between the two sides of the cliff, but not between what would support them and what would not. It looked as though experience with space through locomotion was necessary for being able to tell by looking what would offer support for the body. Fear of the cliff was correlated with previous falls, cuddliness, and protest at separation from the mother.

Fear of strangers ordinarily occurs in the second half of the first year and rarely before then. The babies in the study described above showed no fear of strangers until 7 months, moderate fear between 7 and 12, and more fear after 12 months [72]. A certain amount of maturity is necessary before unfamiliar images and expectations must be built up first, in order to have a basis for comparison [19].

Sex differences in fear of strangers were found in another study [70]. The age of onset of fear of strangers was taken as the first month in which the baby showed a clear-cut avoidance response to an unfamiliar adult. For girls, the mean age for this measure was 6.7 months and for boys, 9.1 months. Fear of strangers is also related to the number of social contacts an infant has, both within and outside his family. First-born children showed fear of strangers at younger ages than did later-borns [74].

Fear of strangers becomes meaningful when viewed in the sequence of attachment behavior described on page 216. Positive attachments to the mother and other important human beings are built up, and then discrimination against others

Ellen S. Smart

Figure 4–7. Fear of a stranger shown by clinging to mother.

is developed. In the previously mentioned study [75] of attachment in infancy, 77 percent of babies were found to show their first fear of strangers about one month after they showed the beginnings of specific attachments. At 8 to 9½ months, the amount of looking at a stranger has been found negatively related to the infant's fear of strangers [70]. Ainsworth [2], from her observations of infants in Uganda, describes a developmental sequence in response to strangers during the first year of life: (1) No observable discrimination between strange and familiar people. (2) Different responses to mother and strangers, but accepts strangers. (3) The baby stares at strangers but does not show fear reactions. (4) The baby does not approach strangers but allows them to hold him, showing some uneasiness. (5) Fear reactions, ranging from slight apprehension to panic.

Fear of strangers decreases during the second and third years of life, as shown by increasing willingness to accept comfort from a stranger [53]. Fear of being left alone and fear of the dark probably have a large hereditary, maturational basis. It would be very dangerous for a young, wild primate to be left alone, especially in the dark. His fears and protestations would have real survival value. What meaning does this have for human parents? If they think of such fears as natural outcomes of development in infancy, then they will expect to provide comfort and reassurance if such fears are aroused and to be patient until children grow beyond them.

Applying Knowledge from Research on Fear

1. Avoid separations of the baby from his attachment objects except for brief periods. Since mothers are sometimes necessarily absent, it is wise to encourage

the building of other attachments, which the infant is likely to do with anyone who responds to him and who offers interesting stimulation.

2. Avoid separations and frightening experiences especially at the time when fear of strangers is developing and at its peak. Hospitalization and painful treatments are best postponed if possible. If such experiences are essential, keep the child with a loved person. If the parent is powerless to provide this safeguard to emotional well-being, then provide an object to which the child is attached, such as his blanket, or an object belonging to a person to whom he is attached, such as his mother's purse.

3. Introduce the infant gradually to new situations so as to prevent fears arising from sudden stimulus changes.

4. Provide new situations and gradual changes along with reassurance so as to help the child tolerate novelty and cope with newness.

5. If the baby is afraid of the dark, give him a night light.

6. Use reconditioning, when appropriate. A fear of a specific object or situation may be overcome by experiencing it along with something pleasant and comfortable.

Anger

Anger is the distress that accompanies being restrained or blocked in progress toward some sort of fulfillment. Anger involves lashing out rather than withdrawing as in fear. The crying and bodily activity of infants under conditions of bodily tension, such as hunger, look like anger. They seem to be reacting similarly to children and adults who are known to be angry. During the first year, babies learn to use anger for solving some of their problems, to a greater or lesser degree, depending on how successful it is. Some anger expressions seem to be only release of emotional energy.

During the second year, when the desire to establish autonomy is strong, interference with choice making is likely to bring angry resistance, crying, screaming, kicking, perhaps hitting, throwing, and biting. For establishment of a sound sense of autonomy, a baby grows by having many experiences in successful choice making and few in choosing activities where he cannot succeed.

Goodenough's comprehensive and classic study, *Anger in Young Children*, describes and analyzes 1878 anger outbursts of children in the first 8 years of life [39]. Since the observations were recorded by parents, the cases were necessarily selected from families where parents were unusually cooperative and intelligent. As can be seen in Figure 4–8 there was a marked peak in anger outbursts during the second year and then a rapid decline. Little sex difference appeared in infancy, but during the preschool period, boys had significantly more outbursts than girls. At all ages, however, differences between individuals were greater than differences between the sexes.

Anger behavior changed with age. Most of the outbursts during the first 3 years involved display or undirected energy. Such behavior included crying, screaming, stiffening the body, throwing self on floor, stamping, jumping up and down. With age, such primitive bodily responses tended to be replaced with more directed, less violent, more symbolic expressions. The duration of outbursts changed very little, however.

Physical factors were influential. Anger occurred before mealtimes more than at

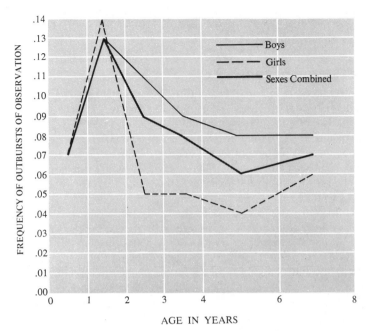

Figure 4–8. Number of anger outbursts in ten hours by age and sex.
SOURCE: Adapted from F. L. Goodenough [39].

any other times of day. Children were angry more when ill, even with slight colds or constipation. Outbursts were more frequent among those who had recovered from one or more fairly serious illnesses than among children who had not been ill.

Many psychological factors were shown to be significant. Children who were being toilet-trained showed more anger on days following bedwetting than on days following dry nights. The more adults in the home, the more likely was a child to become angry. When parents shifted from one method of control to another, the child tended to have more outbursts. "Giving the child his own way" was reported more often for children who had many outbursts than for those who had few.

Goodenough comes to this conclusion:

> the control of anger in children is best achieved when the child's be-
> havior is viewed with serenity and tolerance, when the standards are
> adhered to with sufficient consistency to permit the child to learn through
> uniformity of experience, without such mechanical adherence to routine
> that the child's emotional or physical well-being is sacrificed to the de-
> mands of an inflexible schedule. However, when departures from the
> established schedule are made, they should be determined by a recogni-
> tion of the needs of the child and not simply by the convenience or mood
> of the adult in charge. Self-control in the parents is, after all, likely to be
> the best guarantee of self-control in the child.

Hostile aggression is a type of anger expression which frequently shows up in relation to the preschool child. The roots of hostile aggression may lie in the infant–mother relationship [77, pp. 221–226]. If it happens that the mother answers the baby's calls after he has become angry through frustration, he may learn to be aggressive with his mother. She thus reinforces his angry behavior because she follows it with satisfactions. He also learns that it hurts her when he does not do what she wishes. If he repeatedly perceives hurt in the other person as he achieves his ends (overcomes his frustrations), then hurting another person may become pleasant to him.

Regulation of Behavior

Before the end of the first year, the infant who has lived in a harmonious relationship is inclined to cooperate with the important people in his life, those to whom he is attached. The origins of socialization can be seen in the baby's obedience to simple commands and prohibitions given by his parents. Studies on infant obedience show how wrong was the old notion of babies as purely selfish creatures who had to be coerced into social acceptability. The attachment bond seems to predispose the infant to comply with requests signaled by loved people [78]. Thus does cooperation grow out of trust.

In their efforts to regulate what a baby does and when, where, and how he does it, parents are influenced by what they believe to be good for the baby and good for the rest of the family and by their own needs. "Good for the baby" involves what is good for him now and what will help him to grow into the right kind of child, adolescent, and adult. "Good for the rest of the family" means considering all the other people in the home and even some beyond the home, perhaps grandparents. Parents' "own needs" include those that they recognize as existing and also needs of which they are unaware or only dimly aware. The behavior influenced by parental guidance includes thinking and feeling as well as overt action.

Family life has many rhythms. The fitting of small rhythms to one another and into larger wholes is a dynamic process. The ways in which infant and family adapt to one another have important outcomes for both.

Timing

The term *mutual regulation* is perhaps more apt than *scheduling* to describe what ideally happens in a home with a young baby. Since the newborn baby cannot wait for food and comfort, the family has to adjust pretty much to *his* rhythms if he is to be kept comfortable and helped to feel that the world is worth trusting. After 2 or 3 months, however, a baby can wait briefly for food and attention. With the development of physiological stability, some confidence, and some interest in sensorimotor exploration, he can begin to fit into some of the rhythms of the family. Perhaps he'll sit happily on Daddy's lap for five minutes while Mother finishes her dessert, even though he is hungry. In another month or two, the baby can eat larger meals and can last for longer times between meals. Although he may have some preference as to mealtimes, a mother can fit them into convenient times by gradual change and planning the staying qualities of meals and snacks.

In the matter of sleeping, too, a baby accommodates himself more and more to family rhythms as he matures and as he is guided to do so. In the beginning, sleep follows eating, and waking brings a demand for food. Gradually he stays awake for longer periods and sleeps for a longer time at night, when the rest of the family sleeps. In societies where babies are always with other people, going to bed when the family goes to bed, and sleeping when sleepy during the day, there is no problem of scheduling sleep. American life, especially middle-class American life, is tightly scheduled. Infants have to have naps and go to bed early in order to get enough sleep and also in order for their mothers to get their housework and other jobs done. Parents tend to feel that they need some free, quiet hours without children present, in the evening. Thus getting the baby to go to sleep at certain times often comes to be a problem. It is usually solved by exerting pressure on the baby's own changing rhythms, waking him from previous sleep in time to have him need sleep appropriately, timing meals, arranging baths, play, and outings to induce just enough fatigue.

Babies often come to resist being put to bed, sometimes because they are put to bed when they really are not tired and sleepy. An infant may feel mistrust and lack of confidence in the family who is overeager to get him out of the way. Fears and excitement can prevent and disturb sleep. Sometimes the most careful attention to schedules and emotional security is not enough, and a tired baby cries when put to bed. In such a case, crying is usually brief.

Scheduling includes planning baths, toileting, and dressing at times that fit both the family and baby. Times for play of different kinds and in different places, walks and rides, visiting and receiving guests—all are part of planning for the baby's well-being and for family living. Thus the family, especially the mother, structures the infant's life in time and space, in terms of maintaining his life, stimulating his development, and building relationships with him.

Physical well-being hinges on a schedule that fits the baby. Health and optimal growth require adequate nutrition, rest, and exercise. It takes careful planning and management to see that the baby gets all of these while family living goes on to everyone's benefit. What the baby seems to want at the moment is not always what is best in the overall picture, at least as viewed by the adult. A toddler may want to get into the thick of a game with his kindergartner sister and her friends, not realizing that the results for him would be great excitement, frustration, and fatigue. Or he may be hungry and yet refuse to come in for lunch just because it feels so good to be climbing outdoors.

Cognitive development results from good scheduling, too. For the baby too young to sit up by himself, a frequent change of position and scenery is necessary for giving him mental food (visual and tactual stimulation). When he enlarges his own sphere of operations, first by sitting, then by creeping and walking, his family can still enlarge the scene for him by moving him to different rooms and different furniture and taking him places. Scheduling does not mean that the mother has to pick the baby up at 9 and 11 but rather that she carry on a plan of household activity which includes a change of scene and action for the baby at fairly regular intervals. Her management of his toys has a bearing on mental growth, too. He benefits from some system of rotating toys, so that he gets only a few at a time and frequent changes. Thus a schedule can assure a steady flow of stimulation.

Emotional health is fostered by a suitable schedule. When the infant's physical needs are met before they become overwhelming, he is spared anxiety and frustration. He enjoys the good feeling of trust. Regular holding and cuddling further build up his sense of trust, allaying fears and anxiety and stimulating his senses. Because he trusts, he learns to wait and hope and thus to cooperate as a family member.

Control and Autonomy

Parents everywhere set limits on their infants' behavior. If they did not, there would be no more babies, since babies creep and toddle right into danger, whether it be off the platform of a house built on poles over the sea or under a station wagon parked in the driveway. There are always dangers to be kept from exploring fingers and mouths, too—a dung fire in the corner, incense burning before a household god, an electric socket. Little fingers and mouths have to be prevented from destroying precious objects, such as a threaded loom, a clay water pot, or a piece of Steuben glass.

Cultures vary widely in whether babies are expected to learn self-control from the limits placed on their behavior. In some societies, keeping the baby safe is just that and no more. Somebody is expected to look out for him during his early years to see that he does himself no harm. But in many societies, including the American culture, keeping safe is, of course, a prime motive, but a variety of other aims makes for a wide range of practices.

One dimension of parent–child behavior is autonomy-control or permissiveness-restrictiveness [6]. Parents vary according to how strict or permissive they are with children, or how much autonomy they permit, versus how much they try to control the child. Some parents permit wide autonomy, others a little less; some are very controlling, others somewhat controlling. Parents vary on this dimension within the same culture, and cultures also vary in autonomy-control in adult–child relationships. The teaching manual *Soviet Preschool Education* [24, pp. 24–25] spells out, for example, that the child at 18 months should be taught not to take toys away from others, not to interfere with them, to sit at a table calmly, to obey adults, to feed himself neatly, to wash his hands, to pull up his socks and overalls . . . and more. Probably most Americans would think that this picture presents a great deal of control and not much permissiveness for autonomy.

Ideals in America are probably more diverse than they are in the Soviet Union. Individual freedom and self-expression, however, are high on the lists of many people. The development of a strong sense of autonomy, according to Erikson, requires freedom for a toddler to make choices and planning by adults that will ensure a large proportion of successful choices. Thus the toddler comes to feel, "I can decide" and "What I choose is all right." Some confirmation of the importance of autonomy in infancy for later personality development is offered by longitudinal study on infants and their mothers [59]. During the infancy period, the mothers of the babies were observed and rated on how much autonomy they permitted and how much they tried to control their children. For example, would the mother let the baby decide when he had had enough to eat, or would she try to get him to take more? When the children reached preschool age, they were rated on a number of personality characteristics, and these ratings correlated with the mothers' autonomy-control behavior. Significant correlations were found, showing that there were relations between the mothers' behavior during infancy and the children's preschool behavior. Table 4–3 shows the size of correlations between mothers' permission for autonomy and characteristics of preschool-age boys. Another study indicates that boy babies and girl babies react differently, in terms of their intellectual development, to opportunities for autonomy and the degree of control given by their mothers [5].

Adaptations in the home which make possible the permission of wide limits include the provision of spaces where little damage can result from play and exploration. Fussy, breakable objects can be put away. Furniture can be upholstered or slip-covered in tough, washable fabrics. Floor coverings and draperies can be of relatively indestructible materials. A baby is able to creep in this kind of room

Table 4–3 Relationship Between Autonomy Permitted by Mother in Infancy and Personality Characteristics of Preschool-Age Boys

Correlation Coefficient	Personality Characteristic
0.614	Capacity to maintain internal integration
0.571	Ability to limit or fend off excessive stimulation
0.511	Resistance to discouragement
0.610	Ability to mobilize energy to meet challenge or stress
0.784	Sense of self worth
0.646	Clarity in sex role
0.700	Separation (differentiation of self and others)

SOURCE: Reprinted by permission from L. V. Murphy, *The Widening World of Childhood* (New York: Basic Books, 1962). Copyright © 1962, Basic Books, Inc.

without hurting himself or anything else. A toddler climbs, explores, runs his cars, and pushes a doll carriage. The bathroom can be arranged so that a toddler can climb steps in front of the washbasin and there enjoy freedom with water play. Some of the cupboards in the kitchen may offer young children freedom to pull out pots and pans and perhaps put them back again.

Toilet Training

Here is a kind of restriction that requires the child to bring a reflex activity under conscious control, and which, according to some writers, has far-reaching effects upon personality. Freud, for example, saw toilet training as the important influence on such traits as orderliness, messiness, stinginess, and generosity, but at least one empirical study has failed to show such specific relationships [48].

All societies impose some toilet regulation on children. Toileting is a simple matter for the bare-bottomed babies and toddlers in India and other poor countries with warm climates. Umersingh (whose baths we described in Chapter 2) wore only a shirt until he was about 4 years old. During his first few months, Leela kept a piece of cloth under him in his little bed. When he was in her arms, she held him aside as he started to urinate or defecate. They spent most of their time outdoors and if Umersingh happened to eliminate in the house, it was only on a mud floor, anyway. When children can walk, they squat down to eliminate, perhaps with assistance at first, but also in imitation of their elders, who are often seen squatting by the roadside or in the field. Thus neither clothing nor modesty poses any problem for an Indian toddler in a peasant family. The girls must later learn modesty, but the boys remain free to go as and when they feel moved to do so.

In the United States and in many other societies, as well, toilet training can cause problems for mothers and babies. The Soviet manual says, in regard to toileting, "It is extremely important to train a child from the very first year of life to be neat" [24]. An investigation of what a group of American mothers said they actually did shows considerable latitude in practice in this country. A few mothers began training when the child was under 5 months, 41 percent began between 5 and 9 months and 30 percent began between 10 and 14 months [77]. Seven months was the average length of time it took to complete bowel training, but there was a range from a few weeks to a year and a half. The later the training was begun, the less time it took. Maturation made learning easier.

Mollie Smart

Figure 4–9. A bare bottom makes toileting easy.

Punishment and scolding did not decrease the length of time required but did increase the amount of upset in babies whose mothers were relatively cold and undemonstrative. Severe training had no upsetting effect when mothers were warm in their relationships with the child. The time of beginning training was related to upset, with both early (before 6 months) and late starters (15 to 19 months) more disturbed than those who began between 6 and 10 months. Children trained after 20 months tended to learn quickly and to have little upset. Figure 4–10, taken from an earlier study, shows how much more quickly a child is likely to learn bladder control when his training is started after he has had time for sufficient maturation. Achievement curves for two twins show the slow progress made by Hugh, who began at approximately 7 weeks. By 2 years, Hugh's training was almost complete and Hilton's was begun. Almost immediately, Hilton did as well as Hugh.

The facts in the paragraph above cannot be taken uncritically as a guide to toilet training. At first glance, it would seem logical to say, "Let every mother wait until 20 months to toilet-train her baby." More is involved here than the age of the baby, mainly the personality of the mother. The Sears study of American practices also showed that mothers who were high in sex anxiety tended to begin training early. Perhaps because sex and toileting are connected in the minds of many people, in addition to sheer amount of extra work entailed in laundry, there is a desire to get it over with quickly in those mothers with high sex anxiety. Anxiety cannot be reasoned away. It is a real part of the person. If a mother has strong feelings that

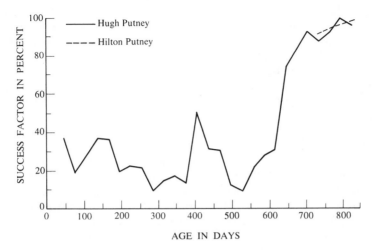

Figure 4–10. Records of toilet training of twins, one of whom started early and one late.
SOURCE: McGraw, Myrtle, B.: Neural maturation as exemplified in achievement of bladder control, *J. Pediat.*, **16**:580–590, 1940.

she should begin toilet training early, she may have a healthier relationship with the baby by training him early than by forcing herself to wait. However, when parents are comfortable about allowing the baby a high degree of autonomy, the second half of the second year is the time for easiest learning to use the toilet. By that age most children can perceive signals of imminent elimination, can hang on long enough to get to the toilet, and can release the sphincter muscles at will. The toddler will probably go by himself if his clothing is very easy to manage or if he can be left without pants at appropriate times, and if he has a child's toilet chair nearby. One little girl who had recently learned with such arrangements taught a visiting toddler to go to her toilet chair, after the toddler's mother had met only resistance to her efforts in toilet training.

Sex Teaching

Babies learn the names of eyes, nose, mouth, fingers, toes, and many more parts of the body as parents tell them, often playing games such as "This little piggy went to market." A child's concept of self is built as he learns about his physical self in this way. In a happy, affectionate context, he feels good about himself and his body.

When a baby fingers his genitals, as all do, there is probably one chance in ten that the mother who lovingly names his toes will exclaim happily, "There's your penis." More likely, she will say nothing, possibly removing his hands from his penis and distracting him with a toy or something to look at or listen to. Infants are sensitive to sexual stimulation, showing signs of relaxation and pleasure when the genital areas are touched. Newborn boys have erections of the penis. Both boys and girls learn to stimulate their genitals during infancy, through the process of exploring their bodies.

Although some societies permit expression of infant sexuality, Americans and many Europeans take a stern attitude toward it. An exploration of what American mothers said they did with their young children shows ways in which they tried to minimize their children's awareness of sex [77]. They tried to prevent stimulation. Modesty training, to prevent development of sexual interests, began in early infancy in some families. Such a mother kept a diaper on the baby at all times, wrapped him in a towel quickly after his bath, hurrying to get him dressed. Although children might be bathed together when very young, the practice was stopped when they showed any interest in each other's genitals. Parents kept themselves modestly covered.

Assuming that masturbation might result from irritation, mothers kept their babies very clean, using oil and powder regularly. Distraction was a favorite technique. The mother moved the child's hands away from his genitals and gave him something else to do with them, such as playing pat-a-cake. The mother might simply say, "Stop that. It isn't nice," but she was more likely to add a reason that was not quite accurate, such as, "It's dirty." Or she might ask, "Are you itchy?" or "Do you have to go to the toilet?" Many families used no terms for sexual organs and activities; others used vague terms, like "down there"; and still others said baby words, such as "wee-wee." The implication is that if the child has no term for an organ or action, he won't notice it. One mother said, "I think it is very important for them to hardly realize any difference between different parts of their body" [77].

Nobody knows whether minimizing sexual stimulation in the first years of life will suppress sexual activity before marriage. Whatever the rational aspects of the situation may be, it is likely that the restrictive parents act more from what they *feel* to be right than from having thought it out objectively. Sex training differs in an important way from the other kinds of inhibitory training a mother does. When she asks her child to give up his bottle and his diapers, there are more mature forms of behavior to replace babyish ways. With sexual behavior, there is nothing to do but to stop it.

Parent educators have long believed that it was wise to use the names of organs and functions and to permit babies to explore their bodies. Reasons for this point of view include promoting cognition (increased knowledge of the world, a clear body image), building a positive self concept, and laying a foundation for good sexual adjustment as an adult.

Problems of Deprivation

When a child is deprived, he is not receiving something that he needs or ought to have. The terms *maternal deprivation* and *cultural deprivation* are often used today, but their meanings are not always clear. Maternal deprivation can mean having no mother at all, as in an institution, having a mother whose presence is discontinuous, as when the mother works or the baby is hospitalized, or it can mean having a mother who is with the baby but neglecting or mistreating him. Deprivation can also be thought of in nonpersonal terms, especially sensory, emotional, nutritional, and protectional. *Cultural* deprivation usually implies inadequate experience with objects and language. Often, but not always, a deprived infant is suffering from both maternal and cultural deprivation, since the absence of the mother's care and attention often results in inadequate experience with objects and language. The timing and duration of various kinds of deprivation are important variables. So is the age at which the effects of deprivation are evaluated.

Stimulus Deprivation

Since children cannot be used in deprivation experiments, the only *experimental* evidence on deprivation comes from animals. This research strongly indicates that stimulation is necessary for the development of basic behavioral capacities [76]. Chimpanzees and cats raised in darkness had varying degrees of visual impairment, depending upon the extent of the deprivation. Puppies raised without their mothers have to have stimulation which approximates licking in order to eliminate, and their feeding behavior is impaired [76].

When children are deprived through unfortunate circumstances, their development can be observed. This has been done in orphanages, and many reports have been made of institutionalized children showing physical, intellectual, language, and emotional retardation [23, 76]. The previous chapter describes an institution in Iran where sensory deprivation was extreme, and the babies showed marked retardation in mental and motor development. When a baby is kept lying in a crib, especially on his back, when the crib sides are covered with plain material, when he has no toys, when people rarely speak to him or touch him, then he is deprived of normal perceptual experiences. This type of deprivation may or may not happen in an institution. It could happen in a home or anywhere. In recent years, child-care institutions have taken note of babies' need for stimulation, and some of them make provisions for it. Groups of institutionalized infants have been studied and found normal in intelligence and behavior [67]. In countries such as the Soviet Union, where institutions for child care are planned to offer personal interaction and rich perceptual experiences, several studies have shown no significant differences between family-reared and institution-reared children [33, p. 12].

Enrichment experiments have been carried on with both humans and animals in the exploration of the effects of stimulation on development. Extra handling, resulting in enriched tactile stimulation, was given to experimental groups in two institutions [22, 85]. In the first study infants were given [22] extra stimulation for 20 minutes a day for 10 weeks. At the end of that time the experimental group scored higher than the control group on the Gesell tests for adaptive, language, and personal-social behavior. In the second study [85], infants were given extra tactile stimulation for 20 minutes a day for 30 days, from the sixth to thirty-sixth day of life. These infants, when compared with their control group, showed significantly more visual attentiveness. Enrichment through stimulation by talking has been shown to promote language production [23]. Massive, carefully planned enrichment of the environment (including tactile, visual, and opportunities for contacting objects with hands) resulted in accelerated visual attention and reaching [85].

There seems to be little doubt that stimulus deprivation and enrichment can have significant short-term effects. The question of how long-lasting such effects might be is an important one. A reviewer of a large number of deprivation studies concludes that unless the deprivation lasts for a long time, there is little evidence that it will have long-term effects [61]. Environmentally deprived children tend to improve when they are placed in normal environments.

Maternal Deprivation

In studying what happens to the child who does not have enough mothering, the timing and the setting of the separation need to be considered.

Timing. The results of separation from the mother vary with the timing of the separation, as to age of child, and duration of separation. Stereotyped rhythmic behavior is frequent in infants reared in institutions, as well as in animals completely deprived of maternal care [19]. Rocking, head-banging, and thumb-sucking are repetitive actions which seem to be soothing to distressed infants and which apparently reduce tensions associated with maternal deprivation. A fear of visual novelty has often been noted in children who use frequent stereotyped rhythms. Autism, a pathological condition in which the baby interacts very little with people, is characterized by all sorts of rhythmic, repetitive actions. Although it is not clear whether the mother or the baby initiates the deprivation, autism is a situation of deprivation for both, since the baby's failure to look at the parents, smile, talk, and reach leads to lack of response on their part. Chimpanzee and monkey infants, as well as humans, use rocking and thumb-sucking as soothing devices when they are deprived of maternal care early in life [19].

Many studies indicate that babies are most likely to be seriously disturbed if they are separated from their mothers after attachment has been established, at about 6 months of age [17]. A study of the impact of maternal environment on children under 6 months showed that when a baby was changed from one foster mother to another, he was likely to show blunted social responses, increased tension, disturbance of routines, physiological disturbances, and developmental regression. The severity and pervasiveness of the disturbance increased with increasing age from 3 to 12 months. At 3 months, only a few showed any disturbance; at 4 months, 50 percent did; at 6 months, 86 percent were disturbed; and at 7 months, all of the infants showed upset upon being moved. When the relationship with the first mother was a close one, the immediate disturbance on separation was more severe; when the relationship between infant and mother was superficial, disturbance was milder [90]. If the disruption of the infant–mother tie is followed by sensory deprivation and lack of a mother substitute, the baby is likely to become depressed and disorganized [15].

When evaluated in adolescence, problems were more severe in children separated from their mothers before 6 months of age than in those separated after 6 months of age [17]. Since this comparison involves two studies, one done in Britain and one in the United States, and since the degree of similarity of the two institutions is not clear, this result should be taken with some caution. Nevertheless, the early-separated children showed greater intellectual deficit and more emotional problems, especially difficulties in forming relationships, inability to concentrate, restlessness, and craving for affection. Both samples of institutionalized children showed more problems at adolescence than did children brought up in foster homes. The institution children exceeded the foster home children in poor school achievement, inability to concentrate, hyperactivity, and craving for affection. These studies indicate that early placement in institutions (separation from the mother with no maternal substitute) is likely to result in intellectual and emotional problems in adolescence, the problems being more severe in those separated before 6 months. The result in adolescence of separation is the reverse of the result in infancy, when the later-separated babies showed most disturbance. The disturbance of the later-separated babies in infancy was probably due to the breaking of the established bond, whereas the adolescent disturbance of the never-attached babies must have been due to not having had experiences essential for development, a situation that might be stimulus deprivation. Or we could think of it in terms of not having had the opportunities to develop attachment behavior and to become attached at the period critical for the growth of attachment.

When effects of separation were evaluated in adulthood, the picture changed again. The small body of research on this topic indicates that harmful effects seem to level out as the child grows up [17]. The authors generally speak of the absence of psychological disorder, which of course is not identical with optimal psychological functioning. One such study [52] involved a follow-up of 20 adults who had been preschool children in London during World War II. Their parents had placed them in residential nurseries. The young adults were studied by means of interviews, projective tests, interviews of their parents, reviews of medical and social agency files, and nursery school records. The subjects were rated on feeling life, inner controls, relationships with people, role performances, and intellectual functioning. The findings showed relatively normal adjustment, with most of the group not significantly different from a normal population. Adjustment varied, however, with the type of nursery, the age at which the child was placed, and his family experiences before and since. Children's villages in Austria and Yugoslavia are institutions where children live in groups with foster parents, from infancy through adolescence [89]. Comparisons at adolescence, with family-reared children, showed no significant differences in intellectual performance, personality development, values, and problems. Nor was there any difference between early and later admissions to the institutions. These studies affirm the plasticity of human personality. They also indicate that institutional care does not necessarily result in disturbed psychological development.

Multiple Mothering

When an infant's care is shared by two or more women, the situation can be called multiple mothering. Although the infant may be deprived of his own mother for part of the time, he has the care and attention of one or more other women who look after him while he is apart from his mother. Or he may be separated permanently from his own mother and have the joint care of several women. The latter situation was true for children who spent their infancy in home management houses which served as laboratories for colleges of Home Economics throughout the United States. A home management house baby received excellent physical care and rich sensory and social stimulation from many students and several faculty members. The subsequent personality development and academic achievement of some of these children were studied after the children had spent several years as adopted children, living in regular families [35]. The experimental group was compared with a control group of children who had been born into their families and who matched the experimental subjects in age, sex, and intelligence. No difference between the groups was shown in school achievement, anxiety, and social adjustment. A test of personal adjustment favored the control group, suggesting that the children who had had multiple mothering were at a slight disadvantage emotionally.

Children in the Israeli kibbutzim are interesting in regard to multiple mothering, because they see their own mothers only briefly and periodically, while another woman and her assistants take care of them otherwise. A group of kibbutz-reared babies were found to score lower than home-reared on the Griffiths scale, especially in the area of personal-social development. Probably it is more complex for a baby to learn to adjust his motor and social responses to several adults than to one. However, by age 10, the kibbutz-reared children surpassed the home-reared Israeli ones on tests of intelligence and competency [64]. It might be expected here that the children would be slower in forming attachment to their mothers, due to less contact with them. One would also expect the nature of the attachment to be different, less intense, while attachment to nurse, teachers, and peers would also be different from that of home-reared children. Considering the demands of life on a communal farm, it is not surprising that a communally reared child, by age 10, would be better able than a home-reared child to cope with the tasks facing him. Most observers agree that personality development in the kibbutz is different from that in the cities of Israel or in the United States. Bettelheim, a psychiatrist, uses Erikson's model of personality development as a base for describing and speculating on his observations of personality development in kibbutz children. He sees the kibbutz nursery as stimulating less basic trust, since no adult is immediately available at night, and less basic mistrust, since with other infants always present, there is no danger of being left completely alone [9, pp. 304–307]. In each of Erikson's stages of development, Bettelheim finds differences in the kibbutz child, culminating in an adult who escapes despair, but at some cost to personal identity, emotional intimacy, and individual achievement [9, pp. 317–318]. While multiple mothering doubtless contributes heavily to the differences seen in infancy, the whole culture of the kibbutz is basic. The differences between adult kibbutzniks and Americans or other Israelis cannot be considered as due chiefly to multiple mothering, since so many other influences have been at work throughout the various stages of development.

Multiple mothering also occurs in the Soviet Union in the nurseries described in a previous section of this chapter. The teachers in the nurseries carry out carefully constructed, clearly described programs of care and instruction which are consistent with Communist ideals. As in the kibbutz, the child is nurtured and controlled by a complex social order, of which multiple mothering is only a small and integrated part [56].

Multiple mothering can occur at home, as well as in an institution or school. In the joint family of Asia and in some lower- and upper-class families in the West, several or many adults may take care of the baby and have warm relationships with him. Even in large families where a baby is exposed to many people, it takes a certain level of maturity to distinguish between those he knows and those he does not know and a certain amount of progress in attachment behavior in order to care who people are. Mead [82] describes how, in villages she has studied, a baby will be brought up with 30 or 40 people around him all the time and yet at 8 or 9 months, he suddenly rejects all but the 20 or so who have been taking a lot of care of him. A "stranger" from four houses down the street can be very frightening. Mead observes that children cared for by the mother only have more fear of people (and less acceptance) than those cared for by several or many people. She thinks that the adult adjustment of the latter is easier, but points out that the result of one kind of upbringing fits into one culture, the other into another.

Taken all together, the studies on multiple mothering seem to amplify Mead's conclusion. If multiple mothering is a normal part of the culture, then it seems to work well in preparing the child to fit into that culture. If multiple mothering is not, then the child may experience some ill effects from it.

Maternal Deprivation without Separation

A different form of deprivation, as compared with separation from the mother, occurs when the mother does not respond to the baby and does not care for him in normal ways. In such cases the child is deprived, even though his mother is physically present.

Evidence of what happens when the mother says she did not want the baby comes from a study done in Brussels [32]. Interviewing mothers within a few days after the birth of their babies, the question was asked, "Did you want to have a baby at the time when your child was born?" Later, from age 4 weeks to 3 years, the 215 unwanted babies were compared with a control group of wanted babies. Significant differences indicated that the desired children had fewer allergies, fewer emotional disturbances, less hostility, and better motor and intellectual development.

Some infants, living in families, fail to gain weight and to grow at normal rates, in spite of no organic pathology. A study of 50 such cases showed inadequate mothering and a disturbed mother–child relationship to be basic to the baby's failure to thrive [20]. There were deficiencies in the ways that the mothers fed, held, and otherwise responded (or did not respond) to the children. Often the mother herself was seriously disturbed, or there was an upset family situation. Sometimes there was something about the infant which made it hard or impossible for the mother to respond nurturantly to him. For example, a very active or hard-to-console baby may be extremely stressful to a mother.

Battered Babies and Parents. Since only a small proportion of child abuse cases are reported to legal authorities, the number reported gives little idea of the magnitude of the problem. A Brandeis University survey of adults throughout the United States showed that between $2\frac{1}{2}$ and 4 million people knew of incidents of child abuse during the previous year [36]. Some of these incidents were probably known to more than one person. On the other hand, many attacks on children are known only to the family involved.

Abuse takes two main forms: neglect and attack. Neglect usually results in malnutrition, sometimes in starvation. Diaper rashes, severe skin damage, infestation, and infections also come from neglect. A list of the wounds and fractures inflicted on infants by caretakers makes painful reading for students of child development. The pictures in the book "The Battered Child" [47] are even more heartbreaking than the words. Injuries to infants and toddlers included bruises, burns, abrasions, lacerations, fractures, hemorrhages, and bruises to the brain and internal organs.

There is only a shade of difference between neglect and abuse as threats to physical growth and health. They are also results of disturbed emotional relationships between parents and children. The results of physical abuse, which was diagnosed by skeletal injuries revealed by X ray, were the focus of a follow-up study of 50 children [31]. When the study began, 9 of the children had died from injuries, malnutrition, or at the hands of their mothers. Of the 20 who were eventually studied, 8 were emotionally disturbed, 10 had IQs below 80, and 7 had quite severe physical handicaps stemming from their old injuries. Of the 10 still living in their old homes, 6 were below normal in physical growth.

A hint of what adulthood holds for the battered child is given by studies of parents of battered children. Parents who abused their infants were studied in depth by two psychiatrists [80] who found a pattern of thinking and feeling which was characteristic of such parents. These parents expected and demanded from their babies a kind of behavior that was far beyond the ability of a baby. Such a parent expects maturity and love from the baby, while ignoring the baby's needs, limited abilities, and helplessness. Being immature themselves, and in great need of love, these parents seem to see the babies not as infants, but as parts of themselves, or as the causes of their troubles. An example of such a case is Kathy, mother of 3-weeks-old battered Kenny, who said, "I have never felt really loved in all my life. When the baby was born, I thought he would love me; but when he cried all the time, it meant he didn't love me. So I hit him" [80, p. 110].

Henry, the father of 16-month-old Johnny, whose ear was partially torn from his head, explained it thus, "He knows what I mean and understands it when I say, 'Come here.' If he doesn't come immediately, I go and give him a gentle tug on the ear to remind him of what he's supposed to do" [80, p. 110].

The life histories of the child-attackers show that they themselves were battered children, or at least raised in a similar style. Several had been severely beaten. All had had extremely demanding parents who had early expectations of submissive behavior, prompt obedience, no mistakes, sympathy, approval, and help for parents. Whatever they did, it was never enough, never quite right, it was at the wrong time; it disgraced the parents. These children grew up feeling unloved, disregarded, unfulfilled, and wrong. In some cases the psychiatrists were able to interview and observe the grandmothers of their battered infant patients. They found that the grandparents had experienced as babies the same kind of distorted mothering which they later applied to their own children, who in turn became impossibly demanding, disregarding, and abusing parents [80].

The psychiatrists observed that these abusing parents are not isolated instances, but only extreme instances in the culture in which they live. Many parents in North America and in Europe believe in "Spare the rod and spoil the child," "Children have to be taught to obey," and that children owe it to their parents to do what the parent wants and to be a comfort to the parents. It is just a step to the extreme notion that children exist primarily to satisfy their parents' needs and that children who do not fulfill this obligation should be punished.

Cultural support for the attitude that spawns child abuse has existed in the form of laws that emphasize parents' rights rather than society's rights in regard to control over children. Since the systematic study of the battered child syndrome in the 1960s, laws have been changed in the direction of protecting children more adequately. Before that time, California was the only state in which parental abuse of the child was a crime. Now all states have such laws. Solution of the problem, however, requires more than laws. Parents who abuse children need extensive help. So do children who must be removed from their parents.

A severely deprived infant is likely to grow into a battering adult, not only in the human world, but also among monkeys. Harlow's famous experiments with baby monkeys raised with substitute mothers showed that the infants spent more time with warm, rocking, cloth-covered surrogates than with stationary wire surrogates, even if wire mothers gave milk. Harlow reported that as far as the experimenter could observe, the baby monkey's attachment to a cloth mother was as strong as for a real mother and that the security he gained from a cloth mother was as great as from a real mother [42]. However, when the cloth-mothered babies grew to maturity, neither males nor females were interested in mating. The females who were impregnated and gave birth did not take adequate care of their babies. All showed abnormal behavior ranging from indifference to abuse. They would avoid the infants, knock them down, step on them, beat them, and rub their faces on the floor. They were "helpless, hopeless, heartless mothers devoid, or almost devoid, of any maternal feeling" [43].

The battered child presents a complex social problem. For his physical rehabilitation (if possible) and protection, he needs prompt help in getting hospital treatment and being separated from the person who injured him. Little is known about how successful emotional rehabilitation can be, although there are cases of neglected and damaged children being treated and then adopted by loving parents, whereupon the child seemed to blossom.

Uniqueness of Individual Development. The genetic endowment of the infant determines how he first interacts with the environment into which he is born. So also does the environment determine how the baby can interact. The baby's successive experiences affect his future interactions. A given external condition has different meaning and significance for different babies. In other words, a given external condition offers differing experiences to different individuals. And it is the *experience*, rather than an external condition, which is significant for development [33, pp. 59–65]. For example, take as the external condition Mother A who handles a baby often and vigorously, speaks and sings to him frequently and loudly, keeps him with her while she works, and maintains contact with him. Baby A is relatively insensitive to perceptual stimulation, showing no reaction to slight stimulation and moderate reactions to what his mother offers. Mother B picks up her baby only when he is in distress or otherwise needs care and leaves him alone when he is quiet. She speaks softly and handles him gently. If Baby A belonged to Mother B, he would be understimulated. Baby B, however, is highly sensitive. Mother A would be much too stimulating for him, keeping him in a state of intense arousal frequently; Mother B gives him the amount and quality of stimulation that he can handle easily. Although their mothers provide widely different external environments, Baby A and Baby B have similar experiences in regard to adequacy of stimulation.

Roots of Individuality [33] is the title of a book describing the behavior dimensions and interactions through which an infant elaborates his uniqueness. The study shows relationships between experience and development. One of the important dimensions that bears upon experience is perceptual sensitivity, as seen in the preceding paragraph. Another is activity, "the amount and vigor of body motion typically shown by a given infant in a variety of situations" [33, p. 22]. As has been shown earlier in this chapter, the activity level of an infant can strongly affect his family relationships and hence his experiences. The present study gives some contrasts in behavior of active and relatively inactive infants which are relevant to what is experienced [33, pp. 239–241]. Active infants were more coordinated and complex in their spontaneous behavior, focusing more on the environment including distant stimuli. They vocalized more intensely and in more complex ways. Inactive infants were affected more than active ones by social stimulation and by efforts to interest them in toys. The active ones responded vigorously to people and toys even when little or no effort was made to elicit response. Inactive babies used more sucking and oral activity and were able to soothe themselves through mouth activity. Active babies reacted more strongly to hunger than did inactive ones. As Figure 4–11 shows, crying or screaming in hunger was typical of five of six active babies and of only one out of six inactive infants. It is easy to see how a mother would hurry to assuage the hunger pangs of a screaming baby while the

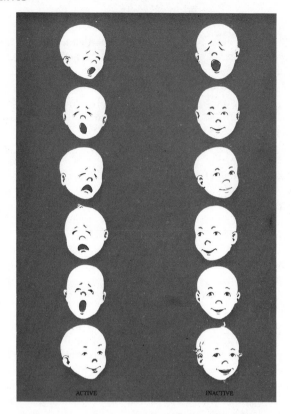

Figure 4-11. Twelve hungry babies, showing typical behavior for active and inactive infants.

mother of a hungry but silent infant might delay. The ways in which these two groups of babies are dependent on their caretakers show two contrasts: the active babies can find stimulation relatively easily for themselves but need soothing and comfort more; the inactive babies need help in finding interesting things to see and do but can manage quite well in overcoming distress and maintaining equilibrium. This one set of findings explains some of the differences in the ways that individual children react to deprivation situations.

The "roots of individuality" include additional dimensions of infant behavior and further differentiation of parent behavior. Experiences at each age affect subsequent interactions and development.

Summary

The culture into which a child is born determines the limits of his opportunities for physical, cognitive, and social development. Role prescriptions and ideals for child-rearing, although clear in simple, stable societies, are often confusing in a rapidly changing culture. In the United States methods of child-rearing change relatively fast. A variety of attitudes and methods exist at any one time, varying with such factors as economic level and stage of family development. The infant himself is active in determining how people respond to him. Appearance, sex, and temperament are significant. Sex-linked behavior is influential in shaping mother–infant interactions. An infant's well-being is affected by the fit between his temperament and his family.

Scheduling or timing is basic in the care and guidance of infants. The needs of all family members have to be balanced and adjusted in mutual regulation, taking special account of the baby's immaturity. At the same time that the family takes care of the infant's requirements for food, rest, exercise, and cleanliness, they also build relationships and attitudes. Intellectual development is influenced through all experiences, as well as during play and stimulating interactions. Infant care also includes restrictions, many of which are applied in order to ensure safety and health, others of which exist for the purpose of making life comfortable for other family members. Especially during the stage of development of the sense of autonomy, healthy growth requires clear, firm, minimal restrictions, within which the child can operate freely. Toilet training is accomplished more quickly when begun later, rather than earlier, in infancy. The mother's personality, especially her warmth or coldness, is a factor in success. In toilet training, the mother requires the child to substitute a more mature form of behavior for an immature pattern. In restricting sex activity, however, the mother asks the child to give up an activity without substituting for it.

Emotions become differentiated as the child develops. Love, a term with many implications, has been studied in the context of attachment. An infant shows attachment to another person when he shows desire for the presence, contact, and response of that person. Attachment is shown by selective smiling and vocalizing and by crying at separation from the attachment object. The mother is usually the first attachment object, the father the second. Babies tend to select responsive, stimulating people as objects for their affection. Exploration is facilitated by the presence of an attachment object. The child leaves the mother briefly as attachment bonds become elastic.

Intense infant–mother relationships are frequent in cultures where the mother has little help with the care of her baby. When separated from the mother to whom he is firmly attached, the baby shows disturbance and disorganization. Separation and other love-deprivation experiences have to be interpreted in the life context of the child. Experiments with monkeys suggest that play with peers may compensate somewhat for deprivation in infant–adult affectional relationship. Infant peer relationships are fostered in collective societies.

Infants show fear reactions to intense stimuli, pain, and sudden changes in stimulation. Fear of strangers develops after attachment. The dark is often frightening. Fear of novelty requires having built some schemas which permit discrimination of the familiar and the new. In coping with fear-provoking situations, an infant, like all people, only more so, gains courage and reassurance from the presence of a person to whom he is attached.

Anger involves tension and attack in connection with a blocking situation. Anger outbursts occur most frequently during the second year, when the child is very eager to make choices and yet lacks experience and skills necessary for independent successful action. Parents can minimize young children's anger outbursts by meeting their physical needs before tensions become acute and by maintaining firm, consistent, yet reasonable, control.

Maternal deprivation can take many forms, each of which derives some meaning from the cultural context. Recovery of the child depends upon the form and timing of the deprivation and the form and timing of ameliorative efforts. The battered child is a result of severe parental disturbance in a nonsupportive social setting.

References

1. Ainsworth, M. D. S. Patterns of attachment behavior shown by the infant in interactions with his mother. *Merrill-Palmer Quart.*, 1964, **10**, 51–58.
2. Ainsworth, M. D. S. *Infancy in Uganda: Infant care and the growth of love.* Baltimore: Johns Hopkins Press, 1967.
3. Ainsworth, M. D. S., & Bell, S. M. Attachment, exploration, and separation: Illustrated by the behavior of one-year-olds in a strange situation. *Child Devel.*, 1970, **41**, 49–67.
4. Applebaum, R. M. Best to start disciplining early. *Baby Talk*, 1969, **34**:11, 10.
5. Bayley, N., & Schaefer, E. S. Correlations of maternal and child behaviors with the development of mental abilities: Data from the Berkeley growth study. *Mono. Soc. Res. Child Devel.*, 1964, **29**:6.
6. Becker, W. C. Consequences of different kinds of parental discipline. In M. L. Hoffman & L. W. Hoffman (Eds.), *Review of child development research.* Vol. 1. New York: Russell Sage Foundation, 1964, pp. 171–208.
7. Bell, R. Q. A reinterpretation of the direction of effects in studies of socialization. *Psychol. Rev.*, 1968, **75**, 81–95.
8. Bell, S. M. The development of the concept of object as related to mother-infant attachment. *Child Devel.*, 1970, **41**, 291–311.
9. Bettelheim, B. *The children of the dream.* New York: Macmillan, 1969.
10. Bigner, J. J. Fathering: Research and practice implications. *Fam. Coord.*, 1970, **19**, 357–362.
11. Biller, H. B. Father absence and the personality development of the male child. *Devel. Psychol.*, 1970, **2**, 181–201.
12. Bowlby, J. *Child care and the growth of love.* London: Penguin, 1953.
13. Bowlby, J. The nature of the child's tie to his mother. *Int. J. Psychoan.*, 1958, **39**, 1–24.
14. Bowlby, J. *Attachment and loss.* Vol. I: *Attachment.* London: Hogarth, 1969.
15. Brody, G. F. Socioeconomic differences in stated child-rearing practices and in observed maternal behavior. *J. Marr. Fam.*, 1968, **30**, 656–660.
16. Bronfenbrenner, U. Socialization and social class through time and space. In E. E. Maccoby, T. M. Newcomb, & E. L. Hartley (Eds.), *Readings in social psychology.* New York: Holt, Rinehart and Winston, 1958, pp. 400–425.
17. Bronfenbrenner, U. Early deprivation in mammals: a cross-species analysis. In G. Newton & S. Levine (Eds.), *Early experience and behavior.* Springfield, Ill.: Charles C Thomas, 1968, pp. 727–764.
18. Bronfenbrenner, U. Introduction. In H. Chauncey (Ed.), *Soviet preschool education.* Vol. 1: *Program of instruction.* New York: Holt, Rinehart and Winston, 1969, p. xiii.
19. Bronson, G. W. The development of fear in man and other animals. *Child Devel.*, 1968, **39**, 407–431.
20. Bullard, D. M., et al. Failure to thrive in the neglected child. *Am. J. Orthopsychiat.*, 1967, **37**, 680–690.
21. Caldwell, B. M., & Richmond, J. B. Social class level and stimulation potential

of the home. In B. Staub & J. Hellmuth (Eds.), *Exceptional infant.* Vol. 1. Seattle: Special Child Publications, 1967.

22. Casler, L. The effects of extra tactile stimulation on a group of institutionalized infants. *Genet. Psychol. Mono.*, 1965, **71**, 137–175.
23. Casler, L. Perceptual deprivation in institutional settings. In G. Newton & S. Levine (Eds.), *Early experience and behavior.* Springfield: Charles C Thomas, 1968, pp. 573–626.
24. Chauncey, H. (Ed.). *Soviet preschool education.* Vol. 1: *Program of instruction.* New York: Holt, Rinehart and Winston, 1969.
25. Chess, S. Temperament in the normal infant. In B. Staub & J. Hellmuth (Eds.), *Exceptional infant.* Vol. 1. Seattle: Special Child Publications, 1967.
26. Chess, S., Thomas, A., & Birch, H. G. Behavior problems revisited: Findings of an anterospective study. In S. Chess & A. Thomas (Eds.), *Annual progress in child psychiatry and child development 1968.* New York: Brunner/Mazel, 1968, pp. 335–344.
27. Clausen, J. A. Family structure, socialization and personality. In M. L. Hoffman & L. W. Hoffman (Eds.), *Review of child development research.* Vol. 2. New York: Russell Sage Foundation, 1966, pp. 1–53.
28. Clay, V. S. The effect of culture on mother-child tactile communication. *Fam. Coord.*, 1968, **17**, 204–210.
29. Collard, R. R. Social and play responses of first-born and later-born infants in an unfamiliar situation. *Child Devel.*, 1968, **39**, 325–334.
30. Dennis, W., & Najarian, P. Infant development under environmental handicap. *Psychol. Mono.*, 1957, **71**:7.
31. Elmer, E., & Gregg, G. S. Developmental characteristics of abused children. *Pediat.*, 1967, **40**, Part I, 596–602.
32. Emery-Hauzeur, C., & Sand, E. A. Enfants désirés et non désirés. *Enfance*, 1962, **2**, 109–126.
33. Escalona, S. K. *The roots of individuality.* Chicago: Aldine, 1968.
34. Freud, A., & Dann, S. An experiment in group upbringing. *Psychoanal. Stud. Child*, 1951, **6**, 127–168.
35. Gardner, D. B., Hawkes, G. R., & Burchinal, L. G. Noncontinuous mothering in infancy and development in later childhood. *Child Devel.*, 1961, **32**, 225–234.
36. Gil, D. G. Incidence of child abuse and demographic characteristics of persons involved. In R. E. Helfer & C. H. Kempe, *The battered child.* Chicago: University of Chicago Press, 1968, pp. 19–40.
37. Goldberg, S., & Lewis, M. Play behavior in the year-old infant: early sex differences. *Child Devel.*, 1969, **40**, 21–31.
38. Golden, M., & Birns, B. Social class differentiation in cognitive development: A longitudinal study. Paper presented at the meeting of the Society for Research in Child Development. Santa Monica, Calif., March 27, 1969.
39. Goodenough, F. L. *Anger in young children.* Minneapolis: University of Minnesota Press, 1931.
40. Gordon, M. Infant care revisited. *J. Marr. Fam.*, 1968, **30**, 578–583.
41. Haas, M. B., & Harms, I. E. Social interaction between infants. *Child Devel.*, 1963, **34**, 79–97.
42. Harlow, H. F. The nature of love. *Am. Psychol.*, 1958, **13**, 673–684.
43. Harlow, H. F. The heterosexual affectional system in monkeys. *Am. Psychol.*, 1962, **17**, 1–9.

44. Harlow, H. F. The maternal affectional system. In B. M. Foss (Ed.), *Determinants of infant behaviour II*. New York: Wiley, 1963, pp. 3–34.
45. Harlow, H. F., & Harlow, M. K. Social deprivation in monkeys. *Sci. Am.*, 1962, **207**:5, 136, 146.
46. Heinicke, C. M., & Westheimer, I. *Brief separations*. New York: International Universities Press, 1965.
47. Helfer, R. E., & Kempe, C. H. *The battered child*. Chicago: University of Chicago Press, 1968.
48. Hetherington, E. M., & Brackbill, Y. Etiology and covariation of obstinacy, orderliness and parsimony in young children. *Child Devel.*, 1963, **34**, 919–944.
49. Honzik, M. P. Environmental correlates of mental growth: Prediction from the family setting at 21 months. *Child Devel.*, 1967, **38**, 337–364.
50. Hunt, R. G., & Winokur, G. Some generalities concerning parental attitudes with special reference to changing them. In J. C. Glidewell (Ed.), *Parental attitudes and child behavior*. Springfield, Ill.: Charles C Thomas, 1961, pp. 174–187.
51. Koch, H. L. *Twins*. Chicago: University of Chicago Press, 1966.
52. Maas, H. S. Long-term effects of early separation and group care. *Vita Humana*, 1963, **6**, 34–56.
53. Maccoby, E. E. Tracing individuality within age-related change. Paper presented at the meeting of the Society for Research in Child Development, Santa Monica, Calif., March 27, 1969.
54. Mason, W. A. Determinants of social behavior in young chimpanzees. In A. M. Schrier, H. F. Harlow, & F. Stolenits (Eds.), *Behavior of non-human primates*. Vol. 2. New York: Academic Press, 1965, pp. 287–334.
55. Maurer, A. The game of peek-a-boo. *Dis. Nervous System*, 1967, **28**, 118–121.
56. Meers, D. R., & Marans, A. E. Group care of infants in other countries. In C. A. Chandler et al. *Early child care*. New York: Atherton, 1968.
57. Mitchell, G. D. Attachment differences in male and female infant monkeys. *Child Devel.*, 1968, **39**, 611–620.
58. Moss, H. A. Sex, age and state as determinants of mother-infant interaction. *Merrill-Palmer Quart.*, 1967, **13**, 19–53.
59. Murphy, L. B. *The widening world of childhood*. New York: Basic Books, 1962.
60. Neubauer, P. (Ed.). *Children in collectives: Child-rearing aims and practices in the kibbutz*. Springfield, Ill.: Charles C Thomas, 1965.
61. O'Connor, N. Children in restricted environments. In G. Newton & S. Levine (Eds.), *Early experience and behavior*. Springfield, Ill.: Charles C Thomas, 1968, pp. 530–572.
62. Pearlin, L. I., & Kohn, M. L. Social class, occupation and parental values: A cross culture study. *Am. Soc. Rev.*, 1966, **31**, 466–479.
63. Prothro, E. T. Socialization and social class in a transitional society. *Child Devel.*, 1966, **37**, 219–228.
64. Rabin, A. I. Behavior research in collective settlements in Israel. *Am. J. Orthopsychiat.*, 1958, **28**, 577–586.
65. Rapp, D. W. Childrearing attitudes of mothers in Germany and the United States. *Child Devel.*, 1961, **32**, 669–678.
66. Rebelsky, F., & Hanks, C. Fathers' verbal interaction with infants in the first 3 months of life. *Child devel.*, 1971, **42**, 63–68.

67. Rheingold, H. L. The effect of environmental stimulation upon social and exploratory behavior in the human infant. In B. M. Foss (Ed.), *Determinants of infant behavior*. Vol. I. New York: Wiley, 1961, pp. 143–177.
68. Rheingold, H. L., & Eckerman, C. O. The infant's free entry into a new environment. *J. Exper. Child Psychol.*, 1969, **8**, 271–283.
69. Ricciuti, H. N. Social and emotional behavior in infancy: Some developmental issues and problems. *Merrill-Palmer Quart.*, 1968, **14**, 82–100.
70. Robson, K. S., Pedersen, F. A., & Moss, H. A. Developmental observations of diadic gazing in relation to the fear of strangers and social approach behavior. *Child Devel.*, 1969, **40**, 619–627.
71. Rosenhan, D. Preface. In H. Chauncey (Ed.), *Soviet preschool education*. Vol. II: *Teacher's commentary*. New York: Holt, Rinehart and Winston, 1969, pp. v–xii.
72. Scarr, S., & Salapatek, P. Patterns of fear development during infancy. *Merrill-Palmer Quart.*, 1970, **16**, 53–90.
73. Schaefer, E. S., & Bayley, N. Maternal behavior, child behavior and their intercorrelations from infancy through adolescence. *Mono. Soc. Res. Child Devel.*, 1963, **28**:3.
74. Schaffer, H. R. The onset of fear of strangers and the incongruity hypothesis. *J. Child Pyschol. Psychiat.*, 1966, **7**, 95–106.
75. Schaffer, H. R., & Emerson, P. E. The development of social attachments in infancy. *Mono. Soc. Res. Child Devel.*, 1964, **29**:3.
76. Scott, J. P. *Early experience and the organization of behavior*. Belmont, Calif.: Brooks/Cole, 1968.
77. Sears, R., Maccoby, E. E., & Levin, H. *Patterns of child rearing*. Evanston, Ill.: Row, Peterson, 1957.
78. Stayton, D. J., Hogan, R., & Ainsworth, M. D. S. Infant obedience and maternal behavior: The origins of socialization reconsidered. Paper presented at the meeting of the Eastern Psychological Association, Atlantic City, 1970.
79. Stechler, G. A., & Carpenter, G. Viewpoint on early affective development. In B. Staub & J. Hellmuth (Eds.), *Exceptional infant*. Vol. 1. Seattle: Special Child Publications, 1967.
80. Steele, B. F., & Pollock, C. B. A psychiatric study of parents who abuse infants and small children. In R. E. Helfer & C. H. Kempe (Eds.), *The battered child*. Chicago: University of Chicago Press, 1968.
81. Stern, G. G., Caldwell, B. M., Hersher, L., Lipton, E. L., & Richmond, J. B. A factor analytic study of the mother-infant dyad. *Child. Devel.*, 1967, **40**, 163–181.
82. Tanner, J. M., & Inhelder, B. *Discussions on child development*. Vol. II. New York: International Universities, 1954.
83. Wahler, R. G. Infant social attachments: A reinforcement theory interpretation and investigation. *Child Devel.*, 1967, **38**, 1079–1088.
84. Waters, E., & Crandall, V. J. Social class and observed maternal behavior from 1940 to 1960. *Child Devel.*, 1964, **35**, 1021–1032.
85. White, B. L., & Held, R. Plasticity of sensorimotor development in the human infant. In B. Staub & J. Hellmuth (Eds.), *Exceptional infant*. Vol. 1. Seattle: Special Child Publications, 1967, pp. 291–313.
86. White, B. L., LaCrosse, E. R., Litman, F., & Ogilvie, D. M. The Harvard preschool project: An etho-ecological study of the development of competence.

Symposium presented at the meeting of the Society for Research in Child Development, Santa Monica, Calif., March 27, 1969.

87. Willerman, L., Broman, S. H., & Fiedler, M. F. Infant development, preschool IQ and social class. *Child Devel.*, 1970, **41**, 69–77.

88. Wolfenstein, M. Trends in infant care. *Am. J. Orthopsychiat.*, 1953, **33**, 12–130.

89. Wolins, M. Young children in institutions: Some additional evidence. *Devel. Psychol.*, 1970, **2**, 99–109.

90. Yarrow, L. J. Maternal deprivation: Toward an empirical and conceptual re-evaluation. *Psychol. Bull.*, 1961, **58**, 459–490.

91. Yarrow, L. J. Research in dimensions of early maternal care. *Merrill-Palmer Quart.*, 1963, **9**, 101–114.

92. Yarrow, L. J. The development of focused relationships during infancy. In B. Staub & J. Hellmuth (Eds.), *Exceptional infant.* Vol. 1. Seattle: Special Child Publications, 1967, pp. 425–442.

93. Yarrow, L. J., Rubenstein, J. L., & Pedersen, F. A. Dimensions of early stimulation: Differential effects on infant development. Paper presented at the meeting of the Society for Research in Child Development, Minneapolis, Minn., April 4, 1971.

Readings in
Relationships with People

This section is an unusually long one because research in the area of relationships with people is prolific. Consideration of positive social and emotional development is especially relevant to problems in today's world. How do people come to love one another and what can go wrong? The study of social relationships in infancy gives some information about the foundations of feeling, caring, and giving. Although experimentations with human beings in these areas is usually unacceptable, additional insights and clues are contributed by animal research and by comparisons with other cultures.

The first article, by John Paul Scott, reviews facts known about animals other than man in order to give the background for his message about the social development of human beings. The subject of imprinting, first observed in birds, is introduced by Scott in this article. Later articles in this chapter will develop the topic further. The concept of critical periods is also used by other authors, not only in this chapter but throughout this book, because it is one of the important child development concepts. Among the applications to human existence that Scott makes is the timing of the adoption of children by foster parents.

Mary D. Salter Ainsworth has investigated the attachment of the infant to his mother and has written extensively on this topic. Here, with Silvia M. Bell, she shows that it is possible to experiment with babies and mothers without harming them. Using a miniature sample of a real-life situation Ainsworth and Bell studied the relation between attachment and exploratory behavior.

Michael Lewis and Susan Goldberg found a difference in the way mothers treated boys and girls when they studied sex differences in play behavior of one-year-olds.

Peer relationships in infancy have not been studied very much in the United States, because until recently, babies have not often come together in groups. In the kibbutzim of Israel, however, infants live closely together. A famous psychiatrist, Bruno Bettleheim, describes infant–infant relationships in "Crib Mates," an excerpt from his book The Children of the Dream.

The last article is included as a balance for the others. Although personality development is greatly influenced by the people with whom the child interacts, the individual also has his own unique characteristics, from the beginning. A pediatrician, Herbert Birch, and two psychiatrists, Stella Chess and Alexander Thomas, have collaborated on a longitudinal study of temperament or behavioral style. Their dimensions of temperament are helpful in understanding individuals, in appreciating individuality, and in realizing that parent–child interaction is the product of the child just as much as it is of the parent.

Critical Periods of Social Development

John Paul Scott
BOWLING GREEN STATE UNIVERSITY

Among animals living under natural conditions, the social environment is often the most stable feature of the surroundings. A lamb living in a flock of mountain sheep experiences changing weather conditions from day to day, and even from hour to hour as rain ceases and the sun comes out. Predators may be present one day and gone the next, and even the food supply varies enormously with the seasons. However, other members of the flock are always present. Individuals die and are replaced by younger ones, but reproduction always takes place in the same way year after year, and behavior develops in a very consistent fashion in succeeding generations.

Because of its stability, the important effects of the early social environment do not become apparent until experimenters interfere with it by drastic methods. For example, the behavior of domestic sheep develops in ways very similar to those of mountain sheep, generation after generation; but the simple act of taking a young lamb from its mother at birth and rearing it on a bottle away from the flock produces a radically different animal, one that stays apart from the flock and attempts to follow people everywhere like Mary's little lamb in the nursery rhyme.

Two general methods are used in this kind of experiment. One is to take a young mammal or bird from its parents at birth or hatching and rear it by hand away from its own kind. The second method is to take young animals and rear them in isolation, providing the equivalent of parental care by mechanical means. By these methods the important phenomenon of primary socialization, or imprinting, was discovered.

PRIMARY SOCIALIZATION (IMPRINTING)

One of the major functions of most highly developed animal societies is the care and protection of the young. In order for this to work efficiently the young animal must become attached to the members of its own species. It will not suffice for the newborn animal to have a generalized positive reaction to all members of its own species, for efficient care depends on its staying with particular individuals who are ready and equipped to give that care. Therefore, it must become attached to particular individuals and be able to discriminate between these and others. We call this process primary socialization, implying that this is the first way in which the behavior of the young animal becomes modified in relation to the rest of society, and we can define it as the formation of the first social relationships, and particularly the formation of emotional attachments. All the highly social animals which have been so far studied have a short period early in life when this process takes place.

From *Early Experience and the Organization of Behavior*, pp. 61–76, by John Paul Scott. © 1968 by Wadsworth Publishing Company, Inc., Belmont, California 94002. Reprinted by permission of the publisher.

Imprinting in Birds   Birds are characteristically flying animals, but all are flightless as they emerge from the egg. Characteristically, most of them develop very rapidly so that they can reach the relative safety of the air as soon as possible. Some of the small perching birds are able to fly twelve or fourteen days after hatching, and even large birds like ducks and geese are very nearly full grown in about six weeks. The Japanese quail, a domestic bird noted for rapid development, may produce eggs as soon as eight weeks after its own egg was originally laid.

Some birds, like chickens and ducks, are born in a precocious state and are able to walk as soon as they are hatched. If eggs of these species are hatched in an incubator and the newly emerging young are shown only a model of a parent bird, they will soon begin to follow it. The model need not have any great resemblance to a bird, as young chicks will readily become attached to square boxes or round balloons. They will also become attached to almost any other living thing, from white rats to human beings. Using the right technique, it is easy to produce the comical effect of a chick following a person as if he were its mother. The peak of the imprinting effect occurs about seventeen hours after hatching and declines rapidly thereafter. By three or four days of age, young chicks become quite fearful of strange objects, and getting them to form an attachment becomes increasingly difficult (Hess, 1962).

Other birds are born in a very immature state. Most people are familiar with the blind and naked nestlings of the perching birds. These birds also form emotional attachments, but at a much later date and in a much more gradual way, with the result that hand rearing has little effect until a week or so after hatching. In doves and pigeons, whose newly hatched young are also helpless, the degree of attachment to a human being varies inversely with the age at which the young squab is removed from its parents' nest. Klinghammer (1967) found that mourning doves taken before 8 days never developed fears of human handlers, but those taken a day or two later showed fears as adults.

When begun at the proper time, hand-rearing has drastic effects on a bird's later behavior. A hand-reared male turkey, for example, may be able to mate with his own kind as an adult, but if he has a choice between another turkey and a human being, he will go to the human being—and perseveringly repeat the behavior patterns of courtship in spite of the fact that these do not produce any response. The result of primary socialization, or imprinting, has been to transfer the development of social relationships from one species to another. Because experience in the early period of primary socialization not only determines the nature of primary relationships but also indirectly determines the later ones, the period of primary socialization is a critical period for later development.

Primary Socialization in Mammals.   Like birds, some mammals are precocious and others are born in various stages of immaturity. The large herd animals are all precocious, and the effects of hand rearing such animals are well known. Bottle-raised fawns become extremely tame and attached to people and lose so many of their "instinctive" fears that they are seldom able to survive if turned loose in the wilds afterwards.

Of all the herd animals we know most about domestic sheep and goats. If a young lamb is taken from its mother at birth and reared on a bottle, it becomes a most unsheeplike sheep, following people everywhere, unafraid of dogs, and independent of its own kind. It is unresponsive to other sheep even if raised in the same field with the flock, but the behavior which prevents its becoming attached to other sheep is that of the adult females rather than its own. The young lamb will approach the females but they always butt it away and reject it as they would any strange lamb. The young orphan lamb soon learns to stay away from them and develops its relationships only with people.

The length of the critical period for primary socialization in the young lamb has never been determined, but it must begin soon after birth and last for at least a week. On the other hand, the critical period for a mother forming an attachment to her own lamb is a matter of hours. If a mother has her lamb taken away at birth, she will accept it if it is brought back again within two to four hours and will "own" it during a somewhat longer period if she is kept isolated from other sheep in the meantime (Hersher et al., 1963). This emphasizes the fact that the relationship between mother and offspring is a dual one and that the mother forms an attachment to her offspring as well as the reverse.

The situation in slowly developing animals like the dog is quite different. The young puppy is born in a very immature state with respect to its sense organs, being both blind and deaf. Even the sense of smell is poorly developed. This means that the newborn puppy is unable to discriminate between one individual and another, and the process of forming an emotional attachment does not begin until the puppy is about three weeks of age.

By this time the sense organs have matured, and for the next several weeks the young puppy is able to form new relationships rapidly with any strange dog or human being. Although the first reaction to a stranger of a young puppy between three and seven weeks of age is to crouch down or escape, this response is only momentary. Within a few seconds or minutes it will approach and investigate, nosing the stranger's clothes, and wagging its tail. In one experiment, Freedman, King, and Elliot (1961) raised puppies in a one-acre field that was surrounded by a high board fence so that the animals could not see people. They were fed through a hole in the fence, and their only human contact came when they were removed for a week's socialization in the laboratory at different ages. By fourteen weeks of age, those pups which had no human contact were acting like little wild animals, but those with previous contact showed different degrees of positive attraction. This experiment showed that the peak of the ability to rapidly form a new social relationship occurs between six and eight weeks of age, declining thereafter with the increasingly prolonged fear responses to strangers. It is perhaps no accident that the peak of this capacity occurs very close to the time when a mother normally weans her puppies completely from the breast. At this age neither dogs nor their wild ancestors, the wolves, are truly self-sufficient, and wolf cubs continue to be fed by their elders, including other members of the pack as well as parents. It is therefore highly adaptive for the puppy to be able to form new relationships readily at this time. Whether similar timing occurs in other species is a matter for investigation.

Duration and Nature of the Critical Period   As we have seen from these various examples, the critical period for primary socialization can be as short as a few hours in a rapidly developing animal like the chicken, or it can extend over a period of several weeks in a slowly developing mammal like the dog. All of the animals in which this phenomenon has been studied are alike in that they can form social attachments quite rapidly during the critical period.

In the dog, lasting effects can be produced by daily contacts extending over a period of as little as a week. Puppies reared in isolation during the critical period will develop normal relationships with people if allowed as little as two twenty-minute periods of contact per week throughout the whole period of several weeks. All animals in which primary socialization has been studied are also alike in that the critical period comes early in life, although not necessarily at the point immediately after hatching or birth.

What determines the length of the critical period and what brings it to a close? These questions raise the problem of the basic nature of the process involved. What exactly happens to an animal forming a strong social attachment? One clue comes from the fact that the attachments are made before the animal develops a strong fear response to strangers. A young chick or puppy does not quickly form a social relationship with a stranger after the critical period because its first response is to run away and stay away, thus effectively preventing any prolonged contact. Furthermore the fact of becoming attached to one individual and staying with it, as a chick stays with its mother, will keep it out of contact with other hens, not to mention other species of animals and particularly predators such as foxes.

Although this still does not answer the question of the nature of the positive mechanism of forming an attachment, all evidence indicates that emotional responses are involved. A young puppy will exhibit distress vocalization as soon as it is removed from the familiar objects and individuals to which it becomes attached during the critical period. At six or eight weeks of age, a temporarily isolated puppy may average 140 vocalizations per minute and keep up this rate for hours. This obvious emotional distress is relieved by the presence of another individual or by familiar surroundings. Thus the puppy experiences an uncomfortable emotion which is relieved by staying with its own kind. The emotional reaction itself appears to be a very simple primary response that has the effect of maintaining an attachment between the animal and another member of its own species. Furthermore, the effect of artificially producing other unpleasant emotions, such as fear responses to noise or electric shock, is to intensify the reaction of staying with its own kind and to speed up the general process of attachment. The young animal must learn very quickly that being separated from familiar individuals is unpleasant and that being with them relieves this unpleasantness. In terms of learning theory, staying with familiar animals and persons is reinforced by the punishing effect of separation and the relief afforded by reunion (Scott, 1967).

General Theory of Critical Periods   The concept of a critical period may be examined on several levels of complexity. Most superficially, a critical period is based on time, and within this dimension a critical period can be defined as a time when a large effect can be produced by a smaller change in conditions than in any later or earlier period in life. From this viewpoint, critical periods have enormous practical importance for the modification of behavior through training and education. In the case of the critical period for primary socialization, a small amount of contact at an early period in life will determine which individuals will be the close social relatives of the animal in its infancy and often for the rest of its life. A similar period of contact in adult life may produce only momentary reactions to passing strangers.

Considered more deeply, critical periods must depend on internal processes. There must be changes taking place within the animal which are correlated with time and hence account for the existence of critical periods. Time itself is a term of description and measurement rather than an explanatory concept. A fundamental question is: what changes go on within the individual which make a critical period in life different from any other? The most general answer is that a critical period is one in which rapid organization of some kind is taking place. While this is going on, it is easy to change the nature of the organization. However, organization in itself has a tendency to produce stability. *Therefore, any period in life when rapid organization is taking place is a critical period,* since the changes which are easily and often accidentally produced at that time become a fixed and relatively permanent feature of the stabilized organization (Scott, 1962). In the case of primary socialization, the young animal is organizing its first social relationships.

By extension we can reason that *any period in life when a major new relationship is being formed is a critical one for determining the nature of that relationship.* Such a period would occur in later life during courtship and mating and the resulting formation of the first sexual relationship, and we have already seen an example of a critical period in the formation of a relationship by the mother sheep for her offspring. Such a period should occur in any mammal when the young are born. The period of primary socialization is an unusually critical one in that it may indirectly affect the formation of these later relationships.

Periods and Processes   From what has been said above it is obvious that the important thing about the process of primary socialization is not time, although this permits us to easily describe and predict events, but the actual process itself. Therefore, the things to look for in development are times at which organizational processes are proceeding at a maximum speed.

Primary Socialization in Human Infants   . . . There appears to be a definite neonatal period in human infants, extending from birth to about five or six weeks of age. During this period all behavior is organized around the problems of neonatal life, particularly that of neonatal nutrition, which is accomplished by suckling. Marked by the appearance of the smiling response to human faces, there is a period of rapid improvement in the capacity for visual perception. By six months of age, the decrease in rate of smiling to strangers indicates that the infant readily distinguishes between familiar and unfamiliar faces. The period from approximately five or six weeks to six or seven months of age is thus the period during which the process of primary socialization, or the formation of the first social relationships, takes place (Gray, 1958). One consequence of the timing of this period is that a young baby will usually form its first social relationships with its own parents. Since it usually has more contact with its mother than any other individual, the earliest, and presumably strongest, relationship will be formed with her, although under other conditions of child rearing it would be possible for a baby to form a strong relationship with any individual who took care of it. We have no data on how long a baby takes to form a lasting social relationship, but if results with other animals are any guide, it probably needs very little time. The baby's reactions are consistent with those of other animals in that its positive responses to a stranger during this period are easily and quickly evoked. The puppy during the critical period of socialization wags its tail at strangers, and the human infant smiles.

THE EFFECTS OF ISOLATION

Drastic experiments with social isolation of human infants are never performed for obvious reasons, and what evidence we have is confined to accidental cases in which children have been hidden from the outside world for criminal or emotional reasons. The most famous case is that of the "Nuremberg boy," Kaspar Hauser, who was discovered wandering in the streets as a young adult in the year 1828. He could at first speak little more than his own name but later reported that he had been kept in a dungeon without companions and that his only playthings were a toy dog and two hobbyhorses. He was therefore not only a social isolate but also the product of rearing in a barren environment. No information was available as to how early he was placed in isolation, and all that can be said is that he showed a considerable degree of recovery from its effects.

Results of Animal Experiments on Isolation   Rearing a young bird or mammal in isolation from its own kind (and from any other species with which it might associate) produces bizarre and striking effects on behavior. The longer the isolation is continued the more drastic are the results. An isolated male Indian jungle fowl will as an adult attempt to go through the usual motions of courtship to a female but direct these toward his own body so that he spins and whirls in behavior never seen in ordinary roosters (Kruijt, 1964). A puppy isolated during the critical period will often show bizarre postures such as standing still in the corner of a room with one paw raised above its head and forced into the angle of the walls (Fuller and Clark, 1966a, 1966b).

From our understanding of the process of primary socialization, we would predict that the isolated animal would become attached to whatever was available in the environment during the critical period. The only living thing present is the animal itself. We would therefore predict that a chicken reared in isolation would become imprinted upon its own body and, indeed, the reaction of the isolated adult is consistent with this expectation. From experiments with attachments to inanimate models we would also predict that the isolated animal would become attached to anything present in the physical surroundings, such as food dishes or even the walls of the confining chamber. Thus isolated puppies after their release from confinement will sometimes play for hours with food and water dishes each in a solitary fashion. More than this, the effects of isolation upon the subsequent behavior of a puppy are bound up with the development of the capacity of fear. During isolation there is very little to frighten the young animal, but it nevertheless develops a capacity for a complete fear response. The result is that the release from isolation produces a strong fearful reaction which becomes associated with the entire outside world. The puppy standing in the corner is probably attempting to escape as far as possible from all the strange stimulation around it, or perhaps it is trying to draw some comfort from contact similar to the walls of its box.

Results of Semi-isolation on Human Behavior   As indicated above, drastic isolation experiments are never done on children, but isolation occurs commonly enough in normal experience for us to know something of its effects. Short periods of isolation produce crying and a strongly unpleasant emotional reaction; in fact, temporary isolation was formerly often used as a method of punishment for young children, just as solitary confinement is still occasionally used as a drastic punishment for adult prisoners.

Children's lives differ a great deal with respect to the number and closeness of social contacts that are permitted during early development. Some children grow up in remote rural areas with a limited group of family acquaintances, and others are deliberately exposed to a large number outside the family, as in the case of those who are sent to nursery school. We would predict that the result of semi-isolation would be the development of shyness with strangers, and this seems to be the case with children brought up in isolated rural environments where they may never see anyone except members of their immediate families during their early years. However, there is undoubtedly wide variation in emotional responses among children, and some should have a much greater hereditary capacity for the development of shyness than others. Effects of rearing in such an environment should therefore vary among individuals.

A much more serious disturbance of behavior is the development of autism. An autistic child tends to play entirely by himself and to be unresponsive to others. The symptoms, at least, are very similar to those of young animals raised in isolation, but the circumstances are different. Such children usually live in what seem to be normal family surroundings. Some evidence indicates that their parents are not warmly emotional, but this explanation hardly seems adequate, especially in view of the tendency of animals to become attached to completely unresponsive objects. The autistic child behaves as if he had become socialized only to himself. We can hypothesize that there has been some derangement of the whole process of socialization, that the derangement is definitely connected with the development of emotional reactions, and that it may have a partially hereditary basis.

RESULTS OF BREAKING A SOCIAL RELATIONSHIP

Unlike rearing in isolation, the breaking off of a social relationship is something which frequently happens in human development as a result of death, illness, financial misfortunes, and other disruptions of family life. The practical problems of replacing such relationships through adoption, together with its frequently unfavorable results, have inspired a considerable amount of observational work. The psychiatrist John Bowlby (1951) became interested in the results of broken relationships when he studied the case histories of a group of juvenile thieves and discovered that a large number of them had been separated from their mothers for long periods during infancy. He and his associates then made first-hand studies of children as they were separated from their parents, particularly in cases of hospitalization, which can necessitate an abrupt, drastic and long-lasting separation from familiar surroundings. They found that children are indeed seriously upset by these experiences, and their results have prompted many children's hospitals to change their practices through encouraging frequent visits by parents and by decreasing the time of separation as much as possible.

Primary Results of Separation in Infants   As we saw in Chapter 2, Schaffer (1958) found two kinds of reactions in babies returned to their homes after a period of separation in hospitals. Before seven months such babies show what he calls a "global syndrome," becoming depressed and staring anxiously at everything in the room, living and non-living. After seven months, the babies show an "overdependency syndrome." They cry a great deal and try to avoid being separated from anyone who is caring for them. The earlier reaction is related to change in the physical environment and indicates that the babies have become attached to their surroundings and are disturbed by leaving them. This reaction is undoubtedly related to the process of localization, or becoming attached to a particular place. . . . The changed reaction after seven months indicates that the baby is now reacting primarily to the separation from people, which is equivalent to the temporary breaking of a social relationship.

Permanent separation produces more drastic effects. Yarrow (1964) studied a group of seventy-five infants that were transferred to a foster mother sometime during their first year. A few showed distress when transferred as early as three months, but by six months 86 per cent showed serious emotional disturbances, and all infants over seven months showed reactions severe enough to be called emotional trauma.

Bowlby (1960) and his colleagues have also studied the degree of emotional disturbance produced by separation at various ages. During the second half of the first year, the emotional reaction to separation may appear after only a few hours. As a child grows older, he becomes more and more capable of managing separation for long periods, particularly after he has learned to talk and begins to have some concept of the time at which his parents may return.

Most parents are familiar with the emotional symptoms of separation when they leave their children for a few days to travel or take a vacation. The baby-sitter or caretaker of course finds that the children are emotionally disturbed and hard to handle, being given to frequent crying and periods of depression. An experienced baby-sitter soon learns to try to keep the children amused and stimulated and thus counteracts the emotion of depression in her charges. On their return, the parents find the children tearful, demanding, and sometimes antagonistic. They often conclude that this behavior is the result of the baby-sitter's "spoiling" them. Actually, the children have been emotionally hurt by their parents and react in various ways. Some of these seem to be simple attempts to punish the parents. If the separation has been unusually long, a child may react with real coldness, as if reluctant to enter into a close social relationship again and thus run the risk of future separations and the resulting emotional pain. Obviously, breaking a social relationship, even temporarily, is a serious matter for a child.. Although separation can never be completely avoided, and perhaps should not be, parents should manage it as carefully as possible, especially in the case of younger children.

Adoption   From a theoretical viewpoint, any emotional damage which might result from adoption should be the effect not of forming a new relationship but of breaking off an old one. The more well established the original relationship, the more the child should be disturbed by breaking it, but this principle is limited by the fact that as a child becomes older he can understand the circumstances better and protect himself against their emotional consequences. We shall discuss here only the effects of breaking a relation in infancy.

The theoretically ideal time for an adoption is, of course, soon after birth and no later than the end of the neonatal period. At this age the baby should react to its adopted parents just as it would to its real ones, and their only concern should be to give it the good physical care that any baby should have. If adoption takes place during the period of socialization, extending from five or six weeks to approximately six or seven months, a new relationship should be formed with ease, but most easily toward the beginning of the period rather than the end. Some immediate emotional upset would be expected, in accordance with Schaffer's observations, but this should be as much the result of the change in locality as the break in a primary social relationship.

Once the primary social relationship has been strongly established and the fear reaction to strangers has begun to appear, a much more severe emotional upset should result. Indeed, such objective evidence as is available indicates that children who have been separated from familiar persons and surroundings and adopted in the second half of the first year are more likely to show later difficulties of personal adjustment than those adopted in the first. It is, however, difficult to tell how much of this maladjustment is due to permanent emotional damage suffered by the infant at the time, and how much is due to the pattern of parent-child relationships which is being organized for the first time immediately after adoption and whose effects continue long into the future. Any continuing social relationship is a two-way affair, and unless foster parents are aware of the problems of adoption and are able to make emotional readjustments of their own, the habits and attitudes that they set up during their own critical period of emotional adjustment and behavioral organization will almost certainly be different toward a fearful, emotionally disturbed infant than toward a normally clinging and welcoming one.

Various circumstances such as death or lack of foster parents available to take an orphan at the most suitable time may make adoption necessary at various periods later than the optimum. If such an unavoidable situation arises care should be taken to make the transition as smooth as possible. For example, the prospective parents can be introduced to their new child in his own familiar environment and their visits repeated over a period of several hours or even days in such a way that the child can overcome his fear of strange people without having to contend with the fear of strange surroundings at the same time. Second, the transition can be made in such a way that the child is taken into his new environment for a few hours only and then returned to his original home before being taken away for good. Returning the child more often might also be desirable in order to preserve some continuity between his former and future existences.

To summarize: All evidence from both human development and that of other social mammals indicates that even temporarily breaking contact with individuals and surroundings to which a primary attachment has taken place is a strongly disturbing emotional experience. This reaction has undoubtedly evolved as an adaptation to being lost or separated from the familiar. For a young and dependent social mammal, such a situation is often extremely dangerous. Unless the infant gives an immediate emotional reaction and starts signaling its whereabouts, its life may be lost within a few hours. Hence the distress vocalization of young puppies and the crying responses of human babies when left alone in strange places have strong survival value.

The results of permanent separation and the consequent complete break in a strongly developed social relationship are serious at any time in life, as anyone knows who has experienced the death of a close relative or the breakup of a marriage. For a young infant, the problem of permanent separation is usually settled by adoption, and here we can learn much from experiments with dogs, whose adoption (by the human species) is a normal occurrence. Much can be done to alleviate the painful emotions produced by separation, but the adopted puppy almost inevitably becomes more sensitive to separation and, consequently, more dependent on its human foster parents. These characteristics are desirable in a dog, as few people want a completely independent pet, but less so in a child, who should eventually develop into an independent and responsible adult. The answer seems to be to manage the child's separation in such a way as to decrease the painful emotional reactions as much as possible and to allow him an opportunity to integrate and organize the two portions of his existence.

References

BOWLBY, J. Maternal Care and Mental Health. Geneva: World Health Organization, 1951. Review of effects of disrupting maternal care.

———. Separation anxiety. *International Journal of Psychoanalysis*, 1960, *41*, 1–25. Summary of observations of infants' emotional reactions to separation from their mothers.

FREEDMAN, D. G., KING, J. A., and ELLIOTT, O. Critical period in the social development of dogs. *Science*, 1961, *133*, 1016–1017. The best experimental study of the critical period for primary socialization in this species.

FULLER, J. L., and CLARK, L. D. Genetic and treatment factors modifying the post-isolation syndrome in dogs. *Journal of Comparative and Physiological Psychology*, 1966a, *61*, 251–257. Some dog breeds are more severely affected by isolation than others; results of attempted therapy.

———, Effects of rearing with specific stimuli upon post-isolation syndrome in dogs. *Journal of Comparative and Physiological Psychology*, 1966b, *61*, 258–263. Visual isolation has more severe effects than restriction of space alone.

GRAY, P. H. Theory and evidence of imprinting in human infants. *Journal of Psychology*, 1958, *46*, 155–166. Review of the evidence concerning the effects of adoption at different ages.

Hersher, L., Richmond, J. B., and Moore, U. A. Maternal behavior in sheep and goats. In H. L. Rheingold (Ed.), *Maternal behavior in mammals.* New York: Wiley, 1963. Pp. 203–232. The herd animals rapidly form an exclusive bond with their young, as well as the young becoming attached to their mothers.

Hess, E. H. Imprinting and the critical period concept. In E. L. Bliss (Ed.) *Roots of behavior.* New York: Harper, 1962. Pp. 254–263. The primary socialization process in the domestic chick.

Klinghammer, E. Factors influencing choice of mate in altricial birds. In H. W. Stevenson, E. H. Hess, and H. L. Rheingold (Eds.), *Early behavior: Comparative and developmental approaches.* New York: Wiley, 1967. Pp. 5–42. Experiments with imprinting in ring doves and mourning doves with a review of work on other altricial species.

Kruijt, J. P. *Ontogeny of social behavior in Burmese red jungle fowl.* Leiden: Brill, 1964. Descriptive and experimental studies of behavioral development in the wild ancestor of the domestic chicken.

Schaffer, H. F. Objective observations of personality development in early infancy. British Journal of Medical Psychology, 1958, *31,* 174–183. Age changes in emotional reactions to separation from relatives.

Scott, J. P. Critical periods in behavioral development. *Science,* 1962, *138,* 949–958. General review of facts and theory relating to critical periods.

———. The process of primary socialization in the dog. In G. Newton and S. Levine (Eds.), *Early experience and behavior.* Springfield, Ill.: Thomas, 1967. Summarizes experiments with this process in the dog.

Yarrow, L. J. Separation from parents during early childhood. In M. L. Hoffman and L. W. Hoffman (Eds.), *Review of child development research.* New York: Russell Sage Foundation, 1964. Pp. 89–136. Good critical review of the literature on this topic.

Attachment, Exploration, and Separation: Illustrated by the Behavior of One-Year-Olds in a Strange Situation*

Mary D. Salter Ainsworth and Silvia M. Bell
JOHNS HOPKINS UNIVERSITY

The concepts of attachment and attachment behavior are considered from an ethological-evolutionary viewpoint. Attachment behavior and exploration are viewed in balance, and the biological functions of each are discussed. As an illustration of these concepts, a study is

Reprinted from *Child Development,* 41, 50–67. Copyright © 1970 by The Society for Research in Child Development, Inc. By permission.

* An earlier version of this paper was prepared while the first author was a fellow of the Center for Advanced Study in the Behavioral Sciences. It was presented at the annual meeting of the American Psychological Association, at San Francisco, September 1968, in a symposium, "Attachment Behaviors in Humans and Animals." The extended project which yielded the data has been supported by grant 62-244 of the Foundations' Fund for Research in Psychiatry, and by USPHS grant RO1 and HD 01712; this support is gratefully acknowledged. We are also appreciative of help given by the following in various aspects of the "strange situation" study: George D. Allyn, John Conklin, Elizabeth A. Eikenberg, Edwin E. Ellis, William C. Hamilton, Mary B. Main, Robert S. Marvin II, Eleanor S. McCulloch, and especially Barbara A. Wittig who helped in the original planning of the strange situation.

reported of 56 white, middle-class infants, 49–51 weeks of age, in a strange situation. The presence of the mother was found to encourage exploratory behavior, her absence to depress exploration and to heighten attachment behaviors. In separation episodes such behaviors as crying and search increased. In reunion episodes proximity-seeking and contact-maintaining behaviors were heightened. In a substantial proportion of Ss, contact-resisting behaviors were also heightened in the reunion episodes, usually in conjunction with contact-maintaining behaviors, thus suggesting ambivalence. Some Ss also displayed proximity-avoiding behavior in relation to the mother in the reunion episodes. These findings are discussed in the context of relevant observational, clinical, and experimental studies of human and nonhuman primates, including studies of mother-child separation. In conclusion, it is urged that the concepts of attachment and attachment behavior be kept broad enough to comprehend the spectrum of the findings of this range of studies.

. . . It is the purpose of this paper to highlight some distinctive features of the ethological-evolutionary concept of attachment, by citing reports of the inter-actions between the infant's attachment behavior and other behaviors men-tioned above; to illustrate these interactions by a report of the behavior of 1-year-olds in a strange situation; and to note parallels between strange-situa-tion behavior and behavior reported in other relevant observational, clinical, and experimental contexts.

Let us begin with some definitions and key concepts distinctive of the ethological-evolutionary viewpoint, as proposed by Bowlby (1958, 1969) and Ainsworth (1964, 1967, 1969). *An attachment* may be defined as an affectional tie that one person or animal forms between himself and another specific one— a tie that binds them together in space and endures over time. The behavioral hallmark of attachment is seeking to gain and to maintain a certain degree of proximity to the object of attachment, which ranges from close physical contact under some circumstances to interaction or communication across some distance under other circumstances. *Attachment behaviors* are behaviors which promote proximity or contact. In the human infant these include active proximity- and contact-seeking behaviors such as approaching, following, and clinging, and signaling behaviors such as smiling, crying, and calling.

The very young infant displays attachment (proximity-promoting) behaviors such as crying, sucking, rooting, and smiling, despite the fact that he is insufficiently discriminating to direct them differentially to a specific person. These initial behaviors indicate a genetic bias toward becoming attached, since they can be demonstrated to be either activated or terminated most effectively by stimuli which, in the environment of evolutionary adaptedness, are most likely to stem from human sources. When these behaviors, supplemented by other active proximity-seeking behaviors which emerge later—presumably through a process of learning in the course of mother-infant interaction— become organized hierarchically and directed actively and specifically toward the mother, the infant may be described as having become attached to her.

The intensity of attachment behavior may be heightened or diminished by situational conditions, but, once an attachment has been formed, it cannot be viewed as vanishing during periods when attachment behavior is not evident. Therefore, it seems necessary to view attachment as an organization of be-havioral systems which has an internal, structural portion that endures throughout periods when none of the component attachment behaviors have been activated.

Viewed in the context of evolutionary theory, infant-mother attachment may be seen to fulfill significant biological functions, that is, functions that promote species survival. The long, helpless infancy of the human species occasions grave risks. For the species to have survived, the infant has required protection during this period of defenselessness. It is inferred, therefore, that the genetic code makes provision for infant behaviors which have the usual (although not necessarily invariable) outcome of bringing infant and mother together.

Exploratory behavior is equally significant from an evolutionary point of view. As Hamburg (1968) has pointed out, a prolonged infancy would miss its adaptive mark if there were not also provisions in the genetic code which lead the infant to be interested in the novel features of his environment—to venture forth, to explore, and to learn. The implication is that the genetic biases in a species which can adapt to a wide range of environmental variations provide for a balance in infant behaviors (and in reciprocal maternal behaviors) between those which lead the infant away from the mother and promote exploration and acquisition of knowledge of the properties of the physical and social environment, and those which draw mother and infant together and promote the protection and nurturance that the mother can provide.

The interaction between exploratory and attachment behaviors has been highlighted in field studies of ground-living nonhuman primates (e.g., Southwick, Beg, & Siddiqi, 1965; DeVore, 1963; Goodall, 1965; Schaller, 1965) as well as studies of such species in captive colonies (see Hinde, Rowell, & Spencer-Booth, 1964, 1967) and in laboratories (e.g., Harlow, 1961; Harlow & Harlow, 1965; Mason, 1965.) Although at first infant and mother are in almost continuous close contact, soon they are in collusion to make more elastic the bonds that unite them. The infant ventures forth to investigate his environment and to play with other infants, and gradually spends more and more time "off" his mother. His expeditions take him further and further away from her, and she becomes increasingly permissive and retrieves him less promptly and less frequently. Alarm or threat of separation, however, quickly brings mother and infant together again.

Naturalistic studies of the attachment-exploration balance are very time consuming; the interaction between the two sets of behaviors must be observed over a wide range of situations. A short-cut alternative is to utilize a controlled strange or unfamiliar situation in which the child, with and without his mother, is exposed to stressful episodes of different kinds. So powerful is this technique in evoking behavioral changes that it is likely to be used with increasing frequency in studies of mother-infant interaction. The ethological-evolutionary view of the attachment-exploration balance is a useful model to use when planning and when interpreting the findings of strange-situation studies.

Of strange-situation studies already reported in the literature, only two have been guided by an ethological-evolutionary point of view. Harlow (1961) used a strange situation to demonstrate the security function of surrogate cloth mothers for infant rhesus macaques. Ainsworth and Wittig (1969) made a preliminary report of the attachment-exploration balance in human 1 year olds. Other studies—Arsenian (1943), Cox and Campbell (1968), Rheingold

(1969)—focused on exploratory behavior and reported that the presence of the mother supports it, but paid scant attention to attachment behavior and its hierarchical manifestations in reunion episodes as well as during separation.

The strange-situation procedure provides more than an opportunity to observe how exploratory behavior is affected by mother-present, mother-absent, or other conditions. It is a laboratory microcosm in which a wide range of behaviors pertinent to attachment and to its balance with exploratory behavior may be elicited. Attachment behaviors may be seen as complicated by "negative" behaviors, such as avoidance and aggression. And yet, since the laboratory situation provides but a very small sample of mother-infant interaction, strange-situation findings are not self-interpreting. Perception of the implications of the behaviors that occur in it is facilitated by reference to the findings of other studies—naturalistic, clinical, and experimental. For this reason the ensuing report of a strange-situation study is presented as a useful *illustration* of the shifting balance between exploratory and attachment behavior implicit in the ethological-evolutionary view of attachment. The discussion which follows the presentation refers to relevant findings of other studies. The propositions offered in conclusion comprehend these other relevant considerations as well as the findings of the illustrative strange-situation study.

THE STRANGE SITUATION

In the course of a longitudinal, naturalistic investigation of infant-mother attachment during the first year of life, there was little opportunity in the home environment to observe the balance of attachment and exploratory behaviors under conditions of novelty and alarm. Therefore, a laboratory situation was devised as a test situation to which the Ss were introduced when nearly 1 year old. It was desired to observe the extent to which the infant could use his mother as a secure base from which he could explore a strange environment, with fear of the strange kept in abeyance by her presence. It was also intended to observe the extent to which attachment behavior might gain ascendancy over exploratory behavior under conditions of alarm introduced by the entrance of a stranger and under conditions of separation from and reunion with the mother.

METHOD   *Subjects*   The 56 Ss were family-reared infants of white, middle-class parents, who were originally contacted through pediatricians in private practice. One subsample of 23 Ss, who had been observed longitudinally from birth onward, were observed in the strange situation when 51 weeks old. The second subsample of 33 Ss, studied in the context of an independent project (Bell, 1970), were observed when 49 weeks old.

Procedure   The strange situation was comprised of eight episodes which followed in a standard order for all subjects. The situation was designed to be novel enough to elicit exploratory behavior, and yet not so strange that it would evoke fear and heighten attachment behavior at the outset. The approach of the stranger was gradual, so that any fear of her could be attributed to unfamiliarity rather than to abrupt, alarming behavior. The episodes were arranged so that the less disturbing ones came first. Finally, the situation as a whole was intended to be no more disturbing than those an infant was likely to encounter in his ordinary life experience. A summarized account of the procedure has been given elsewhere (Ainsworth & Wittig, 1969) but will be reviewed here.

The experimental room was furnished—not bare—but so arranged that there was a 9 × 9-foot square of clear floor space, marked off into 16 squares to facilitate recording of location and locomotion. At one end of the room was a child's chair heaped with and surrounded by toys. Near the other end of the room on one side was a chair for the mother, and on the opposite side, near the door, a chair for the stranger. The baby was put down in the middle of the base of the triangle by the three chairs and left free to move where he wished. Both the mother and the female stranger were instructed in advance as to the roles they were to play.

Episode 1 (M, B, O). Mother (M), accompanied by an observer (O), carried the baby (B) into the room, and then O left.

Episode 2 (M, B). M put B down in the specified place, then sat quietly in her chair, participating only if B sought her attention. Duration 3 minutes.

Episode 3 (S, M, B). A stranger (S) entered, sat quietly for 1 minute, conversed with M for 1 minute, and then gradually approached B, showing him a toy. At the end of the third minute M left the room unobtrusively.

Episode 4 (S, B). If B was happily engaged in play, S was nonparticipant. If he was inactive, she tried to interest him in the toys. If he was distressed, she tried to distract him or to comfort him. If he could not be comforted, the episode was curtailed—otherwise it lasted 3 minutes.

Episode 5 (M, B). M entered, paused in the doorway to give B an opportunity to mobilize a spontaneous response to her. S then left unobtrusively. What M did next was not specified—except that she was told that after B was again settled in play with the toys she was to leave again, after pausing to say "bye-bye." (Duration of episode undetermined.)

Episode 6 (B alone). The baby was left alone for 3 minutes, unless he was so distressed that the episode had to be curtailed.

Episode 7 (S, B). S entered and behaved as in episode 4 for 3 minutes, unless distress prompted curtailment. (Ainsworth & Wittig 1969, planned a somewhat different procedure for episode 7, which was attempted for the first 14 Ss but, as it turned out, approximated the simpler procedure reported here, which was used for the remaining Ss.)

Episode 8 (M, B). M returned, S left, and after the reunion had been observed, the situation was terminated.

The behavior of the Ss was observed from an adjoining room through a one-way vision window. Two observers dictated continuous narrative accounts into a dual channel tape recorder which also picked up the click of a timer every 15 seconds. (This represents the procedure we now consider standard. For the first 14 Ss, however, the dual channel recorder was not available, so one observer dictated, while the other made written notes. For the second sub-sample of 33 *S*s, author Bell was the sole observer.) The protocols were sub-sequently transcribed and consolidated, then coded. Reliability of observation was checked by separate codings of the dictated reports made by the two authors in four cases observed by both. Product-moment coefficients of .99 were found for each of locomotor, manipulatory and visual exploration, and one of .98 for crying.

The narrative record yielded two types of measure. A frequency measure was used for three forms of exploratory behavior—locomotor, manipulatory, and visual—and for crying. A score of 1 was given for each 15-second time interval in which the behavior occurred. The maximum was 12 for an episode, since the standard length of an episode was 3 minutes, and longer or shorter episodes were prorated. Frequency measures were obtained for episodes 2 through 7. Product-moment reliability coefficients for two independent coders for eight randomly selected cases were as follows: exploratory locomotion, .99; exploratory manipulation, .93; visual exploration, .98; crying, .99.

The second measure was based upon detailed coding of behaviors in which the contingencies of the mother's or stranger's behavior had to be taken into consideration. The codings were then ordered into 7-point scales on the assumption that not only could the same behavior be manifested in different degrees of intensity, but that different behaviors could serve the same end under different intensities of activation. There were five classes of behavior thus scored.

Proximity- and contact-seeking behaviors include active, effective behaviors such as approaching and clambering up, active gestures such as reaching or leaning, intention movements such as partial approaches, and vocal signals including "directed" cries.

Contact-maintaining behaviors pertain to the situation after the baby has gained contact, either through his own initiative or otherwise. They include: clinging, embracing, clutching, and holding on; resisting release by intensified clinging or, if contact is lost, by turning back and reaching, or clambering back up; and protesting release vocally.

Proximity- and interaction-avoiding behaviors pertain to a situation which ordinarily elicits approach, greeting, or at least watching or interaction across a distance, as when an adult entered, or tried to engage the baby's attention. Such behaviors include ignoring the adult, pointedly avoiding looking at her, looking away, turning away, or moving away.

Contact- and interaction-resisting behaviors including angry, ambivalent attempts to push away, hit, or kick the adult who seeks to make contact, squirming to get down having been picked up, or throwing away or pushing away the toys through which the adult attempts to mediate her interventions. More diffuse manifestations are angry screaming, throwing self about, throwing self down, kicking the floor, pouting, cranky fussing, or petulance.

These four classes of behavior were scored for interaction with the mother in episodes 2, 3, 5, and 8, and for interaction with the stranger in episodes 3, 4, and 7.

Search behavior was scored for the separation episodes 4, 6, and 7. These behaviors include: following the mother to the door, trying to open the door, banging on the door, remaining oriented to the door or glancing at it, going to the mother's empty chair or simply looking at it. Such behaviors imply that the infant is searching for the absent mother either actively or by orienting to the last place in which she was seen (the door in most cases) or the place associated with her in the strange situation (her chair.)

In scoring these five classes of behavior, the score was influenced by the following features: the strength of the behavior, its frequency, duration, and latency, and by the type of behavior itself—with active behavior being considered stronger than signaling. Detailed instructions for scoring these behaviors as well as for coding the frequency measures are provided elsewhere.[1]

Reliability coefficients (rho) for two independent scorers for 14 randomly selected cases were, for behaviors directed to the mother, as follows: proximity- and contact-seeking, .93; contact-maintaining, .97; proximity- and interaction-avoiding, .93; contact-resisting, .96; search, .94.

FINDINGS   The findings to be reported here are of behaviors characteristic of the sample as a whole. Individual differences were conspicuous, instructive, and significantly correlated with other variables. Some of these have been reported elsewhere (Ainsworth & Wittig, 1969; Ainsworth & Bell, 1970; Bell, 1970) but they cannot be considered here.

Exploratory Behavior   Figure 1 shows how three forms of exploratory behavior vary in successive episodes from 2 through 7. There is a sharp decline in all forms of exploratory behavior from episode 2 when the baby was alone with his mother to episode 3 when the stranger was present also. (This and all other interepisode differences reported here are significant at the .01 level or better, as tested by the binomial test, unless noted otherwise.) Exploration remains depressed through episode 4 when the baby was left with the stranger. Visual and manipulatory exploration (visual at the .02 level) recover significantly in episode 5, aided by the mother's attempts to interest the baby again in play, although similar efforts by the stranger in episodes 4 and 7 were ineffective. Visual and manipulatory exploration decline again in episode 6 after the mother departs for a second time, leaving the baby alone. All forms of exploratory behavior decline to their lowest point in episode 7 after the stranger had returned but while the mother was still absent.

To supplement the visual exploration score, which measured visual orientation to the physical environment, visual orientation to the mother and to the stranger were also coded. The only noteworthy findings may be summarized as follows: In episode 2, the baby looked at the toys and other aspects of the physical environment much more frequently than at the mother, at whom he glanced only now and then, keeping visual tabs on her; in episode 3, the stranger, the most novel feature of the environment, was looked at more than the toys, and the mother was looked at no more frequently than before.

[1] The following materials have been deposited with the National Auxiliary Publications Service: instructions for conducting the strange situation procedure, instructions to the mother, instructions for coding behaviors for frequency measures, and instructions for coding socially interactive behaviors. Orders NAPS Document 00762 from ASIS National Auxiliary Publications Service, c/o CMM Information Sciences, Inc., 22 West 34th Street, New York, New York 10001; remitting $3.00 for microfiche or $1.00 for photocopies.

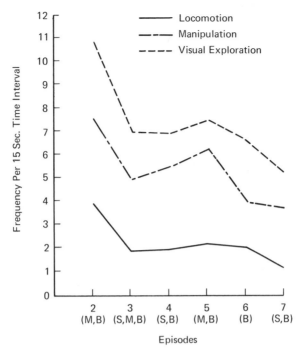

FIGURE 1.   *Incidence of exploratory behavior.*

Crying   Figure 2 suggests that the strange situation does not in itself cause alarm or distress, for crying is minimal in episode 2. Crying does not increase significantly in episode 3 ($p = .068$), which suggests that the stranger was not in herself alarming for most Ss, at least not when the mother was also present. The incidence of crying rises in episode 4 with the mother's first departure; it declines upon her return in episode 5, only to increase sharply in episode 6 when she departs a second time, leaving the baby alone. It does not decrease significantly when the stranger returns in episode 7, which suggests that it is the mother's absence rather than mere aloneness that was distressing to most of the babies, and that the greater incidence of crying in episode 6 than in episode 4 is largely due to a cumulative effect.

Search Behavior During Separation   The mean strength of search behavior was moderate in episode 4 (3.0), significantly stronger in episode 6 (4.6), and moderate again in episode 7 (2.5). Although this might suggest that search behavior is especially activated by being left alone and reduced in the presence of the stranger, this interpretation is not advanced because of the contingencies of the stranger's behavior and her location near the door. Some infants (37 percent) cried minimally if at all in episode 6, and yet searched strongly. Some (20 percent) cried desperately, but searched weakly or not at all. Some (32 percent) both cried and searched. All but four Ss reacted to being left alone with either one or other of these attachment behaviors.

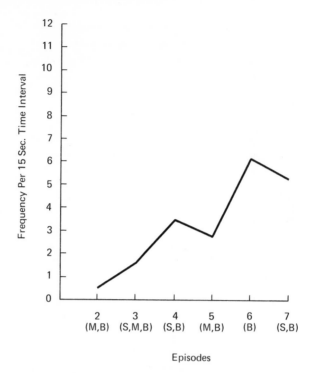

FIGURE 2.   *Incidence of crying.*

Proximity-Seeking and Contact-Maintaining Behaviors   Figure 3 shows that efforts to regain contact, proximity or interaction with the mother occur only weakly in episodes 2 and 3 but are greatly intensified by brief separation experiences. Contact-maintaining behavior is negligible in episodes 2 and 3, rises in the first reunion episode (5), and rises even more sharply in the second reunion episode (8). In the case of both classes of behavior the increase from episodes 2 through 5 to 8 is highly significant ($p < .001$). Some Ss showed these behaviors in relation to the stranger also. Thus, for example, a few infants approached the stranger in each of the episodes in which the stranger was present, but substantially fewer than those who approached the mother. Some infants were picked up by the stranger in episodes 4 and 7—in an attempt to comfort them—and some of these did cling to her and/or resist being put down again. Nevertheless proximity-seeking and contact-maintaining behaviors were displayed much less frequently and less strongly to the stranger than to the mother.

Contact-Resisting and Proximity-Avoiding Behaviors   Table 1 shows the incidence of contact-resisting and proximity-avoiding behaviors directed to both mother and stranger. Contact-resisting behavior directed toward the mother occurred very rarely in the preseparation episodes because the mother had been instructed not to intervene except in response to the baby's demands, and therefore episodes 2 and 3 are omitted from the table. In the reunion episodes,

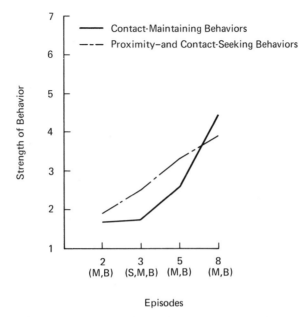

FIGURE 3.   *Strength of proximity-seeking and contact-maintaining behaviors directed toward the mother.*

some *S*s resisted contact with the mother, but many did not. Therefore Table 1 shows the incidence of this behavior rather than its mean strength.

About one third of the sample showed contact-resisting behavior to the mother in episode 5, at least to some degree, and about one half showed it in episode 8. All but one infant who scored relatively high (4 or higher) in contact-resisting behavior received a comparably high score on contact-maintaining behavior. Thus, at least when directed to the mother, contact-resisting behavior seems to represent classic ambivalence—wanting to be held, wanting to be close, and at the same time angrily resisting contact.

Contact and interaction with the stranger were also resisted but somewhat less frequently than with the mother. Six *S*s showed fairly strong contact- or interaction-resisting behavior (scores of 4 or higher) with both stranger in episode 7 and with mother in episode 8, but, for the most part, babies who tended to resist the mother did not resist the stranger and vice versa.

Proximity- and interaction-avoiding behavior did not occur in relation to the mother in the preseparation episodes, for the mother's nonparticipant role made no claim on the baby's attention. But, as shown in Table 1, it occurred to some degree in about half the sample in each of the reunion episodes, 5 and 8. About one third of the sample avoided the stranger at some time in episode 3 —ignoring her, avoiding meeting her eyes, or moving further away from her. The incidence of these behaviors declined in episode 4, and even in episode 7 remained less than in episode 3. About half the sample avoided neither mother nor stranger, but those who showed this behavior in any strength (score of 4 or over) to one did not show it to the other.

TABLE 1

Incidence of Contact-Resisting and Proximity-Avoiding Behavior to Mother and Stranger

STRENGTH OF BEHAVIOR	BEHAVIOR TO MOTHER		BEHAVIOR TO STRANGER		
	EPISODE 5	EPISODE 8	EPISODE 3	EPISODE 4	EPISODE 7
RESIST CONTACT					
6–7	4	6	0	6	7
4–5	5	8	5	3	12
2–3	9	13	2	3	3
1	38	29	49	44	34
AVOID PROXIMITY					
6–7	7	5	4	1	1
4–5	17	13	7	3	6
2–3	3	7	7	1	2
1	29	31	38	51	45

DISCUSSION

These findings illustrate the complex interaction between attachment behavior, response to novel or unfamiliar stimulus objects and situations, and responses to separation from the attachment object and to subsequent reunion. First, let us consider response to novelty. It is now commonly accepted that novelty may elicit either fear and avoidance or approach and exploration, depending both on the degree of novelty and upon circumstances. One of the conditions which facilitates approach and exploration of the novel is the presence, in reasonable but not necessarily close proximity, of the mother—the object of attachment. The infants of the present sample showed little alarm in the preseparation episodes of the strange situation. Their attachment behavior was not activated; they tended not to cling to the mother or even to approach her. They used her as a secure base from which to explore the strange situation. This finding is not new. Similar observations have been reported by Arsenian (1943), Cox and Campbell (1968), Ainsworth and Wittig (1969), and Rheingold (1969) for human subjects, and by Harlow (1961) for rhesus macaque infants. The presence of the mother can tip the balance in favor of exploring the novel rather than avoiding it or withdrawing from it.

Absence of the mother tends to tip the balance in the opposite direction with a substantial heightening of attachment behavior and concomitant lessening of exploration. During the mother's absence, proximity-promoting behaviors (crying and search) are evident. The mother's return in the reunion episodes did not serve to redress the balance to its previous level. Attachment behaviors—proximity- and contact-seeking and contact-maintaining behaviors

—remained heightened. Crying did not immediately subside in many cases and, despite the mother's attempts to evoke a renewed interest in exploring the properties of the toys, exploration remained depressed below its initial level.

It was assumed that separation episodes totaling 9 minutes at most would not have any lasting effect on the balance between attachment and exploratory behavior, and indeed the posttest behavior of the infants tended to confirm this assumption. Nevertheless these minuscule separations evoke behaviors which are similar in kind to those provoked by longer separations, although differing in duration and intensity. The behavior of these 1-year-old humans in response to separations lasting only a few minutes bears remarkable resemblance to the behavior of infant monkeys in response to separation for longer periods—a week (Spencer-Booth & Hinde, 1966) or a month (Kaufman & Rosenblum, 1967). In these experiments the mother was removed, and the infant left in his familiar social group. Attachment behavior, including distress calling and search for the mother, was heightened, and exploratory and play behavior was depressed during the separation. The infants responded more intensely to frightening stimuli during separation than when the mother was present. As separation continued there was some lessening of the intensity of distress and search, and some recovery of exploration and play—a recovery not manifest by the human infants in this sample in their very brief separations. When the mother was restored, however, the infant monkeys clung to her more and explored less than they had before separation—differing in this from nonseparated controls—and these effects lasted for three months or more.

The response of infant monkeys to experimental separations strongly resembles the behavior of young children, aged from 8 months to 3 years, when they undergo separations of several days, weeks, or even months away from home in hospitals or residential nurseries. Robertson and Bowlby (1952), Bowlby (1953), Schaffer (1958), and Heinicke and Westheimer (1965) have shown that the child is at first acutely distressed, protests the separation, and attempts to regain the mother by all means at his disposal. This initial phase of response tends to give way to despair, which in turn may give way—if the separation endures long enough—to a brightening of affect and renewed responsiveness to companions and to things in the environment. Attachment behavior directed toward the mother may have disappeared, but reunion with the mother tends to reactivate it and indeed to intensify it beyond its pre-separation level. This heightened level tends to persist for a more or less prolonged period, usually much longer than the separation itself. During the period after reunion when the child's attachment behavior is heightened, he is focused on his mother, attends less to other people and to things in his environment, explores less, and presumably learns less. An unduly prolonged heightening of attachment behavior may be viewed as a distortion of the attachment-exploration balance. Some long-term follow-up studies (e.g., Bowlby, Ainsworth, Boston, & Rosenbluth, 1956) suggest that this kind of behavior, often described as overdependent, may in some instances be a lasting effect of long, depriving separations.

Let us turn from attachment behavior to consider those behaviors that work against contact- and proximity-seeking, namely, contact-resisting and proximity- and interaction-avoiding behaviors. Contact-resisting behavior, as directed toward the mother, usually occurred in conjunction with contact-seeking behavior, and hence, as suggested earlier, implies an ambivalent response. Ambivalent or rejecting and angry responses are reported as common in young children returning home after brief separations (e.g., Heinicke & Westheimer, 1965.) Separation heightens aggressive behavior of this kind as well as attachment behavior, and predisposes the child toward angry outbursts upon minimal provocation. Spencer-Booth and Hinde (1966) report similar increase of aggression in monkeys: Unusually intense tantrums occur in response to any discouragement of contact-seeking behavior during the period of reunion after separation. Some of our strange-situation Ss showed contact-resisting behavior toward the stranger. Although in some cases this may indicate fear of the strange person, it seems likely that in some, perhaps most, it is a manifestation of aggression evoked by the mother's departure.

Proximity-avoiding behavior, on the other hand, seems likely to stem from different sources in the case of the stranger than in the case of the mother, even though the overt behavior seems the same in both cases. Ignoring the stranger, and looking, turning, or moving away from her probably imply an avoidance of the unfamiliar and fear-evoking person. This is suggested by the fact that these responses are more frequent (as directed toward the stranger) in episode 3, when the stranger has first appeared, than in later episodes. Similar avoidance of the mother cannot be due to unfamiliarity, and seems unlikely to be caused by fear. Such behavior occurs in the reunion episodes, and is more frequent than avoidance of the stranger.

Proximity- and interaction-avoiding behavior in relation to the mother is shown in striking form by some young children upon reunion after separations lasting for weeks or months. Robertson and Bowlby (1952) and Heinicke and Westheimer (1965) report that some children do not seem to recognize their mothers upon reunion, and that for a longer or shorter time they remain distant from her and treat her like a stranger. Bowlby (1960) has termed this kind of distanciation "detachment." During a prolonged separation, detachment tends to succeed protest and despair reactions, and after reunion it may persist for a long time—even indefinitely in cases in which separations have been very long and depriving. Such behavior has not yet been reported in nonhuman primates—perhaps because their experimental separations have been brief, perhaps because of species differences.

Avoidance responses of the kind observed in the strange situation in relation to the mother—looking away, turning away—may be detachment in the making and so constitute a primitive kind of defense. The constellation of individual differences in the strange-situation sample supports this hypothesis, although it is impossible here to present detailed evidence.

It may be pertinent, however, to refer to a similar looking-away response found in two experiments on the conditioning and extinction of attachment behaviors. Brackbill (1958) worked with the smiling response. During the conditioning period she provided contingent reinforcement for smiling by responding socially to the baby each time he smiled—and smiling increased in frequency. During the extinction period she met the baby's smile with an impassive face. Not only did the frequency of smiling decrease, but when the experimenter failed to respond to a smile, the baby fussed and looked away. It became increasingly difficult to catch the baby's eye. He looked away from the person who had previously reinforced his attachment behavior but who no longer did so. Similar results are reported for an experiment on babbling by Rheingold, Gewirtz, and Ross (1959).

These findings highlight the fact that in extinction—as indeed learning theorists have often themselves emphasized—there is an active process of blocking the response by another, antithetical behavior, rather than or in addition to the weakening of the strength of smiling (or babbling) behavior itself. This suggests that detached behavior may consist of responses, incompatible with attachment behavior, which have, often temporarily, gained the greater strength. That attachment can endure despite a period of detachment is shown by the strength with which attachment behavior can break through into overt expression in the case of young children who do not at reunion seem to recognize their mothers, but who subsequently manifest much heightened proximity-seeking and contact-maintaining behavior.

In summary, continuities have been noted between attachment and exploratory behavior and their activating and terminating conditions, observed in the microcosm of the laboratory strange-situation, and similar behaviors and conditions as reported by field studies, clinical studies, and experimental studies for both humans and nonhuman primate subjects. It is urged that the concept of attachment and attachment behavior employed as a guide in future studies be given a broad enough perspective to comprehend the spectrum of findings relevant to attachment which have been sampled in this discussion.

PROPOSITIONS FOR A COMPREHENSIVE CONCEPT OF ATTACHMENT

The following propositions are suggested as essential to a comprehensive concept of attachment. They are based on an ethological-evolutionary point of view, and have been formulated on the basis of reports of a broad range of investigations, including naturalistic studies of mother-infant interaction, and studies of mother-child separation and reunion in both human and nonhuman primates, as well as the illustrative strange-situation study reported here.

1. Attachment is not coincident with attachment behavior. Attachment behavior may be heightened or diminished by conditions—environmental and intraorganismic—which may be specified empirically. Despite situationally determined waxing and waning of attachment behavior, the individual is nevertheless predisposed intermittently to seek proximity to the object of attachment. It is this predisposition—which may be conceived as having an inner, structural basis—that is the attachment. Its manifestations are accessible to observation over time; a short time-sample may, however, be misleading.

2. Attachment behavior is heightened in situations perceived as threatening, whether it is an external danger or an actual or impending separation from the attachment object that constitutes the threat.

3. When strongly activated, attachment behavior is incompatible with exploratory behavior. On the other hand, the state of being attached, together

with the presence of the attachment object, may support and facilitate exploratory behaviors. Provided that there is no threat of separation, the infant is likely to be able to use his mother as a secure base from which to explore, manifesting no alarm in even a strange situation as long as she is present. Under these circumstances the relative absence of attachment behavior—of proximity-promoting behavior—cannot be considered an index of a weak attachment.

4. Although attachment behavior may diminish or even disappear in the course of a prolonged absence from the object of attachment, the attachment is not necessarily diminished; attachment behavior is likely to reemerge in full or heightened strength upon reunion, with or without delay.

5. Although individual differences have not been stressed in this discussion, the incidence of ambivalent (contact-resisting) and probably defensive (proximity-avoiding) patterns of behavior in the reunion episodes of the strange situation are a reflection of the fact that attachment relations are qualitatively different from one attached pair to another. These qualitative differences, together with the sensitivity of attachment behavior to situational determinants, make it very difficult to assess the strength or intensity of an attachment. It is suggested that, in the present state of our knowledge, it is wiser to explore qualitative differences, and their correlates and antecedents, than to attempt premature quantifications of strength of attachment.

References

AINSWORTH, M. D. The development of infant-mother interaction among the Ganda. In B. M. Foss (Ed.), *Determinants of infant behaviour II.* London: Methuen, 1963. Pp. 67–112.

———. Patterns of attachment behavior shown by the infant in interaction with his mother. *Merrill-Palmer Quarterly*, 1964, **10**, 51–58.

———. *Infancy in Uganda: infant care and the growth of love.* Baltimore: Johns Hopkins University Press, 1967.

———. Object relations, dependency and attachment: a theoretical review of the infant-mother relationship. *Child Development*, 1969, **40**, 969–1025.

———, & BELL, S. M. Some contemporary patterns of mother-infant interaction in the feeding situation. In J. A. Ambrose (Ed.), *The functions of stimulation in early post-natal development.* London: Academic, 1970.

———, & WITTIG, B. A. Attachment and exploratory behavior of one-year-olds in a strange situation. In B. M. Foss (Ed.), *Determinants of infant behaviour IV.* London: Methuen, 1969. Pp. 111–136.

ARSENIAN, J. M. Young children in an insecure situation. *Journal of Abnormal and Social Psychology*, 1943, **38**, 225–249.

BELL, S. M. The development of the concept of the object as related to infant-mother attachment. *Child Development*, 1970, *41*, 291–311.

BOWLBY, J. Psychopathological processes set in train by early mother-child separation. *Journal of Mental Science*, 1953, **99**, 265–272.

———. The nature of the child's tie to his mother. *International Journal of Psychoanalysis*, 1958, **39**, 350–373.

———. Separation anxiety. *International Journal of Psychoanalysis*, 1960, **41**, 69–113.

———. *Attachment and loss.* Vol. 1. *Attachment.* London: Hogarth, 1969; New York: Basic Books, 1969.

————; Ainsworth, M. D.; Boston, M.; & Rosenbluth, D. The effects of mother-child separation: a follow-up study. *British Journal of Medical Psychology*, 1956, **29**, 211–247.

Brackbill, Y. Extinction of the smiling response in infants as a function of reinforcement schedule. *Child Development*, 1958, **29**, 115–124.

Cairns, R. B. Attachment behavior of mammals. *Psychological Review*, 1966, **73**, 409–426.

Cox, F. N., & Campbell, D. Young children in a new situation with and without their mothers. *Child Development*, 1968, **39**, 123–131.

DeVore, I. Mother-infant relations in free-ranging baboons. In H. L. Rheingold (Ed.), *Maternal behavior in mammals*. New York: Wiley, 1963. Pp. 305–335.

Gewirtz, J. L. A learning analysis of the effects of normal stimulation, privation and deprivation on the acquisition of social motivation and attachment. In B. M. Foss (Ed.), *Determinants of infant behaviour*. London: Methuen, 1961. Pp. 213–299.

————. Mechanisms of social learning: some roles of stimulation and behavior in early human development. In D. A. Goslin (Ed.), *Handbook of socialization theory and research*. Chicago: Rand McNally, 1969. Pp. 57–212.

Goodall, J. Chimpanzees of the Gombe Stream Reserve. In I. DeVore (Ed.), *Primate behavior: field studies of monkeys and apes*. New York: Holt, Rinehart & Winston, 1965. Pp. 425–473.

Hamburg, D. A. Evolution of emotional responses: evidence from recent research on non-human primates. In J. Masserman (Ed.), *Science and psychoanalysis*. Vol. **12**. New York: Grune & Stratton, 1968. Pp. 39–52.

Harlow, H. F. The development of affectional patterns in infant monkeys. In B. M. Foss (Ed.), *Determinants of infant behaviour*. London: Methuen, 1961. Pp. 75–97.

————, & Harlow, M. K. The affectional systems. In A. M. Schrier, H. F. Harlow, & F. Stollnitz (Eds.), *Behavior of nonhuman primates*. Vol. **2**. New York: Academic, 1965. Pp. 287–334.

Heinicke, C. M., & Westheimer, I. *Brief separations*. New York: International Universities Press, 1965.

Hinde, R. A., Rowell, T. E.; & Spencer-Booth, Y. Behaviour of socially living rhesus monkeys in their first six months. *Proceedings of the Zoological Society of London*, 1964, **143**, 609–649.

————. The behaviour of socially living rhesus monkeys in their first two and a half years. *Animal Behaviour*, 1967, **15**, 169–196.

Kaufman, I. C., & Rosenblum, L. A. Depression in infant monkeys separated from their mothers. *Science*, 1967, **155**, 1030–1031.

Maccoby, E. E., & Masters, J. C. Attachment and dependency. In P. Mussen (Ed.), *Carmichael's manual of child psychology*, New York: Wiley, 1970.

Mason, W. A. Determinants of social behavior in young chimpanzees. In A. M. Schrier, H. F. Harlow, & F. Stollnitz (Eds.), *Behavior of nonhuman primates*. Vol. **2**. New York: Academic, 1965. Pp. 287–334.

Morgan, G. A., & Ricciuti, H. N. Infants' responses to strangers during the first year. In B. M. Foss (Ed.), *Determinants of infant behaviour IV*. London: Methuen, 1969. Pp. 253–272.

Rheingold, H. L. The effect of a strange environment on the behavior of infants. In B. M. Foss (Ed.), *Determinants of infant behavior IV*. London: Methuen, 1969. Pp. 137–166.

————; Gewirtz, J. L.; & Ross, H. W. Social conditioning of vocalizations in the infant. *Journal of Comparative and Physiological Psychology*, 1959, **52**, 68–73.

Robertson, J., & Bowlby, J. Responses of young children to separation from their mothers. II. Observations of the sequences of response of children aged 16 to 24 months during the course of separation. *Courrier Centre International de l'Enfance*, 1952, **2**, 131–142.

ROBSON, K. S. The role of eye-to-eye contact in maternal-infant attachment. *Journal of Child Psychology and Psychiatry*, 1967, **8**, 13–25.

SCHAFFER, H. R. Objective observations of personality development in early infancy. *British Journal of Medical Psychology*, 1958, **31**, 174–183.

———. The onset of fear of strangers and the incongruity hypothesis. *Journal of Child Psychology and Psychiatry*, 1966, **7**, 95–106.

———, & EMERSON, P. E. The development of social attachments in infancy. *Monographs of the Society for Research in Child Development*, 1964, **29**, (3, Serial No. 94).

SCHALLER, G. B. The behavior of the mountain gorilla. In I. DeVore (Ed.), *Primate behavior: field studies of monkeys and apes*. New York: Holt, Rinehart & Winston, 1965. Pp. 324–367.

SCHWARZ, J. C. Fear and attachment in young children. *Merrill-Palmer Quarterly*, 1968, **14**, 313–322.

SOUTHWICK, C. H.; BEG, M. A.; & SIDDIQI, M. R. Rhesus monkeys in North India. In I. DeVore (Ed.), *Primate behavior: field studies of monkeys and apes*. New York: Holt, Rinehart & Winston, 1965. Pp. 111–159.

SPENCER-BOOTH, Y., & HINDE, R. A. The effects of separating rhesus monkey infants from their mothers for six days. *Journal of Child Psychology and Psychiatry*, 1966, **7**, 179–198.

WALTERS, R. H., & PARKE, R. D. The role of the distance receptors in the development of social responsiveness. In L. P. Lipsitt & C. C. Spiker (Eds.), *Advances in child development and behavior*. Vol. 2. New York: Academic, 1965. Pp. 59–96.

Play Behavior in the Year-Old Infant: Early Sex Differences*

Susan Goldberg
UNIVERSITY OF ZAMBIA

Michael Lewis
EDUCATIONAL TESTING SERVICE

32 boys and 32 girls, 13 months old, were observed with their mothers in a standardized free play situation. There were striking sex differences in the infants' behavior toward their mothers and in their play. Earlier observation of the mothers' behavior toward the infants at 6 months indicates that some of these sex differences were related to the mothers' behavior toward the infants. It was suggested that parents behave differently toward girls and boys,

Reprinted from *Child Development*, 40, 21–31. Copyright © 1969 by The Society for Research in Child Development Inc. By permission.

* This research was conducted at the Fels Research Institute and was supported in part by grants HD-00868, FR-00222, and FR-05537 from the National Institute of Mental Health, U. S. Public Health Service. Editorial assistance was supported by research grant 1 P01 HD01762 from the National Institute of Child Health and Human Development. Portions of this paper were presented at the 1967 meeting of the Society for Research in Child Development, New York. We would like to thank Lynn Godfrey, Cornelia Dodd, and Helen Campbell for their aid in data analysis.

*even as infants, reinforcing sex-appropriate behavior. This study emphasizes the importance
of observing the freely emitted behavior of the very young child.*

Until recently, the largest proportion of studies in child development gave
attention to nursery and early grade school children. The literature on sex
differences is no exception. A recent book on development of sex differences
which includes an annotated bibliography (Maccoby, 1966) lists fewer than 10
studies using infants, in spite of the fact that theoretical discussions (e.g., Freud,
1938 [originally published in 1905]; Piaget, 1951) emphasize the importance
of early experience. Theoretical work predicts and experimental work confirms
the existence of sex differences in behavior by age 3. There has been little
evidence to demonstrate earlier differentiation of sex-appropriate behavior,
although it would not be unreasonable to assume this occurs.

Recently, there has been increased interest in infancy, including some
work which has shown early sex differences in attentive behavior (Kagan &
Lewis, 1965; Lewis, in press). The bulk of this work has been primarily experimental studying specific responses to specific stimuli or experimental conditions.
Moreover, it has dealt with perceptual-cognitive differences rather than
personality variables. There has been little observation of freely emitted
behavior. Such observations are of importance in supplying researchers with
the classes of naturally occurring behaviors, the conditions under which
responses normally occur, and the natural preference ordering of behaviors.
Knowledge of this repertoire of behaviors provides a background against which
behavior under experimental conditions can be evaluated.

The present study utilized a free play situation to observe sex differences
in children's behavior toward mother, toys, and a frustration situation at 13
months of age. Because the Ss were participants in a longitudinal study,
information on the mother-child relationship at 6 months was also available.
This made it possible to assess possible relations between behavior patterns at
6 months and at 13 months.

METHOD

SUBJECTS   Two samples of 16 girls and 16 boys each, or a total of 64 infants,
were seen at 6 and 13 months of age ($\pm$6 days). All Ss were born to families
residing in southwestern Ohio at the time of the study. All were Caucasian.
The mothers had an average of 13.5 years of schooling (range of 10–18 years)
and the fathers had an average of 14.5 years of schooling (range of 8–20 years).
The occupations of the fathers ranged from laborer to scientist. Of the 64
infants, 9 girls and 10 boys were first-born and the remaining infants had from
1 to 6 siblings.

THE 6-MONTH VISIT   The procedure of the 6-month visit, presented in
detail in Kagan and Lewis (1965), included two visual episodes and an auditory
episode where a variety of behavioral responses were recorded. The infant's
mother was present during these procedures. At the end of the experimental
procedure, the mother was interviewed by one of the experimenters, who had
been able to observe both mother and infant for the duration of the session.

The interviewer also rated both mother and infant on a rating scale. The items rated for the infant included: amount of activity, irritability, response to mother's behavior, and amount of affect. For the mother, the observer rated such factors as nature of handling, amount of playing with the baby, type of comforting behavior, and amount of vocalization to the baby. Each item was rated on a 7-point scale, with 1 indicating the most activity and 7 the least. For the purpose of this study, it was necessary to obtain a measure of the amount of physical contact the mother initiated with the child. Since scores on the individual scales did not result in sufficient variance in the population, a composite score was obtained by taking the mean score for each mother over all three of the touching-the-infant scales. These included: amount of touching, amount of comforting, and amount of play. The composite touch scores (now called the amount of physical contact) resulted in a sufficiently variable distribution to be used for comparison with the 13-month touch data.

THE 13-MONTH VISIT   Kagan and Lewis (1965), who employed the same 64 infants for their study, described the procedures used at 6 months, which were similar to those of the present (13-month) study. The only addition was a free play procedure, which will be discussed in detail below.

The playroom, 9 by 12 feet, contained nine simple toys: a set of blocks, a pail, a "lawnmower," a stuffed dog, an inflated plastic cat, a set of quoits (graduated plastic doughnuts stacked on a wooden rod), a wooden mallet, a pegboard, and a wooden bug (a pull toy). Also included as toys were any permanent objects in the room, such as the doorknob, latch on the wall, tape on the electrical outlets, and so forth. The mother's chair was located in one corner of the room.

PROCEDURE   Each S, accompanied by his mother, was placed in the obser- vation room. The mother was instructed to watch his play and respond in any way she desired. Most mothers simply watched and responded only when asked for something. The mother was also told that we would be observing from the next room. She held the child on her lap, the door to the playroom was closed, and observation began. At the beginning of the 15 minutes of play, the mother was instructed to place the child on the floor.

MEASUREMENT   Two observers recorded the S's behavior. One dictated a continuous behavioral account into a tape recorder. The second operated an event recorder, which recorded the location of the child in the room and the duration of each contact with the mother.

Dictated Recording   During the initial dictation, a buzzer sounded at regular time intervals, automatically placing a marker on the dictated tape. The dictated behavioral account was typed and each minute divided into 15-second units, each including about three typewritten lines. The typed material was further divided into three 5-second units, each unit being one typed line. Independent experimenters analyzed this typed material. For each minute, the number of toys played with and amount of time spent with each toy was recorded.

Event Recorder   To facilitate recording the activity and location of the child, the floor of the room was divided into 12 squares. For each square, the observer depressed a key on the event recorder for the duration of time the child occupied that square. From this record it was possible to obtain such measures as the amount of time spent in each square and the number of squares traversed. A thirteenth key was depressed each time the child touched the mother. From this record, measures of (a) initial latency in leaving the mother, (b) total amount of time touching the mother, (c) number of times touching the mother, and (d) longest period touching the mother were obtained.

The data analysis presented in this report provides information only on sex differences (a) in response to the mother and (b) in choice and style of play with toys. Other data from this situation are presented elsewhere (Lewis, 1967).

RESULTS

RESPONSE TO MOTHER (13 MONTHS)   *Open Field*   Boys and girls showed striking differences in their behavior toward their mothers (see Table 1). First, upon being removed from their mothers' laps, girls were reluctant to leave their mothers. When Ss were placed on the floor by their mothers, significantly more girls than boys returned immediately—in less than 5 seconds ($p < .05$ for both samples by Fisher Exact Probability Test). This reluctance to leave their mothers is further indicated by the time it took the children to first return to their mothers. Girls, in both samples, showed significantly shorter latencies than boys. Out of a possible 900 seconds (15 minutes), girls returned after an average of 273.5 seconds, while boys' average latency was nearly twice as long, 519.5 seconds. This difference was highly significant ($p < .002$, Mann-Whitney U test). All significance tests are two-tailed unless otherwise specified.

TABLE 1

Summary of Infant Behavior to Mother in Free Play Session

BEHAVIOR	GIRLS	BOYS	p
Touching mother:			
$\bar{x}$ latency in seconds to return to mother	273.5	519.5	< .002
$\bar{x}$ number of returns	8.4	3.9	< .001
$\bar{x}$ number of seconds touching mother	84.6	58.8	< .03
Vocalization to mother:			
$\bar{x}$ number of seconds vocalizing to mother	169.8	106.9	< .04
Looking at mother:			
$\bar{x}$ number of seconds looking at mother	57.3	47.0	< .09
$\bar{x}$ number of times looking at mother	10.8	9.2	NS
Proximity to mother:			
$\bar{x}$ time in squares closest to mother	464.1	351.4	< .05
$\bar{x}$ time in squares farthest from mother	43.8	44.3	NS

Once the children left their mothers, girls made significantly more returns, both physical and visual. Girls touched their mothers for an average of 84.6 seconds, while boys touched their mothers for only 58.8 seconds ($p < .03$, Mann-Whitney U test). Girls returned to touch their mothers on an average of 8.4 times, and boys 3.9 times ($p < .001$, Mann-Whitney U test). For the visual returns, the number of times the child looked at the mother and the total amount of time spent looking at the mother were obtained from the dictated material. The mean number of times girls looked at the mother was 10.8 (as compared with 9.2 for boys), a difference which was not significant. The total amount of time looking at the mother was 57.3 seconds for girls and 47.0 seconds for boys ($p < .09$, Mann-Whitney U test).

Finally, vocalization data were also available from the dictated material. The mean time vocalizing to the mother was 169.8 seconds for girls and 106.9 seconds for boys ($p < .04$, Mann-Whitney U test).

Another measure of the child's response to his mother was the amount of physical distance the child allowed between himself and his mother. Because the observers recorded which squares the child played in, it was possible to obtain the amount of time Ss spent in the four squares closest to the mother. The mean time in these squares for girls was 464.1 seconds; for boys, it was 351.4 seconds ($p < .05$, Mann-Whitney U test). Moreover, boys spent more time in the square farthest from the mother, although the differences were not significant.

Barrier Frustration   At the end of the 15 minutes of free play, a barrier of mesh on a wood frame was placed in such a way as to divide the room in half. The mother placed the child on one side and remained on the opposite side along with the toys. Thus, the child's response to stress was observed.

TABLE 2

Summary of Infant Behavior During Barrier Frustration

BEHAVIOR	GIRLS	BOYS	p
$\bar{x}$ number of seconds crying	123.5	76.7	$< .05$
$\bar{x}$ number of seconds at ends of barrier	106.1	171.0	$< .001$
$\bar{x}$ number of seconds at center	157.7	95.1	$< .01$

Sex differences were again prominent, with girls crying and motioning for help consistently more than boys (see Table 2 and Fig. 1). For both samples, amount of time crying was available from the dictated record. Girls' mean time crying was 123.5 seconds, compared with 76.7 seconds for boys ($p < .05$, Mann-Whitney U test). Boys, on the other hand, appeared to make a more active attempt to get around the barrier. That is, they spent significantly more time at the ends of the barrier than girls, while girls spent significantly more time in the centre of the barrier—near the position where they were placed ($p < .01$, Mann-Whitney U test).

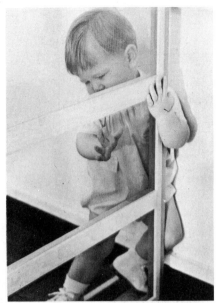

FIGURE 1.   *These two pictures illustrate typical sex differences in children responding to a frustration situation. The girl, at the left, is standing at the middle of the barrier and crying helplessly, while the boy, at the right, though showing signs of distress, is making an active attempt to get around the barrier.*

TOY PREFERENCE (13 MONTHS)   A second area of experimental interest was toy preference. When the nine toys were ranked in order of the total amount of time they were played with, girls and boys showed similar patterns of preference.

Table 3 presents each toy and the amount of time it was played with. Play with the dog and cat were combined into one category. The toys which were used most were the lawnmower, blocks, and quoits, and those that were used least were the stuffed dog and cat. On a *post hoc* basis, it seems as if the toys which received the most attention were those that offered the most varied possibilities for manipulation.

Although there were no sex differences in overall toy preference, there were significant sex differences in the amount of time spent with individual toys and in the ways toys were used. Girls played with blocks, pegboard, and with the dog and cat (the only toys with faces) more than boys did ($p < .03, p < .03, p < .01$, respectively, Mann-Whitney U test).

In terms of style of play, there were also sex differences (see Fig. 2). Observation of girls' play indicates that girls chose toys which involved more fine than gross muscle coordination, while for boys, the reverse was true— building blocks and playing with dog and cat versus playing with mallet and rolling the lawnmower over other toys. Moreover, boys spent more time playing with the nontoys (doorknob, covered outlets, lights, etc.; $p < .005$, Mann-Whitney U test).

In terms of overall activity level, boys were more active than girls. Girls

TABLE 3

Mean Time Playing with Toys, by Sex

	GIRLS	BOYS	*p*
Total time with:			
Mallet	51.7	60.8	−
Bug	50.2	45.3	−
Pail	34.6	22.9	−
Blocks	126.5	77.5	< .03
Lawnmower	220.3	235.6	−
Cat plus dog (combined)	31.0	9.1	< .01
Quoits	122.7	130.3	−
Pegboard	37.2	28.7	< .05
Nontoys	6.9	31.0	< .005
Putting toys in pail	28.2	43.0	−
Banging toys	19.7	34.8	< .05
Lawnmowing on other toys	2.8	9.8	−
Other manipulation of two toys	28.2	10.3	< .05

tended to sit and play with combinations of toys ($p < .05$, Mann-Whitney U test), while boys tended to be more active and bang the toys significantly more than girls ($p < .05$, Mann-Whitney U test). In addition, the children were rated by two observers on the vigor of their play behavior; a rating of 1 was given for high vigor, 2 was given for medium vigor, and 3 for low vigor. These ratings were made from the dictated material for each minute, so that the final

FIGURE 2.   *These pictures illustrate some of the sex differences observed in play behavior. The little girl, at the left, is squatting in one place, cuddling a soft animal. In contrast, the little boy, right, is actively swinging and banging the lawnmower over other toys.*

score for each S represented a mean of 15 vigor ratings. The interobserver reliability was $\rho = .78$. The boys played significantly more vigorously than girls (mean for boys was 2.45, varying from 1.2 to 3.0; for girls, the mean was 2.65, varying from 1.9 to 3.0 [$p < .05$, Mann-Whitney U test]). This vigor difference was also seen in the style of boys' play; for example, boys banged with the mallet and mowed over other toys. Thus, there were not only significant differences in the choice of toys, but also in the way the toys were manipulated. The data indicate that there are important and significant sex differences in very young children's response to their mothers, to frustration, and in play behavior.

Mother-Infant Touch (6 Months)   One possible determinant of the child's behavior toward the mother in the playroom is the mother's behavior toward the child at an earlier age. The 6-month data indicated that mothers of girls touched their infants more than mothers of boys. On the composite score, where 1 indicated most touching and 7 least, there were twice as many girls as boys whose mothers were rated 1–3 and twice as many boys as girls whose mothers were rated 5–7 ($p < .05$, χ^2 test). Moreover, mothers vocalized to girls significantly more than to boys ($p < .001$, Mann-Whitney U test), and significantly more girls than boys were breast-fed rather than bottle-fed ($p < .02$, Mann-Whitney U test). Thus, when the children were 6 months old, mothers touched, talked to, and handled their daughters more than their sons, and when they were 13 months old, girls touched and talked to their mothers more than boys did. To explore this relationship further, mothers were divided into high, medium, and low mother-touch-infant groups (at 6 months), with the extreme groups consisting of the upper and lower 25 per cent of the sample. For the boys at 13 months, the mean number of seconds of physical contact with the mother indicated a linear relation to amount of mother touching (14, 37, and 47 seconds for the low, medium, and high mother-touch groups, respectively; Kruskal-Wallis, $p < .10$). Thus, the more physical contact the mother made with a boy at 6 months, the more he touched the mother at 13 months. For the girls, the relation appeared to be curvilinear. The mean number of seconds of touching the mother for the low, medium, and high mother-touch groups was 101, 55, and 88 seconds, respectively (Kruskal-Wallis, $p < .10$). The comparable distribution for number of seconds close to the mother was 589, 397, and 475 seconds (Kruskal-Wallis, $p < .03$). A girl whose mother initiated very much or very little contact with her at 6 months was more likely to seek a great deal of physical contact with the mother in the playroom than one whose mother was in the medium-touch infant group.

Observation of the mothers' behavior when their infants were 6 months old revealed that five of the seven mothers of girls who showed little physical contact were considered by the staff to be severely rejecting mothers. The data suggest that the child of a rejecting mother continues to seek contact despite the mother's behavior. This result is consistent with Harlow's work with rejected monkeys (Seay, Alexander, & Harlow, 1964) and Provence's work with institutionalized children (Provence, 1965; Provence & Lipton, 1962) and suggests that the child's need for contact with his mother is a powerful motive.

DISCUSSION

Observation of the children's behavior indicated that girls were more dependent, showed less exploratory behavior, and their play behavior reflected a more quiet style. Boys were independent, showed more exploratory behavior, played with toys requiring gross motor activity, were more vigorous, and tended to run and bang in their play. Obviously, these behavior differences approximate those usually found between the sexes at later ages. The data demonstrate that these behavior patterns are already present in the first year of life and that some of them suggest a relation to the mother's response to the infant in the first 6 months. It is possible that at 6 months, differential behavior on the part of the mother is already a response to differential behavior on the part of the infant. Moss (1967) has found behavioral sex differences as early as 3 weeks. In interpreting mother-infant interaction data, Moss suggests that maternal behavior is initially a response to the infant's behavior. As the infant becomes older, if the mother responds contingently to his signals, her behavior acquires reinforcement value which enables her to influence and regulate the infant's behavior. Thus, parents can be active promulgators of sex-role behavior through reinforcement of sex-role-appropriate responses within the first year of life.

The following is offered as a hypothesis concerning sex-role learning. In the first year or two, the parents reinforce those behaviors they consider sex-role appropriate and the child learns these sex-role behaviors independent of any internal motive, that is, in the same way he learns any appropriate response rewarded by his parents. The young child has little idea as to the rules governing this reinforcement. It is suggested, however, that as the child becomes older (above age 3), the rules for this class of reinforced behavior become clearer and he develops internal guides to follow these earlier reinforced rules. In the past, these internalized rules, motivating without apparent reinforcement, have been called modeling behavior. Thus, modeling behavior might be considered an extension or internalization of the earlier reinforced sex-role behavior. However, it is clear that the young child, before seeking to model his behavior, is already knowledgeable in some appropriate sex-role behavior. In that the hypothesis utilizes both early reinforcement as well as subsequent cognitive elaboration, it would seem to bridge the reinforcement notion of Gewirtz (1967) and Kohlberg's cognitive theory (1966) of identification.

The fact that parents are concerned with early display of sex-role-appropriate behavior is reflected in an interesting clinical observation. On some occasions, staff members have incorrectly identified the sex of an infant. Mothers are often clearly irritated by this error. Since the sex of a fully clothed infant is difficult to determine, the mistake seems understandable and the mother's displeasure uncalled for. If, however, she views the infant and behaves toward him in a sex-appropriate way, our mistake is more serious. That is, the magnitude of her displeasure reveals to us the magnitude of her cognitive commitment to this infant as a child of given sex.

Regardless of the interpretation of the observed sex differences, the free play procedure provides a standardized situation in which young children can be observed without interference from experimental manipulation. While behavior under these conditions may be somewhat different from the young child's typical daily behavior, our data indicate that behavior in the play situation is related to other variables, that behavior can be predicted from earlier events, and that it is indicative of later sex-role behavior. The results of the present investigation as well as the work of Bell and Costello (1964), Kagan and Lewis (1965), and Lewis (in press) indicate sex differences within the first year over a wide variety of infant behaviors. The fact that sex differences do appear in the first year has important methodological implications for infant research. These findings emphasize the importance of checking sex differences before pooling data and, most important, of considering sex as a variable in any infant study.

References

BELL, R. Q., & COSTELLO, N. S. Three tests for sex differences in tactile sensitivity in the newborn. *Biologia Neonatorum*, 1964, **1**, 335–347.

FREUD, S. Three contributions to the theory of sex. Reprinted in *The basic writings of Sigmund Freud*. New York: Random House, 1938.

GEWIRTZ, J. The learning of generalized imitation and its implications for identification. Paper presented at the Society for Research in Child Development Meeting, New York, March, 1967.

KAGAN, J., & LEWIS, M. Studies of attention in the human infant. *Merrill-Palmer Quarterly*, 1965, **11**, 95–127.

KOHLBERG, L. A cognitive-developmental analysis of children's sex role concepts and attitudes. In E. Maccoby (Ed.), *The development of sex differences*. Stanford, Calif.: Stanford University Press, 1966.

LEWIS, M. Infant attention: response decrement as a measure of cognitive processes, or what's new, Baby Jane? Paper presented at the Society for Research in Child Development Meeting, symposium on "The Role of Attention in Cognitive Development," New York, March, 1967.

———. Infants' responses to facial stimuli during the first year of life. *Developmental Psychology*, in press.

MACCOBY, E. (Ed.) *The development of sex differences*. Stanford, Calif.: Stanford University Press, 1966.

MOSS, H. Sex, age and state as determinants of mother-infant interaction. *Merrill-Palmer Quarterly*, 1967, **13** (1), 19–36.

PIAGET, J. *Play, dreams and imitation in childhood*. New York: Norton, 1951.

PROVENCE, S. Disturbed personality development in infancy: a comparison of two inadequately nurtured infants. *Merrill-Palmer Quarterly*, 1965, **2**, 149–170.

———, & LIPTON, R. C. *Infants in institutions*. New York: International Universities Press, 1962.

SEAY, B., ALEXANDER, B. K., & HARLOW, H. F. Maternal behavior of socially deprived rhesus monkeys. *Journal of Abnormal and Social Psychology*, 1964, **69**(4), 345–354.

Crib Mates

Bruno Bettelheim
UNIVERSITY OF CHICAGO

This importance of the peer group begins in the very first days of life. We do not know whether, in the human being, something akin to the imprinting of animals takes place. But there is no doubt that the earliest experiences make a deep impact and are hence apt to shape all later ones in some measure.

Imprinting is thus nothing but an extremely important early experience. And in our own culture, at this most impressionable age, it is only or mainly the mother's image that is scanned by the infant as he nurses. In the kibbutz, by comparison, what greets the infant who wakens to feed, and looks around at his world? As likely as not, and from the very beginning, he sees just as much of the metapelets and other mothers tending their babies, as he does his own mother. She only emerges as separate and special when she puts him to breast.

Much more important in time and emotional impact are the constant companions who live in his room. Them he always sees and reacts to. Much of the waking time spent by the middle-class infant watching his parents, the kibbutz infant spends watching his roommates. As a matter of fact, so important may be the infant in the crib next to him, for example, that if his crib mate is moved to another room he may lose his appetite and get run down, a condition that improves when his "friend" or "twin" is returned.

Separation anxiety in the kibbutz is thus very typically experienced around the absence of a peer. And it can never be felt as acutely as by the middle-class infant whose mother leaves him, because however important the infant in the next crib, he is not the only one in the room, nor the only one life revolves around. At least two others are still left for companionship. And while the positive attachment to one person (the mother) seems diluted, when compared to our settings, separation anxiety is much less acute because of the continuing presence of several important others (metapelet, other infants). Thus again if we consider only the positive attachments, things seem to favor the middle-class child. But if we consider the ratio between security gained from positive attachment versus separation anxiety, it may very well be that kibbutz infants again enjoy the advantage.

While all children are "children of the kibbutz," and feel essentially like siblings, this is not just a matter of semantics. Those children who, from birth on, live together as an age-group, experience each other not only as siblings but as twins, since they were nurslings together and close crib companions. True, they do not share identical parents, and their heredity is radically different. But because of their otherwise "twinlike" existence they show some of the psychological features that characterize twins: the deep dependence and reliance on each other, the feeling that no one but their twin can ever fully understand them or share their innermost being. Only instead of one twin they have several, and of both sexes.

Because of this, though for other reasons too, the polarization, through which one twin often asserts his identity by being as different as possible from the other twin, I did not find in the kibbutz. I got to know one set of twins rather well. From all appearances (and from what I was told) they were identical twins, and by that time quite grown up. While extremely close to each other, they showed few of the characteristics I observe among identical twins in our setting. They were neither "half" a person without the other, nor did they show any need to develop in opposite ways to feel secure in their personal identity. My guess is that, having lived "like twins" from birth on with several others, and not just their own twin, they did not feel as dependent on each other as seems true of twins in our families.

Perhaps the difference in parentage and natural endowment gives enough real differentiation to those who from birth on grow up like twins so that there is no need to strive for any more on their own. It is not enough, though, to cancel out the strange situation that four or more infants share all vital steps in growing up and developing, as would be true with us only of twins or of infants growing up in institutions.

This is why the kibbutz child, in his relatedness to other children, feels closest to his very own age-group, in many ways more so than to his natural siblings, who come next, and third, to all other kibbutz children.

What does this collective life look like, for the older infant from the time he can crawl? These infants, when they wake, are placed in large playpens; then, as soon as they can walk, in rather large, fenced-in play spaces. For many periods of the day, even when the metapelets are supposedly taking care of a group of infants or toddlers, they are left to their own devices. Often this is for hours at a stretch, while the metapelets clean the house, fetch the food, sort the laundry, do the mending. During this time the infant, and later the small child, is never alone, as an infant raised at home might be even if the mother is just busy in another room.

In playpen and play yard the children crawl over each other, push each other down, and while at first the pushed down child may wail, he soon learns his place in the pecking order and adjusts accordingly. But life is not just bad times and getting pushed down; most of the time the children play successfully together. Since no parent interferes with the pecking order, and even the metapelet does so only rarely, each child stays in his given place and soon learns to play according to the hierarchy established. As long as he does, and soon they all learn to do it for most of the time, there is always someone to play with; they are never alone.

American readers will wonder what happens to the low man on the totem pole, to the weak child or the meek one who—were this a society based on nothing but the pecking order—would always come last, would never come into his own except by withdrawing or submitting. And this might well happen in our competitive society where winning is so highly valued. But things are not so in the kibbutz.

I did not see a single case of a bully or of bullying. I did see the weaker infants pushed over by stronger ones, but never deliberately—if one can speak of being deliberate in such things before the age of two—nor gloatingly. And thereafter such a child was usually picked up and comforted by another child, sometimes by the one who pushed him down. Depending, of course, on the relative maturity of the child, this stage may be reached anywhere between age two and two-and-a-half.

By toddler age, then, life is truly with the group; the children are comrades, not competitors. If one is stronger, he will use and occasionally misuse his strength, but not for long. Very soon the group spirit asserts itself, and he feels the disapproval and desists. The spirit of helpfulness among them is much more evident than the desire for dominance. Since there are no parents around for whom to vie, and since the competitive spirit is frowned on, the push is toward acting like brothers and sisters, where the stronger one exerts some controlling influence, but also feels called on to use it in the interests of his brothers and sisters. And this is well established by the toddler age. But even before then, they have all learned to be self-reliant to a degree most uncommon in our middle-class settings.

How early they are forced by the arrangements to learn self-reliance may be illustrated by two observations made in one of the oldest and wealthiest of left-wing kibbutzim. The first one concerns babies and occurred while I was interviewing an elderly metapelet, in charge of the infants' house there for many years. I was asking how many babies she had in her care, and she told me there were sixteen in the nursery, but that each metapelet was only responsible for four. "I work four hours in the morning," she said, "from 7:00 to 11:00, and then I return again at 12:30."

I wondered what happens then, between 11:00 and 12:30? (The time, then, was shortly after 11:00, and the babies were in a playpen on the porch, just outside the room where we spoke.) The answer was: "They don't need anybody, they're in the playpen during that time." Nevertheless, we could hardly hear each other at times because the wailing of the babies was so loud. So I said I could hear them crying right now so they seemed to need someone to look after them, and the metapelet told me: "If they cry too long, some other metapelet will look to see what's the matter. There is always one metapelet in the house serving all four groups."

The crying continued, and I went out to see what went on. I found seven babies in a large playpen out in the sun, with some nice toys in it. Two bigger babies crawled all over a little one and took a toy away from him. He cried for a long time while the one metapelet on duty was occupied with washing furniture. Finally she came out on the porch and picked up the crying one for a moment but without comforting him. He continued to cry, but more quietly now. So she put him down at another spot in the playpen and left. And soon he stopped crying and went about his business.

As soon as the being picked up may have raised some hopeful expectations in the baby, he was returned to the old situation to fend for himself as best he could. If many such experiences are repeated, as they are, it may force the infant (and all other infants who watch it) to give up hoping for comfort from a mother figure, or any desire for her presence.

It was not that the metapelet was insensitive. She was merely convinced that the baby had to learn to get along in his group, and not to rely on the intercession of someone outside it; that her comforting would only retard a piece of learning that was more important than temporary discomfort.

And a year or two later, when they are toddlers, they have indeed learned much: how to fend for themselves, how to get along with the group, how to find comfort there and satisfaction. One day, for example, I observed an entire toddlers-house group who had been playing for quite a while in the large play space in front of their house while the metapelet was away fetching their lunch from the communal kitchen and her adolescent helper was inside setting the table. On her return the metapelet called to the children to come in for lunch.

Scrambling to get there, one little boy fell and started to cry; he had obviously hurt himself. The metapelet very nicely went over to him, picked him up, but then set him down a moment later, before she had really discovered what was wrong, and long before he had quieted down or been reassured. She then went indoors because she had to, since there were now some fourteen children inside to be taken care of and fed by her and her helper.

Eventually after some hard inner struggle the boy fought down his crying. The others were too busy with their meal and each other to offer comfort at this moment, so the best thing was to join them as soon as he could. But first he took a knife from the table and went back outside where he sat down to scrape the dirt off his slightly bleeding knee. This took some time, and quite a few minutes later, he was still there and had not yet come to the table.

The metapelet could not have returned to him easily, even had she wished Her other duties forbade it. But after some ten minutes the boy had got complete hold of himself and rejoined the group. He really had no true choice in the matter. Had he stayed behind, he would have gotten no comfort for his hurt and would not only have missed out on lunch but also the companionship of the children and metapelet.

During this same toddler age, though, the peer group also comes to be a source of comfort in lieu of adults. It was charming, for example, to see a three-year-old come up to an age-mate who was upset about something, inviting him to play, cheering him up, leading him back to the group. But because of it, the small child is more and more relieved of having to struggle by himself with an inner experience. Because even (or especially) if no other comfort is available. the group and its doings are always there to divert his attention to an external experience with them, and away from the one with himself.

At critical times, such as at night, small children have only their mutual comforting to rely on, since it may take quite a while for the single night watch to hear a child who wakes up crying, and a bit longer till he or she comes around. Though no one in the small community is entirely a stranger, the night watch rotates among members from day to day, or week to week. So even when the night watch is finally summoned by the child's anxious cry, the person who comes when the child thus awakens from a nightmare, deeply shaken, is more or less a stranger and can therefore give only small comfort. But as likely as not, when the night watch finally gets there, he finds that some other child has already soothed the anxious one.

Thus when in deep emotional distress, the kibbutz child soon learns to rely on the help of another child for comfort and security. Later on, too, it will more likely be a more advanced or a bit older child in his peer group and not the metapelet who will help him on the toilet, with getting dressed, and at all other times when he cannot manage by himself.

Behavior Problems Revisited:
Findings of an Anterospective Study*

Stella Chess and Alexander Thomas
NEW YORK UNIVERSITY SCHOOL OF MEDICINE

Herbert G. Birch
ALBERT EINSTEIN COLLEGE OF MEDICINE

A number of theoretical formulations have been advanced to explain the origin and nature of behavior problems in childhood. These have included the constitutionalist view in which the symptoms of disturbance are considered to be the direct expression of a predetermined constitutional pattern in the child, the psychoanalytic view in which disturbance is seen as the outcome of conflicts between instinctual drive seeking expression and satisfaction and repressing forces seeking to inhibit or contain them, the learning theory approach in which symptoms are viewed as conditioned maladaptive learned patterns based on conditioned reflex formations, and the culturist view in which symptoms are considered to be the more or less direct expression of sociocultural influences.

A unique opportunity to investigate the genesis and evolution of behavior problems and to test the validity of these theories has presented itself during the course of our New York longitudinal study of individuality in behavioral development. In this study, in progress since 1956, 39 of the 136 children who have been followed from the earliest months of life onward by a variety of data-gathering techniques have developed behavior disturbances of various types and varying degrees of severity.

Until now, none of the numerous studies in the field has provided a body of evidence sufficient to validate one or another of the extant theoretical formulations. Aside from any other questions as to the adequacy of the data offered as evidence, the approaches have relied primarily on data gathered retrospectively. A number of recent studies, including several from our own center, have revealed significant distortions in retrospective parental reports on the early developmental histories of their children (Robbins, 1963; Wenar, 1963; Chess et al., 1966). It has become clear that retrospective data are insufficient for the study of the genesis of behavior disorders and that anterospective data gathered by longitudinal developmental studies are essential.

Reprinted from *The Journal of the American Academy of Child Psychiatry*, 1967, *6*, 321–331. Copyright © 1967 by International Universities Press, Inc. By permission.

* This investigation was supported by Grant MH-03614 from the National Institute of Mental Health.

Previous longitudinal studies—at Berkeley (MacFarlane et al., 1954), the Fels Institute (Kagan and Moss, 1962), Yale (Kris, 1957), and Topeka (Murphy et al., 1962)—have made certain contributions to the understanding of the evolution of behavior disorders. The possible significance of temperamental characteristics of the child in interaction with parental functioning has been indicated. A lack of correlation between the child's patterns of psychodynamic defenses and the occurrence of behavioral dysfunction has been found. Symptoms typical of various age-periods have been tabulated, their vicissitudes over time traced, and correlations among different symptoms determined. However, each of these studies has been limited either by small sample size, which has not permitted generalization of the findings, or by the absence of systematic psychiatric evaluation of the children, which has severely restricted the possibility of categorizing the behavior disturbance and of making meaningful correlations with the longitudinal behavioral data.

Our New York longitudinal study has had available, by contrast, both a total sample of substantial size and the data resulting from independent clinical psychiatric evaluation in all of the children with behavior problems. The data on the total sample include information gathered longitudinally and anterospectively at sequential age levels from early infancy onward on the nature of the child's own individual characteristics of functioning at home, in school, and in standard test situations; on parental attitudes and child care practices; on special environmental events and the child's reactions to such events; and on intellectual functioning. In addition, psychiatric evaluation has been done in each child presenting symptoms by the staff child psychiatrist. Wherever necessary, neurological examination or special testing, such as perceptual tests, have been done. Clinical follow-up of each child with a problem has also been carried out systematically.

Details of the data-gathering procedures and of the techniques of data analysis have been reported elsewhere (Chess et al., 1962; Thomas et al., 1963). Since the developmental data were gathered before the child was viewed as a problem by either the parent or the psychiatrist, they were uncontaminated by the distortions which inevitably attend retrospective histories obtained after the appearance of the behavioral disturbance. Data as to environmental influences, such as parental practices and attitudes, changes in family structure, illnesses and hospitalization, and the character of the school situation, were also obtained in advance of the behavioral disturbance and so were also not distorted by the fact of pathology.

The size of the sample and the nature of the data have made possible various quantitative analyses comparing children with and without behavior problems as well as individual longitudinal case studies. In all our analyses we have been concerned with tracing the ontogenesis and development of each behavioral disturbance in terms of the interaction of temperament and environment, as well as the influence of additional factors in specific cases, such as brain damage, physical abnormalities, and characteristics of intellectual functioning. *Temperament*, in our usage, refers to the behavioral style of the individual child and contains no inferences as to genetic, endocrine, somatologic or environmental etiologies. It is a phenomenological term used to describe the characteristic tempo, energy expenditure, focus, mood, and rhythmicity typifying the behaviors of the individual child, independently of their contents. We have used nine categories of reactivity within which to subsume temperamental attributes. They are activity level, rhythmicity, adaptability, approach withdrawal, intensity of reaction, quality of mood, sensory threshold, distractibility, and persistence and attention span.[1] A child's temperamental organization, therefore, represents his characteristic mode of functioning with respect to these features of behavioral organization. It refers to the *how* rather than to the *what* or the *why* of behavior. No implications of permanence or immutability attach to such a conception.

The prevalence rate of behavior problems in our study population approximates that found in other studies (Lapouse and Monk, 1958; Glidewell et al., 1963). The types of symptoms were typical of those usually coming to notice in preschool and early school age children of middle-class highly educated parents.

In each of the thirty-nine children with behavior problems the psychiatric assessment has been followed by a detailed culling of all the anterospective data from early infancy onward for pertinent information on temperament, environmental influences, and the sequences of symptom appearance and development. It has been possible in each case to trace the ontogenesis of the behavioral disturbances in terms of the interaction of temperament and environment. Temperament alone did not produce behavioral disturbance. Instances of children of closely similar temperamental structure to the children with behavior problems were found in the normally functioning group. Rather, it appeared that both behavioral disturbance as well as behavioral normality were the result of the interaction between the child with a given patterning of temperament and significant features of his developmental environment. Among these environmental features intrafamilial as well as extrafamilial circumstances such as school and peer group were influential. In several cases, additional special factors such as brain damage or physical abnormality were also operative in interaction with temperament and environment to produce symptoms of disturbed development.

A number of case summaries illustrating typical interactive patterns of development in children with and without behavior problems have been presented in several previous publications (Chess et al., 1963; Birch et al., 1964). At this time we would like to present some of the characteristic temperamental patterns found among the children, the environmental demands which are typically stressful for children with each of these temperamental constellations, and the parental and other environmental approaches which intensify such stressful demands to the point of symptom formation. Symptoms manifested by the children included tantrums, aggressive behavior, habit disorders, fears, learning difficulties, nonparticipation in play activities with other children, and lack of normal assertiveness.

A temperamental pattern which produced the greatest risk of behavior problem development comprises the combination of irregularity in biological functions, predominantly negative (withdrawal) responses to new stimuli, nonadaptability or slow adaptability to change, frequent negative mood, and

---

[1] See Thomas et al. (1963) for criteria of each of the nine categories and for details of the scoring method.

predominantly intense reactions. As infants, children with this pattern show irregular sleep and feeding patterns, slow acceptance of new foods, prolonged adjustment periods to new routines, and frequent periods of loud crying. Their laughter, too, is characteristically loud. Mothers find them difficult to care for, and pediatricians frequently refer to them as the "difficult infants." They are not easy to feed, to put to sleep, to bathe, or to dress. New places, new activities, strange faces—all may produce initial responses of loud protest or crying. Frustration characteristically produces a violent tantrum. These children approximate 10 percent of the total study population but comprise a significantly higher proportion of the behavior problem group (Rutter et al., 1964). The stressful demands for these children are typically those of socialization, namely, the demands for alteration of spontaneous responses and patterns to conform to the rules of living of the family, the school, the peer group, etc. It is also characteristic of these children that once they do learn the rules, they function easily, consistently, and energetically.

We have found no evidence that the parents of the difficult infants are essentially different from the other parents. Nor do our studies suggest that the temperamental characteristics of the children are caused by the parents. The issue is rather that the care of these infants makes special requirements upon their parents for unusually firm, patient, consistent, and tolerant handling. Such handling is necessary if the difficult infant is to learn to adapt to new demands with a minimum of stress. If the new demand is presented inconsistently, impatiently or punitively effective change in behavior becomes stressful and even impossible. Negativism is a not infrequent outcome of such suboptimal parental functioning.

The problems of managing a difficult child not infrequently highlight a parent's individual reaction to stress. The same parents who are relaxed and consistent with an easy child may become resentful, guilty, or helpless with a difficult child, depending on their own personality structures. Other parents, by contrast, who do not feel guilty or put upon by the child's behavior may learn to enjoy the vigor, lustiness, and "stubbornness" of a difficult infant.

At the opposite end of the temperamental spectrum from the difficult infant is the child who is regular, responds positively to new stimuli (approaches), adapts quickly and easily to change, and shows a predominantly positive mood of mild or moderate intensity. These are the infants who develop regular sleep and feeding schedules easily, take to most new foods at once, smile at strangers, adapt quickly to a new school, accept most frustrations with a minimum of fuss, and learn the rules of new games quickly. They are aptly called "easy babies" and are usually a joy to their parents, pediatricians, and teachers. By contrast to the difficult infant, the easy child adapts to the demands for socialization with little or no stress and confronts his parents with few if any problems in handling. However, although these children do as a group develop significantly fewer behavior problems proportionately than do the difficult infants, their very ease of adaptability may under certain circumstances be the basis for problem behavior development. Most typically we have seen this occur when there is a severe dissonance between the expectations and demands of the intra- and extrafamilial environments. The child first adapts easily to the standards and behavioral expectations of the parent in the first few years of life. When he moves actively into functional situations outside the home, such as in peer play groups and school, stress and malfunctioning will develop if the extrafamilial standard and demands conflict sharply with the patterns learned in the home. As a typical example, the parents of one such child had a high regard for individuality of expression and disapproval of any behavior or attitude in their child which they identified as stereotypical or lacking in imagination. Self-expression was encouraged and conformity and attentiveness to rules imposed by others discouraged even when this resulted in ill manners and a disregard of the desires of others. As the child grew older she became increasingly isolated from her peer group because of continuous insistence on her own preferences. In school her progress was grossly unsatisfactory because of difficulty in listening to directions. The parents were advised to restructure their approach, to place less emphasis on individuality and instead to teach her to be responsive to the needs of others and to conform constructively in behavior in class and in activities with her peers. The parents, acutely aware of the child's growing social isolation and the potential seriousness of her educational problem, carried out this plan consistently. At follow-up, six months later, the child had adapted to the new rules easily, the conflict between standards within and without the home had become minimal, and she had become an active member of a peer group and had caught up to grade level in academic work.

It is certainly true that a severe dissonance between intra- and extra-familial environment demands and expectations may produce stress and disturbance in psychological development for many types of youngsters, including the difficult child. In our case series, however, it has been most readily apparent as a dominant pathogenic factor in these easy children.

Another important temperamental constellation comprises the combination of negative responses of mild intensity to new stimuli with slow adaptability after repeated contact. Children with this pattern differ from the difficult infants in that their withdrawal from the new is quiet rather than loud. They also usually do not have the irregularity of function, frequent negative mood expression, and intense reactions of the difficult infants. The mildly expressed withdrawal from the new is typically seen with the first encounter with the bath, a new person, a stranger, or a new place. With the first bath the child lies still and fusses mildly, with a new food he turns his head away quietly and lets it dribble out of his mouth, with a stranger who greets him loudly he clings to his mother. If given the opportunity to re-experience new situations without pressure, such a child gradually comes to show quiet and positive interest and involvement. This characteristic sequence of response has suggested the appellation the "Slow to Warm Up" as an apt if inelegant designation for these children. A key issue in their development is whether parents and teachers allow them to make an adaptation to the new at their own tempo or insist on the immediate positive involvement which is difficult or impossible for the slow-to-warm-up children. If the adult recognizes that the slow adaptation to a new school, new peer group or new academic subject reflects the child's normal temperamental style, patient encouragement is likely. If, on the contrary, the child's slow warm-up is interpreted as timidity or lack of interest, adult impatience and pressure on the child for quick adaptation may occur. The child's reaction to this stressful pressure is typically an intensification of his withdrawal tendency. If this increased holding back in turn stimulates increased impatience and pressure on the part of the parent or teacher, a destructive child-environment interactive process will be set in motion.

In several other instances in our study population, nursery school teachers have interpreted the child's slow initial adaptation as evidence of underlying anxiety. In still another case, an elementary school teacher estimated that a child's slow initial mastery of a new accelerated academic program indicated inadequate intellectual capacity. In these cases, the longitudinal behavioral records documented a slow warm-up temperamental style and made possible the recommendation that judgment be suspended until the child could have a longer period of contact with the new situation. The subsequent successful mastery of the demands of the new situation clarified the issue as one of temperamental style and not psychopathology or lack of intellectual capacity.

A contrast to the slow-to-warm-up child is the very persistent child who is most likely to experience stress not with his initial contact with a situation but during the course of his ongoing activity after the first positive adaptation has been made. His quality of persistence leads him to resist interference or attempts to divert him from an activity in which he is absorbed. If the adult interference is arbitrary and forcible, tension and frustration tend to mount quickly in these children and may reach explosive proportions.

Type-specific stress and maladaptive child-environment patterns can be identified for other temperamental patterns, such as the very distractible or highly active child, but the scope of this presentation does not permit their description.

Currently influential psychoanalytic theories of the ontogenesis of behavior problems place primary emphasis on the role of anxiety, intrapsychic conflict, and psychodynamic defenses. Our findings do not support these concepts. Our data suggest that anxiety, intrapsychic conflict, and psychodynamic defenses, when they do appear in the course of behavior problem development, are secondary phenomena which result from the stressful, maladaptive character of an unhealthy temperament-environment interaction. Once any or all of these secondary factors appear they can add a new dimension to the dynamics of the child-environment interaction and substantially influence the subsequent course of the behavior problem. It is not surprising that in retrospective studies which begin when the child already presents an extensively elaborated psychological disturbance the prominent phenomena of anxiety and conflict should be labeled as primary rather than secondary influences. Also, if the fact of temperamental individuality is not given serious attention, certain temperamental patterns, such as those of the difficult child or the child with a slow warm-up, are easily misinterpreted as the result of anxiety or as defenses against anxiety.

Our findings also challenge the validity of the currently prevalent assumption that a child's problem is a direct reaction of a one-to-one kind to unhealthy maternal influences. The slogan "To meet Johnny's mother is to understand his problem" expresses an all too frequent approach in which a study of the mother is substituted for a study of the complex factors which may have produced a child's disturbed development, of which parental influences are only one. Elsewhere we have described this unidirectional preoccupation of psychologists and psychiatrists with the pathogenic role of the mother as the "Mal de

Mere" syndrome (Chess, 1964). The harm done by this preoccupation has been enormous. Innumerable mothers have been unjustly burdened with deep feelings of guilt and inadequacy as a result of being incorrectly held exclusively or even primarily responsible for their children's problems. Diagnostic procedures have tended to be restricted to a study of the mother's assumed noxious attitudes and practices, with investigations in other directions conducted in a most cursory fashion, or not at all. Treatment plans have focused on methods of changing maternal attitudes and ameliorating the effects of presumed pathogenic maternal attitudes on the child and have ignored other significant etiological factors.

Our data on the origin and development of behavior problems in children emphasize the necessity to study the child—his temperamental characteristics, neurological status, intellectual capacities, and physical handicaps. The parents should also be studied rather than given global labels such as rejecting, overprotective, anxious, etc. Parental attitudes and practices are usually selective and not global, with differentiated characteristics in different areas of the child's life and with marked variability from child to child. Parent-child interaction should be analyzed not only for parental influences on the child but just as much for the influence of the child's individual characteristics on the parent. The influence of other intra- and extrafamilial environmental factors should be estimated in relation to the interactive pattern with each specific child with his individual characteristics rather than in terms of sweeping generalizations.

Our finding that an excessively stressful maladaptive temperament-environment interaction constitutes a decisive element in the development of behavior problems suggests that treatment should emphasize the modification of the interactive process so that it is less stressful and more adaptive. This requires first of all an identification of the pertinent temperamental and environmental issues. Parents can then be armed with this knowledge in the service of modifying their interactive pattern with the child in a healthy direction. Parent guidance rather than parent treatment should be the first aim. If the parent cannot learn to understand his child and utilize this understanding effectively, it then becomes pertinent to inquire into the factors which may be responsible for such a failure of parent guidance. In our experience such failures are in a minority. Most parents do appear able to cooperate in a parent guidance program. When this is accomplished, the parent and psychiatrist can truly become allies in the treatment of the child's problem.

References

Birch, H. G., Thomas, A., & Chess, S. (1964), Behavioral development in brain-damaged children: three case studies. *Arch. Gen. Psychiat.*, 11:596–603.
Chess, S. (1964), Mal de Mere. *Amer. J. Orthopsychiat.*, 34:613–614.
———, Hertzig, M., Birch, H. G., & Thomas, A. (1962), Methodology of a study of adaptive functions of the preschool child. *This Journal*, 1:236–245.
———, Thomas, A., & Birch, H. G. (1966), Distortions in developmental reporting made by parents of behaviorally disturbed children. *This Journal*, 5:226–234.
———, Thomas, A., Rutter, M., & Birch, H. G. (1963), Interaction of temperament

and environment in the production of behavioral disturbances in children. *Amer. J. Psychiat.*, 120:142–148.

GLIDEWELL, J. C., DOMKE, H. R., & KANTOR, M. B. (1963), Screening in schools for behavior disorders: use of mother's report of symptoms. *J. Educ. Res.*, 56:508–515.

KAGAN, J. & MOSS, H. A. (1962), *Birth to Maturity: A Study in Psychological Development*. New York: Wiley.

KRIS, M. (1957), The use of prediction in a longitudinal study. *The Psychoanalytic Study of the Child*, 12:175–189. New York: International Universities Press.

LAPOUSE, R. & MONK, M. A. (1958), An epidemiologic study of behavior characteristics in children. *Amer. J. Pub. Hlth.*, 48:1134–1144.

MACFARLANE, J. W., ALLEN, L., & HONZIK, M. P. (1954), *A Developmental Study of the Behavior Problems of Normal Children between Twenty-one Months and Fourteen Years* [University of California Publications in Child Development, Vol. II]. Berkeley: University of California Press.

MURPHY, L. B. et al. (1962), *The Widening World of Childhood*. New York: Basic Books.

ROBBINS, L. C. (1963), The accuracy of parental recall of aspects of child development and of child-rearing practices. *J. Abnorm. Soc. Psychol.*, 66:261–270.

RUTTER, M., BIRCH, H. G., THOMAS, A., & CHESS, S. (1964), Temperamental characteristics in infancy and the later development of behavioral disorders. *Brit. J. Psychiat.*, 110:651–661.

THOMAS, A., CHESS, S., BIRCH, H. G., HERTZIG, M., & KORN, S. (1963), *Behavioral Individuality in Early Childhood*. New York: New York University Press.

WENAR, C. (1963), The reliability of developmental histories: summary and evaluation of evidence. *Psychosom. Med.*, 25:505–509.

Chapter 5

Courtesy the Peace Corps by Ray Witlin

An Overview of Human Life and Growth

All of existence is continuous and related. A search for beginnings and causes of life reveals psychological, physiological, biological, biochemical, and physical structures built upon and of each other.

Every organism and its environment have dynamic, reciprocal relationships. Affecting each other and being affected by each other, neither can be understood without the other, nor can either be what it *is* without the other. The cool air under the tree does not exist without the tree, nor would the tree exist without air. An interesting interaction between plants and landscape can be seen in coastal areas where conservation projects are carried out. A beach which was washed away by a hurricane now stretches smoothly into the Atlantic, backed by sand dunes built by plants. The plants were dead Christmas trees stuck into the sand and then reinforced by living plants which, finding nutrients and moisture enough in the sand, sent down a network of tough roots, which held the sand in the dunes.

More remarkable even than the building of beaches is the interaction of the human baby with his environment, his family. A human baby grows into a human child as he lives in a human family, calling forth maternal and paternal responses from two adults whose behavior could not be parental if he were not there.

Varieties of Interaction Between the Individual and His World

The story of child development begins with the interactions of a small package of DNA and ends with an adult human being living in a complex social network. Everyone has some beliefs and hypotheses as to how these many changes take place. Nobody has explained it all in a comprehensive theory, but many theorists have described and explained parts of it. A theory depends first of all on the point of view from which the observer looks at the human scene and consequently on the phenomena which he observes. Theories of growth and development usually have a biological flavor. Learning experiments may suggest the influence of physics. Research in social relationships often involves sociology and perhaps anthropology. This chapter deals with six types of interactions which represent different ways of looking at human phenomena. They are: equilibration, growth and development, learning, maturation, evolutionary adaptation, and heredity.

Equilibration

The organism constantly regulates its life processes so as to maintain physical and mental states within certain limits.

Homeostasis

Homeostasis is a balance which the organism maintains within itself during the processes of living and as environmental influences affect its internal conditions. Since the balance is continually upset and re-created, through a complex of interactions, it can be called a dynamic equilibrium. Through activities that are mostly unconscious, the individual keeps his blood sugar at a definite level, his water content within a given range, his oxygen content just so. Breathing and heartbeat speed up or slow down from their average rates to restore disturbed balances. The mechanisms of homeostasis regulate sleeping and waking states, activity and rest. Pressures and depleted tissues may register consciously as felt needs, leading to such purposeful interactions with the environment as eating, drinking, and eliminating.

Looming large in the life of a newborn infant, the problems of homeostasis dwindle throughout infancy and childhood. By about 3 months of age basic physiological processes are well controlled. At any time throughout the life span, however, when the balance is seriously threatened, when biological demands become crucial or urgent, the individual drops his higher-order activities, such as giving a lecture or playing tennis, in order to restore the balance within his body.

Psychological Equilibrium

The search for balance occurs in the mental realm as well as in the physical. Equilibration is the process of achieving a state of balance. Sooner or later, the state of equilibrium is upset and a new one must be created. Equilibration includes selecting stimuli from the world, seeking this or that kind, more or less, paying attention to some of them and using some in more complex mental operations. When you consider all the sounds, sights, tastes, and other perceptions available, it follows that a person could not possibly attend to all of them at once. There must be ways of selecting stimuli and avoiding or reducing psychological conflict. In Walter's words: "... there are mechanisms within the brain which act like traffic cops for information and actually damp down and modify the action of the receptors themselves. It has been shown that the information which is allowed to reach the brain from the outside world is a function of its novelty and significance. The level of the receptor itself, the actual eye or ear, is cut down, as though the central nervous system were to say: 'I'm not interested in what you're sending me'" [48, p. 109]. What Walter is describing is very much akin to homeostasis of physiological functions, the maintenance of satisfactory internal conditions.

Equilibration is one of Piaget's principles of mental development [34, pp. 5–8]. Action can be provoked when equilibrium is upset by finding a new object, being asked a question, identifying a problem; in fact, by any new experience. Equilibrium is reestablished by reaching a goal, answering a question, solving a problem, imitating, establishing an effective tie or any other resolution of the difference between the new factor or situation and the mental organization already existing. Equilibration results in the successive stages of intelligence which Piaget describes.

Equilibration, in Piaget's theory, includes two complementary processes through which the person proceeds to more complex levels of organization—*assimilation*, which is the taking in from the environment what the organism can deal with and *accommodation*, the changing of the organism to fit external circumstances. Just as the body can assimilate foods and not other substances, so the mind can take in certain aspects and events in the external world and not others. Existing structures or *schemas* incorporate experiences which fit them or which almost fit them.

A schema is a pattern of action and/or throught. A baby develops some schemas before he is born and has them for starting life as a newborn. With simple schemas, he interacts with his environment, working toward equilibration. He achieves equilibrium over and over again, by using the schemas available to him at the moment. For example, a baby has a furry toy kitten which he knows as *kitty*. When given a small furry puppy he calls it *kitty*, strokes it and pats it, assimilating the puppy to an existing schema. A new little horse on wheels requires accommodation, since it is too different to be assimilated into the schema for dealing with *kitty*. It looks different; it feels different; it is not good for stroking and patting, but something can be done with the wheels which cannot be done with *kitty*. A new pattern of action is required. The child accommodates by changing and organizing existing schemas to form a schema for dealing with *horsey*. Thus the child grows in his understanding of the world and his ability to deal with his experiences in meaningful ways. Assimilation conserves the structural systems that he has while accommodation effects changes through which he copes more adequately with his environment and behaves in increasingly complex ways.

When homeostasis presents no problems, such as hunger, thirst, or fatigue, a person looks for something to do, something interesting, a new experience. If equilibrium were completely satisfying in itself, then surely he would sit or lie quietly doing nothing. In looking for action, the child seems to be trying to upset his state of equilibrium, as though equilibration were fun! And so it is. Activity is intrinsic in living tissue, brain cells included. Curiosity, exploration, competence, and achievement motivation are all outgrowths of the human propensity for enjoying the process of equilibration. The first stage of the process, perception of a problem, an incongruity or discrepancy, involves tension and a feeling of incompleteness. Something is missing or something is wrong.

The baby pushes himself forward to grasp a toy that is out of reach. The 4-year-old makes a mailbox which is necessary for his game of postman. The first grader sounds out a new word. Each child reduces a feeling of tension as he creates a new equilibrium. The equilibration (achievement of new balance) makes him into a slightly different person from what he has been, a person who can move forward a bit, a person who has made his own mailbox and can therefore make other things, a person who can read another word. Thus equilibration is a way of describing behavior development. New and more complex behavior occurs as it is demanded by the person's relationship with his surroundings.

When a person's schemas are adequate to deal with the situation in which he finds himself, he reacts automatically. For example, the response of a hungry breast-fed baby of 3 months would be quite automatic when offered his mother's breast. A 10-year-old would automatically answer the question "What is two times two?" When the schemas are not quite adequate to the situation, the child uses what he has, changing them slightly into actions which do solve the problem. For instance, the baby would change his behavior sufficiently to cope with a bottle and the 10-year-old with "$2x = 4$. What does x equal?" The change which takes place at the same time within the child is the development of a new behavior pattern or schema. A pleasant feeling of curiosity and satisfaction accompanies successful adjustments to demands for new behavior.

A person feels uneasy when he encounters a situation in which his resources are very inadequate. In order to provoke uneasiness, the problem must be somewhat similar to those which a person can solve, but not similar enough for him to succeed with. Such a problem for the baby mentioned might be a cup of milk. For the 10-year-old it might be an equation such as $5x - 49/x = 20x/5$. If the situation is so far removed from a person's past experience that his schemas for dealing with it are extremely inadequate, then he will have no reaction to it. He will not notice it. He will not select from the environment the stimuli which would pose the problem. The baby will not try to drink out of a carton full of cans of milk. The child won't attempt to solve $xY - x5 - 144 = 1062 + 2300$.

Familiar objects in unfamiliar guise produce unpleasantness, uneasiness, or even fear. (Chimpanzees are afraid of the keeper in strange clothes, an anesthetized chimp, a plaster cast of a chimp's head. Human babies are afraid of strangers.) In order to be frightened or to get the unpleasant feeling, the subject must first have residues of past experience with which to contrast the present experience. Thus does incongruity arise, with its accompanying unpleasant feeling tone. If the individual can cope with the situation successfully, he achieves equilibration and its accompanying pleasant feeling tone. Stimuli preferred and chosen are those that are slightly more complex than the state of equilibrium that the individual has already reached. Thus he moves on to a new state of equilibrium [36].

Growth and Development

The child's body becomes larger and more complex while his behavior increases in scope and complexity. If any distinction is made between the two terms, growth refers to size, and development to complexity. However, the two are often used interchangeably and this is what we have done. The terms *growth* and *development* were borrowed from the physical field, but they are commonly understood in connection with mental and personality characteristics. One can say, "He has grown mentally," or "He has developed mentally." The statement means "He is now functioning on a more complex intellectual level." Or one can speak of growth of personality and development of attitudes. Listening in on second grade and fifth grade classrooms in the same school building will reveal differences in subject matter interests and in mode of thinking.

Growth or development can be shown to have taken place either by comparing younger and older individuals at the same moment of time or by comparing the same individuals at two different points of time. When the measures of some characteristic of a number of individuals are averaged by age groups, the averages of the successive age groups show what growth has taken place. If each individual is measured only once, that is, if there are different people at each age, the study is *cross-sectional*. If the same individuals are measured at each successive age, the study is *longitudinal*. If some individuals do not remain available for continued study and new ones are added, the study is called *mixed longitudinal*. In a cross-sectional study, growth status at each age is investigated, and inferences regarding growth are drawn from *differences* between any groups. *Change* in status from age to age can be inferred only if the individuals at the two ages can be assumed to be comparable in all relevant ways. In a longitudinal study both growth status at each age and change in status from age to age can be investigated more precisely, because the same individuals are involved and actual growth patterns are established for individuals.

Principles of Growth

There are a number of generalizations about growth which are more apparent with respect to physical growth but which, as far as research can show, are also true for psychological growth. We will elaborate on nine such statements about growth at this point, some of them with subheadings.

Variation of Rates. Rates of growth vary from one individual to another, and they vary within one individual. An organism grows at varying rates, from one time to another. The organs and systems grow at varying rates, at different times. There is a sex difference in rates and terminals. Various group differences can be shown. It is no wonder that comparisons of growth require facts obtained by highly controlled methods.

An organism and its parts grow at rates which are different at different times. The body as a whole, as measured by height and weight, shows a pattern of velocity that is fast in infancy, moderate in the preschool period, slow during the school

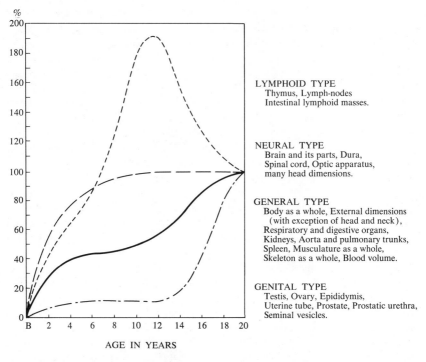

Figure 5–1. Growth curves of the body as a whole and of three types of tissue. Values at each age are computed as percentages of values for total growth.

SOURCE: Reproduced by permission from J. A. Harris, C. M. Jackson, D. G. Paterson, and R. E. Scammon, *The Measurement of Man*. Minneapolis: University of Minnesota Press, 1930.

years, and fast in the beginning of adolescence. Figure 5–1 illustrates growth velocities of different types of tissue, expressed as percentages of maturity for each age. The general type of growth, which represents not only height and weight, but muscles, skeleton, and most of the internal organs, is illustrated by a sigmoid curve, an elongated S. The brain and related tissues grow in a different pattern of velocity, very fast during the first 2 years, moderately until about 6, and very little after that. The growth curve for genital tissue is almost the reverse of that of neural tissue. The genital system grows very little during infancy and childhood and very fast in adolescence. The fourth curve in Figure 5–1 represents the lymph system which grows rapidly throughout infancy and childhood, reaches a peak just before puberty, and then decreases in size throughout adolescence.

Rates of growth vary from one individual to another. Some children are fast growers, some moderate, and some slow in regard to the number of years taken to reach maturity. Periods of fast and slow growth vary as to when they occur and for how long. One child begins the pubescent growth spurt earlier or later than another, grows faster or slower during the spurt, and finishes sooner or later.

There are sex differences in rates. Early in fetal life, girls show evidence of maturing faster than boys, especially in skeletal development. At birth, girls are four weeks ahead of boys skeletally. Boys' skeletal development is about 80 percent of that of girls' from birth to maturity [44, p. 43]. Girls are ahead of boys in dentition, as measured by eruption of permanent teeth. Although sex differences in height and weight before the preadolescent growth spurt are very slight, favoring boys, sexual maturity and its antecedent growth spurt occur in girls about two years before they do in boys. Therefore, there is a period of about two years when girls are taller and heavier than boys. At all ages, girls are more mature physiologically.

Individual Differences in Terminals. It is obvious, yet it is essential in understanding growth, to recognize that for different people maturity comes at different points. You have only to walk down the street to observe that some people grow until they are over 6 feet tall, others stop at 5 feet, and most people stop in between. Measurable mental growth stops at different times for different individuals too. The average girl reaches height and weight terminals before the average boy. Little is known about mental growth terminals.

Dynamic Interrelations in Growth. It would be surprising if different measures of growth were not related to each other. A tremendous number of studies have probed into the question of interrelationships of growth-controlling and regulating mechanisms.

Correlations between measures of growth can be between measures in the same field (physical–physical, mental–mental, and so on), or in different fields (physical–mental, mental–emotional). Skeletal development, assessed by X rays of the wrist, is at present the best indicator of physiological maturity, although if body proportions could be quantified and scaled in some manageable way, this might prove even more useful. Fat thickness in childhood is also a measure of general physiological maturity [16]. Sexual maturity and eventual height can be predicted with good accuracy from measurements of skeletal maturity. A general factor of bodily maturity operating throughout the growth period influences the child's growth as a whole, including his skeleton, size, physiological reactions, and possibly intelligence. Influencing factors of more limited scope operate independently of the general factor and of each other. One of these limited factors controls baby teeth, another permanent teeth, another the ossification centers in the skeleton and probably several others regulate brain growth. This is why various measures of physical growth have low positive correlations with each other. If there were only one controlling factor, then the different measures would presumably all correlate highly or even perfectly with one another [44].

Studies of the relation between physical and mental growth show a small but consistent positive correlation, bearing out the hypothesis of a general factor which influences all growth processes. This relationship has been studied from age 6½ onward, comparing the mental ages or academic achievement, or both, of early maturing youngsters with those of late maturers [1, 24, 39, 40, 42]. A study of children at the extremes of distributions of mental traits showed gifted boys to be significantly ahead of retarded boys in measures of physical growth [24]. A small positive correlation between mental ability and size is also found in adults [45]. As an example of the relationships between growth and personality, there is good evidence that early maturers feel more adequate and more comfortable about themselves than do late maturers [23, 31].

Optimal Tendency. An organism behaves as though it were seeking to reach its maximum potential for development in both structure and function. Even though growth is interrupted, such as in periods of inadequate food supply, the child (or organism) makes up for the lean period as soon as more and better food is available, returning to his characteristic pattern of growth. Only if the deprivation is severe, or if it occurs throughout a critical period, will he show permanent effects from it.

During the deprivation period, the organism adapts by slowing growth and cutting down on the use of energy.

All sorts of adaptive arrangements are worked out when there are interferences with the normal course of development, as though the child is determined to reach his best potential by another route when one is blocked. The child with poor eyesight seeks extra information from his other senses. Babies with a tendency toward rickets drink cod liver oil freely if permitted to, selecting their own diets from a wide variety of simple foods [7]. For northern white children, the characteristics of the home were found to be most important in determining how well the child did at school, but for southern black children the characteristics of the school were more important than those of the home. "It is as if the child drew sustenance from wherever it was available. When the home had more to offer, it became more determining; but when the school could provide more stimulation than the home, then the school became the more influential factor." [5, p. 106].

"Every breach in the normal complex of growth is filled through regenerative, substantive, or compensatory growth of some kind. . . . Insurance reserves are drawn upon whenever the organism is threatened. . . . Herein lies the urgency, the almost irrepressible quality of growth" [18, p. 165]. This principle has been recognized as working in physical realms as well as organic, where there seems to be a self-stabilizing or target-seeking property of certain systems [49].

Differentiation and Integration. From large global patterns of behavior, smaller, more specific patterns emerge. Later the small, specific patterns can be combined into new, complicated, larger patterns. For example, a photographic study of human beginnings shows an $11\frac{1}{2}$ weeks' fetus reacting to being stroked on the right cheek [18, p. 25]. The fetus contracted the muscles of his neck, trunk, and shoulder, causing his whole body to bend away from the stimulus and the arms and hands to move backward. When a newborn infant is stroked on the cheek he turns toward the stimulus, pursing his lips and opening his mouth when his lips touch something. Thus he shows a new, specialized response pattern which involves a small part of his body instead of the whole. As he grows older, the rooting response changes and becomes integrated with other behavior patterns. Instead of turning toward food when he is touched near the mouth, he turns toward the breast or bottle when he sees it. His hands come into play in guiding food toward his mouth. Later he uses a knife and fork. He is integrating behavior patterns of eyes and hands with the rooting pattern, forming a smoothly functioning whole.

Examples can also be taken from purely intellectual fields, such as mathematics. There is a stage of maturity at the end of infancy when a child knows *one*, *two* and *a-lot-of*. At 5, he has differentiated *three* and *four* out of *a-lot-of*. By 6, numbers up to ten have true meaning. Using these differentiated concepts, he next combines them in addition and subtraction to form new and more complicated concepts. Conceptual differentiation and integration are at work as the student moves up through algebra and geometry into higher mathematics. There remains an undifferentiated sphere where each person stops in his progress in mathematics.

Developmental Direction. Certain sequences of development take place in certain directions, in reference to the body. The motor sequence takes two such directions, cephalocaudal (head to tail) and proximodistal (midline to outer extremities). Like all animals, the child grows a relatively large, complex head region early in life, whereas the tail region or posterior is small and simple. As he becomes older, the region next to the head grows more, and finally, the end region grows. Coordination follows the same direction, the muscles of the eyes coming under control first, then the neck muscles, then arms, chest, and back, and finally the legs. The motor sequence illustrates the proximodistal direction by the fact that the earliest controlled arm movements, as in reaching, are large movements, controlled mostly by shoulder muscles. Later the elbow is brought into play in reaching, then the wrist, and then the fingers.

Normative Sequence. The sequence of motor development has long been noticed and understood as one of the ways of nature. "A child must creepe ere he walke."

As the structures of the body mature in their various sequences, they function in characteristic ways, provided that the environment permits appropriate interaction. The resulting behavior patterns appear in an orderly sequence. Sequences have been described for locomotion, use of hands, language, problem solving, social behavior, and other kinds of behavior [6, 19, 20]. During the decade of the thirties, the bulk of research in child development was normative, delineating sequences of development and designating average ages for the patterns observed. The classic viewpoint, exemplified by Gesell, stressed normative sequences as an unfolding. Although the role of the environment was implicit in these early writings, the focus was on regulation from innate forces. Today interaction between organism and environment is emphasized as basic to development. The change in viewpoint has come about to some extent because of the broadening of areas of child study to include a variety of cultures, at home and abroad. Although child development continues to take place in orderly sequences, exceptions can be found [8]. Hence normative sequences cannot be considered as universal, but must be understood as occurring in particular kinds of environments.

Epigenesis. Growth takes place upon the foundation which is already there. New parts arise out of and upon the old. Although the organism becomes something new as it grows, it still has continuity with the past and hence shows certain consistencies over time. Through interactions with the environment, the organism continues to restructure itself throughout life, being at each moment the product of the interaction which took place in the previous moment between organism and environment. A toddler's body results from interactions of a baby's body with food, water, and air. The motor pattern of walking is derived and elaborated from creeping and standing. Writing is built from scribbling.

Critical Periods. There are certain limited times during the growth period of any organism when it will interact with a particular environment in a specific way. The result of interactions during critical periods can be especially beneficial or harmful. The prenatal period includes specific critical periods for physical growth. The first three months are critical for the development of eyes, ears, and brain, as shown by defects in children whose mothers had German measles during the first three months of pregnancy. Apparently those organs are most vulnerable to the virus of German measles when they are in their periods of rapid growth.

Experiments on vision with human and animal infants reveal critical ages for the development of visual responses, times when the infant will either show the response without experience or will learn it readily [14]. If the visual stimulus is not given at the critical age (as when baby monkeys are reared in darkness), the animal later learns the response with difficulty, or not at all.

Psychological development also shows critical periods in the sense that certain behavior patterns are acquired most readily at certain times of life. Critical periods in personality development include the period of primary socialization, when the infant makes his first social attachments [38] and develops basic trust [11]. A warm relationship with a mother figure is thought to be essential among the experiences which contribute to a sense of trust [4]. This type of critical period is probably not so final and irreversible as is a critical period for the development of an organ in the embryo. If the term "critical period" is applied to the learning of skills such as swimming and reading, then it should be understood that it signifies the most *opportune* time for learning and not the only one [30].

Stage Theories of Development

The last three principles of growth are incorporated in theories of child development which present growth occurring in stages. Each stage is created through epigenesis, behavior patterns being organized and reorganized in an orderly sequence. Thus past, present, and future development are related and can be understood as an ongoing process. Small pieces of behavior can be interpreted in terms of the stage when they occur instead of being invested with one meaning. For example, crying at 1 month of age was seen to be an active attempt to overcome interference with sucking, whereas crying at 1 year of age was found to be a passive mode of response to environmental frustration [26]. Stage theories encourage research which establishes ways of predicting future development [22].

This book is organized in stages of development, leaning heavily on two stage theories: Erikson's theory of personality growth, and Piaget's theory of the growth of intelligence. The ages which correspond with the various stages are only approximations or rough landmarks. While it is useful to be able to anchor stage concepts to some sort of chronology, it is important to realize that stages are only age-related and not age-determined. The growth principle, *variation of rates*, applies here.

Erikson's Stages. Erikson's theory might be called epigenetic in a double sense. Not only does it portray epigenetic stages, but it was built upon Freud's theory and yet is a new organization and a unique creation. Freud proposed psychosexual stages of development, each of which used a certain zone of the body for gratification of the id (the unconscious source of motives, strivings, desires, and energy). The ego, which mediates between the demands of the id, the outside world, and the superego, "represents what may be called reason and common sense, in contrast to the id, which contains the passions" [15, p. 15]. The superego or ego ideal corresponds roughly to *conscience*. Freud's psychosexual stages are: *oral*, when the mouth is the main zone of satisfaction, about the first year; *anal*, when pleasure comes from anal and urethral sensations, the second and third years; *phallic*, the third and fourth years, a time of pleasure from genital stimulation; *oedipal*, also genital but now, at 4 and 5 years, the child regards the parent of the opposite sex as a love object and the same-sex parent as a rival; *latency*, from 6 to around 11, when sexual cravings are repressed (made unconscious) and the child identifies with the parent and peers of his own sex; *puberal* when mature genital sexuality begins.

Erikson uses Freud's concepts in his theory of psychosocial development, adding to the complexity of each stage and also adding three stages above the puberal, thus dealing with adulthood as a time for growth. Progress through the stages takes place in an orderly sequence. In making his stages psychosocial as well as psychosexual, Erikson recognizes the interaction between individual and culture as contributing to personal growth. While Freud's theory has a great deal to say about pathology, Erikson's offers a guide to both illness and health of personality. For each stage, there are problems to be solved within the cultural context. Thus each stage is a critical period for development of certain attitudes, convictions, and abilities. After the satisfactory solution of each crisis, the person emerges with an increased sense of unity, good judgment and capacity to "do well" [12, p. 92]. The conflicts are never completely resolved nor the problems disposed of forever. Each stage is described with a positive and negative outcome of the crisis involved. The stages are [11, pp. 247–274]:

1. *Basic trust versus basic mistrust.* Similar to Freud's oral stage, the development of a sense of trust dominates the first year. Success means coming to trust the world, other people, and himself. Since the mouth is the main zone of pleasure, trust grows on being fed when hungry, pleasant sensations when nursing, and the growing conviction that his own actions have something to do with pleasant events. Consistent, loving care is trust-promoting. Mistrust develops when trust-promoting experiences are inadequate, when the baby has to wait too long for comfort, when he is handled harshly or capriciously. Since life is never perfect, shreds of mistrust are woven into the fabric of personality. Problems of mistrust recur and have to be solved later, but when trust is dominant, healthy personality growth takes place.

2. *Autonomy versus shame and doubt.* The second stage, corresponding to Freud's anal period, predominates during the second and third year. Holding on and letting go with the sphincter muscles symbolizes the whole problem of autonomy. The child wants to do for himself with all of his powers: his new motor skills of walking, climbing, manipulating; his mental powers of choosing and deciding. If his parents give him plenty of suitable choices, times to decide when his judgment is adequate for successful outcomes, then he grows in autonomy. He gets the feeling that he can control his body, himself, and his environment. The negative feelings of doubt and shame arise when his choices are disastrous, when other people shame him or force him in areas where he could be in charge.

3. *Initiative versus guilt.* The Oedipal part of genital stage of Freudian theory, 4 and 5 years, is to Erikson the stage of development of a sense of initiative. Now the child explores the physical world with his senses and the social and physical worlds with his questions, reasoning, imaginative, and creative powers. Love relationships with parents are very important. Conscience develops. Guilt is the opposite pole of initiative.

4. *Industry versus inferiority.* Solutions of problems of initiative and guilt bring about entrance to the stage of developing a sense of industry, the latency period of Freud. The child is now ready to be a worker and producer. He wants to do jobs well instead of merely starting them and exploring them. He practices and learns the rules. Feelings of inferiority and inadequacy result when he feels he cannot measure up to the standards held for him by his family or society.

5. *Identity versus role diffusion.* The Freudian puberal stage, beginning at the start of adolescence, involves resurgence of sexual feelings. Erikson adds to this concept his deep insights into the adolescent's struggles to integrate all the roles he has played and hopes to play, his childish body concept with his present physical development, his concepts of his own society and the value of what he thinks he can contribute to it. Problems remaining from earlier stages are reworked.

6. *Intimacy versus isolation.* A sense of identity is the condition for ability to establish true intimacy, "the capacity to commit himself to concrete affiliations and partnerships and to develop the ethical strength to abide by such commitments" [11, p. 263]. Intimacy involves understanding and allowing oneself to be understood. It may be, but need not be, sexual. Without intimacy, a person feels isolated and alone.

7. *Generativity versus self-absorption.* Involvement in the well-being and development of the next generation is the essence of generativity. While it includes being a good parent, it is more. Concern with creativity is also part of it. Adults need to be needed by the young, and unless the adults can be concerned and contributing, they suffer from stagnation.

8. *Ego integrity versus despair.* The sense of integrity comes from satisfaction with one's own life cycle and its place in space and time. The individual feels that his actions, relationships, and values are all meaningful and acceptable. Despair arises from remorseful remembrance of mistakes and wrong decisions plus the conviction that it is too late to try again.

Figure 5–2 shows the normal timing of Erikson's stages of psychosocial development. The critical period for each stage is represented by a swelling of the rope which stretches throughout life. The ropes indicate that no crisis is ever solved completely and finally, but that strands of it are carried along, to be dealt with at different levels. As one rope swells at its critical period, the other ropes are affected and interact. Solutions to identity problems involve problems in all the other stages. The metaphor of the rope can also be extended by thinking of the personalities of a family's members as being intertwined ropes. When the parents' Generativity strands are becoming dominant, the infant's Trust strand is dominant. The two ropes fit smoothly together, indicating a complementary relationship between the personalities of infant and parents.

Piaget's Stages. Figure 5–2 shows Piaget's stages in the development of intelligence. Piaget is concerned with the nature of knowledge and how it is acquired. His studies of infants and children have revealed organizations of structures by which the child comes to know the world. The structural units are *schemas*, patterns of action and/or thought. As the child matures, he uses his existing schemas to interact, transforming them through the process of equilibration. Each stage of development is an advance from the last one, built upon it by reorganizing it and adapting more closely to reality. Reorganization and adaptation go on continuously, but from one time to another the results differ from each other. Piaget has broken this series of organizations of structures into units called periods and stages. There are three periods, each of which extends the previous one, reconstructs it, and surpasses it [35, pp. 152–159]. Periods are divided into stages which have a constant sequence, no matter whether the child achieves them at a slow or fast pace. Progress through the periods and stages is affected by organic growth, exercise and experience, social interaction or equilibration. The periods are:

1. *Sensorimotor.* Lasting from birth until about 2, sensorimotor intelligence exists without language and symbols. Practical and aimed at getting results, it works through action-schemas [35, p. 4]. Beginning with the reflex patterns present at birth, the baby builds more and more complex schemas through a succession of six stages. Figure 5–2 lists the names of the stages. They are described in Chapter 3. During this period the baby constructs a schema of the permanence

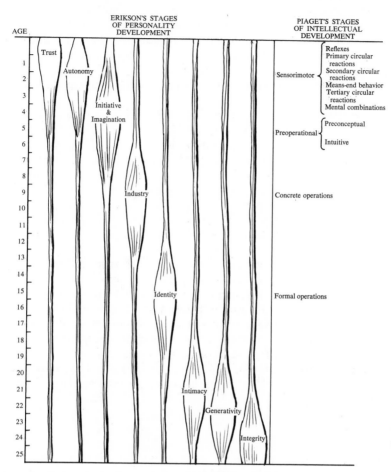

Figure 5–2. Schematic representation of Erikson's stages of psychosocial development, with names of Piaget's stages of the development of intelligence.

of objects. He comes to know that things and people continue to exist even when he cannot see them and he realizes that they move when he is not looking. He learns control of his body in space. He begins to use language to imitate and to make internal representations of reality.

2. *Preoperational.* Sometimes this period, from about 2 to 7, is considered a sub-period of the whole time from 2 to 11. It is distinctly different, however, from the sensorimotor period and the period which comes around 7, the period of concrete operations. Two stages, preconceptual and intuitive thought, are included. The preoperational period is marked by the *semiotic* function and imitation. The semiotic function, often called symbolizing, is the use of an indicator or sign as distinct from the object or event to which it refers [35, pp. 52–91]. For example, the bell that announces dinner is perceived as distinct from the food but as indicating food. Achievements show much use of his new representational abilities, in deferred imitation (imitation starting after the

model has disappeared), symbolic play, drawing, mental images, and verbal representation. The child thinks that names are essential parts of the objects to which they refer. When he gives a reason, it is in terms of how he wants things to be. He sees no need to come to the same conclusions as anyone else because he does not realize the existence of viewpoints other than his own. Throughout this stage the child becomes more flexible in his thinking, more able to use past experience and to consider more than one aspect of an event at a time.

3. *Concrete operations.* The period from about 7 to 11 years of age is essentially the time when the child can think about real, concrete things in systematic ways, although he has great difficulty in thinking about abstractions. He orders, counts, classifies, and thinks in terms of cause and effect. He develops a new concept of permanence, called *conservation*, through which he realizes that amount, weight, volume, and number stay the same when outward appearances of objects or groups are changed. Although he finds it difficult to change his hypotheses, he learns to take other people's points of view and comes to feel that his reasoning and his solutions to problems should check with other people's. His thinking has become socialized.

4. *Formal operations.* The period of formal operations or logical thought begins at about 11 and continues to develop until about 15, when the individual has the mental operations for adult thinking. Instead of having to think about concrete objects, he can think and reason in purely abstract terms. He can think systematically, combining all factors in a situation so as to exhaust all possibilities. He makes hypotheses and tests them. This type of thinking is basic to logic and to the scientific method. The limitation of this stage is a confusion of what could and should be with what is practically possible. The adolescent resists the imperfections in the world when he can construct ideal arrangements in his mind.

Learning

Learning occurs when behavior changes as a result of experience. Experiments on newborn infants have demonstrated learning. As children grow older and their behavior more complex, the variables which influence behavior also increase in number and complexity. Thus different types of learning are described.

Conditioning

Conditioning, or learning by association, is the establishing of a connection between a stimulus and a response. In *classical conditioning*, the kind made famous by Pavlov, a neutral stimulus is presented with another stimulus which elicits an innate response. After several such presentations, the neutral stimulus is given without the other stimulus and the response occurs. Pavlov sounded a buzzer when he gave food to his dog. Eventually the dog salivated at the sound of the buzzer.

Operant, or instrumental, conditioning is done by rewarding the desired response whenever it occurs. Operant conditioning techniques have been developed for use in a wide variety of situations, with animal and human subjects. By rewarding small pieces of behavior, complex patterns can be built up, thus "shaping" or modifying the behavior of the subject. This technique has proved very useful in treating behavior disorders in infants, children, retardates, and the mentally ill.

Conditioning has been used to explore the abilities of infants and to show that newborn babies do learn [27]. Papoušek taught newborn babies to turn their heads to the sound of a buzzer by using a combination of classical and operant conditioning methods [32]. A bell was sounded and if the infant turned to the left, he was given milk. If he did not turn, head-turning was elicited by touching the corner of his mouth with a nipple. Then he was given milk. Newborns were slow to condition, taking an average of 18 days, whereas at 3 months, only 4 days were required and by 5 months, 3 days. Two-month-old infants learned to operate a mobile by means of head-pressing on their pillows [49]. Until recently, the problem for experimenters was to find a way of delivering rewards which would be contingent on a response that the infant was able to make. The ingenious arrangement of the mobile and an activating device in the pillow revealed not only that infants could learn instrumentally (by operant conditioning) but also that they showed enormous involvement and pleasure in the process of controlling stimulation.

Reinforcement

One of the laws of learning which Thorndike formulated in 1905 is the law of effect: "Any act which in a given situation produces satisfaction becomes associated with that situation, so that when the situation occurs, the act is more likely to recur also" [46, p. 203]. This principle is the basis of learning through reinforcement or rewards and punishment. Rewards and punishments, or positive and negative reinforcements, can be given to oneself or to others. It is not always possible to predict what will be rewarding and punishing, since previous experience and the state of the person at the time contribute to the meaning the particular reinforcement has. Havighurst has shown that rewards and punishments change with the age and maturity of the individual and that the development of the reward-punishment system varies from one culture to another [21]. These findings have important implications for educating children from minority subcultures.

Different schedules of reinforcement have different effects on learning by operant conditioning. Response strength is measured by the number of nonreinforced trials required to extinguish the behavior. Intermittent (random) reinforcement results in a much stronger response than does continuous reinforcement. This finding has practical implications for parents and teachers. For example, if the child finds that whining is never rewarded, he will soon stop whining, but if his parents give in occasionally and reward him with what he wants, then whining will be strengthened [41].

Punishment can be very effective in controlling children's behavior, but used without understanding of its complexity, punishment can have undesired effects. Important variables are timing, intensity, relationship between agent and recipient, cognitive structure (reasoning), and consistency [33].

Verbal Mediation

After the child acquires language, he grows in the ability to use words in solving problems and learning. By 5 or 6 years, the ability can be demonstrated by the child's solution of problems which are most easily done with the aid of a principle such as "Always choose the big one" or "It's the color that counts in finding the answer."

Observational Learning

Children learn many behavior patterns through watching and listening and then patterning their behavior according to what they have observed. Social learning, especially, is facilitated by modeling or imitating. Bandura and his associates have done many experiments to show the conditions under which children will learn through observation. One important finding is that children will imitate without any external reinforcement being given. That is, modeling is its own reward. Bronfenbrenner [5] has summarized information on factors affecting the modeling process, under three headings:

Characteristics of the Subject. The child must be able to perceive and to perform the actions and to be interested in observing and imitating.

Characteristics of the Stimulus Act. It is easier to imitate a complex action if it is broken into a series of components and labeled. The child then takes part in increasingly complex interactions.

Characteristics of the Model. The power of the model to induce imitation increases as:

1. The child sees the model as competent, high in status and controlling resources.
2. The child has already experienced the model as rewarding and nurturant.
3. The model is an important source of the child's comfort and support, such as parents, peers, and older children.
4. The child sees the model as similar to himself.
5. Several models show the same behavior.
6. The behavior demonstrated is typical of a group to which the child belongs or wants to belong.
7. The child sees the model rewarded for his behavior. (If he sees the model punished, he is likely not to imitate the behavior unless he gets into a situation where he does not anticipate punishment for performing the actions.)

Bronfenbrenner points out that the Soviets employ all of these principles of modeling in their educational system, where great use is made of the peer group for inducing adult-approved behavior in children. The teacher serves as a competent, high-status, resource-controlling model. The other characteristics of potent models are exemplified by peers.

Social Learning

When a child learns how to think, feel and behave as a member of a certain group, or in a particular role, the process is called social learning. *Socialization* refers to the teaching done by members of the groups or institution in order that social learning may occur in the child. Social learning occurs in people of all ages, but much of it takes place in childhood, as the individual learns appropriate values, attitudes and behavior patterns. Parents are the primary socializers. Siblings and other family members also teach. Teachers and peers are important socializing agents, and then other members of the community.

Socialization refers to both the present and the future. The child learns to behave appropriately as the child he now is, but he also learns attitudes, values and skills that he will use in the future. From interacting with his father, he learns the father role as well as the son role. Similarly, he observes his various socializers as worker, manager, host, citizen, teacher, and in all the many roles that they play in his society. His socializers make varying use of the different methods of teaching implied by the types of learning sketched above. The child learns some specific information and skills, as well as values and attitudes. Thus he is gradually socialized into his family, community and nation through a process which maintains the values and behavior patterns of that group.

Maturation

As the child's bodily structures grow, they change in size and complexity, becoming more and more the way they will be in the mature state. Bodily functions likewise change as the structures do. The whole process is called maturation. Although maturation is controlled by hereditary factors, the environment must be adequate to support it. The growth principle of normative sequence is reflected in maturation, since structures and functions mature in an orderly, irreversible sequence. Since maturation is little affected by experience, its effects are the same throughout a species. An impoverished environment slows the process of maturation more than it changes quality or sequence.

Certain behavior patterns are due to maturation more than to learning because they are relatively independent of experience. Many developmental processes involve both maturation and learning. Examples of processes which are largely maturational are the motor sequence and the emergence of language. In all but the most abnormal environments, infants go through regular sequences of raising the head, raising the chest, sitting, creeping, standing with support, and so on.

Some theories of development stress the role of maturation in determining behavior. Gesell is one of the best known of these theorists, since his writings had a great deal of influence on parents and child care authorities of his time. Gesell's descriptions of behavior stages led many parents to feel that they could do little to influence their children's behavior and that they must enjoy his good stages and wait patiently while he grew out of unattractive, annoying, or disturbing stages. While Piaget recognizes the importance of maturation, he also stresses the necessity for the child to interact, explore, and discover for himself in order to build his mental structures. Mental growth cannot be forced or hurried, however, since its counterpart is physical maturation. "Mental growth is inseparable from physical growth: the maturation of the nervous and endocrine systems, in particular, continues until the age of sixteen" [35, p. vii].

Evolutionary Adaptation

The behavior patterns which develop through maturation can be traced back in the history of the species or the phylum. These fixed action patterns evolved as the animal adapted to a certain environment. *Ethology* is the study of the relation between animal behavior and environment. Ethology has influenced the study of human development, offering insight into certain kinds of behavior which cannot be explained as learning or fully understood as maturation. Lorenz pointed out the implications of ethology for understanding certain forms of human behavior [28]. Bowlby has integrated psychoanalytic theory with ethology [4]. Ainsworth [2] has done extensive research on attachment behavior, the main focus of the ethological approach to human development.

The adaptive behavior pattern becomes fixed in form, appearing as an innate skill in every member of a species, even though he has not had opportunities to learn [9]. A specific stimulus from the environment activates the particular behavior pattern, as though it were a key, unlocking the mechanism. Thus the behavior is sometimes called an *innate response mechanism,* or IRM. For example, a toad's catching response is released by a small, moving object, a 9-week-old gosling gives an intense fear reaction to his first sight of a hawk, and a stickleback fish will attack a red spot that resembles the red underbelly of another stickleback.

Bowlby points out that the environment to which a species is adapted is the environment in which it evolved into its present form [4, p. 59]. Most likely, when man first emerged as a distinct species, he lived by hunting and gathering in a savannah environment, much like today's most primitive societies and not unlike the ground-dwelling primates [2]. Mother–infant reciprocal behavior was adapted to protecting the infant so as to insure his survival. The baby's unlearned, spontaneous patterns of crying, clinging, and sucking brought him (and still bring him) into contact with the mother. Other aspects of attachment behavior, maturing a little later, serve to maintain and strengthen the contacts with the mother, who was (and still is) adapted or genetically programmed to respond with specific action patterns. In the urban environment of today, close physical contact of mother and baby is not necessary for protecting the baby from predators, but babies still behave as though it were and mothers still respond to their infants' behavior with innate action patterns. Closeness of mother and baby has other advantages, however, in terms of normal development.

Human behavior is largely labile, with relatively few fixed action patterns. The individual can make many adaptations, can learn a great deal. He is equipped with a few innate behavior mechanisms, such as attachment behavior and certain patterns of fear behavior, which have various kinds of value.

Heredity

While most students of child development will study the mechanisms of heredity in a biology course, we include a brief account here. After all, the mechanisms of heredity are what start the child developing and what control the course of development.

Biological Inheritance

The human being is composed of two main types of cells. By far the larger number of cells are the *body* cells. These are the cells which compose the skeleton, skin, kidneys, heart, and so on. A minority of cells are the *germ* cells. In the male, germ cells are called *spermatazoa* (the singular is spermatazoon), usually shortened to *sperm*: in the female, the germ cells are *ova* (the singular is *ovum*).

Each body cell is composed of several different parts, the most important of which for our present discussion are the *chromosomes,* of which there are 46, arranged in 23 pairs. The sizes and shapes of the chromosomes can be determined by viewing a prepared cell through an electron microscope. Twenty-two of the pairs of chromosomes are composed of two highly similar chromosomes, though each pair differs in certain respects from every other pair. These 22 pairs are similar

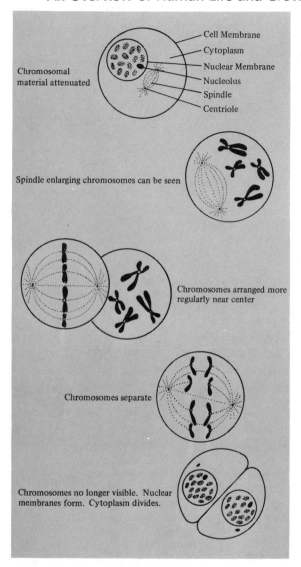

Figure 5–3. Stages in the process of mitosis.
Source: Adapted from P. A. Moody, *Genetics of Man*, Figure 3.2, p. 28. W. W. Norton, 1967.

in males and females. In males, the twenty-third pair is composed of two chromosomes which are unequal in size. The larger one is an *X chromosome*; the smaller is a *Y chromosome*. In females, the twenty-third pair is composed of two X chromosomes. When, in the course of growth, a body cell divides to form two new cells, it goes through the process of *mitosis*. The result of mitosis is that each of the new cells has exactly the same kind and number of chromosomes as the first cell had before it divided. Figure 5–3 shows the process of mitosis.

DNA, a substance in the chromosomes, is the carrier of the genetic code which transmits characteristics from one generation to the next. Figure 5–4 shows a

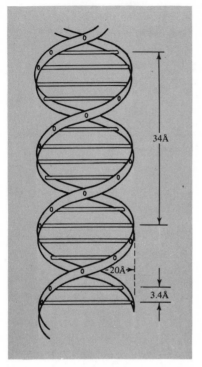

Figure 5-4. DNA takes the form of a double helix.

SOURCE: Adapted from G. W. Burns, *The Science of Genetics*. New York: The Macmillan Company, 1969, Figure 14-9, p. 258.

model of the DNA molecule, in the shape of a double helix or spiral ladder. The genes, carriers of specific instructions for growth, are arranged in linear order on the spirals. The two spirals can come apart like a zipper. Then each half produces another half.

Dominant and Recessive Genes. A recent story [43], which might be called *science prediction* rather than *science fiction*, went like this: a young couple had been quietly holding hands in a secluded corner of the campus. Then one of them said, "Let's match cards." Each pulled out a printed card containing a few holes. They put one on top of the other. None of the holes matched. They embraced happily. Like most human beings, each carried a few dangerous recessive genes out of the thousand or more which can cause birth defects. Since it takes a recessive gene from each parent to produce a characteristic which does not show in either parent, the young couple could safely plan to have children. Or if not with complete assurance, at least they would know that they were not endangering their future children as far as their own dangerous recessives were concerned. Suppose two of the holes had matched. Each of the couple was carrying a recessive gene for cystic fibrosis. For each conception, chances would be one in four for a child with two recessives and hence having cystic fibrosis, two in four for a child carrying one recessive, like the parents, and not showing the defect, and one in four for a normal child with two normal genes. And suppose they conceived a defective embryo. It could be diagnosed early in pregnancy and aborted, if they so chose.

Although at the moment when this is being written, the story is only prediction, the technology on which it is based is of the present. Many physical characteristics, including a large number of defects, are inherited according to simple Mendelian law, as illustrated in our story. Some other defects, such as color-blindness, are sex linked, which means that they are dominant in the male and recessive in the female. A male shows the defect when he carries only one gene for it, but the female does not suffer unless she has two such genes.

Heredity works in more complicated ways, also. Genes work in concert with one another and with the environment. The mechanisms of *crossing over* and *independent assortment* add enormously to the variety of genetic combinations possible. Genes "turn on" and off at various times during the life cycle. For example, the control of sexual maturation is considerably influenced by heredity.

Gene Blends. Many characteristics are the results of more than one pair of genes. Skin color in human beings is such a characteristic. It is not determined in all-or-none way, as is seed color in peas. Rather, in spite of popular belief to the contrary, a child's skin color is almost never darker than the skin of the darker parent, nor lighter than the skin of the lighter parent. If the child's skin is darker than either parent's, it is only a shade darker. At least two pairs of genes are considered to be active in determining skin color; there may be three or more.

Standing height is another human characteristic which is the result of many different genes working at least in part in a literally additive way, although blending of the kind which determines skin color may also be operating. A human being's height is the sum of the lengths of many different bones and many pieces of cartilage. Each bone's length is probably determined by one or more genes, and varies somewhat independently of the length of every other bone. Height is therefore a *polygenic* trait. (In addition, of course, the variation in heights of a group of individuals is affected by environmental factors such as diet and disease.)

Meiosis. Although each individual receives the chromosomes from germ cells of the parents, the offspring of the same parents do not receive identical chromosomes. The explanation of this difference between brothers and sisters lies in the process of *miosis*, the formation of germ cells, sperm, and ova.

Figure 5–5 shows the development of sperm which contain only 2 single chromosomes, since to show 23 would be unnecessarily complicated. In the diagram the primordial germ cell, the *spermatogonium*, is shown as containing two pairs of chromosomes. In the process of meiosis, the spermatogonium divides into two cells called *secondary spermatocytes*, each of which has one of the members of each pair of chromosomes. Each chromosome is composed of two *chromatids*. Each spermatocyte divides into two *spermatids*, each of which has one of the chromatids from the eight chromatids which are shown to have been in the original spermatogonium. From each spermatid develops a sperm. Therefore, from each male primordial germ cell result four sperm, each containing 23 single chromosomes.

The development of each ovum is similar to the development of each sperm, except that from each female primordial germ cell (called an *obgonium*) there result not four ova, but one. But it, like each sperm, contains 23 chromatids from among the 92 chromatids present in the obgonium. Since the obgonium begins meiosis with two X chromosomes, every ovum contains an X chromosome. The spermatogonium, which begins meiosis with one X and one Y chromosome, results in four sperms, two of which contain an X apiece and two a Y. If an X-bearing sperm fertilizes an ovum, the new individual will have two X chromosomes, and will be female. If a Y-bearing sperm fertilizes an ovum, the new individual will have one Y chromosome and one X chromosome, and will be a male.

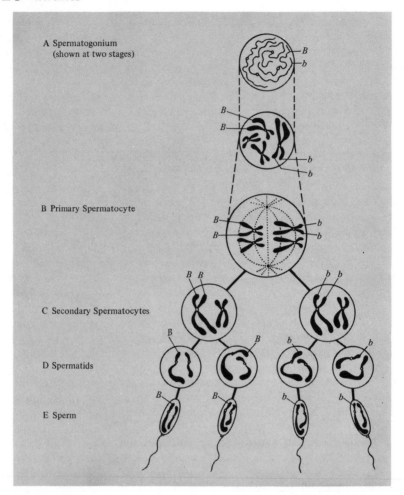

A Spermatogonium
(shown at two stages)

B Primary Spermatocyte

C Secondary Spermatocytes

D Spermatids

E Sperm

Figure 5–5. Meiosis provides the mechanism by which a heterozygous male produces sperm of two kinds: half of them containing the dominant gene, *B*, half of them containing its recessive allele, *b*.

SOURCE: Adapted from P. A. Moody, *Genetics of Man*, Figure 3.7, p. 34. W. W. Norton, 1967.

In the same way, if one parent has two genes for any trait, each offspring will receive from that parent the same kind of genetic material as any other offspring. But if a parent has unlike genes for a trait, half of the offspring (other things being equal, which they often are not) will receive one kind of gene (e.g., the dominant gene) and half will receive the other. The process of meiosis explains part of the genetic difference between brothers and sisters, including the fact that a given father and mother are likely to have both sons and daughters.

Behavior Genetics

Not only are body form and coloration inherited from generation to generation, but different kinds of functioning are, also. The ability to roll the tongue is one of these functions. One of the authors of this book (MCS) can roll her tongue; RCS cannot. All three of their daughters can. Since this ability is known to be a dominant characteristic, we know that RCS is homozygous recessive. Some of our grandchildren may turn out to be like Grandpa. Our daughters are heterozygous for this characteristic. If their husbands are also heterozygous, we could predict that our grandchildren will be tongue-rollers in the ratio of 3:1.

(Incidentally, the genetic ratios hold only for large populations, not for small samples. Since we expect that the total number of our grandchildren will be six, they might all be tongue-rollers.)

The inheritance of certain defects in mental functioning can be described in terms of chromosomes [29]. Down's syndrome (Mongolism), a type of mental retardation accompanied by distinctive physical anomalies, occurs when an extra chromosome is attached to the chromosome numbered 21, making a total of 47 instead of the normal 46 chromosomes. Klinefelter's syndrome, incomplete sexual development along with lowered intelligence in males, involves two X chromosomes in addition to a Y. Turner's syndrome, in which females have only one X chromosome, includes defective spatial abilities. Males with an XXY condition are more likely than normals to be tall, aggressive, and mentally defective.

The transmission of all-or-none traits, such as tongue-rolling and Down's syndrome, can be explained by basic rules of genetics. When many genes are involved and when the characteristic is highly complex, such as intelligence or emotional stability, *heritability* is studied by *quantitative genetics*. Heritability of a characteristic can be estimated by comparing correlations between groups of known genetic similarity. Since the heredity of animals can be controlled, they can be used for experimental work in heredity. In working with humans, investigators have to use groups which vary in known degrees, from identical twins to unrelated persons. Results of many studies on inheritance of intelligence and personality indicate that there are indeed significant hereditary components in both [47].

Intelligence. Figure 5–6 shows median (average) sizes of correlations between measured intelligence of persons of different degrees of genetic similarity [13]. Unrelated persons living apart show no correlation (−.01). Identical twins reared together are very similar (.87). Identical twins reared apart are more closely correlated than those in any other relationship group (.75). Intelligence of parents and children correlates significantly (.50). Heredity components have been found in the following intellectual abilities, listed in order of weight of influence by heredity: word fluency, verbal ability (including spelling and grammar), spatial ability, clerical speed and accuracy, reasoning, number ability, and memory [47].

Personality. There is evidence for heritability of several dimensions of personality, the main ones of which are usual activity level; expression of emotions frankly in interpersonal relationships; degree of planning ahead rather than behaving impulsively [47]; extraversion–introversion [37].

Age Trends. Correlations between intelligence of children and parents are low negative in early infancy, zero at around a year, low positive at the end of the second year, and moderate (.5) in early childhood and thereafter [10]. This pattern is true of children and parents living apart, as well as of those living together. Correlations between stature of parents and children also increase throughout the early preschool years [16].

Sex Differences in Heritability. There is evidence that girls are controlled by heredity more than boys are, most likely because the X chromosome, of which girls have two and boys one, carries more hereditary material than does the Y

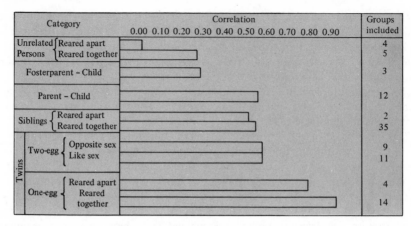

Figure 5–6. Median correlation coefficients for intelligence test scores showing degree of similarity between performances of people of varying degrees of relatedness under different and similar environmental conditions.

SOURCE: Data from L. Erlenmeyer-Kimling and L. F. Jervik. *Science*, 1964, **142**, 1477–79.

chromosome. After age 13, measurements of stature correlate more highly for father–daughter than for father–son and for mother–daughter than for mother–son [17]. Data from the Berkeley Growth Study indicated that girls' intellectual functioning is more genetically determined than boys and that the impact of the environment is greater upon boys than upon girls [3]. High school boys and girls, studied by a twin control method, showed stronger heritability for girls than for boys on a battery of tests of achievements and aptitudes [25].

Summary

A baby, like all organisms, interacts continuously with his environment. He and his parents influence each other and change each other. Child development is described from different theoretical viewpoints, offering different ways of interpreting and understanding. Six types of interaction are described briefly in this chapter.

Equilibration is a process of regulation which the organism carries on in physical and intellectual modes. Homeostasis is the maintaining of the organism within certain physical limits such as those of chemical content and temperature. Psychological equilibrium involves regulating stimulation to an optimal level and also progressing toward more complex levels of mental organization. Piaget's notion of equilibration includes two complementary processes, accommodation and assimilation. Assimilation is the taking in and using of material from the environment; accommodation is changing the schemas to adjust to reality as it is experienced. Equilibration is enjoyable, as shown by children's curiosity and exploration, looking for problems and incongruities to be solved.

Growth and development, terms which can be used interchangeably, refer to increasing size and complexity of structure and function. The following principles or generalizations hold for many kinds of growth and development: variation in rates between individuals, between sexes, within the organism and of the organism in time; individuals differ in time of reaching maturity; measures of growth are interrelated; organisms behave as though they were seeking to achieve maximum potential, searching for substitute sources of nurture when the usual ones are not available; specific patterns of behavior are differentiated out of larger, global patterns, and then specific patterns are integrated into larger, complex patterns; certain sequences of physical and motor development take place in directions (cephalo-caudal and proximo-distal) in relation to the body; certain behavior patterns mature in orderly sequences; growth is based on a foundation, the organism interacting with the environment to transform itself; critical periods are specific times when the organism will interact with the environment in specific ways which may be harmful or beneficial.

Stage theories, including Erikson's and Piaget's, explain development as proceeding epigenetically, being reorganized on more and more complex levels which occur in an orderly sequence. Erikson's psychosocial theory uses Freud's psychosexual stages as a base and develops a theory of the healthy personality. The eight stages of man's development involve the development of basic trust versus basic mistrust; autonomy versus doubt and shame; initiative versus guilt; industry versus inferiority; identity versus role diffusion; intimacy versus isolation; generativity versus self-absorption; ego integrity versus despair. Piaget shows how children develop intelligence in the process of dealing with the world and coming to know it. His sensorimotor period, spanning infancy, is subdivided into six stages. The preoperational period, from around 2 to 7, includes the stages of preconceptual and intuitive thought. The period of concrete operations comprises the school years, and the period of formal operations (logical thought), adolescence.

Learning is the change in behavior due to experience. Different methods of learning include classical conditioning, when a neutral stimulus becomes associated with a response due to pairing of the neutral stimulus with a stimulus which normally elicits the response; operant conditioning, when a response is established as a result of rewarding it, a method used widely for shaping behavior; verbal mediation, the use of words in problem solving or self-instruction; observational learning, a complex process of imitating some of the behavior of other people, according to the characteristics of the child himself, the stimulus, and the model. Reinforcement includes rewards and punishments, both of which operate in complex ways.

Maturation is the growth toward maturity of the body, its structures, and functions—growth which is relatively independent of experience. Most developmental processes involve both maturation and learning.

Evolutionary adaptation accounts for certain behavior patterns which mature quickly into a complex and relatively fixed form. The environment to which a species is adapted is the one in which it emerged in its present form. Attachment behavior in the human infant is most easily understood in terms of evolutionary adaptation.

Hereditary characteristics in human beings are sometimes the result of single pairs of genes, but often of numbers of genes working together. Most human beings carry several dangerous recessive genes, which will do no harm unless matched with the same dangerous genes from the partner in reproduction. Birth defects can be predicted on a chance basis, and some with certainty. An ovum contains an X chromosome, a sperm either an X or a Y. The source of sex differences is in the X and Y chromosomes, including differences in heritability, females being more influenced by heredity. These functions include intelligence and many of its components and also certain personality dimensions. Correlations between physical and mental measurements of parents and children increase during the preschool period.

References

1. Abernethy, E. M. Relationships between physical and mental growth. *Mono. Soc. Res. Child Devel.*, 1936, **1**:7.
2. Ainsworth, M. D. S. Object relations, dependency and attachment: A theoretical review of the infant–mother relationship. *Child Devel.*, 1969, **40**, 969–1025.
3. Bayley, N., & Schaefer, E. S. Correlations of maternal and child behaviors with the development of mental abilities: Data from the Berkeley growth study. *Mono. Soc. Res. Child Devel.*, 1964, **29**:6.
4. Bowlby, J. *Attachment and loss.* Vol. I: *Attachment.* London: Hogarth, 1969.
5. Bronfenbrenner, U. *Two worlds of childhood.* New York: Russell Sage Foundation, 1970.
6. Bühler, C. *The first year of life.* New York: Day, 1930.
7. Davis, C. M. Self-selection of diet by newly weaned infants. *Am. J. Dis. Child.*, 1928, **36**, 651–679.
8. Dennis, W. Causes of retardation among institutional children: Iran. *J. Genet. Psychol.*, 1960, **96**, 46–60.
9. Eibl-Eibesfeldt, I. Concepts of ethology and their significance in the study of human behavior. In H. W. Stevenson, E. H. Hess, & H. L. Rheingold (Eds.), *Early behavior.* New York: Wiley, 1967, pp. 127–146.
10. Eichorn, D. H. Developmental parallels in the growth of parents and their children. In *Newsletter of Division on Devel. Psychol.*, Washington, D. C.: *American Psychological Association*, Spring, 1970.
11. Erikson, E. H. *Childhood and society.* New York: Norton, 1963.
12. Erikson, E. H. *Identity, youth and crisis.* New York: Norton, 1968.
13. Erlenmeyer-Kiling, L. K., & Jarvik, L. F. Genetics and intelligence: A review. *Sci.*, 1964, **142**, 1477–1479.
14. Fantz, R. L. The origin of form perception. *Sci. Am.*, 1961, **204**, 66–72.
15. Freud, S. *The ego and the id.* New York: Norton, 1962.
16. Garn, S. M. Fat thickness and developmental status in childhood and adolescence. *J. Am. Medic. Assoc.*, 1960, **99**, 746–751.
17. Garn, S. M. Body size and its implications. In L. W. Hoffman & M. L. Hoffman (Eds.), *Review of child development research.* Vol. 2. New York: Russell Sage Foundation, 1966, pp. 529–561.
18. Gesell, A. *The embryology of behavior.* New York: Harper, 1945.
19. Gesell, A., & Thompson, H. *The psychology of early growth.* New York: Macmillan, 1938.
20. Halverson, H. M. An experimental study of prehension in infants by means of systematic cinema records. *Genet. Psychol. Mono.*, 1931, **10**, 107–286.
21. Havighurst, R. J. Minority subcultures and the law of effect. *Am. Psychol.*, 1970, **25**, 313–322.
22. Hunt, J. M., & Bayley, N. Explorations into patterns of mental development and prediction from the Bayley scales of infant development. Paper presented at the Fifth Minnesota Symposium on Child Psychology, Minneapolis, May 2, 1970.

23. Jones, M. C., & Mussen, P. H. Self-conceptions, motivations, and inter-personal attitudes of early- and late-maturing girls. *Child Devel.*, 1958, **29**, 492–501.

24. Ketcham, W. A. Relationship of physical and mental traits in intellectually gifted and mentally retarded boys. *Merrill-Palmer Quart.*, 1960, **6**, 171–177.

25. Klinger, R. Sex differences in heritability assessed by the Washington pre-college test battery of achievement/aptitude measures. Paper presented at the meeting of the Society for Research in Child Development, Santa Monica, Calif., March 27, 1969.

26. Lewis, M. The meaning of a response, or why researchers in infant behavior should be oriental metaphysicians. *Merrill-Palmer Quart.*, 1967, **13**, 7–18.

27. Lipsitt, L. P. Learning in the human infant. In H. W. Stevenson, E. H. Hess, & H. L. Rheingold (Eds.), *Early behavior.* New York: Wiley, 1967, pp. 225–247.

28. Lorenz, K. *King Solomon's ring.* New York: Crowell, 1952.

29. McClearn, G. E. Behavioral genetics: An overview. *Merrill-Palmer Quart.*, 1968, **14**, 9–24.

30. McGraw, M. B. Major challenges for students of infancy and early childhood. *Am. Psychol.*, 1970, **25**, 754–756.

31. Mussen, P. H., & Jones, M. C. The behavior-inferred motivations of late- and early-maturing boys. *Child Devel.*, 1958, **29**, 61–67.

32. Papoušek, H. Experimental studies of appetitional behavior in human new-borns and infants. In H. W. Stevenson, E. H. Hess, & H. L. Rheingold (Eds.), *Early behavior.* New York: Wiley, 1967, pp. 249–277.

33. Parke, R. D. Effectiveness of punishment as an interaction of intensity, timing, age, nurturance and cognitive structuring. *Child Devel.*, 1969, **40**, 213–235.

34. Piaget, J. *Six psychological studies.* New York: Random House, 1967.

35. Piaget, J., & Inhelder, B. *The psychology of the child.* New York: Basic Books, 1969.

36. Sackett, G. P. Effects of rearing conditions upon the behavior of rhesus monkeys (Macca Mulatta). *Child Devel.*, 1965, **36**, 855–868.

37. Scarr, S. Social introversion-extraversion as a heritable response. *Child Devel.*, 1969, **40**, 823–832.

38. Scott, J. P. Early experience and the organization of behavior. Belmont, Calif.: Brooks/Cole. 1968.

39. Shuttleworth, F. K. The physical and mental growth of girls and boys age six to nineteen in relation to age at maximum growth. *Mono. Soc. Res. Child Devel.*, 1939, **4**:3.

40. Simon, M. D. Body configuration and school readiness. *Child Devel.*, 1959, **30**, 493–512.

41. Stevenson, H. W. Learning and reinforcement effects. In T. D. Spencer & N. Kass (Eds.), *Perspectives in child psychology.* New York: McGraw-Hill, 1970, pp. 325–355.

42. Stone, C. P., & Barker, R. G. Aspects of personality and intelligence in post-menarcheal and premenarcheal girls of the same chronological age. *J. Comp. Psychol.*, 1937, **23**, 439–455.

43. Sullivan, W. If we master the gene. *New York Times*, June 14, 1970.

44. Tanner, J. M. *Education and physical growth.* London: University of London Press, 1961.

45. Tanner, J. M. Relation of body size, intelligence test scores and social circumstances. In P. Mussen, J. Langer, & M. Covington (Eds.), *Trends and issues in developmental psychology.* New York: Holt, Rinehart and Winston, 1969.
46. Thorndike, E. L. *The elements of psychology.* New York: Seiler, 1905.
47. Vandenberg, S. G. Human behavior genetics: Present status and suggestions for future research. *Merrill-Palmer Quart.*, 1969, **15**, 121–154.
48. Walter, G. Comments in J. M. Tanner & B. Inhelder (Eds.), *Discussions on child development.* Vol. I. New York: International Universities, 1953.
49. Watson, J. S., & Ramey, C. T. Reactions to response-contingent stimulation in early infancy. Unpublished paper. University of California at Berkeley, 1970.

Readings in
An Overview of Human Life and Growth

In an earlier and possibly in some ways happier time, man was considered the final and triumphant item of creation, the master and user of other living things. Even the early evolutionary biologists considered that man stood at the apex of evolution; they did not seem aware of the possibility that the process of evolution might continue, resulting in the appearance of new species. They seemed even less aware of the possibility that the evolutionary process of man resulted in a creature who had within him the seeds of his own destruction, like the sabre-toothed tiger, whose overdeveloped canine teeth prevented him from ingesting his prey.

Ecology is the branch of biology which studies the relationship of living things to their environment, including other living things. Recently ecologists have included man as the subject of their study. In general the results of their investigations have been frightening. Especially in North America man is seen as a fouler of his environment—air, water, and soil—to such an extent that ecologists say that if present trends go unchecked, man may make his continued existence impossible.

In the first article in this chapter William W. Ballard, a biologist, describes some of the facts about man's evolutionary development and speculates about the future. He makes the important distinction between man as a species and men as individuals who together make up the species. Each individual has characteristics of the species which have arisen during the course of evolution, but each individual has his own personal history, during which he has learned some ways of behaving that may be, in the long run, maladaptive for the species.

Lawrence K. Frank, the author of the second article, gave form, direction, and impetus to the field of child development. Frank's genius provided a flow of ideas for research, education, and theory. He was responsible for establishing child development centers, the parent education movement, and interdisciplinary research. In the article presented here, Frank shows his characteristic warmth and wonder while analyzing the growth processes at work in infants. He shows how the child elaborates his individuality through interaction. In the terms used by Ballard in the first article, Frank shows how the "second computer" begins, based on the beginnings of the "first computer."

Erikson and Piaget, the authors of the third and fourth selections, are also primarily concerned with the development of the "second computer." But both are explicit in their statement that their theories are based on biology. Although both are dealing with psychological material, they start from biological characteristics of man.

The epigenetic theory of Erik H. Erikson is represented by the next essay, taken from his book Identity, Youth and Crisis. An artist, teacher, and philosopher thoroughly *trained in Freudian psychoanalysis, Erikson has made enormous contributions to the field of child development. His theory is built upon Freudian theory, which he extends and develops into a way of understanding and describing the healthy personality throughout life. Erikson describes stages of personality growth, showing for each one a relation of personality to bodily development and to interaction with the culture. Each stage is derived from and built upon the one preceding it. The organization of this book is shaped by Erikson's stages in childhood and adolescence. The content is influenced by his thinking.*

Jean Piaget, the world-famous Swiss psychologist, is the author of the fourth piece in this section. Piaget is primarily a genetic epistemologist, a scientist-philosopher who investigates the production of knowledge. He has developed a comprehensive theory of the mental structures through which human beings build their concept of reality and deal with it. Piaget has stimulated psychological research all over the world. Americans have produced hundreds of studies in response to his theories and findings. Like Erikson's theory of personality development, Piaget's account of the growth of intelligence is epigenetic and interactional. Piaget's theory is very compatible with a child development point of view, because the child's mind is seen as resulting from biologically given beginnings, actively engaged with the environment.

In the concluding selection in this chapter, Myrtle McGraw admonishes students of child development, particularly students of the development of very young children, that those who study growth need to be aware of the complexity and interrelatedness of their subject matter. To those who make applications of research knowledge about children she makes a plea for the careful consideration of terms, the continuous viewing of the child as a multifaceted organism, and the importance of adult guidance which changes synchronously with the child's development.

The Rise and Fall of Humanity

William W. Ballard

The reading which follows is the last part of a lecture titled " The Rise and Fall of Humanity." In the first part Ballard summarizes the development of living things during the course of 4 billion years of earth history, the accelerating growth of knowledge in the last few thousand years, and the serious threats to man's continued existence which have stemmed from this knowledge. Basically, Ballard says, the present crisis has arisen because there are too many people on the earth and they are demanding more than the earth can provide. These things have happened because man as a species of animal is composed of men as individuals.

To maximize the amount of life that can be supported in a given ecosystem, a large number of species of plants, animals and decomposers are brought into

Reprinted from *Dartmouth Alumni Magazine*, 1970, 62 (6), 60–64. By permission of the author, the Dartmouth Alumni College, and the *Dartmouth Alumni Magazine*.

balance, each occupying its own niche and following its own instructions to make the best of the things available to it while contributing to the flow of energy and the recycling of materials. If one species in the ecosystem gets out of balance the whole community develops an instability that may either result in an irreversible change in its character, or in the control or rejection of the destabilizing element.

The human species has been manipulating its environment since the invention of agriculture, favoring the plants and animals that serve it for food, repressing or even exterminating others. Where this was overdone—e.g., Mesopotamia, the Near East, Yucatan—ghost cities and records of dead cultures remain to show how powerfully nature can strike back. Quite recently we have begun to use the treasure trove of fossil fuels to grow the food to satisfy the multiplying demands of our own population, and we congratulate ourselves on having temporarily freed ourselves from the normal restrictions of the natural world. It is a dangerous game we are playing.

No good asking why the human *species* takes these risks. A species is an invention of the mind, a generalization. Only human *individuals* actually walk and breathe and make decisions and it is the collection of individuals who have been doing what I say the species has been doing. What went wrong with human individuals, that they have gotten their species and their environment into such a mess? The other face of this question is, what is an individual supposed to be doing, and within what limits is he supposed to be held?

The Primary Computer   To simplify, I shall restrict the latter question to animals rather than plants or decomposers. I shall pick animals that are not on a rampage, animals that have (so far as we can tell) no conscious reasoning ability, no thoughts, loyalties, hopes or faiths. Some kind of earthworm or some frog will do. I assume that whatever one of these animals does, any choice that it makes, is determined by its inherited computer system. It receives from its ancestors a scanning mechanism which reports what all the circumstances around and inside it are at the moment. This information is checked against an inherited memory encoded in its central nervous system. The computer then not only orders up the strategy and tactics that had met that sort of situation successfully before, but directs what every cell, what every organ, what the whole earthworm or frog must be doing to contribute to that response. (Directions for unsuccessful responses are not encoded in this primary computer, because they simply are not inherited.)

To see what this genetic computer requires the individual worm or frog to do, let us follow his life history, watching him obey and reconstructing from what he does the nature of the commands.

1. As a member of a bisexual species he (or she) starts as a fertilized egg, a single diploid individual with unique heterozygous genic individuality. First, *he develops*. Since the fertilized egg is insulated to a degree from the outside world, his computer works at first mostly on internal information. It refers to the inherited memory in the chromosomes and brings out instructions of various intricate sorts to the ultrastructures of the cell, programmed so that the cell divides into two, then four, then eight cells . . . until the word gets back to the multiplied computers in the multiplied cells that it is time to activate their

inherited instructions for differentiation. Tissues and organs are formed, in such sorts and such patterns as have enabled the species to survive so far. The new individual acquires the sensory and neural apparatus for bringing in more and more information from the outside, and this is referred to the more and more specialized computer developing out of the inherited instructions, in a central nervous system (in the case of a frog, a brain and spinal cord). He begins to move about, respire, feed, excrete, defend himself, in directions and at rates calculated to be appropriate to the sensed state of affairs from moment to moment. This is quite a trick for a self-built computer to bring off, and as an embryologist I wish I understood more of how it is done.

2. The young earthworm or pollywog, having broken loose from its protective envelopes and used up its dowry of yolk, is next under orders to *reach adulthood*. He recognizes dangers and opportunities by continually referring the information flowing in from his sensory apparatus to his inherited memory. He certainly has not learned his behavioral responses from his parents, never having met them. It is the inherited computer which tells him what to do from one millisecond to the next. He survives or not, partly by luck but also partly according to whether his own inherited variant of the species-specific computer will deliver the right answers to the problems of his own day and place. (The *species* survives by offering up enough varieties so that some individuals will have what the new situations demand, the wastage of the other individuals being a necessary part of the cost. No other way has yet been discovered for meeting the demands of an unpredictable future, i.e. winning a game the rules for which have not yet been written.)

3. Our earthworm or frog, if lucky, finds himself a sexually mature individual, with his instructions to reproduce now turned on. These instructions, activated by seasonal or other environmental signals, operate upon particular genes, particular cells, particular organs, and particular behavioral mechanisms set off through the nervous system. Without knowing it, much less knowing why, the animal seeks out a mate, copulates, and shares in the production of fertilized eggs that bring us again to phase 1 of the cycle.

4. Having blindly and without thought followed his instructions to (1) develop, (2) make do, survive, gain strength, and (3) reproduce, our earthworm or frog subsequently (4) *dies*. It is the ancient law. So far as the interests of the individual are concerned, it is absurd.

But now how about man? How unique is he? Does he not learn by experience and education, manage his own life, consciously determine what jobs he shall tackle, what ends he shall serve? My argument that he too is run by an inherited computer program rests partly on the observed fact that (1) he develops, (2) he makes every effort to reach maturity, (3) if lucky enough he sets the cycle going again, and (4) he dies. There is nothing unique about that. Experience, learning, individual preferences serve only for minor embellishments.

I select one case to illustrate that an animal's program is mostly inherited. Four to six weeks after fertilization (depending on temperature) a salamander embryo will have used up its yolk and must by then have acquired an elaborate repertoire of locomotor, hunting-sensory, food-grabbing and swallowing behavior to keep itself fed and growing. Does the individual learn this behavior by trial and error? No. Starting a day before any of his muscles were mature enough to contract, you can rear him in a dilute anesthetic solution until he has reached the feeding stage. Put him back into pond water, and in twenty minutes the anesthetic will have worn off and he is swimming, hunting, grabbing and swallowing like a normal tadpole. One is seeing here the computer-controlled maturation of a computer-controlled behavior. No practice, no learning. The individual within which this remarkable apparatus matures is an expendable pawn, and the apparatus is not for his enjoyment of life, it is to keep the species going.

The Secondary Computer   There is such an inherited program in the human individual, but there is much more. The baby does not so much learn to walk as to develop the inherited capacity to walk; but then he can learn a dance that no man has ever danced before, he can paint a picture with a brush clasped between his toes. During late fetal life and his first six or eight years he gradually matures a second computer system superimposed on, controlling and almost completely masking the ancient frog-type computer. The evolutionary history of this new device is traceable back to, and in some respects beyond, the time of origin of the modern mammals 70 million or more years ago. It has progressed farthest in particular mammalian orders—the carnivores, hoofed animals, bats, whales and primates, and least in the egg-laying mammals and marsupials.

The new trend has worked certain real advantages, and has been kept under reasonable control, in the higher mammals, but it is my strong suspicion that its over-development in man is the root of our trouble. Like the dinosaurs, we contain in our own structure the reason why we will have to go. Robinson Jeffers[1] said it: "We have minds like the fangs of those forgotten tigers, hypertrophied and terrible."

Up to a point, the development of brain and spinal cord follows the same course in frog and man. Sense organs, cranial and spinal nerves, principal subdivisions of the brain, basic fiber tract systems, all form in strictly comparable fashion in both. But the adult human brain is a far different thing from the adult frog brain. It continues the multiplication and interconnection of neurons during a far longer growth period, and adds to the elementary or frog-type apparatus two principal complicating tissues that far overshadow the earlier developments. One is often called reticular substance, the other is the cerebral cortex.

The reticular substance is so called because it is an interweaving of small centers of gray substance with short bundles and interspersed mats of axons (the white substance), quite different from the simple contrast between gray and white substance seen in primitive animals and in early embryos. The frog brain is not without this sort of tissue, but in the brains of advanced vertebrates like the teleost fishes, the reptiles and the birds, it becomes indescribably complex. The modern mammals push this development to still higher orders of magnitude.

Although neurological science is not yet ready with answers to most specific questions about what happens where in the central nervous system, the

[1] R. Jeffers, "Passenger Pigeons," in *The Beginning and the End.*

new techniques of exploration within the brain suggest that in and through the reticular substance the connections for integrating sensory information with the devices for evaluation and for making decisions and coordinated responses are multiplied exponentially.

Thus, an electrode planted within a single neuron in the reticular substance of the hindbrain can give startling evidence that this one cell is receiving and reacting to sensations reported from widely scattered parts of the body, and sending out coded pulses as a calculated response. Your own brain contains hundreds of millions, probably billions of such cells, every one individually a computer.

The neurologists can now stimulate chosen localized areas through implanted electrodes, either hooked up to wires dangling from the cage ceiling or activated through miniaturized transmitters healed in under the scalp and controlled by radio transmission. In such experiments, stimuli delivered to many parts of the reticular substance cause the animal to react as though he were flooded with agreeable sensation. If the cat or rat or monkey learns how to deliver the stimulus to himself by pressing a pedal, he will do so repeatedly and rapidly, until he falls asleep exhausted. As soon as he wakes up, he goes to pounding the pedal again.

There are other reticular areas which have the reverse effect. If the stimulus comes at rhythmical intervals and the animal discovers that he can forestall it by pressing the pedal, he quickly learns to regulate his life so as to be there and step on it just in time. What kind of sensation such a stimulus produces in him can only be guessed by the experimenter. One might suppose that these areas of reticular substance which have such opposite effects are there to add into the computer's analysis of the situation at the moment a go signal or a stop signal for particular alternative choices, or a sense of goodness or badness, satisfaction or distress, urgency or caution, danger or relaxation. A value judgment, in other words.

It is not difficult to see the survival value of such a device. No doubt the basic mechanism exists in the brains of fishes and frogs, though I am not aware that experiments have been done to locate it. In the reticular substance of mammals, however, we see it hugely developed. The result of overdoing this might produce an awareness of the good and bad features of so very many facets of a situation as to delay and perplex the individual in calculating his single coordinated response.

Mammals are also conspicuously good at remembering experiences from their own lives as individuals, and these memories are loaded with value judgments. There is still no clear answer as to where or in what coded form these new personal memories are stored. But an animal with all this added to the ancestral memory, enhanced with perhaps casually acquired and unwisely generalized connotations of goodness and badness, might predictably be endowed with excessive individuality, prone to unnecessarily variable behavior, chosen more often for self-satisfaction than in the interest of species survival.

The other evolutionary development, the formation of the cerebral cortex, is almost unknown in vertebrates other than mammals, and is feeble in some of these. Cerebral cortex is a tissue of awesome complexity, and our techniques for analyzing what happens in it are still highly inadequate. Stimulation of willing human subjects, in chosen spots exposed surgically, or radio stimulation of these areas through permanently installed electrodes operated by healed-in transistor devices, evoke feelings referred to a particular part of the body, or cause normal-appearing localized movements, e.g. the flexion of an arm or a finger, time and again, upon repetition of the signal. Other areas produce more generalized sensory or motor or emotional or physiologic effects. The patient, his brain exposed under local anesthesia, does not know when the stimulus is applied. When the electrode touches a particular spot of his cortex he may report that he is suddenly remembering a scene identifiable as to time and place, but the memory blacks out when the current is off. Stimulation of other areas may elicit emotions of sexual attraction or anxiety or rage graded according to the intensity of the signal.

More wide-ranging experiments with cats, monkeys or barnyard stock, singly or in groups, free to move in large caged areas, show the possibility of turning on and off a great range of complex emotions, behavior, and even person-ality traits, by local stimulation.[2] The effect produced through a permanently planted electrode is area specific. Though not predictable before the first stimulus is given, the response is repeated with each stimulus, many times a day or over periods of months or years.

In subjective comparison of mammals with greater or less personal individuality one gets the impression that the degrees of freedom of choice, of imaginative recognition of possible ways to react to situations, of storage capacity and retentiveness of memory, and the richness of association, are correlated with the intricacy and amount of the cerebral cortex and reticular substance. Animals highest on both scales include porpoises, elephants, cats and dogs, apes, and people.

One cannot underestimate the effects on the human species of other evolutionary trends that came to a climax in us, for instance the development of upright posture that frees the hands, the reshaping of the fingers for grasping and manipulating, the perfection of binocular vision that can bring into focus either the hands or the far distance at will. Far more significant than these was the development of speech, made possible by and controlled in a particular small area of the new cerebral cortex. This expanded the powers of the human secondary computer by orders of magnitude, even in comparison with that of close relatives like apes.

We no longer communicate with each other by baring teeth, raising hackles and flaunting rumps, but in symbolic language. We can make abstractions and generalizations and artificial associations. Through speech we can feed into the recording apparatus of each other's secondary computers not only the vast and rather accidental store of individually acquired and long-lasting memories of our own experience, but also the loads of approval or disapproval which we deliberately or unwittingly put upon them. We increasingly remove ourselves into created worlds of our own, calculating our choices by reference to a memory bank of second-hand ghosts of other people's experiences and feelings, prettied up or uglified with value judgments picked up who knows where, by whom, for what reason.

[2] J. M. R. Delgado, 1969, *Physical Control of the Mind.*

Language gave a fourth dimension to the powers of the secondary computer, and writing a fifth dimension. We can now convince each other that things are good or bad, acceptable or intolerable, merely by agreeing with each other, or by reciting catechisms. With writing we can color the judgments of people unborn, just as our judgments are tailored to the whim of influential teachers in the past.

Symbols have given us the means to attach a value judgment to some abstract noun, some shibboleth, and transfer this by association to any person or situation at will. We invent, we practice, we delight in tricks for saying things indirectly by poetry and figures of speech, that might sound false or trite or slanderous or nonsensical if we said them directly. A more normally constructed animal, a porpoise or an elephant, mercifully spared such subtleties, might well look at human beings and see that each one of us has become to some degree insane, out of touch with the actual world, pursuing a mad course of options in the imagined interest of self rather than of species.

The primary computer is still there, programmed in the interest of species survival. With his new powers, man should do better than any other animal at understanding the present crisis and generating an appropriate strategy and tactics. Instead, the effort is drowned out in the noise, the flicker-bicker, the chattering flood of directives from the personalized secondary computer. In pursuit of his own comfort and his own pleasure, man wars against his fellows and against the good earth.

The frame of each person is like a racing shell with two oarsmen in it, back to back, rowing in opposite directions. The one represents the ancient computer system, comparing the personal situation of the moment with an inherited value system and driving the person to perform in such a way that the species will survive, irrespective of how absurd his own expendable life may be. The other represents the secondary computer system, probably located in reticular substance and cerebral cortex, surveying chiefly the memories of childhood and adult life, and deciding how to act according to the value-loaded store of personal experience.

It is this runaway evolutionary development of our superimposed second computer that has produced our inventors, our artists, our saints and heroes, our poets, our thinkers. Our love and hate, ecstasy and despair. The infinite variety of human personalities. It has also atomized the species into a cloud of ungovernable individuals. We split our elections 48 to 52, make laws to break them, and either ignore community priorities or establish them by political blind-man's-buff in frivolous disregard of real emergencies. Six experts will come violently to six different decisions on how to meet a crisis because their personal histories lead them to weight the same data differently. Each of us can see bad logic and conflicts of interest affecting the judgment of most of our associates; it is more difficult to detect them in ourselves. Our individually acquired prejudices have been built into our secondary computers.

Yet it is a glorious thing to feel the uniqueness, the power of decision, the freedom of being human. Who would prefer to be even so wonderful a creature as a dog, an elephant, a horse, a porpoise? I believe nevertheless that just this ungovernable power of the human individual, the essence of our humanity, is the root of our trouble.

The California biologist Garrett Hardin, in a famous essay called "The Tragedy of the Commons," showed that this accounts for practically all the facets of our apocalyptic crisis, from the population explosion to runaway technology.[3] He is referring to the community pasture where anyone may feed his animals. Overgrazing will bring erosion and irreversible deterioration in it. Each herdsman, calculating the advantage and disadvantage to himself of putting out one more animal to graze, balancing his small share of the possible damage against his sole ownership of the extra income, adds another animal in his own interest, and another, and another. All do, and all lose together. The tragedy is the inescapable disaster when each herdsman pursues his own advantage without limit, in a limited commons. This is the tragedy that leaves us with too many human mouths to feed, soil impoverished and washed or blown away, forests skinned off, lakes ruined, plastic bottles and aluminum cans scattered over the countryside, rivers clogged with dead fish, bilge oil spreading on public waters, streets and highways made obscene with advertisements. It is what gives us choking smog, the stink and corruption below paper mills and slaughter houses, the draining of one well by another in a falling water table, the sneaking of radioactive wastes into the air and the oceans.

All these, Hardin makes clear, are problems with *no technological solution.* To be sure, the technology stands ready, but the trouble starts with some individual, you, me, whose response to a situation is to give highest priority to his personal chance of profit, or his family's, or his country's. He has a vivid sense of the value to himself of his own freedom, but the total effects of all such freedoms on the species and on the natural world which supports it is invisible or far out of focus. The technology might just as well not exist.

Some of these problems that will not be solved by technology alone can indeed be brought under control by compacts, treaties, and other agreements between willing groups, or by laws imposed by the majority upon a minority in the common interest. Hardin, however, puts the finger on the population problem as the worst example of the worst class of problems, in which all of us must restrict the freedom of all of us, when none of us want to. He is properly skeptical of conscience or altruism as forces for uniting the community when nearly all of us are still daring to gamble on the continued capacity of the commons to withstand collapse. What is needed, he says, is a fundamental extension of morality.

My way of agreeing with him is to say that human nature is our chief enemy because the species-preserving function of our primary computer has not yet been built into the secondary computer which generates our human nature. It is by now clear that our nature as individuals is not so much inherited as learned by babies as they grow into people, in and from their individual, accidental and culture-bound experiences. We need to incorporate into the decision-making apparatus that will really control them a new survival morality, a system of values the principal axiom of which is that anything which threatens the welfare of the species is bad, anything that serves to bring the species into harmony with its environment is good. We must, each of us, because of this inner drive, regulate our numbers and our selfish wants as rigorously as the

[3] G. Hardin, 1968, *Science* 162: 1243. The Tragedy of the Commons.

forces of natural selection would have done had we not learned how to set them aside.

Do we know how to create a human nature that can keep the species going without undue sacrifice of the privilege and joy of being human? How much freedom must we give up? Do we want to? Is there time?

Basic Processes in Organisms

Lawrence K. Frank

If we are to understand the infant as a persistent, but ever changing, organism, we need to think in terms that are dynamic, which calls for a recognition of the ongoing processes by which the infant grows, develops, matures and ages while continually functioning and behaving. As a young mammalian organism, the human infant lives by much the same basic physiological processes as other mammals.

The recognition of process has come with the acceptance of such recently formulated conceptions as that of self-organization, self-stabilization, self-repair and self-direction which are characteristic not only of organisms but of various man-made machines such as computers and systems designed to operate a planned sequence of activities with the use of positive and negative feedbacks. (Wiener 1961; Von Foerster and Zopf 1962). The organism may be said to be "programmed" by its heredity but capable of flexible functioning through the life cycle.

Moreover, it must be re-emphasized that each infant differs to a greater or lesser extent from all other infants, exhibiting not only individual variation but also displaying a considerable range of intra-individual variability, or continually changing functioning and physiological states, especially during the early months of life when the infant is not yet fully organized or capable of adequate self-stabilization.

Since most of our knowledge of infancy and childhood is derived from observations and measurements of selected variables, responses to stimuli, at a given time or a succession of times, we do not gain an adequate conception of the continuous, dynamic processes of living organisms, especially since we tend to focus upon the outcomes, without recognizing the processes which produce them. Accordingly, some account of these basic processes and how they operate may provide a conceptual model for understanding the multidimensional development of infants during the first year of life. Whatever is done to and for the infant, what privations, frustrations and deprivations he may suffer, what demands and coercions he must accept, what spontaneous activity and learning he displays, may be viewed as expressions of his basic functioning processes.

Every experience in the life of an infant evokes some alteration in these organic processes whereby he manages not only to survive but to grow and develop, to learn while carrying on his incessant intercourse with the surrounding world. Thus, by focusing on the organic processes we may discover what is taking place when we speak of adjustment, learning, adaptation, and the transitions encountered at critical stages in his development.

The concept of mechanism indicates or implies a deterministic relationship between antecedent and consequent, usually as a *linear* relationship in which the consequent is proportional to the antecedent. The concept of *process* involves a dynamic, *non-linear* operation, whereby the same process, depending upon where, when, how, and in what quantities or intensities it operates, may produce different products which may be all out of proportion to that which initiates or touches off the process. For example the process of fertilization and gestation operates in all mammals to produce the immense variety of mammalian young. But different processes may produce similar or equivalent products, an operation which has been called "equifinality" by Bertalanffy (1950).

A brief discussion of the six basic processes operating in organisms will indicate how the infant organism is able to persist and survive by continually changing and is thereby able to cope with the particular version of infant care and rearing to which he is subjected.

These six processes are: The Growth Process, The Organizing Process, The Communicating Process, The Stabilizing Process, The Directive or Purposive Process and The Creative Process. (Frank 1963.)

The Growth Process   The infant who has been growing since conception continues, with a brief interruption and often some loss of weight, to grow incrementally, adding gradually to his size and weight. His growth may be slowed down by inadequate or inappropriate feeding, by some difficulties in digesting and assimilating whatever foodstuff he be given, or by a variety of disturbances and dysfunctions. A continuing upward trend in weight is expected as an expression of normal development, although recent cautions have been expressed on the undesirability of too rapid increase in weight and the vulnerability of a fat, waterlogged infant.

This incremental growth in size and weight indicates that the infant is maintaining an excess of growth over the daily losses through elimination of urine and feces, through skin and lungs, and also in the replacement of many cells that are discarded. Thus, millions of blood corpuscles are destroyed and replaced each day, the iron of those destroyed being salvaged and reused. Likewise, cells of the skin and lining of the gastrointestinal tract, of the lungs, kidneys, liver, indeed of almost all organ systems, except the central nervous system and brain, are continually being replaced at different rates.

Probably more vitally significant but less clearly recognized is the continual replacement of the chemical constituents of cells, tissues and bony structures, like the skeleton and the teeth in which different chemicals are discarded and new materials are selected out of the blood stream to replace them. Here we see a dramatic illustration of the statement that an organism is a configuration which must continually change in order to survive, a conception which is wholly congruous with the recently formulated assumption of the world as an aggregate of highly organized complexes of energy transformations.

Growth, incremental and replacement, is a major functioning process, gradually producing an enlarging infant as the growing cells differentiate, specialize and organize to give rise to the varied tissues and organ systems in the developing embryo and fetus. In this prenatal development the creative process is also operating to produce the unique, unduplicated human infant along with the operation of the organizing process.

The Organizing Process   Only recently has the process of self-organization been recognized in scientific thinking as basic to all organisms which start with some kind of genetic inheritance and undergo multiplication and duplication of cells with differentiation and specialization of components that become organized into a living organism. (Von Foerster and Zopf 1962.) Thus the initial development of an infant takes place through the operation of the growth and the organizing processes which continue to operate throughout its life, maintaining the organism as it undergoes various transitions and transformations and copes with the many discontinuities encountered in its life cycle.

Since the normal infant arrives fully equipped with all the essential bodily components and organ systems, the growth process and the organizing process operate to incorporate the intakes of food, water and air into its ever changing structure-functioning. Most of the highly organized foodstuffs, proteins, fats and carbohydrates, are progressively broken down, disorganized and randomized, and the products of these digestive operations are then circulated through the blood stream from which the constituent cells, tissues and fluids select out what they need for metabolism and organize these into their specialized structure-functioning components. The recent dramatic findings in molecular biology show how this organizing process operates within the cell as the DNA (the carrier of the genetic information) of the genes directs the production of the various proteins and the utilization of the minerals and vitamins for the growth and multiplication of cells and the maintenance of their functioning.

Also of large significance for the understanding of organic processes are the sequential steps in the utilization of food stuffs for metabolism involving many steps and numerous specialized enzymes and catalysts. Unfortunately some infants suffer from so-called metabolic errors when one or more of these steps in the metabolic sequence is missing or inadequate and therefore his growth and development and healthy functioning are jeopardized.

In the self-organizing organism we encounter circular and reciprocal operations in which every component of the organism by its specialized functioning, gives rise to, and maintains, the total organism of which it is a participant; concurrently, the total organism reciprocally governs when, what and how each of these components must function and operate to maintain the organized whole. This capacity for self-organizing arises from the autonomy of each component of an organism which over millions of years of evolution has developed its own highly individualized and specialized functioning within the total organic complex but functions according to the requirements of the organism in which it operates.

Communication Process   Obviously, these autonomous components which give rise to growth and organization must continually communicate, internally and with the external "surround." The infant has an inherited communication network in his nervous system, his circulatory system, and his lymphatic system. Through these several channels every constituent of an organism continually communicates with all others, directly or indirectly, and with different degrees of speed in communication. Each component continually sends and receives messages whereby its functioning operations are regulated, synchronized, articulated and related to all others, with greater or less immediacy. The infant is born with most of these internal communications already functioning, having been in operation for varying periods of its prenatal development but with the central nervous system still immature. The infant also has the sensory apparatus for various inputs, of light, of sound, touch, taste and smell, also for pain, heat and cold, and for gravity and for atmospheric pressure changes. But the infant is also initially prepared for dealing with the varying intensities and durations of these intakes and impacts, gradually increasing his capacity for filtering, buffering, mingling and transducing these inputs whereby he may monitor these sensory communications according to his ever changing internal, physiological states and the kinesthetic and proprioceptive messages by which he continually orients himself and gradually achieves an equilibrium in space.

The infant must carry on this incessant intercourse with the world more or less protected by adults from too severe or hazardous impacts and provided with the food and care required by his helpless dependency. But the infant often must try to defend himself from what his caretakers try to impose on him or compel him to accept, as in feeding, toilet training, etc. Under this treatment much of the infant's energies may be expended in these efforts to maintain his stability and integrity against unwelcomed and uncongenial treatment which may interfere with his normal functioning and compromise his growth and development and learning as a unique organism. Thus we may say that the growth and organizing processes contribute to and are dependent upon the communication process, which operates through the inherited receptors of the infant which may become progressively altered, refined, and increasingly sensitized through learning. Quite early the infant may become receptive to nonverbal communications such as tones of voice, smiling, tactile comforting, or painful treatment.

Stabilizing Process   Since the world presents so many different and continually varying messages and impacts, organisms must be able to cope with the ever changing flux of experience and maintain their integrity and functional capacities by monitoring all their organic functions. While all other organisms have evolved with their species-specific range of sensory awareness and capacity for perception and for living in their ancestral life zones, the human infant, and a few other mammals are able to live in a wide variety of climates and habitations and maintain their internal world within fairly close limitations upon intraorganic variability. This becomes possible through the operation of the stabilizing process.

The stabilizing process operates through a network of physiological feedbacks, both negative and positive, to maintain a dynamic equilibrium and is not limited to the concept of homeostasis which Cannon used to describe the maintenance of the fluid internal environment. The stabilizing process maintains continually changing physiological states. At birth it is not fully developed or operationally effective and hence the infant needs continual care, protection, and appropriate nutrition. But as he grows and develops he increasingly regulates his internal functioning by responding appropriately to the various inputs and outputs, intakes, and outlets. Obviously an infant who must grow, both incrementally and by replacement, cannot tolerate too stable an internal environment which might prevent or limit such growth and adaptive functioning. With his increasing exposure to the world the infant learns to calibrate all his sensory inputs and increasingly to "equalize his thresholds," as Kurt Goldstein (1939) has pointed out.

Not the least significant and often stressful experience under which an infant must maintain his internal stability are the varying practices of child care and feeding, the efforts of parents to regularize his functioning and compel him to conform to whatever regimen of living they wish to establish. Clearly the stabilizing process is essential to the infant's survival and to his continuing growth and development and the variety of learning which he must master. Happily, most infants achieve a progressive enlargement of their capacity for living and for self-regulation and self-stabilization to assume an autonomy expressing their integrity in the face of often uncongenial treatment and surroundings.

The Directive or Purposive Process   With the achievement of motor coordination and locomotion, by creeping and crawling, and then assuming an erect posture and learning to walk, the infant enlarges the purposive or goal seeking process which involves continual scanning, probing and exploring the world and developing his selective awareness and patterned perception, and especially the ability to ignore or to reject what may interfere or distract him in his endeavor to attain remote or deferred goals. Obviously, the purposive process cannot operate effectively until the infant has achieved a considerable degree of internal stabilization and of neuro-muscular coordination, and the ability to cope with a three dimensional, spatial world.

Since the child initially is attracted or impelled by whatever he may become aware of or has an impulse to seek, to handle, to put into his mouth, or otherwise to manipulate, the purposive process is frequently blocked and the child may be severely punished in his attempts to develop his autonomous mastery of his small world. Thus the purposive process operates differentially in each infant who is likely to be attracted by and responsive to different dimensions of his environment at different times; these early explorations provide an endless sequence of learning experiences which involve, not only the actual world of nature, but the wide range of artifacts and of highly individuated personalities with whom he is in contact. With language the infant learns to deal with people and verbal symbols of language for goal seeking.

The Creative Process   As noted earlier, the creative process begins to operate early in gestation to produce a unique infant as a human organism with the same basic organic functions and similar or equivalent components which, however, are different in each infant. From birth on, therefore, each infant is engaged in creating a highly selective environment or a "life space" that is as congenial and appropriate for his individualized organism, with its peculiar needs and capacities, as is possible under the constraints and coercions imposed by others upon his growth, development, functioning, and learning. In infancy and childhood the individual is more creative than in any other period in his life cycle, but this creativity may be either ignored or discouraged by those who are intent upon making the child conform as nearly as possible to their image or ideal of attainment.

Within recent years the purposive and creative processes have become major foci in the studies of early child growth, development and education, but it must be remembered that the purposive and creative processes cannot operate independently because they are inextricably related to and dependent upon the other four basic processes which reciprocally contribute to the operation of these two processes.

Most of the training and education of the infant and young child involves curbing, regulating, focusing, and patterning, and also evoking the communicating and stabilizing and directive processes which are more amenable to intervention and control by others. Through supervision and regulation of these processes the child is largely molded, patterned, and oriented into the kind of organism-personality favored by his parents and appropriately prepared for living in his cultural and social order. As he grows older the infant is expected to learn the required conduct for group living and to master the various symbol systems by which he can relate cognitively to the world and negotiate with other people. It appears that learning as an expression of the purposive and the creative processes may be compromised and sometimes severely distorted or blocked when the child is expected or compelled to alter the organizing, communicating, and stabilizing processes, as required by his parents and other more experienced persons.

In the discussion of humanization we will see how the young mammalian organism is transformed into a personality for living in a symbolic cultural world and for participating in a social order, through the various practices of infant care and rearing that are focused upon, and directly intervene in, the operation of these six basic organic processes. But each infant is a highly individualized organism who develops his own idiosyncratic personality through the development and utilization of his basic organic processes.

Bibliography

BERTALANFFY, L. VON, "Theory of Open Systems in Physics and Biology," *Science*, CXI, 1950, pp. 27–29. See also Yearbooks of Society for General Systems Research.

FRANK, L. K., "Human Development—An Emerging Discipline," in *Modern Perspectives in Child Development*, In honor of Milton J. E. Senn, Eds. Albert J. Solnit and Sally Provence, New York: International Universities Press, 1963.

———. "Potentiality: Its Definition and Development," in *Insights and the Curriculum*, Yearbook, Association for Supervision and Curriculum Development, Washington, D.C.: National Education Association, 1963.

GOLDSTEIN, KURT, *The Organism*, New York: American Book Company, 1939.

VON FOERSTER, HEINZ, and ZOPF, JR., GEORGE W., Eds., *Principles of Self Organizing Systems*, London: Pergamon Press, 1962.

WIENER, NORBERT, *Cybernetics*, Cambridge and New York: M.I.T. Press and John Wiley and Sons, Inc., 1961.

The Life Cycle: Epigenesis of Identity

Erik H. Erikson
HARVARD UNIVERSITY

Whenever we try to understand growth, it is well to remember the *epigenetic principle* which is derived from the growth of organisms *in utero*. Somewhat generalized, this principle states that anything that grows has a ground plan, and that out of this ground plan the parts arise, each part having its time of special ascendancy, until all parts have arisen to form a functioning whole. This, obviously, is true for fetal development where each part of the organism has its critical time of ascendance or danger of defect. At birth the baby leaves the chemical exchange of the womb for the social exchange system of his society, where his gradually increasing capacities meet the opportunities and limitations of his culture. How the maturing organism continues to unfold, not by developing new organs but by means of a prescribed sequence of locomotor, sensory, and social capacities, is described in the child-development literature. As pointed out, psychoanalysis has given us an understanding of the more idiosyncratic experiences, and especially the inner conflicts, which constitute the manner in which an individual becomes a distinct personality. But here, too, it is important to realize that in the sequence of his most personal experiences the healthy child, given a reasonable amount of proper guidance, can be trusted to obey inner laws of development, laws which create a succession of potentialities for significant interaction with those persons who tend and respond to him and those institutions which are ready for him. While such interaction varies from culture to culture, it must remain within "the proper rate and the proper sequence" which governs all epigenesis. Personality, therefore, can be said to develop according to steps predetermined in the human organism's readiness to be driven toward, to be aware of, and to interact with a widening radius of significant individuals and institutions.

It is for this reason that, in the presentation of stages in the development of the personality, we employ an epigenetic diagram analogous to the one employed in *Childhood and Society* for an analysis of Freud's psychosexual stages.[1] It is, in fact, an implicit purpose of this presentation to bridge the theory of infantile sexuality (without repeating it here in detail) and our knowledge of the child's physical and social growth.

In Diagram 1 the double-lined squares signify both a sequence of stages and a gradual development of component parts. In other words, the diagram formalizes a progression through time of a differentiation of parts. This indicates (1) that each item of the vital personality to be discussed is systematically related to all others, and that they all depend on the proper development in the proper sequence of each item; and (2) that each item exists in some form before "its" decisive and critical time normally arrives.

[1] See Erik H. Erikson, *Childhood and Society*, 2nd ed., New York: W. W. Norton, 1963, Part I.

DIAGRAM 1

	1	2	3	4	5	6	7	8
VIII								INTEGRITY vs. DESPAIR
VII							GENERATIVITY vs. STAGNATION	
VI						INTIMACY vs. ISOLATION		
V	Temporal Perspective vs. Time Confusion	Self-Certainty vs. Self-Consciousness	Role Experimentation vs. Role Fixation	Apprenticeship vs. Work Paralysis	IDENTITY vs. IDENTITY CONFUSION	Sexual Polarization vs. Bisexual Confusion	Leader- and Followership vs. Authority Confusion	Ideological Commitment vs. Confusion of Values
IV				INDUSTRY vs. INFERIORITY	Task Identification vs. Sense of Futility			
III			INITIATIVE vs. GUILT		Anticipation of Roles vs. Role Inhibition			
II		AUTONOMY vs. SHAME, DOUBT			Will to Be Oneself vs. Self-Doubt			
I	TRUST vs. MISTRUST				Mutual Recognition vs. Autistic Isolation			

If I say, for example, that a sense of basic trust is the first component of mental vitality to develop in life, a sense of autonomous will the second, and a sense of initiative the third, the diagram expresses a number of fundamental relations that exist among the three components, as well as a few fundamental facts for each.

Each comes to its ascendance, meets its crisis, and finds its lasting solution in ways to be described here, toward the end of the stages mentioned. All of them exist in the beginning in some form, although we do not make a point of this fact, and we shall not confuse things by calling these components different names at earlier or later stages. A baby may show something like "autonomy" from the beginning, for example, in the particular way in which he angrily tries to wriggle his hand free when tightly held. However, under normal conditions, it is not until the second year that he begins to experience the whole critical alternative between being an autonomous creature and being a dependent one, and it is not until then that he is ready for a specifically new encounter with his environment. The environment, in turn, now feels called upon to convey to him its particular ideas and concepts of autonomy in ways decisively contributing to his personal character, his relative efficiency, and the strength of his vitality.

It is this encounter, together with the resulting crisis, which is to be described for each stage. Each stage becomes a crisis because incipient growth and awareness in a new part function go together with a shift in instinctual energy and yet also cause a specific vulnerability in that part. One of the most difficult questions to decide, therefore, is whether or not a child at a given stage is weak or strong. Perhaps it would be best to say that he is always vulnerable in some respects and completely oblivious and insensitive in others, but that at the same time he is unbelievably persistent in the same respects in which he is vulnerable. It must be added that the baby's weakness gives him power; out of his very dependence and weakness he makes signs to which his environment, if it is guided well by a responsiveness combining "instinctive" and traditional patterns, is peculiarly sensitive. A baby's presence exerts a consistent and persistent domination over the outer and inner lives of every member of a household. Because these members must reorient themselves to accommodate his presence, they must also grow as individuals and as a group. It is as true to say that babies control and bring up their families as it is to say the converse. A family can bring up a baby only by being brought up by him. His growth consists of a series of challenges to them to serve his newly developing potentialities for social interaction.

Each successive step, then, is a potential crisis because of a radical change in perspective. Crisis is used here in a developmental sense to connote not a threat of catastrophe, but a turning point, a crucial period of increased vulnerability and heightened potential, and therefore, the ontogenetic source of generational strength and maladjustment. The most radical change of all, from intrauterine to extrauterine life, comes at the very beginning of life. But in postnatal existence, too, such radical adjustments of perspective as lying relaxed, sitting firmly, and running fast must all be accomplished in their own good time. With them, the interpersonal perspective also changes rapidly and often radically, as is testified by the proximity in time of such opposites as "not letting mother out of sight" and "wanting to be independent." Thus, different capacities use different opportunities to become full-grown components of the ever-new configuration that is the growing personality.

Equilibrium

Jean Piaget
UNIVERSITY OF GENEVA

The psychological development that starts at birth and terminates in adulthood is comparable to organic growth. Like the latter, it consists essentially of activity directed toward equilibrium. Just as the body evolves toward a relatively stable level characterized by the completion of the growth process and by organ maturity, so mental life can be conceived as evolving toward a final form of equilibrium represented by the adult mind. In a sense, development is a progressive equilibration from a lesser to a higher state of equilibrium. From the point of view of intelligence, it is easy to contrast the relative instability and incoherence of childhood ideas with the systematization of adult reason. With respect to the affective life, it has frequently been noted how extensively emotional equilibrium increases with age. Social relations also obey the same law of gradual stabilization.

An essential difference between the life of the body and that of the mind must nonetheless be stressed if the dynamism inherent in the reality of the mind is to be respected. The final form of equilibrium reached through organic growth is more static and, above all, more unstable than the equilibrium toward which mental development strives, so that no sooner has ascending evolution terminated than a regressive evolution automatically starts, leading to old age. Certain psychological functions that depend closely on the physical condition of the body follow an analogous curve. Visual acuity, for example, is at a maximum toward the end of childhood, only to diminish subsequently; and many other perceptual processes are regulated by the same law. By contrast, the higher functions of intelligence and affectivity tend toward a "mobile equilibrium." The more mobile it is, the more stable it is, so that the termination of growth, in healthy minds, by no means marks the beginning of decline but rather permits progress that in no sense contradicts inner equilibrium.

It is thus in terms of equilibrium that we shall try to describe the evolution of the child and the adolescent. From this point of view, mental development is a continuous construction comparable to the erection of a vast building that becomes more solid with each addition. Alternatively, and perhaps more appropriately, it may be likened to the assembly of a subtle mechanism that goes through gradual phases of adjustment in which the individual pieces become more supple and mobile as the equilibrium of the mechanism as a whole becomes more stable. We must, however, introduce an important distinction between two complementary aspects of the process of equilibration. This is the distinction between the variable structures that define the successive states of equilibrium and a certain constant functioning that assures the transition from any one state to the following one.

There is sometimes a striking similarity between the reactions of the child and the adult, as, for example, when the child is sure of what he wants and acts as adults do with respect to their own special interests. At other times there is a world of difference—in games, for example, or in the manner of reasoning. From a functional point of view, i.e., if we take into consideration the general motives of behavior and thought, there are constant functions common to all ages. At all levels of development, action presupposes a precipitating factor: a physiological, affective, or intellectual need. (In the latter case, the need appears in the guise of a question or a problem.) At all levels, intelligence seeks to understand or explain, etc. However, while the functions of interest, explanation, etc., are common to all developmental stages, that is to say, are "invariable" as far as the functions themselves are concerned, it is nonetheless true that "interests" (as opposed to "interest") vary considerably from one mental level to another, and that the particular explanations (as opposed to the function of explaining) are of a very different nature, depending on the degree of intellectual development. In addition to the constant functions, there are the variable structures. An analysis of these progressive forms of successive equilibrium highlights the differences from one behavioral level to another, all the way from the elementary behavior of the neonate through adolescence.

The variable structures—motor or intellectual on the one hand and affective on the other—are the organizational forms of mental activity. They are organized along two dimensions—intrapersonal and social (interpersonal). For greater clarity we shall distinguish six stages or periods of development which mark the appearance of these successively constructed structures:

1. The reflex or hereditary stage, at which the first instinctual nutritional drives and the first emotions appear.

2. The stage of the first motor habits and of the first organized percepts, as well as of the first differentiated emotions.

3. The stage of sensorimotor or practical intelligence (prior to language), of elementary affective organization, and of the first external affective fixations. These first three stages constitute the infancy period—from birth till the age of one and a half to two years—i.e., the period prior to the development of language and thought as such.

4. The stage of intuitive intelligence, of spontaneous interpersonal feelings, and of social relationships in which the child is subordinate to the adult (ages two to seven years, or "early childhood").

5. The stage of concrete intellectual operations (the beginning of logic) and of moral and social feelings of cooperation (ages seven to eleven or twelve, or "middle childhood").

6. The stage of abstract intellectual operations, of the formation of the personality, and of affective and intellectual entry into the society of adults (adolescence).

Each of these stages is characterized by the appearance of original structures whose construction distinguishes it from previous stages. The essentials of these successive constructions exist at subsequent stages in the form of substructures onto which new characteristics have been built. It follows that in the adult each stage through which he has passed corresponds to a given level in the total hierarchy of behavior. But at each stage there are also temporary and secondary characteristics that are modified by subsequent development as a function of the need for better organization. Each stage thus constitutes a particular form of equilibrium as a function of its characteristic structures, and mental evolution is effectuated in the direction of an ever-increasing equilibrium.

We know which functional mechanisms are common to all stages. In an absolutely general way (not only in comparing one stage with the following but also in comparing each item of behavior that is part of that stage with ensuing behavior), one can say that all action—that is to say, all movement, all thought, or all emotion—responds to a need. Neither the child nor the adult executes any external or even entirely internal act unless impelled by a motive; this motive can always be translated into a need (an elementary need, an interest, a question, etc.).

As Claparède (1951) has shown, a need is always a manifestation of disequilibrium: there is need when something either outside ourselves or within us (physically or mentally) is changed and behavior has to be adjusted as a function of this change. For example, hunger or fatigue will provoke a search for nourishment or rest; encountering an external object will lead to a need to play, which in turn has practical ends, or it leads to a question or a theoretical problem. A casual word will excite the need to imitate, to sympathize, or will engender reserve or opposition if it conflicts with some interest of our own. Conversely, action terminates when a need is satisfied, that is to say, when equilibrium is re-established between the new factor that has provoked the need and the mental organization that existed prior to the introduction of this factor. Eating or sleeping, playing or reaching a goal, replying to a question or resolving a problem, imitating successfully, establishing an affective tie, or maintaining one's point of view are all satisfactions that, in the preceding examples, will put an end to the particular behavior aroused by the need. At any given moment, one can thus say, action is disequilibrated by the transformations that arise in the external or internal world, and each new behavior consists not only in re-establishing equilibrium but also in moving toward a more stable equilibrium than that which preceded the disturbance.

Human action consists of a continuous and perpetual mechanism of readjustment or equilibration. For this reason, in these initial phases of construction, the successive mental structures that engender development can be considered as so many progressive forms of equilibrium, each of which is an advance upon its predecessor. It must be understood, however, that this functional mechanism, general though it may be, does not explain the content or the structure of the various needs, since each of them is related to the organization of the particular stage that is being considered. For example, the sight of the same object will occasion very different questions in the small child who is still incapable of classification from those of the older child whose ideas are more extensive and systematic. The interests of a child at any given moment depend on the system of ideas he has acquired plus his affective inclinations, and he tends to fulfill his interests in the direction of greater equilibrium.

Before examining the details of development we must try to find that which is common to the needs and interests present at all ages. One can say, in regard to this, that all needs tend first of all to incorporate things and people into the subject's own activity, i.e., to "assimilate" the external world into the structures that have already been constructed, and secondly to readjust these structures as a function of subtle transformations, i.e., to "accommodate" them to external objects. From this point of view, all mental life, as indeed all organic life, tends progressively to assimilate the surrounding environment. This incorporation is effected thanks to the structures or psychic organs whose scope of action becomes more and more extended. Initially, perception and elementary movement (prehension, etc.) are concerned with objects that are close and viewed statically; then later, memory and practical intelligence permit the representation of earlier states of the object as well as the anticipation of their future states resulting from as yet unrealized transformations. Still later intuitive thought reinforces these two abilities. Logical intelligence in the guise of concrete operations and ultimately of abstract deduction terminates this evolution by making the subject master of events that are far distant in space and time. At each of these levels the mind fulfills the same function, which is to incorporate the universe to itself, but the nature of assimilation varies, i.e., the successive modes of incorporation evolve from those of perception and movement to those of the higher mental operations.

In assimilating objects, action and thought must accommodate to these objects; they must adjust to external variation. The balancing of the processes of assimilation and accommodation may be called "adaptation." Such is the general form of psychological equilibrium, and the progressive organization of mental development appears to be simply an ever more precise adaptation to reality.

Reference

CLAPARÈDE, E. *Le développement mental*. Neuchâtel: Delachaux et Niestlé, 1951.

Major Challenges for Students of Infancy and Early Childhood

Myrtle B. McGraw
BRIARCLIFF COLLEGE

It is not possible to pinpoint any particular ideologies or theories that have given rise to the present interest in early childhood development. The forces were many; they were complex and intertwined. Sputnik shocked the nation out of a state of educational complacency. The disparity of educational opportunities and achievements of children from differing socioeconomic and ethnic groups was brought to light. Then it was determined that children from less favorable environments entered school with their educational handicaps already established. To alleviate this situation, the federal government set up Head Start programs. The outcome of the Head Start programs has led to the claim that even the pre-kindergarten period is too late—education begins in the cradle. Furthermore, since the body of knowledge doubles every 10 years, the amount of knowledge one must master favors an early beginning.

Clearly, the goal of this current wave of concern is to develop the optimum potentials of all children. The pressure is on learning, early learning. It seems clear that the infant and toddler are capable of learning a great deal, *if* the opportunities for learning are properly presented. It also seems evident that the principles of learning derived from laboratory studies of animals or college students are inadequate when it comes to dealing with rapid behavior development of the human infant. The prevailing notion is that these goals can be achieved by manipulation of the environments in which the child lives. To some extent these ideas are reinforced by experiments of the effects of "sensory deprivation," "prolonged isolation," and the comparative effects of "enriched and impoverished" environments. Such studies have been conducted on animals, children, and adults. Once again, the emphasis seems to be shifting to the environmental side of the scale, but it is not locked in with the old heredity-environment dichotomy. It is generally recognized now that nature-nurture are interdependent forces, and to try to separate them clouds inquiry. A few studies (Fowler, 1962; McGraw, 1935; Moore, 1960) have demonstrated that the performances of the young *in particular activities* can be advanced beyond normal expectancy. But we have not as yet learned how to develop to the maximum *all potentials of the growing child*. To do this we shall need new theories or concepts of development that transcend the established principles of learning.

1. *Challenge for the Researchers of Growth*   The present corps of growth scientists are the legatees of a vast body of concepts, theories, and research strategies inherited from the "psychological establishment." Of course, the growth scientists will be drawn from many disciplines and from diverse areas of psychology, other than developmental. Already it is apparent that some

Reprinted from *American Psychologist*, August 1970, *25*, 754–756 by permission of the American Psychological Association.

dyed-in-the-wool experimentalists are selecting the human infant in preference to animals for special investigations. The challenge for all the students of growth —regardless of their scientific expertise and theoretical orientation—is to scan their legacy of knowledge and skills and to have the courage to rule out those theories and techniques that are not applicable to the study of a complex, ever-changing phenomenon, such as growth. Many experimentalists fail to take into account that their own preconceptions may operate as uncontrolled variables within a particular situation. Will the experimentalist, skillful in the manipulation of the variables and instruments of measurement, become able to recognize that the way the infant is held or positioned may also be a factor in the results obtained? Will the examiner be so focused on the toddler's response to the items set before him that he fails to detect that the child's wiggling and climbing off the chair and running toward the door is his way of saying that there is pressure on his bladder? Will researchers trained to use the IQ or just chronological age be able to devise strategies to evaluate a multiplicity of systems constantly in flux, each system influencing another and in different degrees? All growth and development is not in the form of accretion. The growth scientists will need to design methods that reveal the rises and falls, the pulsations and rhythms manifest in the growth of a given function. An understanding of these pulsations and rhythms may become promising guidelines for the development of optimum potentials of the growing child. Strategies developed in other disciplines (e.g., communication theories) may provide suggestive models for evaluating constantly changing phenomena, such as rapid growth during the early years. There is evidence that many of the current investigators (Endler, Boulter, & Osser, 1968) are alert to the problem, and that is the first step to improving methodologies.

2. *The Challenge of Cultural Acceptance of Scientific Theories*   In the past, it has been traditional for scientists, especially those dealing with basic sciences, to be removed from the applied aspects of their findings. They were searching for fundamental truths, and whatever society did with it was none of their concern. On the other hand, many atomic physicists have begun to voice a sense of responsibility for the way society makes use of their knowledge. During this century we have been able to see how many psychological theories have been applied and misapplied to the matter of child rearing and education. If the periods of infancy and the early years are as important for total development as generally contended, then it is reasonable to expect the behavioral scientists to take some responsibility for the way in which their thoughts and theories are adopted into the cultural patterns of child management. Just how this can be done is not clear because it has never been systematically undertaken by any scientific discipline. The general public has faith in science and mass media and is quick to announce, "Science proves thus and so." Sometimes the misapplication of a theory may be ascribed to the use of a particular word, perhaps a word that was originally drawn from another discipline.

Let us consider for a moment some current thoughts that have the potential for creating parental anxiety. Take the question of "critical periods" as applied to learning. The concept was first used by embryologists. It was reinforced by Lorenz's (1935) study of imprinting. Recently, it has been emphasized in connection with studies of the effects of an impoverished environment. It has been asserted that if the impoverishment occurs at critical periods in development, then the damage done may be irreversible. Back in 1935, the writer applied the term "critical periods" to the acquisition of motor skills during infancy. If the agreed meaning of "critical periods" carries the idea that whatever is attained in development or learning must be achieved during a specified period, then the term should not be applied to normal behavioral growth. In the aforementioned instance, it was intended to signify that there are *opportune* times when specific activities can most economically be learned. If one misses that opportune time, then the methods of instruction should be altered for later learning of the same function. It is the irreversibility of damage done that adds emotion and fear to the "critical period" concept.

Just the amount of emphasis attached to certain concepts can also distort their meaning when adopted into the culture. Take, for example, the current emphasis on cognition. No investigator would contend that cognition operates independently of other aspects of learning. Yet, merely because it is the focus of investigative activity, cognition, like personality adjustment of old, is a kind of umbrella for all other goals: expose the child to the right knowledge, in the right way, and at the right time—then the job would be well done.

Perhaps most urgently of all, the growth scientists need to review the accepted principles of learning as they have been articulated and generally accepted. These principles of learning were determined largely by studies of animal subjects in laboratory situations and studies of children in the classroom. As stated above, there is every reason to suspect that they are not applicable to the process of growth taking place during infancy and during the early years. There is a pressing need for totally new guidelines for the benefit of those persons responsible for the management and socialization of the child from birth to three years of age. Obviously the most dominant force is change, change in the organism and change in behavior from day to day. Consistency in parental management does not mean setting up a pattern or rule and sticking to it. It means, rather, dealing with a child in a manner consistent with his developmental changes. To do this effectively requires knowledge, sensitivity, intuition, and flexibility. So the challenge is to orient mothers and teachers toward the concept of change, not toward stability in the ordinary sense. Parents should be taught to observe, to scan, and to detect the nonverbal as well as verbal signals of growth within the child and to design methods of instruction accordingly.

The United States may well be at the threshold of institutional reorganization for the care and education of the young. To develop maximum potentials of children of this age will require special preparation on the part of those responsible for this age group. They need to be not only knowledgeable but intuitive and observant. We have long adhered to the tradition that the biological parents are the ones best qualified to bring up young children. Whether we continue to follow that tradition or turn the education of the young over to specialists—kibbutz fashion—the personnel will require special preparation quite unlike that offered to elementary school teachers or even mothers of today.

The growth scientists are challenged to provide a theoretical frame of reference for the education of this crucial age group. And they are advised also to take account of the way in which their theories and pronouncements are adopted into the culture so that the growing child of today can confidently meet the social changes of the twenty-first century.

References

ENDLER, N. S., BOULTER, L. R., & OSSER, H. *Contemporary issues in developmental psychology*, New York: Holt, Rinehart and Winston, 1968.

FOWLER, W. Teaching a two-year-old to read: An experiment in early childhood reading. *Genetic Psychology Monographs*, 1962, 66, 181–283.

LORENZ, K. J. Der Kumpan in der Umwelt des Vogels. Der Artgenosse als auslösendes Moment sozialer Verhaltungsweisen. *Journal of Ornithology (Leipzig)*, 1935, 83, 137–213.

McGRAW, M. B. *Growth, a study of Johnny and Jimmy.* New York: Appleton-Century, 1935.

MOORE, O. K. *Automated responsive environments.* Hamden, Conn.: Basic Education, Inc., 1960. (Film)

author index

NOTE: Pages referring to bibliographic references are in *italics*. Pages have been given for authors who are mentioned on the text page only by reference number. In those cases, the following italic page must be consulted for the reference number. Pages in **boldface** refer to selections by the authors themselves.

A

Abernethy, E. M., 305, *324*
Adams, A. O., 85, *99*
Adams, G., 79, *98*
Ainsworth, M. D. S., 146, 157, 163, *171*, 205, 214, 216, 219, 220, 221, 225, 228, *244*, **260-276**, 315, 316, *324*
Aitken, F. C., 112, 116, 117, *118*
Akiyama, Y., 122, *125*
Albino, R. C., 142, *171*
Aldrich, C. A., 116, *118*
Alexander, B. K., 283, *285*
Allen, L., 291, *297*
Amatruda, C. S., 144, 147, 156, 167, *173*, 195, *197*
Ames, L. B., 169, *171*
Apgar, V., 72, *98*
Appel, G., 91, *98*
Applebaum, R. M., 201, *244*
Arsenian, J. M., 262, 270, *274*
Aserinsky, E., 122, *125*

B

Bain, K., 112, *118*
Baird, D., 29, *42*
Bakwin, H., 90, *98*, 109, 110, 114, *118*
Ball, R. S., 169, *176*
Ballard, W. W., **328-336**
Barker, R., *188*
Barker, R. G., 305, *325*
Barnes, G. R., Jr., 113, *118*
Barnicot, N. A., 73, *99*
Barrett, I. M., 18, *44*
Barton, S., 88, *98*
Bartsch, G. E., 117, *120*
Bayley, N., 146, 168, 169, *171*, *175*, 212, 230, *244*, 247, 308, 322, *324*
Beaglehole, E., 56, *57*
Beaglehole, P., 56, *57*
Beal, V. A., 18, *42*
Becker, W. C., 202, 230, *244*
Beg, M. A., 262, *276*
Béhar, M., 90, *98*

Stern, G. G., 205, *247*
Stevenson, H. W., 313, *325*
Stevenson, S. S., 115, 117, *120*
Steward, M. S., 36, *43*
Stewart, A., 116, 117, *120*
Stone, C. P., 305, *325*
Stone, D. G. H., 111, *119*
Stott, L. H., 169, *176*
Stuart, H. C., 18, *42*, 132, *176*
Sullivan, W., 318, *325*
Sun, K. H., 85, *101*
Super, C. M., 151, *176*

T

Talmadge, M., 25, *42*
Tanner, J. M., *45*, 73, 74, *99*, *101*, **106-109**, *247*, 304, 305, *325*, *326*
Thomas, A., 211, *245*, **290-297**
Thomas, L. N., *118*
Thompson, H., 307, *324*
Thompson, V. J., 142, *171*
Thomson, A. M., 89, *101*
Thomson, J., 107, *109*, 116, *120*
Thorndike, E. L., 313, *326*
Thurston, D., 36, *43*
Tisdall, F. F., 18, *43*
Todd, T. W., 107, *109*
Toverud, K. U., 110, *120*
Truswell, A. S., 131, *173*
Turner, C. D., 111, *120*
Turner, M. R., 147, *173*
Turnure, C., 167, *176*

U

Uttley, K. H., 56, *57*
Uzgiris, I., 148, 149, 169, *175*, *176*

V

Valadian, I., 132, *176*
Valenti, C., **57-63**
Valquist, B., 117, *120*
Vallbona, C., 74, *102*
Vandenberg, S. G., 321, *326*

Van Marthens, E., 22, *45*
Varga, F., 85, *100*
Von Foerster, H., 336, 338, *341*

W

Wahler, R. G., 216, *247*
Waller, H., 113, *120*
Walter, G., 301, 306, *326*
Walters, C. E., 9, *45*, 146, *176*
Walters, R. H., *276*
Warren, R. J., 117, *118*, *120*
Waters, E., 202, *247*
Watson, E. H., *45*, 72, *102*, 137, 138, 139, *176*
Watson, J. S., 150, *176*, 313, *326*
Webster, R. L., 167, *176*
Weiffenbach, J., 151, *176*
Weiner, J. S., 73, *99*
Welbourn, H. F., 116, *120*
Wenar, C., 290, *297*
Wenner, W., 122, *125*
Werboff, J., 26, *45*
Werner, E. E., 170, *176*
Wertheimer, M., 83, *102*
Westerfield, R., 116, *119*
Westheimer, I., 221, *246*, 272, *275*
Westropp, C., 116, 117, *120*
White, B. L., 81, *99*, 124, *126*, 152, *176*, 205, 235, *247*
White, R. W., 124, *126*
Wiener, G., 38, *45*
Wiener, N., 336, *341*
Willerman, L., 203, *248*
Williams, H. H., 115, 116, *120*
Wilson, J. F., 117, *119*
Winnick, M., 21, *45*
Winokur, G., 199, *246*
Wittig, B. A., 262, 264, 266, 270, *274*
Wolfenstein, M., 200, *248*
Wolff, P. H., 76, 79, 81, 87, 97, *102*, **120-125**, *126*, 162, *176*
Wolins, M., 237, *248*
Woodhill, L. M., 111, *120*
Wortis, H., 38, *45*
Wright, H., *188*

subject index

DATE DUE